WORK TOWN

WORK
TOWN

The Astonishing Story of the
Birth of Mass-Observation

DAVID HALL

WEIDENFELD & NICOLSON

First published in Great Britain in 2015
by Weidenfeld & Nicolson

1 3 5 7 9 10 8 6 4 2

A CIP catalogue record for this book is
available from the British Library.

ISBN: 978 0 297 87168 2

Typeset by Input Data Services Ltd, Bridgwater, Somerset

Printed and bound by CPI Group (UK) Ltd, Croydon CR0 4YY

The Orion Publishing Group's policy is to use
papers that are natural, renewable and recyclable and made
from wood grown in sustainable forests. The logging and
manufacturing processes are expected to conform to
environmental regulations of the country of origin.

Weidenfeld & Nicolson
The Orion Publishing Group Ltd
Carmelite House
50 Victoria Embankment
London EC4Y 0DZ

An Hachette UK Company

www.orionbooks.co.uk

To the memory of Fred
A proud Worktowner

CONTENTS

THE PRINCIPAL CHARACTERS

Mass-Observation Founders

Tom Harrisson
Humphrey Jennings
Charles Madge

BOLTON

Full-time survey leaders

Walter Hood (Politics)
John Sommerfield (The Pub)
Gertrude Wagner (Saving and Spending)
Joe Wilcock (Religion)

Observers

Zita Baker
Brian Barefoot
Penelope Barlow
Frank Cawson
Dennis Chapman
William Empson
Sheila Fox
Bill Lee
Humphrey Pease
Geoffrey Thomas
Woodrow Wyatt

Artists and Photographers

Graham Bell
William Coldstream
Humphrey Spender
Julian Trevelyan
Michael Wickham

Local helpers

Tom Binks
Louie Davies
Jack Fagan
Harry Gordon
Tom Honeyford
Eric Letchford
Joyce Mangnall
Bill Naughton
Bill Rigby

BLACKHEATH

Workers/Volunteers

Priscilla Feare
Bruce Watkin

The Blackheath Group

David Gascoyne
Guy Hunter
Cecily Jennings
Stuart and Margaret Legg
Kathleen Raine
Inez Spender

INTRODUCTION

Mass-Observation was probably the largest investigation into popular culture to be carried out in Britain in the twentieth century. Set up in 1937, this wide-ranging inquiry into the habits, customs and daily routines of the nation became one of the defining cultural phenomena of Britain in the late 1930s. At a time when there were deep divisions in society and differences of opinion over the abdication of Edward VIII, the Spanish Civil War, Hitler's relentless rise in Germany and the economic and social upheavals symbolised by the Jarrow March and Cable Street, the organisation undertook the ambitious task of creating a 'new science of ourselves' – a study of the everyday lives of ordinary working people in Britain.

One of Mass-Observation's most celebrated projects was a community study of Bolton, a Lancashire cotton town which they called Worktown. To carry out the research for the project volunteer teams of Mass-Observers were sent to the town where people's conversations and behaviour were recorded in the street, in shops, at the pub, in dance halls and cinemas, in churches and chapels, in the cotton mills and at meetings and public events. The team of investigators was led by Tom Harrisson, who regarded the working-class Northerners he had come to observe as 'a race apart', as remote from the Establishment as the primitive tribes he had made his name studying in far-off South Sea islands. His team, which was made up predominantly of middle-class students, artists, writers and photographers, was based in a dark, dank terraced house a short walk from the town centre. Number 85 Davenport Street was like a scruffy student flat or hippie commune, described variously by those who lived there as 'bare', 'bleak', 'horrible' and 'bug-ridden'. Here Harrisson instructed his recruits that the best way to understand what real people did was to watch and record them as they went about their everyday lives. This was generally done without their knowledge, leading to accusations that the observers were acting like spies, sitting in pubs with their stopwatches, timing how long it took to down a pint, watching everything that happened in shops, churches, political meetings, cinemas and dance halls, recording conversations, hand gestures, clothing and all kinds of minute detail.

The Worktown team collected an astonishing amount of material, recording in great detail how people worked and lived – their eating and drinking habits, their political and religious beliefs and how they spent their leisure time. Very little of this fascinating material has been published. Although four books were commissioned by the publisher Victor Gollancz, only one, *The Pub and the People*, ever went to press. The Mass-Observation Archive in the University of Sussex Special Collections now houses this invaluable and under-used resource which consists of sixty-five boxes of written observations, typed reports, newspaper cuttings and other related material. It is an outstanding collection, providing excellent source material for social historians and for anybody who is interested in finding out about the lives of ordinary people in Britain during a period of great turmoil and change.

In addition to the written material, around 850 photographs were taken between August 1937 and April 1938 by the pioneering documentary photographer Humphrey Spender. Harrisson wanted the photographs because he believed that the camera was a scientific instrument of precision which could be used to check the accuracy of written observations. Spender's photographs of Bolton have become an important part of the legacy of the Worktown project and provide a unique record of everyday life in the town. Now held in Bolton by the town's Library and Museum Services, they are regarded as internationally significant in the development of documentary photography and have been seen in a wide variety of contexts including exhibitions, books, television documentaries and even by the band Everything but the Girl on the cover of their 1985 album *Love Not Money*.

Mass-Observation's founders were united in a belief, shared by many contemporary writers, artists and intellectuals that there was a gap in any real knowledge of the lives of ordinary working people. They saw Britain as a divided nation with on the one hand a small educated elite, privileged both socially and politically but ignorant of the lives of the vast majority of the population, and on the other a majority, poorly educated and ill informed on political matters. The organisation was concerned with the tension between the Establishment and ordinary working people; between reports on the radio and in newspapers and talk in the pub, the kitchen or the workplace; between the ways in which the media represented public opinion and what people actually felt and thought.

The media generally portrayed the population as having a broad consensus about the issues of the day. When in 1936 the Government forced Edward VIII to abdicate because he wished to marry a divorced woman, Mass-Observation was set up to test this depiction of reality. The need for information seemed imperative, but information was the thing that the majority of the population did not have.

Along with the abdication crisis, there were many events and developments in the 1930s which ran parallel to Mass-Observation and influenced and motivated the observers. There was high unemployment, economic depression and rumours about the possibility of war; the Spanish Civil War divided the left on the issue of pacifism; the National Government pursued a policy of appeasement in the face of Hitler's territorial aggression; and Mosley and his Blackshirts marched through the East End. At the same time experimental television broadcasts were made by the BBC from Alexandra Palace; MORI and Gallup, the opinion poll companies, opened offices in London and market research was becoming established; cinema attendances were booming and the newsreel established itself.

The Documentary Movement was concerned with the production of an 'objective' art which would act as a catalyst for social improvement and reform. The term was first used to describe film, and another of Mass-Observation's founders, Humphrey Jennings, was one of its leading figures, but it soon extended to include photography and literature, such as George Orwell's *The Road To Wigan Pier*. The increasing use of photography in newspapers and magazines led to the establishment of a distinctive style of documentary photojournalism seen at its best in the illustrated weekly news magazine, *Picture Post* which was set up in 1938 to reflect the whole of British life and culture in a way that would be popular and accessible to all. More than any other organization the Left Book Club crystallized the concerns of progressive forces and an emergent middle class radicalism. Strongly anti-fascist at a time when many people in Britain were still ambivalent or ignorant about what was happening in continental Europe, membership was made up mostly of middle-class young professionals with predominantly left-wing sympathies. These were the people who were attracted to Mass-Observation

One of the most interesting aspects of the organisation is that it was both a product of these times and ahead of them as it placed itself in the vanguard of the newly emerging disciplines of sociology, market research and opinion polling. Never before had ordinary working people been studied or asked for their views on issues of the day. Earnest and socially conscious, it was part of a much more complex movement of ideas

concerned with social and political change in the 1930s. It was a time
of great economic, political and moral upheaval, when the Depression
brought the menace of social inequality and dictatorships threatened
democracy. But this was only part of the picture. The 1930s are seen
as a time of dole queues and industrial graveyards, hunger marches and
poverty, a time when a third of the population had an inadequate diet;
the nation that was portrayed by Spender, Orwell and other members of
the Documentary Movement. But the blight they portrayed was largely
regional and barely touched some parts of Britain. Most of the real hardship was concentrated in the North of England, Central Scotland and
South Wales, where the old industries of coal, ship-building and textiles
were in decline. The rest of the country was faring much better and a
North–South divide was beginning to develop as those with jobs, largely
in the more prosperous South, began to enjoy improved standards of
living. Many people who were in work were finding themselves better
off as prices fell and average incomes rose, spawning a consumer boom.
So while large sections of the population were on the breadline, a new
lower-middle class bought electric cookers, vacuum cleaners, radiograms,
telephones and three-piece suites.

On the high street Woolworth's became a popular store where shoppers could browse over goods laid out on the counters rather than having
to ask an assistant to fetch things for them. Thinking there was a need
for cheap, easily available editions of quality, contemporary writing, publisher Allen Lane set up Penguin Books. The first Penguin paperbacks
went on sale in July 1935 and included works by Ernest Hemingway and
Agatha Christie. They cost sixpence, the price of a packet of cigarettes
and were available in chain stores like Woolworth's, tobacconists and
railway station news stands as well as traditional bookshops. It was a revolution in publishing that massively widened public access to literature
and within the first year over three million copies were sold.

It was in this context that Mass-Observation came into being, and the
organisation soon became a melting pot for ideas about society, providing
an opportunity for a diverse group with a wide range of interests and talents
to work together in a new and creative way. Artists and poets influenced
by surrealism and socialist ideologies were attracted to the organisation to
work alongside sociologists and anthropologists to develop an 'anthropology of ourselves'. Implicit in this was a search for identity, but at the time
any definition of ourselves was complicated by the rigidity of the class
system and by such basics as a lack of communication, with dialects and
accents that were class based and mutually incomprehensible. People

were expected to conform to the values and conventions of their own social class and for the majority strict social conventions restricted any attempts at social mobility. For much of working-class Britain 'know your place' was the order of the day and hardships were endured because that was the way of things. Working-class families in the old industrial heart-lands never thought to own their own home or a motor car nor dreamt of having children go to university. In some communities you would even be thought of as a traitor if you tried to better yourself. The artist Julian Trevelyan who came to join the Worktown project was very aware 'of the gulf that separated me from these English workers, the gulf of education, language, accent and social behaviour. It was my constant desire during these years to bridge that gulf, and occasionally I succeeded.' Through his eccentricities, energy and enthusiasm Tom Harrisson attracted many other middle-class writers, artists and intellectuals to join him in Bolton to work on the project; upper-middle-class young men who felt it was their duty to make contact with and to get to know the working class. The motivations for becoming involved ranged from guilt born of a sense of privilege to the excitement of venturing into the unknown, and from a desire to make the world a better place to the simple wish to have a good time.

There have been a number of books and articles analysing Mass-Observation and its place in British cultural history. There have also been edited collections of M-O material, including the popular edited editions of Barrow-in-Furness housewife Nella Last's Second World War diaries which were adapted for television by Victoria Wood. But the story of M-O itself and the characters who shaped it has received surprisingly little attention. The story of the Worktown project in particular – and the people who were attracted to the somewhat bohemian existence in the scruffy terraced house in Bolton – has been left largely untold. Set against the political and historical milestones of the 1930s, my aim is to tell the extraordinary story of how Mass-Observation and the Worktown project came into being and to explore the often fraught relationships of the characters behind it, while giving some insight into the realities of life in a northern industrial town in the days before the outbreak of the Second World War.

When I first approached the story I saw it in terms of the commonly held view that the Worktown project involved a bunch of young middle-class intellectuals engaged in a quest to get in touch with the working class; that this was the upper-middle classes using the lower-middle classes to spy on the working classes. But it soon became clear that this long-held view is misconceived, as James Hinton points out in his recent history of M-O – *The Mass Observers*. It is true that the founders were upper-middle class. Harrisson and Charles Madge had both been born and brought up on the fringes of Empire and colonial administration and sent away to boarding schools, while Jennings had an architect father and a painter mother. The team of investigators who were drawn to Bolton by Harrisson's charismatic personality was also composed largely of middle-class, university-educated Southerners – a background very different from the environment into which they came as observers. But Harrisson made sure that the key full-time workers he recruited had working-class roots – men like Walter Hood, an unemployed miner from the North-east who won a scholarship to Ruskin College, Oxford, and Joe Wilcock, a working-class Christian activist who hailed from a weaving family in nearby Farnworth. From the outset Harrisson also involved local people in the project, and he took on a number of unemployed workers as observers. Harrisson himself claimed that he was able to move at ease between the classes, from the homes of the industrial benefactors who contributed to Mass-Observation's funds to the company of their lowest-paid employers in the pub or on the factory floor.

One of the key elements of the story is this crossing of the class divide that was so deeply entrenched in 1930s Britain. Until the outbreak of war in 1939, British society had a rigid class structure, with the educated upper and middle classes tending to take for granted their own superiority over the working classes. With very few exceptions the holders of power and authority came from an upper- or upper-middle-class background and had, like Mass-Observation's founders, a public school education. They believed in their own moral and cultural superiority and the majority of those lower down the social order seldom questioned their position. It was a social order that was largely fixed from birth with members of different classes rarely able or even willing to move to different social groupings. The 1960s have long been seen as the time when these class barriers broke down and popular culture flowered. These developments, especially with their positive portrayal of the working class, blossomed with the growth of social realism in film and literature. But it was the Mass-Observers back in the 1930s who first began to cross the class divide and bring serious attention to the culture of the masses.

It's a story that came as something of a revelation for somebody like me from a Northern working-class background, who went to university in the 1960s, the first in my family to do so, and was working in television by the

1970s. My studies and the job that followed brought me into a different world and into contact with people from very different backgrounds to my own. In common with many of my contemporaries who had travelled the same road, I believed we were part of a privileged group – the first generation to break away from the stultifying background of our parents with their limited horizons and become part of a seemingly 'classless' group within society with a foot, as it were, in both camps. I travelled the world, met and worked with royalty, politicians, media executives and captains of industry – all a world away from my Manchester council estate – but I always went back to those roots to meet friends and family I'd grown up with, to make programmes with coal-miners and factory workers or to drink with working lads on my way to a football match. Like Tom Harrisson I always felt at ease moving between the classes, but Harrisson and the team he put together for the Worktown project were forty years ahead of me and my baby-boomer contemporaries in crossing the class divide.

In the lean years of the 1930s when Mass-Observation was set up, there were few openings for bright young men and women just out of university – the sort of people who, by the 1960s and 1970s, would like me go into television, advertising or journalism. In the 1930s these opportunities didn't exist, so some went to join Mass-Observation in Bolton. For most of them it was a short stay – a sort of 1930s gap year – but it was an experience that had a big impact on many of them and was to stay with them for the rest of their lives. Brian Barefoot, who wrote a detailed account of his time with Mass-Observation in Bolton, was the son of an architect who had graduated in languages and psychology from Cambridge. He spent as much time as he could in Bolton, and working-class observers Walter Hood and Joe Wilcock became real friends, 'the first friendships I ever made outside my own class', he recalled. 'At the time we were very conscious of class. I was well aware that at Cambridge I knew nothing about the working class and wanted to know more. To be engaged in socialist politics was one way to find an entrance into that mysterious world, as thousands of Oxbridge undergrads were discovering at that time, and M-O was another way in.'

It was a time of new ideas and new ways of seeing society. Artists and intellectuals, inspired by the surrealist movement, which took its inspiration from the language of dreams and revolutionary politics, sought art in popular culture , saw poetry in the everyday and mundane and thought it was their duty to get in touch with the masses and ally themselves with the working class. Richard Crossman, Tom Driberg and Woodrow Wyatt all joined the Labour Party and got involved with Mass-Observation before moving on to distinguished careers as journalists and Labour politicians. But it was a two-way process, and Mass-Observation gave many local Boltonians their first taste of middle-class life and aspirations. Bill Naughton was the coalman who delivered to Davenport Street. He made himself known to the residents because he wanted to teach himself to write, got involved with the project and went on to become a popular author and playwright famous for writing some of the best-known British kitchen-sink dramas such as *All in Good Time* (later filmed as *The Family Way*), *Spring and Port Wine* and that renowned depiction of the swinging 1960s, *Alfie*. Among others whose involvement with M-O contributed to their upward social mobility, Joyce Mangnall, a mill worker who was a constant source of contacts for M-O, emigrated to Australia, got a qualification in child care and went on to a distinguished career as a social worker in Melbourne.

Worktown is a story of larger-than-life characters, many of whom went on to become leading figures in the worlds of art, politics and journalism. It is also a story of major personality clashes and of a group who were disorganised from the outset, took on far too much work and were prone to internal squabbling but who were united in their common desire to make Britain a fairer, more equitable and better-informed society. By focusing on the lives and the stories of some of the people who were involved rather than just reproducing or analysing the reports they wrote for Mass-Observation, we are able to see how, whatever their social background, they had common cause with the broad currents of progressive, anti-fascist policies. M-O's work spread in all directions and became more and more involved with tracking and assessing public opinion and reactions to the major events and changes of the day. The social consciousness of the organisation became a damning critique of the government and of the news media and by the time the Second World War broke out it had become a household name throughout Britain.

The Mass-Observation Archive is a treasure trove of information about the lives and the views of ordinary working people in the late 1930s – an immense and invaluable source for social, economic and cultural historians and for authors, playwrights and screenwriters. In recent years writers and historians have been turning to Mass-Observation and the Worktown project materials in ever increasing numbers when researching social life in the late 1930s and 1940s. Nearly 80 years on, at a time of economic hardship for so many working people in Britain the observations of the Worktown project team and the stories that were told to them help us to appreciate the much greater material deprivation endured by many working people in the 1930s.

The Worktown archive has been described variously as a people's history and as a well-intentioned, idealistic attempt at a kind of general sociological study not often conducted today. It has been criticised as a middle-class adventure at the expense of the working class – nice young men attempting to penetrate into working-class pubs and institutions to try to get to know the workers. There were certainly lots of touches of the dilettante and the Oxbridge effete about the project and, with Harrisson in particular, of just popping up north for an adventure with the natives, but by bringing in working-class observers to join the team the project was able to relate to the 'race apart' on which Harrisson wanted to train his anthropologist's eye. And despite the surrealistic daftness of a lot of the ideas at the beginning, Mass-Observation developed into a serious enterprise, treated with respect even at government level. Whatever view one takes of it, the project collected a huge amount of material that provides a compelling insight into the lives of ordinary people living and working in a pre-war British industrial town and of the observers who came to live among them and put those lives on record.

I

GOING NATIVE

'The ugliness is so complete that it is almost exhilarating.
It challenges you to live there'

J. B. Priestley, *English Journey*

It was half-past seven on a cold, damp October morning in the Lanca-shire cotton town of Bolton. The murky landscape was dominated by great, gaunt spinning mills and bleach works standing by the side of dirty canals and railway tracks. Steam hissed out from their engine houses and the smoke from dozens of towering chimneys filled the air. The whole skyline seemed to be subsumed in a smoking jungle of chimneys, towering over rows of terraced houses, each one belching out clouds of noxious smoke, so that a dirty grey canopy hung over the densely packed cobbled streets. To the sound of clogs in the dark back streets, working men hurried off to their jobs, mostly wearing caps, some carrying their packed lunches in red knotted handkerchiefs. In the distance a tramcar clattered along the road into town and a horse-drawn cart clip-clopped up a cobbled back street.

Along one of these streets a tall dark-haired man in his mid-twenties stepped out on his way to the cotton mill where he worked. The collar of his camel-hair coat was turned up to keep out the early-morning chill as he made his way past row after row of tiny red-brick terraced houses. All looked exactly alike, with never a break between them. As he hurried past them he brushed his long, unkempt hair back with his hand. On either side of the street, doors were opening and people were stepping out of their brightly lit sitting rooms directly on to the gloomy street. Two girls came out of one of the doors and the light that flooded out from the house threw a warm yellow patch on to the paving stones. Both were wearing shawls over their heads – one grey, the other brown. They were joined by lots of other girls, most wearing cloche-style hats pulled down over their heads. They all had it worked out just right so that they'd get to the mill for work just before the gates were shut.

All the streets Tom Harrisson had to walk along to his workplace were cobbled. After a night's rain, the cobbles glistened in the gaslight, making them impossibly slippery in his leather shoes. Nearly everybody else clumped along in the heavy wooden clogs favoured by most mill workers. They clattered on the cobbles, making an almighty din, as more and more workers left their houses and joined the procession to the mill. As Harrisson hurried past one house a bedroom window opened and someone who'd overslept called out and asked the time. He'd be lucky if he made it to work on time.

Every morning, hail, rain or shine, Harrisson joined this stream of fellow mill folk, 'off to t'mill' as they put it. The place he was working at was one of three, built close together on an open piece of ground called, in Lancashire parlance, a croft. Each of them had its own lodge or reservoir to supply water for the steam engines that powered the machinery. Some people walked several miles to their work but, as he got closer, it was not only walkers who converged on the mills; dozens of corporation buses deposited their passengers outside, changing the stream into a flood. Few people spoke but, as they got close to the mill, with its huge glass windows lighting up the darkness, everybody seemed to liven up; people looked as though they were just beginning to wake up. The cotton-mill buildings were six or seven storeys high, and two or three hundred yards long, and at the gate of the mill yard all the streams of people coming from different parts of the town joined together and poured in. Then perhaps one would say something to another about the weather or the price of food. Even then Harrisson observed it was mostly the girls who did the talking in the morning; the men were dour and hardly ever spoke.[1]

Bolton was built on King Cotton, and between the two world wars the scale of the industry there was massive. In the mid-1930s the spinning sector was made up of 112 firms operating from over 120 mills, making sheets, quilts, towels, brocades, twills and dress materials. The names of many of these mills reflected the pretensions of the owners. They included *Ace* and *Majestic*, while others, such as *Cairo* and *India*, indicated strong associations with the old days of Empire. Swan Lane Mills was the largest in the world, and Sunnyside Mill owned by Tootal, Broadhurst and Lee housed 73,000 spindles and 2,529 looms. Their operatives worked on wooden floors, in temperatures between 75 and 98 degrees Fahrenheit. This tropical level of heat and humidity was created and maintained to prevent the cotton threads from drying and snapping. The warmer the mill, the finer the spinning, because cotton is at its softest at high temperature. All through the year the mill workers spent their days in these tropical conditions; and in winter, when moor-encircled Bolton was bitterly cold, they went there each day before the sun, if any, came up and came home each night after the sun had gone down. From the age of fourteen this was the life available for most Boltonians.[2]

It was a life far removed from the one Tom Harrisson had enjoyed before he came to Bolton. Born in Argentina in 1911, he arrived in Britain as a three-year-old when his father, a railway engineer, sailed home to fight in the First World War. Geoffrey Harrisson came back from the war a brigadier-general and promptly returned to Argentina with his wife Marie Ellen, leaving eight-year-old Tom and his younger brother Bill at a prep school broken up by lonely days in guest houses when the holidays came round. During adolescence, he gained a reputation for daring and physically challenging exploits and established what was to become a lifelong daily habit of recording, in largely indecipherable handwriting, detailed observations of the world around him. He also developed a fascination for natural life and took up birdwatching, publishing while he was still at Harrow school a booklet on *Birds of the Harrow District*.[3]

It was this interest in ornithology that led him on to the long and circuitous route that would eventually take him to the industrial North of England. In the summer of 1930, before going up to Cambridge to read natural sciences, Harrisson went on his first overseas scientific expedition, observing bird habits on a month-long trek in Arctic Lapland with the Oxford University Exploration Club. On his return he found Cambridge dull and boring, and it wasn't long before he was distracted from his lectures. He sought out friends who were as intellectual and tough as he thought he was himself and with them he went on pub-crawls, getting very drunk. After little more than a year he abandoned his degree. His father, who by this time had returned to England, was angered by his son's actions and promptly found him a place at King's College London, away from his drunken friends. But instead of going to King's, the young rebel fled to Oxford where he continued to enjoy a riotous and bohemian lifestyle. But it wasn't all drinking and partying, and while he was there he also used his time productively, recruiting and raising money for a six-month undergraduate expedition to study the flora and fauna of Sarawak. Throughout this time he let his father think he was at King's; there was an awful row when the truth came out, and friendly relations between father and son were never again restored.

Under Harrisson's leadership the Sarawak expedition was a great success, and this paved the way for his selection as an ornithologist on what was planned as a year-long expedition to the South Pacific islands of the New Hebrides, led by a friend he had made in Oxford, John Baker. Before setting off, however, Harrisson got involved with Baker's wife Zita, who was ten years older than him, and fell in love with her. She and Baker had two children, but Zita was not the typical Oxford don's wife. She was reputed to have many lovers and she ranked in university circles as something of a femme fatale. She was a slim, slight blonde with a snub nose and Harrisson found her enormously attractive. Part of Zita's appeal for him was that she was very much a modern woman, who had her own opinions and refused to let herself be walked over. But it was her courage and adventurousness that most endeared her to him. He was delighted when he heard that she was going to leave her children in Oxford and come with her husband on the planned expedition in June 1933. While in the New Hebrides Zita and Tom had a passionate affair, but she returned home with her husband at the end of the expedition in February 1934, leaving Harrisson in the South Pacific.

By this time he had sufficient funds to stay on for another three months, exploring, living in close contact with the natives and shifting from ornithology to anthropology. He went to the island of Malekula where, he reported, there were 3,000 cannibals living within 25 miles of the British headquarters. While there he kept his ornithologist's approach. Making himself as unobtrusive as possible he would watch and learn – a birdwatcher's approach to observation. Soon after the Bakers had left, a young Australian, Jock Marshall, arrived, and he and Harrisson immediately struck up a firm friendship. Marshall was a like-minded adventurer and they signed an agreement committing them both to a proposed expedition to New Guinea. When his funds ran out Harrisson planned to return to Britain, but he was able to extend his stay when he managed to secure a six-month appointment as acting British District Agent for Malekula and adjacent smaller islands. Before leaving the South Pacific, he met the Hollywood actor Douglas Fairbanks Sr who proposed to make a film, *Cannibal*, in which Harrisson would tell the story of the Big Nambas people of Malekula.

He eventually came back to England in December 1935 after two and a half years in the South Pacific. Britain was in the depth of an economic depression and there was massive unemployment in the regions as the old staple industries – coal, iron, steel, shipbuilding and textiles – went into further decline. On the continent fascism was on the rise as the Nazi campaign of terror against Germany's Jews was stepped up and Mussolini's Fascist troops marched into Abyssinia. As soon as Harrisson returned he went to Oxford to spend Christmas with the Bakers rather than with his family in Hampshire. He was looking forward to seeing Zita again and hoping, even expecting, that they would pick up where they had left off with their relationship.

But he was in for a disappointment. Zita, he learned, had fallen in love with the journalist and aspiring politician Dick Crossman and had left John Baker for him. His own affair with her, it appeared, had put such a strain on her marriage to Baker that it was almost over when they returned to England. She started her affair with Crossman soon after her return to Oxford. She told her husband that this time it was serious and they talked of divorce. Harrisson regretted that he had not come home sooner, but with no money and no academic qualifications, he couldn't realistically have considered himself as a possible husband for Zita. Now he was back in her presence, however, he realised that he had lost the woman he would later describe as 'the love of my life'.

Although he was alienated from his father and contemptuous of his mother, who he said 'never really did anything', he went back to his parents' home in Hampshire at the beginning of 1936. In the conservative shire he must have been an odd sight with his straggly beard, hair down to his shoulders and a skinny frame weakened by the effects of two and a half years of malnutrition and tropical illness. But he soon began to revive and on 16 March he gave a lecture to the Royal Geographical Society in London on 'Living with the People of Malekula'. He ended with a plea for support for his plan to study primitive man in New Guinea. Setting up the expedition was his prime concern, and he tried to persuade Jock Marshall to come to Britain so that they could proceed with their plans. But, although he arranged for him to drum up enthusiasm for the expedition by lecturing about it to the Royal Geographical Society, financial worries prompted Marshall to hesitate.

Harrisson himself was not well off, but he managed to scrape a living from bits of journalism and radio talks while planning the expedition from a two-room rented flat in Chelsea. Thanks to an old Oxford friend, Mary Adams, who had become the first woman producer for the BBC's newly established television service, he became a frequent BBC guest. During his first year back from Malekula he appeared on radio or television half a dozen times. This work supported him while he wrote a book about his experiences in the New Hebrides. By late March, Victor Gollancz had agreed to publish the book and gave him the surprisingly large advance for a new author of £150. Its title, *Savage Civilisation*, clearly expressed his anthropological point of view that the first step for the explorer of an alien culture was to abandon 'our belief that we are the only civilised ones'.

While waiting to head back to New Guinea, Harrisson looked at what his contemporaries were doing. At the time many idealistic young artists, writers and intellectuals like George Orwell and W. H. Auden were going off to fight for the Republican cause in the Spanish Civil War. The war, which broke out in July, pitted a left-wing, democratically elected Republican government against right-wing Nationalist rebels centred on the army led by the fascist General Franco. To the left in Britain this deeply rooted conflict involving struggles between landowners and peasants, Catholics and secularists, regionalists and centralists was seen as an ideological class war between the forces of reform and those of reaction. It was a potential launch pad for social revolution. But this was not for Harrisson. In a war that set communists and anarchists against fascists and monarchists he would have found it hard to choose between the two evils. Unlike his Marxist friends, he had no wish for an egalitarian society. Comfortable with hierarchy and inherited privilege, he felt that the privileged classes, of which he saw himself as a member, had a duty to lead. To do it well, he believed, leaders needed to be in active dialogue with the common people, to learn from their hopes and their fears, and to teach them better ways of thinking about the world and coping with its challenges.[4]

With this in mind, Harrisson decided to try out his cannibal-watching techniques on different savages who were no better known to the British educated public: the working class of the industrial North of England. By doing this he would be joining the growing ranks of his age and class who were making this same journey. The need to escape from the confines of upbringing and to come into contact with the realities of the lives of the underclass had become a leitmotif for a generation of young intellectuals. Many departed for the industrial North, joined the Communist Party or committed themselves to leftist causes. Throughout the 1930s England was crisscrossed by those intent on pinning down the true state of the nation, largely by heading north, and Harrisson became one of them. The common purpose was to show what J. B. Priestley described as 'outer' England to those in the 'inner' England of Westminster, the City and Fleet Street who would, they hoped, buy their books, read their articles, take notice and maybe even take action.[5]

As soon as the manuscript of *Savage Civilisation* was complete Harrisson went north to Bolton. The town had been suggested to him by John Hilton, a well-known broadcaster, journalist and professor of industrial relations at Cambridge, who came from a working-class Bolton family. Harrisson was all the more responsive to Hilton's suggestion because Bolton was the birthplace of William Lever, the founder of Unilever whose economic empire stretched to the New Hebrides, buying copra (the kernel of the coconut, from which coconut oil is extracted) and selling soap. In a 1960 Mass-Observation interview Harrisson explained that his thinking was based on the fact that the only piece of Britain he found among the cannibal Big Nambas in Malekula was their trading contacts with the Unilever combine. 'So I chose Bolton,' he continued, 'because that was the place where the first Lord Leverhulme was born.'[6]

Harrisson arrived in Bolton in September 1936 to try to observe industrial Britain in much the same way as he had done previously when visiting a little-known foreign country. But in contrast to the vivid colours he had been used to on his previous expeditions he found a place whose colours were basically drab: grey, pale buff and dark reds blackened to dull brown.[7] It was a town of which Priestley had written in his *English Journey*, 'the ugliness is so complete that it is almost exhilarating. It challenges you to live there.'

Harrisson's 'anthropological fieldwork', as he called it, involved working an eleven-hour day in a cotton mill for twenty-seven shillings a week and spending his evenings in the pub or at political meetings. He worked in the mill as a labourer, a job that took him all over the huge building, and he was able to observe at close quarters all the processes involved in spinning cotton. Work in the mill was hard and the hours were long, but he soon found out from his fellow workers that the wages didn't provide a lot of comforts for them and their families. When he asked one worker whether he thought working people good at managing, the man pointed out that they never really had a chance. The wages were condemned before the wife had a chance to lay out the money. 'Now, does she get a chance? She's working all the time on a Debt . . . Fancy these days a man having to go out to work on bread and marge as I did yesterday.' His wife said they did not know how they were going to manage. 'Yesterday it was awful. We only had 6 slices of bread and marge and some potatoes. The kids couldn't understand that there wasn't any butties. It's hard when they go hungry.'

But, unlike his fellow workers, for Harrisson it wasn't all hunger, drudgery and desolate poverty. 'Occasionally in the evenings,' he recalled, 'sprinkled with eau de cologne, I sit at the fireside of prosperous Lever relatives, feeling slightly guilty but softly elated. Not just because I'm being given tea or sherry by a wealthy industrialist, but from the fact that being there proves to me that as an Englishman I can penetrate all classes of English society as easily as I could, as a stranger, enter into the village life of Malekulan cannibals.'[8] But when the opportunity came to take a few days off he seized it, especially as it gave him the chance to be reunited with his beloved Zita.

In October, when Zita took a holiday in Hampshire, not far from his parents' home, Harrisson went to see her. Together they rambled all day through green and pleasant countryside, far removed from the dreary greys of the landscape that he was now calling home. As they walked they would have talked about the magnitude of the problems facing society – economic depression, rising unemployment, scepticism about politicians and the threat posed by the rise of fascism and Communism. In London's East End Oswald Mosley and the British Union of Fascists attempted to march through an area with a high proportion of Jewish residents, and there were violent confrontations between protesters and Mosley's Blackshirts, a corps of paramilitary stewards set up to protect the Fascists' meetings from disruption. On Sunday 4 October the clash that became known as the Battle of Cable Street took place between the Metropolitan Police, who were overseeing a march by the BUF, and anti-fascists including local Jewish, socialist, anarchist and communist groups.

Harrisson didn't see communists or fascists as presenting a way forward for the country. Nor did Britain's National government, which, first under Labour's Ramsay MacDonald, then under the Conservative Stanley Baldwin, had set the tone for Britain for most of the 1930s. Like many of his contemporaries, Harrisson felt that its politics, based on class and regional division, were not acceptable. Many of the older industrial regions had been designated 'special areas'. In popular parlance this meant that most of Northern England, South Wales and the industrial belt of Scotland were depressed areas. As he and Zita talked, Harrisson noted that in London the 207 marchers of the Jarrow Crusade had reached Westminster after walking nearly 300 miles from the shipbuilding town on the Tyne, where the unemployment rate was over 80 per cent, to protest against the lack of jobs and extreme poverty in the North-east. Taking pictures of the marchers for the *Left Review* was the rising documentary photographer Humphrey Spender, whom they both knew of through his brother Michael who had been with them on the New Hebrides expedition.

Harrisson also talked enthusiastically about Bolton. 'Going native' there gave him something new and positive to say to Zita. The real issues of sociology, he pronounced, could be faced only if the sociologist was prepared to plunge deeply under the surface of British life and become directly acquainted with the mass of people who left school before they were fifteen. This was, he said, exactly what he was doing and he insisted there was nothing in his own upbringing, education or accent to prevent him from mixing on equal terms with these working-class people. He claimed that he was a committed socialist, so for him the move to live among the strange Northern working-class people of Bolton was a way of living in accordance with his beliefs. 'Before a man can call himself a live socialist,' he declared, 'he must have lived among working men, be directly conscious of poverty and have been bitten by a workhouse louse.' But he also confided in her that, in spite of all the bravado, it wasn't easy for him. He freely admitted he had less knowledge of the English working class than he had of Malekulan cannibals. But at least the North of England, as a place in which to practise fieldwork techniques, had the advantage of not requiring interpreters.[9]

Back in Bolton at the spinning mill Harrisson talked to his fellow workers and whenever he got the chance sought their views on the jobs they were doing. A thirty-six-year-old spinner said he used to like his job until he discovered that he was not expected to use his brain, and that further promotion was impossible. 'I have just enough interest to keep my job,' he said, 'but wouldn't care very much if the mill closed down.' A thirty-year-old piecer* said he hated his job, but continued for the sake of his children. He said he'd tried repeatedly to get out of the mill but couldn't. A female carder† explained that most women could not afford to give up work after they were married.

Lancashire women are notoriously house-proud, and to have a 'nice home' is certainly something for her to work for. The men are not well paid, particularly in the spinning industry, until they have reached or passed what we would call a marriageable age, about 25 years, and young men and women marrying under these circumstances endeavour to consolidate their position by the wife working a year or two at least.

* A spinner's assistant who had to lean over the spinning machines to repair broken threads.
† Carding is a mechanical process that disentangles, cleans and mixes the raw cotton fibres.

As he got to know his fellow workers he found out more about their working conditions and about some of the dangers. Cancer, he learned, was a disease of the cotton mills, the worst of several. There were also numerous accidents in the mill. The practice of cleaning machinery while it was in motion led to crushed hands and fingers. Broken belts would sometimes fly loose and injure the spinner. But accidents were the least of the cotton workers' troubles. They only happened occasionally, whereas the change from the warm and damp atmosphere of the mill to the normal temperature of the street went on day after day. In consequence cotton operatives were subject to rheumatism and bronchial complaints, and this was not improved by the smoke-filled air of a town like Bolton.

The climax to the day in the mill was when the red bulb flashed for a few seconds at one corner of the great rooms that housed the machinery. Everyone waited and watched for that, clothed and ready for the rush to the doors and out into the air. The workers streamed out through the mill gates – men in cloth caps and mufflers, women in drab coats and headscarves. The route to and from work was so familiar that the only things people took an interest in were the others ahead. They never looked at the shop-windows as they passed in the evening.[10]

Only one worker would look and take an interest in all he saw around him. Harrisson was still fascinated by the sights and sounds of Worktown, as he had now come to call it. Hurrying past the mills on a cold, dark November evening he could see through the big windows of the engine house the gleaming leviathan inside with its great flywheel turning. And up above, there was the clag of black smoke curling out of the chimney as the fireman shovelled coal into the boiler. Trams rattled along the middle of Manchester Road and big noisy diesel lorries lurched along carrying coal and huge bales of cotton to and from the mills. Steam engines were everywhere – in the mills, on the railways and, occasionally, trundling up and down the roads. All over the town there were engineering companies and foundries, loom-makers and textile-machinery manufacturers, large and small, all providing back-up for the textile industry. Harrisson took it all in, making a mental note of everything he saw.

He made his way to the Lever's Arms, a pub on Nelson Square in the town centre, where he had a room. Here he hastily changed out of his work clothes into a smart suit, collar and tie, went down to the hallway and called for a taxi. He may not have had a great deal of money, but old habits die hard and he wouldn't dream of going anywhere on public transport. Mixing with the natives was one thing, but it certainly didn't stretch to travelling around with them on a tramcar. The taxi made its way up one of the hills leading from the town centre towards Egerton, a prosperous area on the edge of the moors where many of the mill owners had their houses. He was heading out for dinner at the home of one of the Lever relatives. W. E. Tillotson was the husband of one of William Lever's nieces. The liberal owner of one of the main local newspapers, he was to become an invaluable ally for Harrisson throughout his time in Bolton. But this evening was to be their first meeting.

Harrisson arrived just before 7.30 and was taken into the front drawing room which was lined with books, the most notable being a series of bound volumes of *The Anglo-Saxon Chronicle*. Tillotson was standing in front of the fire. His daughter sat on a small stool by the hearth. They were soon joined by Tillotson's wife and son, and a butler brought in a tray of pale dry sherries. Over drinks before dinner Tillotson asked Harrisson what had brought him to Bolton. In reply Harrisson began by telling him about his time in the New Hebrides, where, he said, 'the people were still wild and eating each other. But the Big Nambas of Malekula proved to be as pleasant as, and no more difficult to live with than, the English, Irish or Welsh, of whom I had previous experience. And I slowly began to realise that while anthropologists are generously financed to go all over the world studying so-called primitive peoples, no one is making comparable studies of ourselves. When the expedition was over, therefore, I was determined to return to study the cannibals of Britain. So I came back to England and decided to go and immerse myself in a working-class environment and study them objectively. I wanted to study the lives of mill workers, coal-miners and other industrial workers from an anthropological angle by asking them the sort of questions that I had asked the Malekulan natives about their everyday activities. So I came up here to the less savage but to me equally exotic Bolton to apply the anthropological techniques I learned on Malekula to the town which I call Worktown. While I've been here I've worked as a lorry driver and in a cotton mill, eleven hours a day for twenty-seven shillings in wages to try and sort out my ideas and to try out techniques for making studies in the field in England.'

Harrisson held the floor and the Tillotson family listened intently until dinner was announced. The daughter threw half a cigarette into the fire as the family led Harrisson into the dining room. When they were seated, drinks were offered – Sauternes, beer or whisky. Everybody chose the Sauternes except young Tillotson, who had a Magee's Brown Ale. The food was hard-boiled eggs sliced in half, filled with anchovy paste and served on lettuce leaves. This was followed by small portions of cold chicken with tongue and cold mutton. Only one bottle of Sauternes circulated: it was from the Co-operative Wine Society and, Harrisson noted, it was not one of their best choices.[11]

Over dinner his hosts expressed some surprise at the way in which somebody from such a middle-class background felt he could fit in with such a wide range of different people in such divergent societies. Harrisson was almost boastful in answering their questions, bragging that he was 'intelligent, reasonable and independent. Since I was fifteen, I have been doing all sorts of things, living in slums, on trawlers, desert islands, South America, Lapland, and the East, bicycling in Europe, rock-climbing, hop-picking, playing a barrel organ, feeling hungry, staying at Shepheards' Hotel in Cairo, sleeping in lavatories and the baths of hotels, writing articles and a book on natural history and scientific subjects.'[12] It was very easy, he continued, for him to go anywhere and to eat anything at all, or to sleep in the day and stay up all night, or to drink a great deal or not drink a great deal, and if one could do that sort of thing, he maintained, it was easy to get on almost anywhere in the world. The only thing you needed to have along with these attributes of acceptance and non-prejudice was personality. 'No society,' he insisted, 'whether it's a cotton mill in Bolton, or a group of toughs in a long house in the middle of Borneo, want you there as part of the landscape. You must justify your existence either by being extremely good at something, or by having some sort of pep or charm, or being able to stand on your head for forty minutes and tell dirty stories at the same time – or something that is going to amuse and interest people.'[13]

Over dinner that evening he certainly amused the Tillotson family. After a sweet of individual dewberry tarts and jelly with strawberries, followed by Lancashire cheese, Mrs Tillotson and her daughter withdrew and a decanter of port was circulated. This was accompanied by cigars. When asked why he had given Bolton the name Worktown, Harrisson explained that it was simply because its major weekday occupation was industrial work and he felt that as such it was reasonably representative of a largely working-class town. Tillotson senior and junior were both impressed and by the time the older Tillotson got to his fifth port, Harrisson had gained a useful ally for the work he was planning in Bolton.

The town was certainly a good choice. As well as the textile industry, other main occupations in Bolton were engineering machinery, coal-mining, building and food, drink and tobacco. In other sections of enterprise over 10,000 were engaged in commerce and finance, while of the 1,043 professionals the largest group was religion, with 179 males and 48 females earning income from churches. He wanted to be able to observe as many different people and groups within this alien society as possible, so he quit his job in the mill and tried being a lorry driver, a shop assistant and an ice-cream man. The novelty of the different types of work and the opportunity that each of these jobs gave him to spy on the native Boltonians appealed to him. Harrisson was keen to immerse himself in the life of the town as completely as possible so every evening after work, when he wasn't hobnobbing with Bolton's high society, he toured pubs and attended political meetings.

He also started to attend a night-school class on the 'History of the People of Bolton from 1900 to 1937' run by the Workers' Educational Association.* Described as 'an opportunity to work out a new way of studying about ourselves', it was very much in tune with his ideas for an anthropological study of the people of Bolton. The class was run by Albert Smith, a local man who was about the same age as Harrisson. The son of an insurance agent, Smith grew up in Bolton and went to Oxford on a scholarship. He described himself as an anthropologist and ran classes designed to have popular appeal; one of these he labelled 'Striptease to Shakespeare: An Anthropological Study of Drama'. 'History is criticism,' Smith told the class that Harrisson attended, adding that rather than reading vast and dull books about the Industrial Revolution they would bring their own life experiences to the class.[14] Harrisson was already starting to think about volunteer observers for his embryonic Worktown project and in this group of working-class men familiarised with anthropological ideas by Smith's teaching he saw a small group of likely candidates. Smith himself was a good man to know, somebody here on the ground who had similar ideas to his own. After the classes they would go for a drink and discuss these ideas in relation to some of the big issues of the day. For any group of intelligent working men like this the rise of fascism on the continent and the response of Britain's National government was always going to be a hot topic of conversation. Since the First World War there had been a powerful disarmament movement which reached its peak in the mid-1930s and strong support for the League of Nations, which had been created in 1920 to provide a forum for resolving international disputes and maintaining world peace. Ramsay Macdonald, a committed internationalist and pacifist, was an enthusiastic believer that the League

---

* Founded in 1903, the WEA was and still is the UK's largest voluntary-sector provider of adult education.

of Nations could make the world disarm through dialogue. But by the mid-1930s the rise of militant regimes across Europe meant that the idea of 'collective security' espoused by the League was looking increasingly unworkable. There was particular concern about Germany's blatant territorial ambitions. Under the Versailles settlement at the end of the First World War, the Rhineland had been demilitarised, but Hitler claimed that this threatened Germany, so earlier in 1936 he had sent troops into the region. In Britain this was not opposed. The general feeling was that the Germans were merely walking into their own back yard and Prime Minister Stanley Baldwin said that British public opinion would not allow Britain to intervene. But there were many on the left who felt that a stand needed to be taken, particularly as one of the Nazis' ideologies was to reunite all Germans either born or living outside the Reich in order to create an 'all-German Reich'.

The National government's policy was one of appeasement – making political concessions to Germany in order to avoid conflict. That reflected the general mood in the country: anything to keep out of war. It was a policy that stirred up heated discussion, many arguing that making any concessions towards the Nazis was a pro-fascist policy. Towards the end of 1936, however, there was another issue that had come to dominate political debate – the abdication crisis. King George V had died in January and been succeeded by his eldest son, Edward. But there was a problem caused by the new King's intimate friendship with the divorced and remarried American Mrs Wallis Simpson. By the summer, when Mrs Simpson decided that the time had come for a divorce from her second husband, the relationship was beginning to cause concern in official circles. Most of the British public knew little about the relationship because the press had completely covered up the developing constitutional crisis, which began with the news that Mrs Simpson was seeking a divorce.

Edward VIII was popular with the British public, who saw him as 'the people's King'. In the early months of his reign he'd visited many of the depressed regions of his kingdom, shown empathy for the poor and unemployed among his subjects and become a champion of their needs. 'Something must be done,' he declared as he visited South Wales and saw for himself the desperate conditions of the unemployed. None of this made him popular with the government and, as the abdication crisis grew, a fundamental division in British society was laid bare. The National government, led by Stanley Baldwin, resented the King's popularity and his tendency to comment publicly on slums and unemployment. The King's wish to marry Mrs Simpson gave the government the opportunity to force a constitutional crisis by refusing to accept a marriage which would allow her to be his wife but not queen. Just over two weeks after the Simpson decree nisi was granted, Edward summoned Baldwin to Buckingham Palace to inform him of his determination to marry Mrs Simpson and to tell him that if the government and people of Great Britain found this unacceptable, he would abdicate. This unshakeable determination of the King to marry an American commoner who was twice divorced was a major constitutional issue and there were worries within the Establishment as to whether the monarchy would survive.

In the pub after one of Smith's classes Harrisson declared that one of the reasons he had decided to go to live and work in Bolton was to ask ordinary working men and women what they thought about the major issues of the day, not least the abdication crisis. What it revealed for him, he said, was the serious divergence between opinion as published by politicians and the press and the public opinion of the man in the street, who was, he felt, endlessly misinterpreted. 'Working in a place like Bolton,' he went on, 'I have been greatly struck by the complete discrepancy between what all the people I am working with think and what is being reported in the newspapers and on the BBC. The gap between leader and led, between published opinion and public opinion, between Westminster chatter and Lancashire talk has built an invisible barrier, and that is dangerous in our democracy.'[15]

The abdication crisis and the gulf it created between these two worlds was central to Harrisson's thinking about why his project was so important, and he followed developments avidly. After two weeks of debate and attempts to find a compromise, Baldwin returned to the Palace on 4 December to tell the King that if he persisted in his wish to marry Mrs Simpson, he would have to abdicate. Letters flooded into newspaper offices supporting the King. It appeared that the vast majority of the British people were in favour of his marriage. Crowds packed Downing Street chanting 'We want our King!', and women paraded outside Buckingham Palace carrying placards that read 'God save the King from Baldwin'. The crisis had the effect of pushing all the other major stories of the day – the Spanish Civil War, the German threat, the depressed areas – on to the back pages.[16]

As the truth about the King's relationship with Mrs Simpson emerged, the complicated relationship Harrisson had with Zita Baker continued to run its course. In December she was living in rented digs in Devon. Dick Crossman came to visit her and she told him all about Harrisson's job in the cotton mill. 'He writes marvellous letters about it. He really is a one.'

She said she was going to visit him in Bolton but told Crossman not to worry, assuring him that she would be marrying him when her divorce came through. 'Tom', she said, 'is a good friend and I remember fondly the times I had with him. Of course, he is frightfully attractive and for a year he was a wonderful lover, but because I'm with you now I wouldn't sleep with him now even though I would still like to.'[17]

Having given these assurances Zita went to visit Harrisson in Bolton. When she got there the Christmas season was in full swing. The shops with their special displays were crowded; and over all smiled the bearded benevolent face of Father Christmas. 'The old festival of Christmas has a new function in industrial Worktown,' Harrisson told her. 'It is a time when the thwarted wish for abundance and riches can have at least a symbolic satisfaction. At Christmas nearly every coal-house is piled full of coal, partly because fires will be stacked high and their warm glow will be the central feature of domestic comfort, but partly also because of the real pleasure that a householder finds in a full coal-house. It's a pleasure quite like that which the Trobriand Islanders we knew got from elaborately piling up yams in their store-house. From three weeks before Christmas the Worktowners start buying presents – and they give freely. The exchange of presents among grown-ups is on the same principle as in the Trobriands – you usually get much the same as you give.'[18]

The New Hebrides and the passionate affair they'd had there was what bound them together, and Harrisson made frequent references to it in their conversation. 'In Bolton,' he said,

> unless I do something outlandish like going barefoot or wearing my hair long I can be inconspicuous in a way not possible in the Pacific. My biggest thrill has been to find myself so easily accepted in Worktown as an equal in the cotton mills, as a lorry driver or an ice-cream man, in a corner pub or a working man's club. The fact that I have a so-called Oxford accent in no way adds to any suspicion that I am a spy. I only have to claim that I've come from another dialect area a few miles away. In fact no worker in his senses would ever suppose that anyone would come to Worktown for any reason other than of necessity. And it never seems to have occurred to anyone that someone else might want to observe, let alone record, his common everyday actions.[19]

Observation was the key, he insisted. It wasn't enough to ask people what their beliefs and values were. Only by direct observation of behaviour could one hope to understand how a culture operated in practice.

That is how they had operated in Malekula. 'Much of what I saw and heard there I would not have seen and heard if I had not been there a long time; if I had not also won and re-won the confidence of most of the people; if I had not shown a positive sympathy with their culture and an active participation in a large part of it.' This, he said, was exactly the way he was going to have to operate here in Bolton. If it meant roughing it among the labouring classes, that's the way it had to be. And, he reasoned to Zita, to an outside observer, the working classes could be just as fascinating as cannibals. But the reality was that, even with visits from Zita, Bolton was not as much fun as the New Hebrides. Perhaps that is why, despite all the bluff and bluster about Worktown, he was still hoping the New Guinea expedition would come off or that Douglas Fairbanks would give the go-ahead for the *Cannibals* film and that his days in Bolton would be limited.

2

ANTHROPOLOGY AT HOME

*'Nearly everybody who was not born into the working
class regards them as almost a race apart'*

Tom Harrisson

Number 6 Grotes Buildings was a tall Georgian town house just yards
away from Blackheath Village, one of London's more affluent suburbs.
Fronting directly on to the wide open spaces of the common, the home
of the poet and journalist Charles Madge, his partner and fellow poet
Kathleen Raine and their two young children was a world away from
the smoke and grime of industrial Bolton. But within this elegant house
Madge was thinking along very similar lines to Harrisson about the
abdication crisis and the state of British society and, with a group of like-
minded friends, he was beginning to have discussions looking at what
they might be able to do about it.

Madge was the epitome of the upper-middle-class intellectual. A very
refined-looking young man with a long face and slender, artistic fingers,
he belonged to a group of artists, poets, writers and film-makers all based
in Blackheath. He had been a leading literary figure from his early twenties and was also, as a card-carrying member of the Communist Party, one
of a group of extreme left-wingers who came from privileged upper-class
homes.[1] Like Harrisson he came from a colonial background and was
born in South Africa in 1912. His father, who had been a colonel in the
Boer War, worked in colonial administration organising white immigra-
tion. On the outbreak of war in 1914 his father went to fight in France,
where he was killed in 1916. Madge was a clever child, who entered Win-
chester College as a scholar. While he was there he began to write poetry
before going to Magdalene, Cambridge in 1931, where his Latin prose
was hailed as the finest of his year. His poetry was published alongside
that of Auden and Spender in T. S. Eliot's literary magazine the *Criterion*.

Madge had gone up to university committed to Empire and the Conservative Party, but underwent a dramatic change of heart after hunger

marchers from the North-east passed through the Fens on their way to London with their demand for 'work or full maintenance at trade union rates'. 'My attention', Madge recalled, 'was diverted by marchers of the National Unemployed Workers' Movement who bivouacked for the night near my college. These impressively resolute Geordies advised me to get in touch with the University Communist Party; thus began my one active year in that organisation.'[2] While at Cambridge he was swept off his feet by the glamorous Kathleen Raine, who was four years older than him and unhappily married. He abandoned his studies and his selection as the next Secretary of the Communist Party branch and eloped with her. After they had their first child the couple got by initially with occasional fees for reviews and some financial support from Madge's mother. Their finances improved when T. S. Eliot persuaded a journalist friend to find Madge a job as a reporter on the *Daily Mirror* and arranged for Faber to publish his first book of verse, *The Disappearing Castle*. When he got the job on the *Mirror*, early in 1936, the Madges moved into the eighteenth-century house in Blackheath. The job, Madge said, brought him into contact with the 'real concerns of life',[3] and he became increasingly conscious of the gap between what ordinary people thought and what their leaders thought they thought.

Living in Blackheath the Madges found agreeable friends, including Humphrey Jennings and his wife Cecily. Jennings had been a close friend of Madge since their Cambridge days. After graduating from Pembroke College with a first in English, he had a variety of jobs including teaching abroad, photographer, painter and theatre-designer. In 1931, at the age of twenty-four, he went to Paris to design in silk, but his first and greatest love was painting, and he stayed in Paris painting until his money ran out. In 1934, he at last settled down to steady work, making films for the GPO Film Unit which had been set up the previous year under the pioneering Scottish documentary-maker John Grierson to produce sponsored documentary films mainly related to the activities of the General Post Office, which ran both the postal service and the telephone and telegraph systems. For Jennings it was an exciting place to work. Although the unit had been established as part of the GPO's new public relations department, Grierson had a wider vision than mere PR and he oversaw the creation of a unit that he attempted to direct towards a socially useful purpose. Borrowing from the aesthetics of Soviet cinema, the unit's films were at the cutting edge of film technique – demonstrating, as J. B. Priestley observed, what 'camera and sound could really do . . . Grierson and his young men, with their contempt for easy big prizes and soft living, their taut social conscience, their rather Marxist sense of the contemporary scene always seemed to me at least a generation ahead of the dramatic film people.'4 The GPO Film Unit (which became the Crown Film Unit in 1940) was based in Blackheath which brought others into Madge's circle including the documentary film-maker Stuart Legg and his wife Margaret. Other members of the group included Guy Hunter, a communist friend from Madge's Cambridge days, and David Gascoyne, a poet and leading surrealist, who, along with Jennings, had been on the organising committee of a major Surrealist Exhibition in London in June 1936.

The Blackheath group, who began to meet regularly at Madge's house, were very much part of a wider set of leftist, upper-middle-class members of the Auden generation that included in its ranks George Orwell, Stephen Spender, Christopher Isherwood, Louis MacNeice, Humphrey Jennings and William Coldstream. All took up the professions of journalist, photographer or film-maker in an attempt not only to make a living but also to put themselves in touch with real life and expand the meaning of their creative lives. These materially privileged and highly educated young men were acutely aware of their social and political isolation and their ignorance of the conditions in which most people lived. The threat of fascism made the need to examine and understand the real life of the 'masses' and to be aware of their true opinions which were rarely aired in the press seem all the more urgent.

The Blackheath group shared this deep concern. Like Harrisson they were all uneasily aware of the inadequacy of communication between popular opinion and its representation by the powerful in the press and Parliament. The abdication crisis gave them the opportunity to confirm their suspicions and test some of their theories. The fact that, despite his proposed marriage to Mrs Simpson, the King continued to enjoy the support of the British people and that this was not reflected in the press provided the focus for a series of discussions at Madge's house in the autumn and winter of 1936.

Madge was closer to the story than most. As a reporter on the *Daily Mirror* he was covering the events leading up to the abdication. 'Employed now here, now there by my news editor,' he recalled, 'I stood little chance of an overall view of what was going on, but at least what I did know was at first hand, and of potentially more historical interest than the largely fabricated and contradictory accounts that appeared in the newspapers, including my own.' The massive falsification by the press provided Madge with 'an object lesson in how the masses were being misrepresented and excluded'.[5] The *Daily Mirror*'s main concern was with human-interest stories, and in seeking them out Madge knocked on many doors where 'I had glimpses of the lives of a great variety of people. There was strong public support for the King, which was de-emphasised by the press.'[6] The crisis convinced Madge that something would have to be done to bridge the gulf between the newspapers' increasingly anti-Edward editorials and what millions of ordinary people thought and felt. 'The abdication was no isolated national upheaval,' he felt. 'We had already witnessed the Spanish war and the Abyssinia invasion. By the mid-1930s it was easy to see that Europe was heading for rack and ruin. I felt most strongly that while these momentous events were unfolding ordinary people ought to be setting down both their own and other people's reactions – not only for their historical value but also to help gauge movements of opinion.'[7]

The Blackheath group were also intrigued by surrealism, the European artistic movement which took its inspiration from the language of dreams and revolutionary politics while rebelling against the tyranny of prevailing sexual, religious and social conventions. This, they believed, combined with the newly fashionable social sciences of anthropology and sociology, might provide a key to the understanding of modern society. The small group of British surrealists to which they belonged saw significance in accidents and coincidences. One of these, in their view, was the burning down of London's Crystal Palace – the iron-and-glass home of the 1851 Great Exhibition – on the night of 30 November. When this great symbol of Victorian architectural and engineering achievement caught fire, the blaze (one of the largest ever seen in the capital) raged all night, with flames leaping, it was reported, as high as 500 feet. David Gascoyne was on the train home to Richmond after a meeting at Madge's house when he saw the 'great glow in the sky'. For him, the fire 'represented in a sort of symbolic way an image of the world-conflagration which we were already beginning to think of as about to break out'. Other members of the group reacted in the same way. They began to wonder if there could be a meaning in the destruction of such an iconic building, and this prompted them to discuss the symbolic significance in the national consciousness of this and similar events. 'The shock that it seemed to evoke at a symbolic level', Madge said, 'was perhaps akin to the shock that the abdication crisis brought to our stable monarchy.'

On 10 December, the King abdicated in favour of his brother the Duke of York. The story was now out in the open, but the group felt it was significant that the press had delayed reporting the crisis until the last minute – exactly the kind of society-wide repression that the surrealists wanted to break. When the country had been thrown into this constitutional crisis, the need for information seemed imperative: couldn't the King do what he wanted and marry the woman he loved? Who ran the country? Was it the government, the King or the newspapers?[8] The group saw the possibility of studying the abdication and mass reaction to it on anthropological lines. 'Our thinking', Madge recalled, 'was confused, and there was a certain conflict between a more would-be scientific and a more surrealistic tendency within it.' But it led to them producing a questionnaire which began by asking: 'What are your superstitions in order of importance? Do you pay attention to coincidences? What is your class?' It later went on to ask: 'Did you want the King to marry Mrs Simpson and if so why? Were you glad or sorry when the Crystal Palace was burnt down and if so why?'[9]

The group's thinking then led to them looking into the possibility of enlisting volunteers for the observation of social happenings like the abdication and also of 'everyday life' as lived by themselves and those around them. At the same time they began to discuss the formation of a group of writers, painters, photographers and film-makers to start what Madge described as 'an anthropology of ourselves' and decided to write a letter to the *New Statesman* about it. Like Harrisson in Bolton, Madge and Jennings were interested in social investigation, but what they envisaged was a London-based project in which a national panel of volunteers would reply to regular questionnaires on a variety of subjects. For Harrisson the approach was very different. He believed that the best way to understand what ordinary working-class people did and what they thought about the world was to get in among them to watch and record them, without their knowledge, as they went about their everyday lives. This is exactly what he was doing in Bolton. In his various workplaces he was a participant observer, watching all the time as he worked, then coming back at night to write it all up.

Savage Civilisation was published by Gollancz in January 1937 and was received with the greatest enthusiasm by reviewers, particularly H. G. Wells. Harrisson had virtually made his name as an anthropologist overnight. To help launch the book he arranged to have a poem dedicated to Zita Baker that he had written in the New Hebrides three years before published in the *New Statesman* early that month. He didn't have enough money to buy a copy so he went to the library in Bolton to see his poem in print. On the same page he happened to notice the letter written by Charles Madge, under the heading 'Anthropology at Home'. In it Madge claimed that he was the spokesman for a group of people formed to begin an 'anthropology of our own people'. The letter was full of what Harrisson regarded as surrealist jargon. The writer talked of 'mass wish situations' and said that the group he represented used the 'principles of anthropology, psycho-analysis and the sciences dealing with the behaviour of man' and applying them to the 'Crystal Palace–Abdication symbolic situation'. This sounded like pretentious nonsense to the hard-headed Harrisson and he was about to stop reading the letter when his attention was drawn to what followed.

The real observers, the letter went on, were the millions of people who were, for once, irretrievably involved in the public events. 'Only mass observation', it stated, 'can create mass science. The group for whom I write is engaged in establishing observation points on as widely extended a front as can at present be organised. We invite the co-operation of voluntary observers, and will provide detailed information to anyone who wants to take part.' Harrisson was eager to find out more. He cared nothing for the surrealism, but he was interested in the similarity of these aims to his own anthropological study in Bolton. And, above all, he immediately saw the opportunity to turn his one-man project into a major research enterprise. He got in touch with Madge straight away and was invited to a meeting in Blackheath.[10]

When Harrisson arrived at Madge's house for the meeting, David Gascoyne, Kathleen Raine and Humphrey Jennings were also present. Madge explained that he had been dreaming about an 'anthropology of ourselves' since his Cambridge days. They talked about the role of myth and superstition in national life, public opinion and the importance of getting to know more about the lives of working people. The Depression had made workers' misery acute, and, as fascism spread, it seemed crucial to understand what workers wanted and believed.

Harrisson wasn't naturally drawn to this group of 'arty' intellectuals, but he felt that his own project had enough in common with what they wanted to do to make it worthwhile collaborating with them. He told the group that his chief recreation was 'living among strange people and listening to them talk about themselves', and this, he said, included the English working class. 'Nearly everybody who was not born into the working class', he continued, 'regards them as almost a race apart. The wilds of Lancashire or the mysteries of the East End are as little explored as the cannibal interior of the New Hebrides or the head-hunter hinterland of Borneo. In particular my experiences living among cannibals in the New Hebrides taught me the many points in common between these wild-looking, fuzzy-haired, black, smelly people and our own. So when I came home from that expedition I determined to apply the same methods here in Britain. All over the world people like me are going to study other civilisations on a scale of intimacy and detail which has not yet been applied to our own civilised societies and I want to put that right.'

This was an idea that was just coming into its own with the birth of sociology, whose followers were beginning to apply social anthropological methods to the study of developed societies. But these ideas about observing the masses that Harrisson was putting forward were very different from those of the group he'd come to meet; and in Jennings – a great talker, super-confident in manner and an uncontrollable eccentric – he found himself face to face with a man who was as opinionated and dogmatic as he was. Right from the start Harrisson's relationship with Jennings was prickly, and there was no real dialogue between them at this first meeting. As David Gascoyne recalled, 'Humphrey Jennings was a great talker. But Tom Harrisson also turned out to have a great gift and inclination for talking, and what I chiefly remember of the evening is the picture of Humphrey, with his elbow on one end of the mantelpiece, and Harrisson with his elbow on the other end of the mantelpiece, both talking loudly and simultaneously to those present in general, without either of them paying the slightest attention to what the other was saying.'[11]

It must have been obvious to all present that, if Harrisson were to get involved, a major clash of egos within the fledgling movement would be inevitable. Harrisson also had reservations. He was impressed by the cleverness of Madge's circle, but that was about as far as it went. He had no time for what he regarded as their Marxist and surrealist mumbo-jumbo and wasn't prepared to compromise what he saw as his own scientific empiricism. Rather than allow that to happen he made it clear that he wouldn't join forces but would instead continue to pursue his own line in Bolton independently. But Madge, in particular, wanted Harrisson on board and in the days following the meeting he managed to persuade him that there would be something to be gained if they pooled their two very different approaches to the study of popular culture. They decided that the two projects, related in their ideals but different in the techniques they employed to gather information, should join together to form Mass-Observation – an organisation dedicated to developing what they called a 'science of ourselves'. Its stated purpose would be to gather facts about the everyday thoughts, habits and activities of working-class men and women to raise awareness about their lives.

Harrisson stayed on in London and immediately began work with

Madge on a pamphlet, *Mass-Observation*, designed to recruit observers. They made an interesting, if difficult, partnership. Not dissimilar in background, they were polar opposites in personality. Harrisson has been described as 'a classic rogue, determined to be outrageous and succeeding, dominant in whatever company'.[12] Part courageous man of action, part rigorous scholar, part adventurer and part bully, he was an exceptionally charismatic, authoritarian, ferociously independent figure. Many of those who came into contact with him favoured the term 'bloody-minded' or 'cantankerous'. Madge, in contrast, was sensitive in manner, quiet and vulnerable. He bore the personal marks of a gentle and superior upbringing – a diffident and self-effacing manner which hid his passionate and impulsively radical nature.[13]

From the very first days Madge looked as though he was going to be easily dominated by the overbearing Harrisson, and members of the Blackheath group were wary of this bombastic individual who appeared to be taking over their ideas and shaping the newly formed organisation in his own image. In his journal David Gascoyne wrote: 'I at once began to have a pretty clear idea of what direction the movement was going to take. Jennings and Harrisson obviously both had very strong personalities, and it was also obvious on that first occasion of their meeting that they did not take to each other very much, but of the two, practically speaking, Tom Harrisson, unfortunately to my mind, was the stronger. And from then on he began, with Madge at first, and later himself almost entirely to take complete control of what was soon to be well known as Mass-Observation.'[14]

Madge certainly found it a challenge working with Harrisson. 'Attempting to write in collaboration with him was', he admitted, 'one of the most stimulating and difficult tasks one could imagine.'[15] In spite of the problems, they did manage to get the pamphlet completed. In it they explained that Mass-Observation was a new organisation that aimed to do 'sociological research of the first importance', which had hitherto never been attempted. It would 'collect a mass of data based on practical observation of the everyday life of all types of people' and would use it 'for the scientific study of Twentieth Century man in all his different environments'. The primary motive behind the setting up of Mass-Observation was, in Madge's view, 'the perception that a national crisis, in this case the Abdication, which aroused strong feelings and opinions at every level of society, could come and go without any accurate record or scientific analysis being made of it. And there was the further perception that other graver crises lay ahead in which knowledge and understanding of collective response was much to be desired. And side by side with the crises, normal everyday patterns of thought and behaviour were largely unmapped and little understood.'[16]

The original manifesto for Mass-Observation was set out in a letter published in the *New Statesman* on 30 January 1937 entitled 'Anthropology at Home'. In it the founders announced that Darwin, Marx and Freud had a successor – or, more accurately, successors. 'Mass-Observation develops out of anthropology, psychology and the sciences that study man,' the letter read, 'but it plans to work with a mass of observers.' The movement already had fifty volunteers, and it aspired to have 5,000. The letter was signed by Harrisson, Madge and Jennings. But, in a sign of the discord that was to come, Jennings who had not seen the final draft was angry that his name was attached to the letter.

The letter expressed ideals, hinted at revolutionary intent and made reference to contemporary social and political philosophy as well as to popular culture.[17] It included a bizarre plan of campaign listing a strange assortment of topics including the behaviour of people at war memorials, the shouts and gestures of motorists, the aspidistra cult, the anthropology of football pools, bathroom behaviour, the private lives of midwives, the distribution, diffusion and significance of the dirty joke, and beards, armpits and eyebrows. The almost deliberate silliness of the list was very much in accord with surrealist humour. But the authors of the manifesto believed that the data collected would enable the organisers to plot 'weather-maps of public feeling'. Their aim was nothing less than to achieve a complete understanding of modern society, neglecting nothing as unimportant. They were hampered as they set off on their quest, however, by very little knowledge of what social scientists before them had done.[18]

This lack of knowledge of the new discipline of sociology proved to be off-putting for some potential Mass-Observers. One of them was Dennis Chapman. The son of a West Country trade union organiser who had himself served a craft apprenticeship, Chapman had recently graduated from the London School of Economics. 'I came in at the very beginning of M-O,' he recalled,

> but I didn't have much sympathy for their approach, and their unwillingness to admit the existence of literature or skill or training or method. My first contact was with Charles Madge at a flat in Hunter Street, owned or rented by a man called Guy Hunter, who I think had just come down from Oxford. It was a most elegant place and I remember he had a Cona

coffee machine. It was the first time I'd ever seen one. They were discussing the possibility of using volunteers to send in accounts of their lives and particular events. What I think was characteristic of the situation was that Charles Madge knew nothing whatsoever about the history of social research or the methods of social research or the methods of statistics, or scientific methods.[19]

These were all things that were very familiar to an LSE graduate like Chapman, and he expressed astonishment that Madge was so totally ignorant not only of them but also of the enormous amount of material available from nineteenth-century sources – books recording working life and literature associated with the Mechanics' Institutes in which people described work. Madge, Chapman recalled, knew none of this, and this 'total abysmal ignorance' made him very sceptical, so he went off to work for the sociological researcher, social reformer and industrialist Seebohm Rowntree on his study of 'Poverty and Progress' in York.

Madge and Jennings seemed unconcerned about their lack of experience in sociological research. They thought they could identify and record the character of British society from small samples, so a team of volunteers was recruited to fill out reports and diaries. By 12 February, thirty people had been recruited who agreed to set down plainly all that happened to them on the 12th of each month. They were asked to record the everyday concerns of their lives, including their dreams, their hopes and their fears. These 'day-surveys' were designed 'to collect a mass of data without any selective principle'. As well as documenting what happened to people on an 'ordinary' day, the surveys in February, March and April were also trial runs for the survey of 12 May, the day that was set for the Coronation of the new King, George VI.

Right from the start Harrisson had reservations about the usefulness of the panel and the day-surveys. 'An "anthropology of ourselves"', he maintained, 'would have to be primarily direct observation of ordinary Englishmen, men of the working class.'

Scant systematic, long-term fieldwork has been done of such Englishmen before now, and virtually none of it has been done from inside the group, watching what people do when they don't realise they are being observed, as opposed to ringing their doorbells to read out a list of questions in an Oxbridge accent. I don't oppose the idea of having panellists reply to directives and diarists recording what went on during an average day, but my idea of Mass-Observation is that the emphasis should be on direct, objective and, as far as is possible, invisible observation, recording what people are actually doing. Replies to directives and the diaries are useful as secondary sources, recording what people think they are doing.[20]

Despite this crucial difference in approach, Harrisson, Madge and Jennings had one thing they could all agree on quite unequivocally. All three saw Britain as divided: a small educated elite, privileged both materially and politically, but ignorant of the majority; and the majority, poorly educated and uninformed. They also saw a fundamental social division in Britain between modernity and tradition, something that had been laid bare by the abdication crisis. Opinion in the country, they believed, 'had been polarised by a modern king, at ease with air transport and radio broadcasts, supported throughout the crisis by an emergent modern mass society and opposed by Parliament, the Church and the media establishment. Concerned with Fleet Street's 'foisting on the masses . . . ideas and ideals, developed by men apart from it', the three founders hoped to publish accurate records of opinions and diary excerpts from around the country and of the observed behaviour of Bolton's residents. The emphasis was on getting as wide a picture as possible of the social contexts in which people lived and the issues which concerned them. – something that nobody else was doing at that time. Although there was some unity of vision, they were a fractious group from the outset, not even agreeing whether their organisation's name meant observation of the masses or by them, and there was an immediate parting of the ways over research and methodology. Harrisson, it was agreed, would go back to Bolton and collect a team to help him continue what he had been doing there since September, applying his bird- and cannibal-watching techniques to the observation of the North of England's working class. Madge and Jennings would stay in London, directing the national panel of observers and collating the reports they sent in. But the geographical gap between the two arms of the operation mirrored an even bigger ideological divide. While Harrisson regarded himself as a social scientist, Madge and Jennings were more interested in what they saw as the poetic side of Mass-Observation; indeed they believed they were acting as midwives to an entirely new form of literature.

In spite of these differences, Harrisson's commitment to the cause shone through. But, unknown to his new colleagues, he could be a somewhat devious character and as a committed self-publicist, he would sometimes tailor the truth to suit his ends. He used to say, for example, that he had been sent down from both Oxford and Cambridge, when the truth was that he left Cambridge of his own accord but would probably have been sent down had he continued with his rowdy behaviour there. He had never even enrolled at Oxford, but had participated in four Oxford expeditions and was banned from the zoological department. But his phrase 'sent down from Oxford and Cambridge' was in his view close enough to the truth to serve as shorthand for the facts. This was very much the case in relation to his research. He had told a good story about Worktown and all that he was doing there, but, unknown to the Blackheath group, the reality of his own situation was not quite what he was leading them to believe. He had in fact determined on going to Bolton only while waiting for the Douglas Fairbanks film to materialise. And he was still trying to get his New Guinea expedition off the ground. This economy with the truth would lead to friction with the other members of the group.[21]

Harrisson was reminded of the attractions of New Guinea on 14 February, just two days after the first day-reports were written, when Jock Marshall arrived in London from Australia. Harrisson was at the dock to meet him, driving Zita Baker's car. Marshall, fit and tanned after a summer in Australia, greeted a very different-looking man to the one he had last seen in the New Hebrides. Harrisson had a bad cold and looked pasty and worn out after spending a Lancashire winter indoors, sleeping little and eating bad food. Nevertheless he insisted to Jock that, despite being worn down by the 'dreadful, drab desolation of poverty' involved in his present anthropological researches, they were proving to be 'as exciting and extraordinary, as unhealthy and uncomfortable, as any in Malekula'. Harrisson arranged for Marshall to give a series of lectures and to be interviewed on television by his friend Mary Adams, but the much-looked-forward-to reunion didn't work out well because Jock made it clear that he didn't like Tom's new circle of arty, intellectual friends. But if they were able to raise the required funding for the New Guinea expedition he'd be able to get away from all this.

3

YOU DON'T ASK A BIRD ANY QUESTIONS

'The dialect is, at first, unintelligible to the stranger. Full of fine shades
of meaning, reversed grammar, and regular good humour'

First impressions of an observer

During the early months of 1937 Harrisson's enthusiasm for Mass-Observation kept increasing. He was particularly keen to enlist working-class participants, not just left-wing intellectuals for the project. Always good at raising publicity, he got press coverage through an old Oxford friend, Tangye Lean, who was leader editor of the *News Chronicle*. Another friend, Tom Driberg, was also asked to mention Mass-Observation in the much-read gossip column that he wrote for the *Daily Express* under the pen name William Hickey.[1] In spite of his growing fervour, however, he remained suspicious of Madge and Jennings and was careful to preserve the autonomy of his own project in Bolton. He regarded the venture as a 'unique social experiment' in which his team would record 'in painstaking detail, the rituals and behaviour of these exotic and unknown peoples in our own county'.

His primary need was for money. Since leaving Cambridge in 1931 he had received little money from his wealthy father and, on his father's death in February, he was disinherited completely in favour of his younger brother. His only income was from *Savage Civilisation* and from giving the occasional talk or writing a newspaper article about his adventures.[2] Lecturing at Harrow he teased the privileged white boys. 'Are you so superior to these savages? If you were put in their environment you would be stupid, ludicrous, not worth hitting on the head. You couldn't make a fire, a house, a comb . . . or clean your teeth with sand. What good are you?' Attacking the anthropologist's custom of detaching his own daily life from the people among whom he is working to eat his own food, he insisted that the only reliable route to understanding an alien culture was to immerse yourself in it, to live it. Rather than emphasising his outsider status by paying native informants to tell their stories and scribbling them down in notebooks, the anthropologist should go native. 'Most of the time I wrote down nothing, being too busy eating, sleeping, drinking kava, living hard and good until I became almost part of the landscape.'

In Bolton he continued to live hard and good, but here he drank Magee's bitter in the local pubs rather than kava in the thatched huts of Malekulan tribesmen, and the contrast between the mountains, beaches and jungle of his sun-drenched South Pacific island and the brooding conglomeration of factories and houses that he now chose to immerse himself in couldn't have been greater. Here was a mighty centre of filth and fume, a place where the Industrial Revolution had left behind an appalling conglomeration of factories and workshops intermixed with varieties of dismal houses. Steam would hiss and smoke scowl as dozens of chimneys belched forth over the tightly packed terraces of small Victorian houses. It was a town that truly lived under the cloud of the cotton industry and the whole place ran on coal. Homes, hospitals, schools and public buildings were heated by it; mills and factories were powered by it. The grime created by the thick black smoke settled on the slate roofs of 50,000 houses that stood in continuous gardenless rows. Many had no baths and only had exterior lavatories in their cramped little back yards.

Harrisson was just about able to support himself but he had to look elsewhere to fund his project and so, despite the left-wing leanings of Mass-Observation, he turned to two leading Lancashire industrialists for help. Initially he raised at least £1,000 from Sir Thomas Barlow, a Bolton cotton-mill owner, and Sir Ernest Simon, another industrialist. Both were committed to social reform. Other funding came from members of Lord Leverhulme's family.

The funding he raised was soon supplemented by the publisher Victor Gollancz, who provided £500 in monthly instalments as an advance on four planned books dealing with politics, religion, pubs and holidays. Gollancz was one of the men who helped make the 1930s what it was among British intellectuals: idealistic and left-wing, he used his publishing house to promote socialist and pacifist books, and the proposed Worktown books were a good fit for his list. He saw publishing primarily as a means of disseminating political ideas and used his commercially successful list, which included the work of bestselling authors like A. J. Cronin and Dorothy L. Sayers, to subsidise the Left Book Club which he set up in 1936.

By March, with a publishing deal in place, Harrisson had raised enough money to sign a lease on a gloomy, cheerless terraced house at 85 Davenport Street in Bolton, 'huddled among mills less than half a mile from the town centre', and make this the Worktown project headquarters. With this as a base he recruited a team of observers to join him to work on his study of life and people in the town. From the outset he'd planned three main areas of research – the pub, politics and religion – and his first priority was to take people on to lead these three surveys.

To lead the pub research Harrisson brought in the twenty-nine-year-old communist novelist John Sommerfield, who had just returned to England after fighting in Spain with the International Brigades. The son of a newspaper editor, he had been educated at public school, but he'd left school when he was sixteen and, before enlisting in Spain, he'd worked among other things as a carpenter's labourer, a stagehand and a dishwasher on transatlantic steamers – ideal credentials in Harrisson's view, for mixing with the workers of Bolton.[3] 'When Tom Harrisson said, "Well why don't you come up to Bolton on this",' Sommerfield recalled later, 'I thought, "This sounded great." I mean not just because it was some sort of roof and regular meals, but I was interested in the whole idea. So I said, "Maybe I can do the pubs, which is a subject of which I have some knowledge."'

To lead the religion survey Harrisson brought in a local man who came originally from nearby Farnworth. The forty-two-year-old Joe Wilcock was a working-class Christian activist. Born into a weaving family in 1895, he grew up in Lancashire where he was apprenticed to a blacksmith, but his strong religious convictions led him to give up his job to become 'Brother Joe', one of a small sect of tramp preachers who walked the highways and byways of Britain, sleeping rough and preaching a social gospel. He then went on to work as warden of a hostel in the East End rescuing destitute young boys from a life of crime and prostitution, and it was there that a young Harrisson – helping out during school holidays while at Harrow – had first got to know him.

While Wilcock, with his religious background, was to lead the religion project, Walter Hood, who had a background in Labour politics, was recruited to head up a parallel project on political life and activity in Bolton. Hood was in his early thirties and had been brought up in a small Durham mining community. He had started work as a miner and spent three years down the pit while making a name for himself as a socialist orator. His village clubbed together to send him to the Quaker-run Fircroft College in Birmingham and from there he went on to Oxford where he studied for two years at Ruskin College.[4]

Hood later recalled his first meeting with Harrisson on Greek Street in London:

> Now this was new to me, this Soho, and I had to find out where it was. And then he naturally, with his teddy-bear coat, took me off for one of these Soho meals, and I sat there, not necessarily picking me nose and eating it, but just a little bit 'what was all this about?' He had a wonderful manner of talk. He could excite you, and he certainly set himself out to try to get me interested in this. He talked about the art work that would be done . . . and also about the drive that this, what he called Mass-Observation would have and the effect on my future blah, blah, blah. Now this was good, because it showed Tom in a sense at his best. He was very anxious to bring me in, and I, after a matter of two or three hours, agreed that I would join Mass-Observation. Tom's basic idea when he talked to me was that we as people or as authorities knew very, very little about how working people lived, fought, acted, reacted, or what they wanted out of life. And he also realised that we must not interfere with the pattern of people's lives. Therefore if we were mass observing you must stand outside; you're in it, but not of it, and you must be so inconspicuous that you don't change it. Now this was all very exciting to me, and off we set![5]

In addition to the full-timers he recruited, Harrisson had, through his involvement with Albert Smith's WEA classes, a range of local contacts who had already expressed an interest in the project and a willingness to be involved. So as soon as he got back to Bolton he got in touch with the group and they offered to help. Smith himself didn't last for long. He was an opinionated anarchist and soon fell out with Harrisson, but other members of his WEA class stayed with the project. Peter Jackson went on to make a special study of how people use their leisure time on Saturday afternoons, and Eric Letchford, a one-time iron miller and militant atheist, was happy to put his exceptional capacity for beer consumption at the disposal of Mass-Observation's work on pub culture. Other members of Smith's class who stayed involved were Tom Honeyford, a former spinner now running a small beer-house who supplied a list of all the people who drank regularly there, and Tom Binks, an atheist spinner, who was also contributing to the national day-surveys. Joyce Mangnall, a weaver whom Harrisson had got to know during his time working in the mill the previous year, helped with introductions to people in her circle.[6] Harrisson was confident that he'd got a good team together. The main asset, he believed was that all the people on it had direct experience of working-class life.

Whether it was advertisements in a shop window, overheard conversations in pubs, chip shops and gents' toilets, the order of service at a church or children playing in a back street, Harrisson's observers would record the minutiae that went to make up ordinary, everyday life. In this way they hoped to create a picture of life as it was lived in a Northern working-class town in the late 1930s. Their brief was to note down conversations and observe people's behaviour, documenting precisely everything they saw, like cameras. They would not ask questions but would look, listen and observe and use these observations to produce a documentary account of everyday life in the town.

Harrisson himself set out with an open mind and with a genuine curiosity about the lives of others and, despite the difference in his background and education, it soon became clear that he had an aptitude for engaging with the details of people's domestic and material surroundings. Instructing his volunteers on how their anthropological fieldwork should be done, he told them that the ideal tool for their work was a pair of earplugs. 'Watch what people are doing,' he stressed. When questioned about it he said his approach grew out of his experience of birdwatching. 'You don't ask a bird any questions. You don't try to interview it, do you?' He told the volunteers how his commitment to this technique had been strengthened by discovering in Malekula how much you could learn just from watching people whose language you did not understand.

The work the team were carrying out in Bolton was different from any other sociological work that had been undertaken in Britain because, right from the start, the investigators tried to live and move among the investigated, with their headquarters in a working-class area. For Harrisson an important influence was Bronislaw Malinowski, Professor of Anthropology at the London School of Economics, who was a key figure in the development of empirical working methods – observation and fieldwork – as opposed to theory. The principal features of his approach were intensive on-site study of small-scale societies, and an emphasis on direct participation with native informants. It involved close observation, copious note-taking and total immersion in the society and culture under study.[7]

Observers began to record every aspect of life in Bolton from the contents of sweetshop windows to the behaviour of courting couples. They observed and analysed religious occasions such as church services, weddings, christenings and funerals; they attended social and political

meetings, sporting events and leisure activities, and observed their subjects at work and in the street. At a wrestling match where things were
going a bit slow a fellow with a bass voice breaks into song, 'Let me
call you sweetheart'. If the wrestlers are doing plenty of hugging there
are shouts of 'Marry the girl,' and a wrestler tugging his opponent's arm
brings shouts of 'Break it off,' 'Throw me a piece.' Everything was regarded as fair game. Even sexual activity taking place against the walls of
the back alleys, Harrisson maintained, was legitimate subject matter for
the new science of sociology. 'The ideal way to study people', he would
tell his team, 'is to observe them without their knowing it. Of course
if you really want to see how people live together you need flats with
one-way ceilings and bugging. I've even invented a gadget which you
can plug under a mattress to record sexual habits.'[8]

Detailed instructions were given to observers, and they were briefed to
look at small specific actions, such as how people held their cups. Harrisson's obsession with this sort of detail occasionally led him to discoveries
others might have missed but also led him to acquire enormous stacks
of pointless data. No group or activity was regarded as insignificant. Joe
Wilcock went to the Annual Show of the Bolton Budgerigar Society and
reported: 'All the people in the room are of the working class, most of
the men have hands grained and hard . . . As they stood about there was
plenty of chatter, but little about the birds. Observer caught "They let
'em get away with a draw, they'll never whack Liverpool here, they're
frightened o't buggers, that's what it is."'[9] Observations like this were
generally noted without the knowledge of the people who were being
observed.

As Harrisson and his team settled into their observations in Bolton,
the first of the day-surveys had come into Blackheath, and Madge was
encouraged by the results. He characterised the responses that had been
made as scientific, human and therefore, by implication, poetic. But
poetic was not something that Harrisson had in mind. His training as an
ornithologist focused on the undercover detailed observation of minutiae
within an environment for the sake of collecting quantities of catalogued
facts. He believed that the project should be concerned only with ascertaining the facts as accurately as possible; with developing and improving
the methods for ascertaining these facts; and with disseminating the
ascertained facts as widely as possible in books, bulletins, broadcasts and
articles.[10]

Madge worked in his house in Blackheath sifting through growing
piles of material from the national panel of volunteers, searching for

ways to understand the poetry of everyday life. He started off with the idea of using the reports for surrealist purposes, to collect accounts of people's dreams, to search for coincidences, to look for mass fantasies, to uncover the collective unconscious. It was a far cry from Harrisson's aim to observe and record the minutiae of what people actually said and did in their daily lives. Kathleen Raine later wrote that, for Madge, 'who seemed a man inspired almost as a medium is inspired or possessed, the idea of Mass Observation was less sociology, than a kind of poetry, akin to surrealism. He was the expression of the unconscious collective life of England, literally in writing on the walls, telling of hidden thoughts and dreams of the inarticulate masses.'[11] But the trained sociologist Chapman was not impressed. 'What was immediately obvious was that the bulk of the panel was either living in Bloomsbury or Hampstead, were members of the Communist party, vegans, you name it. That is to say, wholly unrepresentative, very literate but very much concerned with their own personal, private political problems. That is, they were not members of the working class reporting on their daily lives. For that reason I was, myself, extremely critical, and couldn't see how they could organise a panel to be successful in this way.'[12]

As the reports flowed in, there was so much to be done that in March Madge left his job on the *Daily Mirror* to give Mass-Observation his full-time attention. 'This was', he recorded in his autobiography, 'financially foolhardy, considering that it left me with no means of my own to support Kathleen and two children, let alone to develop a new organisation.' The *New Statesman* letters had brought in a fair number of volunteers, many of them interesting and seriously interested people, though obviously not a representative cross-section of the 'masses'. Articles which appeared in the *News Chronicle* and a little later in the *Daily Express*, *Daily Herald* and *Reynold's News* brought in many more volunteers from a more broadly based readership. For Madge these were hectic days. 'It was mainly me,' he recalled in a Mass-Observation interview, 'and anyone I could get hold of worked initially in Blackheath on the National Survey. I may have had some help from Cecily Jennings. Kathleen may have given me some help, though she didn't really like the thing.'

In Bolton meanwhile there was no shortage of volunteers. Here Harrisson organised his team of observers and trained them in what he liked to refer to as objective fieldwork. As always, Harrisson's rebellious nature earned him enemies as well as friends. He could be a drunken bully who was difficult to deal with and he offended as many people as he impressed. But he could also be witty, warm, exciting, engaging, encouraging and life enhancing. Through his eccentricities, energy and enthusiasm he attracted many middle-class writers, artists and intellectuals to join him in Bolton to work on the project alongside his full-time observers and his local working-class volunteers. Woodrow Wyatt, Tom Driberg, the literary critic William Empson and Zita Baker's lover Dick Crossman came as social explorers, upper-middle-class young men who felt it was their duty to make contact with and to get to know the hitherto unknown working class. All were united in a desire to work towards a society that was not based on privilege and class.

Most of the observers had no idea what to expect, but they were agreeably surprised, as one of the early visitors reported, that 'most people are sane, pleasant and straightforward, without southern sophistication, local-minded but curious, reasonably credulous, reasonably optimistic. There are extremely few "upper class" people; there is a constant tendency for people who are economically or intellectually successful to leave the town.' The strong local accent was a problem for them, with the same observer noting: 'The dialect is, at first, unintelligible to the stranger. Full of fine shades of meaning, reversed grammar, and regular good humour. On the whole people care about their homes, and their few personal dreams (security, a holiday week at orientalised Blackpool, a fortune in the pools) and nothing else matters very much except the progress made by the town's famous football club, whose stadium draws each Saturday more people than go into pubs or churches, in a once-a-week mass manifestation of enthusiasm, fury and joy.'[13]

One of the early visitors to Davenport Street was Zita Baker, who was at a loose end until August when her divorce would become final. She was shunting between houses of friends outside Oxford so as not to compromise Crossman's reputation, and Harrisson felt this would be his last chance of winning her back. He got her to join the Worktown team and she stayed at Davenport Street with him for a few days in March. But she was clear in her mind, as he soon began to realise, that she was going to marry Crossman.[14] As ever with Zita, Harrisson was very positive and effusive about his project. 'Our research', he affirmed, 'is not just designed as a contribution to social science, but much more importantly as a means of benefiting those being studied. Mass-Observation will do this by helping to bridge the gap between "us" and "them".' He insisted that there was an urgency about the work and that the aim was 'to publish our results as quickly, widely and cheaply as possible in order to reach not just the book buying public but also the ordinary people being studied'.

When she asked him about the reaction of local people to the presence of the observers he did not see any problems. He insisted, 'It was thought that if you started studying Lancastrians as you studied cannibals there would be uproar. Far from it. People were if anything flattered to be taken seriously.' But that wasn't all. It was also, he went on, 'a chance for this silent majority not only to sound their voices but to observe over the fence the more privileged animals, who'd come up to see them.' Although he was predominantly positive he did voice some concerns to Zita about the differences between himself and Madge and Jennings. The problem with the Madge–Jennings approach, he said, was that 'Humphrey and Charles really weren't going to do any observing at all. People were just going to document themselves.' He wasn't completely opposed to their approach, but his idea of Mass-Observation was that the emphasis should be on direct observation of what people were actually doing.

He also expressed his concerns about what he regarded as Madge's 'prejudiced approach via Marxism' and the fact that he thought his communist friend Guy Hunter wanted to use the organisation as an instrument of communist propaganda.[15] Although he was not very active, Madge was still a member of the Communist Party. Harrisson's political affiliations seemed to depend on who he was talking to. He claimed to be a lifelong socialist but his real affiliations lay with the radical wing of the Liberal Party. Political differences, however, were the least of their difficulties. The National government of the day, led by the Conservative Prime Minister Stanley Baldwin, was a coalition of all the main political parties including Labour. But there was growing support for the foundation of a Popular Front against the rising threat of fascism and the National government's appeasement policy in relation to Nazi Germany. The main advocate of the Front was the Labour politician Sir Stafford Cripps, who urged the need for an alliance with the Soviet Union and argued that socialism alone was the remedy for international discord. But supporters came from across the political spectrum – the Labour Party, the Liberal Party, the Independent Labour Party, the Communist Party and even rebellious elements within the Conservative Party. In this political climate, therefore, it was easy enough for a Liberal like Harrisson and a communist like Madge to find common ground in the defence of democracy against the threat of fascism.

It was in this Popular Front political context that Mass-Observation positioned itself. The aim was to enable the masses to speak for themselves, to make their voices heard above the din created by the press and politicians speaking in their name. In this way the organization, they believed, would help to place democracy on a firm and sustainable footing.[16]

This was the major factor motivating the early Mass-Observers. The emergence of fascism in Europe had disturbed the intellectual middle class and for them the project was a way of connecting with a section of society they had no experience of.

So when Harrisson's middle-class volunteers stepped out of Bolton's Trinity Street Station and took their first look at this typical Lancashire manufacturing town, they entered a world the like of which they had never seen before. Factory buzzers sounded to mark the end of shifts, and wagons in the railway sidings squealed and clanked as busy little shunting engines pushed and pulled them around. Arriving early after coming up to the north on the night train from Euston to Manchester they found people in droves filling the streets, rushing to work in mill and factory.

For the visitor from the South there couldn't have been a more dramatic contrast with the green and pleasant land most of them hailed from. Here – in a place where even the trees in the park had smoke-blackened trunks and branches – all was dark and foreboding. The grime created by hundreds of factory chimneys was hard to tolerate and most were appalled by the 'perpetual delicate mist of soot' which would leave a visible layer on a sheet of paper left by an open window within an hour. Then there was the smell. The sulphurous fumes of burning coal that hung in the air was not unpleasant in itself but when mixed with the other smells of industry – the hot, burning oil of the engineering works, the chemicals from the dye works, the boiled hops from Magee's Brewery and the general industrial effluent that poured into the River Croal – it produced a rancid assault on the senses. You couldn't just smell it, you could almost taste it.

For visitors arriving at 85 Davenport Street after a short walk through the centre of town from the station, the neglected state of the garden advertised the bug-ridden squalor that awaited them within. With a group of young, undomesticated males in residence the headquarters of the Bolton 'experiment', as Harrisson called it, was a scruffy, squalid dump with few home comforts. There was sufficient space for each of the four or five regular inhabitants to have their own bedroom, but there were rarely clean sheets, and they had to double up with mattresses on the floor when visitors were staying. The only communal space was the kitchen. Anthony West, a young intellectual invited by Harrisson to help write up some of the material that had been gathered, recalled his first impressions: 'When I got to Bolton he showed me into the room that was to be my office and bedroom. "Here are your files," he said, tapping a small chest of drawers. "You might like to have a dip into them before we eat" . . . There was one chair in the room with a large tin of Keating's insect powder on the seat. I removed this and sat down to begin dipping.'

In this dark and gloomy abode Harrisson directed operations from day to day and briefed new observers as they arrived. He always began with his mantra that one of the clues to development in the social sciences is the actual observation of human behaviour in everyday surroundings. For this he advocated a method of investigation that involved the intimate observation of its subjects and an obsessive concern with the most trivial aspects of everyday life and customs. So, from the earliest days of the project, the minutiae of everyday life began to pour in. At a concert, for instance, it was recorded that 'two men were reading evening papers, apparently looking at the football results'. Then in a dance hall: 'There were no people with bald heads seen by me downstairs, but a considerable number upstairs.' Interviewing was ruled out. 'We don't believe', Harrisson told them, 'this is the best way of getting information. We do not believe that you can short cut to the truth by asking strangers in the street or on the doorstep what they think about every subject. The answer given on impulse to a strange interviewer is never going to disclose the whole depth of a person's understanding or interest. It may even, consciously or unconsciously, misrepresent it, sometimes very seriously.'[17] He added, 'What people say is only one part – sometimes a not very important part – of the whole pattern of human thought and behaviour.'

'Many of the most interesting questions about human beings', he would go on, 'are not quantifiable. By insisting on graphs and pie charts, sociologists are neglecting many important subjects. And even those things that seem amenable to quantification such as replies to questionnaires will yield nonsensical results if nobody checks whether people's actions conform to their answers. What people will say to a stranger on their doorstep about how many baths they take a week, how much beer they drink, how many cigarettes they smoke, whom they plan to vote for, how often they go to church, or if they ever engage in extramarital sex, may prove to be a poor guide to what those questioned actually do.' In response to any concerns they might have about feeling out of place in what for most of them was an alien environment he would always reassure them. 'The fact that one had an accent that was very acceptable on the BBC', he used to say, 'in no way led to suspicion that one was "slumming" or "spying". For one reason no workers ever supposed that anyone came to work in Bolton for any other reason than dire necessity.'

It is not easy to establish how many people Harrisson persuaded to come and help him in Bolton or how long they stayed, but it is clear most came for brief periods in return for minimal board and lodging at Davenport Street, and that many, but not all, came from a background very different from the environment which they now entered. But not all lasted the course. Unable to make head or tail of the material he was asked to look at and sickened by the need to throw insect powder on the sheets before going to bed, Anthony West quit after a couple of days.[18] Harrisson, however, was there to stay. Despite several letters to Fairbanks about the mooted film project, he didn't receive any reply, so he had to presume it was not going ahead. Then in May he resigned the leadership of the New Guinea expedition. Unable to raise the funding he needed for it, he decided that he'd already studied savages in that part of the world. Studying Britons as if they were savages was new and now was the time to do it.

4

WHERE COTTON WAS KING

*'The general feeling in the spinning room is that work is an
evil thing, a thing to be got over as quickly as possible'*

Bolton spinner Tom Binks, quoted in M-O report

Harrisson's aim might have been to build up a detailed picture of all
aspects of life in Bolton – its religion, its politics, its entertainment and
its social life – but, in the early days at least, central to it all was work and
working life. Of the 65,000 people employed in the town's industries,
over half were employed in branches of the cotton industry. These included the manufacture of textile machinery, cotton carding, spinning
and doubling, weaving and bleaching. But in the 1930s the hometown
of the great Industrial Revolution inventor Samuel Crompton and his
ground-breaking spinning mule was in decline. The town still had 247
cotton mills, but foreign competition was beginning to take its toll and by
1936 output was only a third of what it had been in 1912. The number of
registered unemployed was 10,758 or 11 per cent of the working population as compared with the national average of 10.8 per cent, and 6.4 per
cent in London and the South-east. The death rate was 14.2 per 1,000,
or 25 per cent higher than the national average. Bolton's Medical Officer
of Health in 1937 suggested that the high death rate was probably due to
tuberculosis associated with the cotton industry.[1]

'The major industry of this industrial town', one of the first observers
recorded, 'is cotton, but iron, leather, machinery, coal and tripe are also
important industries.' At a time when the Lancashire cotton industry,
faced with competition from the newly developing textile industries of
India, China and Japan, was in decline, Bolton was the most prosperous
of all the cotton towns, 'for it does fine spinning, and so has been least
affected by foreign competition'. But this relative prosperity came at a
price as smoke from towering mill chimneys contaminated the air. The
chimneys had to be tall not just to carry the smoke and noxious fumes
up into the atmosphere but also to create a draught for the boilers in

the mills that raised the steam to power the engines that drove all the machinery. In Bolton there were so many chimneys that around seven tons of soot would fall on each square mile of the town every year.

Thick smogs, or pea-soupers as they were known, would envelop the town for days on end, making it an unhealthy place to live. Bronchitis was a common complaint. The endless rows of red-brick terraced houses added to the mill and factory emissions as the smoke from the coal fires that blazed in their kitchens curled up from hundreds of chimney pots. But it was an environment that was largely taken for granted by most of the inhabitants. One remembered going to the pictures with his mum and dad, and when they came out the smog was so thick that they got lost and couldn't find their way home. It was so bad they couldn't see the street names four or five feet above their heads, so they had to knock on doors asking what street they were in. Another recalled that if you went into town and it got foggy while you were there the buses would still be running but the conductor would have to walk along the edging with a little lamp so that the driver could see where it was.[2]

Lancashire's textile industry was intricately fragmented. Spinning mills bought raw cotton and turned it into yarn or thread. Weaving mills in their turn bought yarn and produced cloth which was then finished by independent dye works, bleach works and print works. Historically, spinning was based in south-east Lancashire around Manchester, Bolton, Oldham and Rochdale, while weaving was concentrated around Blackburn, Burnley and Preston in the north of the county. Bolton's mills specialised in fine spinning, but in some of the bigger, newer mills one company would buy in raw cotton and take it through all the stages of production – spinning, weaving and finishing – on the one site, ending up with a finished roll of cloth.

During his time working in the mill Harrisson kept detailed records of all that he saw and used the material he gathered in a draft for a book on the cotton industry. One of the first stages he described was the card room, where girls prepared and cleaned the cotton for spinning. In here the noise was too great to allow speech, and card-room workers became skilled at lip-reading. He described how odd ends of cotton were 'flying about all over the place. They get into the hair and all over the clothes of the girls who are looking after the machines, which makes them look rather as if they have had a snowball fight. Some of the bits of fluff get into their mouths and are breathed into their lungs so that quite a lot of the girls die after a few years of this work. But it's quite well known that the card-room girls are the most cheerful people in the mill.'

At the heart of the cotton industry were the spinners. It was a job that was done by men and it had changed little from the early days of the Industrial Revolution. They worked in bare feet, walking up and down behind long mule spinning frames with their rows and rows of bobbins of white cotton, the lower platform of the frame continually running backwards and forwards on wheels drawing the thread towards a central alleyway then back with a bump and a clatter. The space between the spinning mules, generally about forty-two yards long and six yards wide, was the wheelgate, sometimes known as the mulegate. In this alleyway three men worked, the spinner, the side-piecer and the little piecer. 'All day long', Harrisson wrote, 'they walk up and down the alleyway, barefoot on the oily surface, stepping without looking over the numerous rails, covering fifteen or twenty miles a day with eyes trained on the whirling lines of cotton. The moment one breaks you must "piece it up", leaning over as the platform goes in towards the fixed part, and twisting quickly with thumb and first finger to rejoin the thread. It's important that the break should be mended at once, because otherwise the broken end might fly about or foul many other threads.'

The heat and humidity, which were so necessary to maintain the quality of the product, were much worse, Harrisson reckoned, than anything he'd ever come across in the tropics. 'The men wear very few clothes. They usually look very pale, and the nickname for them is "Snuffy". They don't talk to each other much because they're too busy moving around. The spinner gets piece rate on a system of payment so complicated that only a few experts can really calculate it. He is the highest-paid worker in Worktown. He is the aristocrat of Worktown's workers, and his union has built a great hall, where most other unions and the Labour Party meet; it is bigger and more ornate than the Conservative or Liberal headquarters.'3

To find out about the life of a spinner, Harrisson and his team didn't have to rely solely on their own observations. Tom Honeyford, the former spinner who had been recruited to the Mass-Observation ranks from Albert Smith's WEA class, was able to give his own first-hand account of his day-to-day routine. Every morning, he recounted, 'I went up the steps at the corner of the building to the spinning room I was working in and got changed out of my street clothes into white overall trousers and working shirt. I opened the sliding door into the mule room. This was constructed in such a way that it closed automatically behind you to keep the heat in the room. And what a heat it was!' The air was thick with cotton dust which could lead to a lung disease called byssinosis. Eye inflammation and deafness were common, and tuberculosis and cancer of the mouth and of the groin (the latter was known as mule spinners' cancer) also resulted from these working conditions. On top of this, long hours, difficult working conditions and moving machinery were a dangerous combination. Accidents were common and could range from the loss of a finger to the occasional death.

Honeyford described how the wooden floors of the mulegate were soaked in oil. That was the result of years and years of spindle lubricant dripping on to the floor as the mules moved backwards and forwards, day in, day out. The oil created a great fire hazard, and it would take only an hour to burn down a six-storey mill. Honeyford went on to describe the working of the machines. They were all driven by a huge steam engine which transmitted its power to them via hundreds of yards of line shafts and belts. The drive from the engine to each floor was by rope, and this was connected by toothed gearing to horizontal line shafts that ran under the roof and connected to each individual machine by a system of leather belts and pulleys. The line shafting ran the whole length of the mill floor, which could be as long as 200 feet. It meant that the whole mill was driven from one engine.

At 7.30 each morning the hooter blew and all the lights of the mill came on full strength and, where earlier the illumination had just been a dull glow, the great room was now filled with light. Where there had been silence before, there was now a rhythmic ticking of the great driving belts as the joints went over the pulleys, not unlike the wheels of a train going over the points. The mules would be running within minutes of the engine starting, and the little piecer would take mugs with tea and sugar in them to the window at the end of the room for a labourer to pour boiling water on.[4] Although working as a spinner was one of the best jobs a man could get in the mills, it wasn't well liked. In a survey Mass-Observation conducted among an unspecified number of spinners, it found that 72 per cent disliked their jobs. One spinner put it bluntly: 'We are doing pretty well at our place. But I think it's a life thrown away. No, I wouldn't put my lad into it.'

Cobden Mill was one of Bolton's big, integrated mills, where spinning, weaving and finishing were carried out in the same establishment. It had about 370 employees, of whom three-quarters were women. In April 1937 Harrisson visited the mill while doing research for the book he was planning on Bolton's cotton industry. The book was never published, but a draft shows that, despite his ban on interviewing for his observers, his information could not have been obtained from observation alone.

Labour recruited directly from the schools or through family connections; labour exchanges hardly ever used. No difficulty in getting labour for machining and packing, and little difficulty for winding, but no one wants to go into weaving. Reasons: weaving is very noisy, dirty, and the shed is inclined to smell of oil; a weaver must stand practically the whole day; more important is that the warehouse people are considered (mainly by themselves) to be of superior status; although weaving is a much more skilled job the wages are generally a little lower on average (for a fully experienced weaver as compared with an experienced machinist or packer).

There is a full-time Welfare Supervisor with an office and rest-room in a central, but quiet, position. She is in charge of all the first aid, which is mostly of a very minor kind. There is little malingering, and the rest-room is often used as little as one hour or two a week – often not at all. In addition to routine first-aid work the Welfare Supervisor arranges for the weekly visits of the factory doctor, who examines all juniors up to eighteen years on arrival and every six months, and sees anyone else necessary, giving advice about teeth and eyes as well as general health. The Welfare Supervisor interviews applicants for jobs and makes recommendations, but does no formal engaging. Up to the present time there has been no shortage of entrants; generally picked boys and girls sent by local headmasters and headmistresses. Now there is a dearth of girls willing to enter the weaving shed, so that the standard required for acceptance may have to be lowered. Also one of the local headmasters wants all his best girls to be office workers rather than skilled operatives.

A square yard of cloth contains about a mile of thread and the weaving sheds where the cloth was made were usually single-storey buildings, with saw-toothed roof lights. As many as 500 looms would be packed tightly between narrow alleyways on a vast floor. Space between looms was limited and workers often had to walk sideways between whirring belting, wheels and picking sticks. Their job was to watch for any breakages in the weft,[*] stop the loom and do the repairs. Most of the weavers were women, and they would be dressed in blouse and skirt over which they spread a 'warkin' brat', or apron. They had a belt with a pouch for the main tools of their trade – reed, hook, comb and scissors. Accidents were not uncommon. 'Many a time', one weaver said, 'I got hit with a shuttle. They'd come flying off the loom into your side or your stomach or your ankle. It just depended which loom it came out of and where you

* Transverse threads woven into warp to make a piece of cloth.

were standing. You were surrounded by looms so they could come from anywhere and there was nothing you could do to stop them. It was just a fault with the loom. It could just be a bit of dust in the warp and if the shuttle caught it, it would send it out.'

The weaving sheds were not as hot as the spinning mills, but they were even noisier – a problem that, just as it was in the card room, was overcome by the weavers' ability to lip-read, which was known as 'mee-mawing'. A good weaver could communicate with a friend across the shed without uttering a sound. The overlooker in the weaving shed, who was also known as the tackler, was responsible for looking after the machinery. A tackler might maintain as many as 160 looms, and his wages were assessed on every £1 earned by the weavers. The tackler would also have to administer the unpopular slate system, which involved details of each weaver's weekly earnings being displayed for all to see.[5] One tackler recalled going into the weaving shed with some visitors who were being shown round:

One of them was a young fella. I was going round with them and before we opened the door to the weaving shed, we told them to prepare them-selves for the noise in there and to put some cotton wool in their ears if they wanted. There were about 300 looms in the shed and when we were showing them round, I could see this young chap and he was looking at all ladies working on the looms. There were 60-year-olds, who'd brought the family up, got bored at home and gone back weaving and there were also 14-year-olds, lovely young women, weaving there. When their ends broke, the girls had to lie on their looms to fix them and when they did they were showing all their legs and everything. I could see this young chap looking at them and while we were walking round, he came to me and shouted over the noise of the looms, 'It won't do for me to work here.' 'Why?' I said, 'because of the noise?' 'No,' he replied. 'Look at them young women there. I could show them a thing or two.' Straightaway one of the weavers who was four looms away, left her loom, walked across to him and said, 'Oh no, you couldn't.' 'Couldn't what?' the chap said. 'You couldn't show me a thing or two,' she said. This young man hadn't realised that all the women in there could lip-read and that she'd been able to see exactly what he was saying about them.[6]

Harrisson found that there was little opportunity for much conversation anywhere except in the machining and packing rooms. Conversations, when and where they could take place, related mostly to such matters as dress; what's going on in Bolton, that is the cinemas, keep-fit classes, young men; gossip about people in the mill and neighbours. Most of the girls worked in shirts and jerseys during the winter and cotton frocks in summer and, of course, overalls. They knitted the jerseys themselves and made the dresses at home. Knitting was allowed in the shed when a loom was stopped – thus needing a tackler – but reading was not allowed. At break times Harrisson reported that 'anybody can order 1d bottles of milk. People who just want milk with their tea, which they brew at least twice a day, can get tickets for milk. Sugar and tea they bring themselves, and there is a hot-water boiler always going in the weaving shed, and another going for the morning and afternoon pauses on the top floor. There are ovens where people can have food heated, but otherwise no feeding arrangements. A large proportion of the people live locally and go home.' Most people worked a five-and-a-half-day week, but two Saturday mornings in the mill convinced Harrisson that Saturday-morning working should be dispensed with. 'There is very little work done,' he observed, 'and the cleaning that takes place, if it must be done then, could be done by specialist cleaners, while the weavers have the whole day off. Everyone in the mill is in favour of it, even if it means an extra half hour on the other days of the week. Practically everyone goes to church or chapel, which means that she never gets a whole clear day.'[7]

The mills were central to the life of the town, providing the backdrop and the soundtrack to the lives of its people. They towered over many of its 55,000 houses that stood mainly in long, continuous rows, with narrow backs, across which washing flapped every Monday. Innumerable clogs clattered before daylight on their way to cotton's forty-eight-hour week, and if that didn't wake you up, then the sound of the great steam engine in the mill at the end of the street would do as it roared into life to turn the belts and the line shafting that drove the clattering machinery – so regular that for some it acted as their alarm clock. There was one story about an engine that had to be repaired during the night to have it working for the start of the shift the next morning. The chief engineer and the maintenance man thought they'd ironed out the problem and decided they would give the engine a trial run in the middle of the night. They started it up and the next thing they knew was that there were about twenty people outside the mill gates. They'd been woken up by the sound of the engine and thought it was seven o'clock in the morning and time to go to work.

Five minutes' walk from the centre of town, with a spinning mill on one corner and a pub on the other, Davenport Street was well chosen as a base for studying the town and observing everything that went on there. The large terraced houses that lined the street were set back from the pavement behind tiny well-tended front gardens. Although they had clearly seen better times and many were now multi-occupied, an air of respectability remained. Harry Gordon, who was a Bolton resident and knew the street well, described the change: 'Now Davenport Street, they used to be people as could afford that ... The people who lived in Davenport Street then (when I was a youngster) they weren't middle class, but they were on that side. But when M-O were there, it was going down then, going down rapidly. And instead of one family living in a house, you might have two or three families, working-class people.'[8]

Harrisson was steadfast in his belief that his accent didn't prevent him from mixing on equal terms with these working class people but he was very much alone in that belief. Harry Gordon, an unemployed fitter who got involved with Mass-Observation, pointed out the advantages of having locals like him helping out on the project. 'I acted as a guide. I found that the accent of some of the observers put some people off. About that time, the Lancashire dialect was more pronounced than today and people like me born and raised in the town were able to clear the air.' Gordon came into contact with Mass-Observation because he had been attending meetings of the Anti-Fascist Committee at the Daven-port Street home of Harold Shaw, the Secretary of the local Communist Party branch. 'We used to have our meetings on the Town Hall steps,' Gordon recalled 'and it were absolutely essential that we commandeered the steps, especially on a Saturday, to keep the Blackshirts away. So on Thursday night we used to have meetings at Harold Shaw's house to decide who went where at what time on Saturday morning. When Tom Harrisson came to live in Davenport Street, Harold took us to number 85 one night and we were introduced to a few people – there were only about four or five in the room. Anyway we volunteered to help, and after a week or two we were taken on to do what we possibly could.'

After spending two weekends working with the team Gordon decided the most useful thing he could do would be to act as guide and occasional translator for the observers. 'The best way to help was to go along with people and introduce the questions. Another thing that caused confusion was the fact that these fellows were very well dressed, in comparison to us. One young fella had a lovely suit on and he was also nice looking. So I approached this girl ... and said, "Excuse me love. Would you mind answering a question or two?" and she said, "What's it about?" I said, "This young fella wants to ask you, for instance, why you go to Blackpool

always for your holidays. Then he'll ask you some other questions after."
And she said, "Ask him is he getting any money. What I want him to do is
to take me to the bloody pictures tonight, not to bother about Blackpool.
That's months and months away."'

Many of the observers got their first real introduction to Bolton and
its people through Gordon. With him as their guide new arrivals would
quickly get to know the geography of this alien place. On leaving number
85, the first place they'd pass on their way into town would be the pub,
their new local. The Royal Hotel was a substantial-looking building
with terracotta tiling and leaded windows on the corner of Davenport
Street and Vernon Street. From there they'd go on to busy St George's
Road dominated by the forty-yard frontage of the Spinners' Hall, the
headquarters of the influential Spinners' Union. An imposing two-storey
stone building with a large central tower, it was full of ornate carvings,
arches, columns and heraldic creatures. Opposite in the middle of an
elegant Georgian terrace was the Labour Party headquarters, and a little
further along the Rialto Cinema where the first talking picture seen in
Bolton had been screened.

Taking a right turn down Knowsley Street in the direction of the
Town Hall the first thing the new boys in town would be struck by was
the rather grand-looking old market hall. From the outside it looked like
a great Victorian rail terminal with an assortment of columns flanking its
grand entrance. The fine-looking red-brick building opposite the market
was the Victoria Hall – the home of Methodism in Bolton and a venue for
concerts and recitals. The next junction took them to Deansgate – one
of Bolton's oldest roads and one of the most important shopping streets.
During the day shoppers walked the pavements under dozens of awn-
ings of retail outlets that sold everything from clothes and jewellery to
furniture and foodstuffs. At night its pubs turned it into one of the town's
liveliest spots. Deansgate could be followed down into Churchgate, with
the parish church of St Peter at the bottom. A great choice of entertainment and drinking could be enjoyed along there at the Grand Theatre,
the Theatre Royal or the Capitol Cinema or any of the seven pubs that
lined the short street.

The crossing where Deansgate and Churchgate met Bradshawgate
and Bank Street was Bolton's busiest junction. As the Tonge Moor tram
rattled along the middle of Bradshawgate towards the cobbled Nelson
Square, Gordon would take his charges past the Fleece and Yates's
Wine Lodge – two splendid terracotta drinking establishments, the
former distinguished by four magnificent gas lamps. Fold Street, just off

Bradshawgate, was the home of many of the town's solicitors, accountants and auctioneers. Next, the elegant and stylish building with mullioned bay windows and pediment over the door on the corner of Bradshawgate and Nelson Square was Bolton's best hotel, the Pack Horse. Outside in the middle of the square was a statue of Bolton's most famous son, Samuel Crompton, the inventor of the spinning mule. Further along the art deco frontage of the Lido Cinema contrasted with the older architecture of the King's Hall just down the street. The Lido, Gordon explained, was the town's latest cinema. Only just opened on 27 March, its internal decorative scheme included scenes of Venice.

Maybe Bolton wasn't too bad after all, the new recruits would think, until on Newport Street, a lively little street with a good range of shops, visitors were stopped in their tracks by a sign exhorting people to buy UCP tripe. United Cattle Products ran a chain of food shops and restaurants across the north of England and tripe – a traditional Lancashire dish of cow's stomach tissue soaked in vinegar was their best-selling product. 'Hot Tripe for Cold Days' the sign read. A visit to the tripe shop was a regular feature in the lives of most households, and provided a cheaper meal than even the ubiquitous fish and chip shop. It slipped down the throat quite easily but tasted of little other than the salt and pepper you put on it. The other delicacy from the tripe shop, Gordon explained, was cowheel – the fatty cartilage from around the beast's foot. What culinary delights were in store for the young visitors from the South.

Gordon would also take the observers to some of the local dance halls, many of which were open in the afternoon. At one of them, he recalled, the newcomer was surprised by the large number of people who were present. Gordon explained that most of them were unemployed and were allowed in at a very reduced rate. This helped some of the couples who were courting to spend some time together. Visits to the cinema were also made. One had a balcony and only courting couples went there. 'The person I took there', Gordon said, 'was quite surprised because no one really watched the film unless it was something outstanding.' As he took them round Gordon would tell them, 'They have a saying up here "Where there's muck there's brass." And that's certainly true of this place. The spinning industry here might be going down a bit and it isn't quite what it was back at the turn of the century, but it's still a world leader so the mill owners are still raking in the brass. But a lot of their workers, still living in cramped, filthy housing conditions and often enduring dirty and dangerous working conditions, are very firmly on the receiving end of the muck.'

Dominating the centre of Bolton, the Town Hall was the most prominent symbol of the brass. The prosperity of the Industrial Revolution brought with it some magnificent public buildings and here in Bolton they had one that ranked among the finest. Designed in the neo-classical style in the form of a Greek or Roman temple with a tall baroque-style clock tower, it was opened by the Prince of Wales in 1867. This bordered a huge waste space, fringed on one side by a new and very striking cinema, and a decomposing industrial belt, with slums immediately adjacent.

'The official centre of Worktown, the nerve centre of the administration,' was how an early Mass-Observation report described the Town Hall. 'Worktowners cannot easily avoid being conscious of it, because of its height, its size, the different brightness of the stone of which it is built. The architects meant it to be conspicuous. The great majority of Worktowners must visit it at some time, to pay their rates, water-rents and other dues. A feature of the Town Hall is the great flight of stone steps leading up to the lofty main doors. Originally it was the ceremonial entrance for civic functions but no one goes in at the door now. Aldermen enter by a more modest door on the north side, two steps from their motor cars. But the entrance through which the great majority of Worktowners go in is at the back of the building and leads into the Borough Treasurer's department. This takes up the whole ground floor. A very long counter. Behind it at 11.15 a.m. were three male clerks at work, taking payments, working cash registers, giving change, giving out forms for signature or to take away.'

This counter was as far as most people went. But sometimes parties were given conducted tours around the rest of the building. The observer managed to get a place on one of these tours. With him went two Worktown housewives, who were both suitably impressed. In keeping with Harrisson's insistence on detail he recorded that during the next two hours as they went round he heard Miss N. and Mrs S. say 'nice' a total of sixteen times, 'lovely' eight times, and 'beautiful' and 'interesting' four times each. He himself was particularly impressed by the brand-new offices in the extension, which, he observed,

are streamlined to maximum efficiency. The rooms are high, walls painted creamy white. Woodwork of doors and window frames dark-stained. The stone corridors are very resonant and echo with the movement of feet, including the clogs of the women cleaners. In offices, committee rooms, council chamber and mayor's parlour are various grades of carpet – the last named having the thickest and most luxuriant. The members of the council have their own retiring rooms, one for lady members, the other for gents, adjoining the council chamber. The ladies' retiring room opens into a spick and span toilet room. The two housewives were impressed by this. 'It's very nice isn't it?' 'Carpets nice, isn't it? They didn't go to Woolworth's for that.' The ladies were especially eager to see the mayor's parlour and they were not disappointed. The furniture was French walnut and thick pile carpet, subdued lighting and huge tasselled armchairs made this the high spot of civic luxuriance. 'Lovely isn't it?' Mrs S. said. 'Peaceful, isn't it' said Miss N. 'But it'll cost something for t'electric, won't it.' Their final verdict, after their guide had stated there were seven floors in the building: 'It'll want some cleaning. It'll cost something.'[9]

The Town Hall extension and the new Civic Centre provided strong evidence of efforts that were being made to improve the town and the quality of life there. In spite of this, however, there was little to take away from an overall impression of 'grimness' that most of Harrisson's volunteers experienced on their arrival in Worktown. Even Walter Hood, who had grown up in the grime of a North-east mining community, didn't find Bolton an ideal place to live. 'It was dirty, mucky, as you wandered around you never seemed clean. You always felt as if you should be washing your hands and face. On the other hand people were good, people were nice to you and you made some friends.'

In Blackheath there was no such grimness for Madge and Jennings as they continued to promote the literary side of the venture, declaring in the journal *New Verse* that Mass-Observation would establish a new standard for literary realism and liberate poetry from the grasp of professionals. This was one of many manifestos the group issued, none of which made the organisation easy to categorise. Reflecting on responses to the first of the day-surveys, Madge and Jennings found in them an authenticity of language and a poetic quality quite absent from the self-consciously literary work of proletarian novelists. But the writing was not predominantly proletarian as most of the volunteer panellists were educated middle class, not the working class who had left school at fourteen.[10]

One exception was Tom Binks, a twenty-eight-year-old ex-Catholic atheist who worked as a side-piecer in a Bolton cotton mill. In the second of the day-surveys on 12 March he reported that he had a slight cold but other than that 'it was normal day for me'. He left home for work at 7.30 a.m. It was raining and very cold. Rather than just inviting his observers to send in accounts of their day, Madge gave them detailed instructions on how to do this and Binks's report followed these instructions to the letter. Information about their health, the weather and the background of local events should be followed by an hour-by-hour report on their day. So when he got to work Binks recorded:

> The engine in the spinning mill starts up about 7.39. Piecers and spinners begin to oil. Wheels are running full swing slightly before 7.45.
>
> This morning our little piecer was late, that is he came into the room about 7.42.
>
> 8.30. The spinner on the next pair of wheels seeing me doing the cleaning said he would give me a lift now and then. I said 'Do it now, not then.'
>
> 9.20 In the room in which I work we have the mill painter, painting the window frames with white paint.
>
> 10.50 On the other side of my pair of mules is a side-piecer who is spinning temporarily. He called to me in bantering tones 'Where shall I see you tonight and I'll buy you a drink?' He is 32 years old, married and whilst spinning will get a rise from 32s whilst piecing to £4 clear.

And so the report goes on – the minutiae of the day conveying some of the tedium of working life. As the day wears on Binks becomes preoccupied with the painter. He thinks he is a slacker. 'I have, along with others,' he wrote, 'noticed how he dodges work. He is working very hard when bosses are around and slacking when he can. This morning I timed him, he came into the room to start painting at 9.20.' This for somebody who was at the mill to start work at 7.45 was not something that Binks and his workmates approved of, especially as there seemed to be one rule for them and another for the painter. 'The overlooker among his jobs prowls around, to see that everyone is working hard.' Binks observed. 'Talking not allowed. But at 9.45 he came to the painter, who is his crony, out of working hours, for a chat.' What annoyed Binks that day was that while the painter seemed to get away with doing as little work as possible, he had extra work to do on top of his own.

> Having no little piecer on this day, the spinner and I had to perform his functions as well as his own. Two men do three men's work. The piecer's wage is divided equally. I mixed some bobbins I had cleaned, red-topped ones with white-topped ones. This should not be done. It is a little piecer's job cleaning the bobbins. A man who carries bobbins from the card room to the spinning room, and who is known as the bobbin

carrier, came to me at 10 o'clock in a bad temper, complaining about the mixed bobbins. 'You'll have to separate them, we can't do it,' but he took the bobbins away and no more was heard of it. At frequent intervals the painter comes down his ladder for a five-minute interval. He just stares at the people working. Just stares and speaks not.

11.30 The wages are brought round by the overlooker, he stays at the end of the room and makes a loud hooting noise. The spinners react visibly, they brighten and become jolly. The spinner receives the entire wage, he pays his piecers. It is a well-known fact that spinners are happier and brighter creatures on Friday (payday).

Binks is still keeping an eye on the painter and as the wages were brought round he vanished. 'This is usual. He had gone to prepare to go home. At 12 o'clock, the temporary spinner showed me with glee his note of cash which he was carrying about with him in his overall's pocket.' At 12.15 p.m. the mill engines stop for dinner hour. There is a general stampede by almost everyone to get out, rushing down eight flights of steps. Outside the mill Binks is still taken up by the painter: 'I passed the painter ambling home, smoking a pipe, well dressed, bowler hat and overcoat.' Back in the mill, after dinner, the afternoon went by uneventfully. It was very hot and stuffy and one little piecer said it was 'like the equator'. At 5.30 the engines stop and again there was a stampede for the door. A side-piecer further down the room said, 'I've worked bloody hard today.' Binks went home and completed his diary entry for the day:

After tea read the *News*. At 6.30 the insurance agent called for the weekly premium. This was a new agent second week on the job. He had gone to the same school as I and at the same period. A Catholic. We chatted for a while. He was a cyclist. I had been. We both had toured Ireland last summer. He had formerly worked in a gent's outfitters at Preston but it held no prospects of promotion or advance in wages so he was trying insurance. He would soon be married. Been courting a long time. Age about 27. My mother who is stone deaf remarked after 'He looks religious.' I completed my notes on this subject and then finished a book I was reading, *The Evolution of Love* by Emil Lucka.

In the instructions they received from Madge observers were told to keep their feelings for a final section. Following this instruction Binks wrote:

The fact that I had a cold, that the atmosphere was particularly vile, and that the day was dull, were first impression, which gave rise to feelings of the rottenness of the system under which we live. The general feeling in the spinning room (worse-paid workers) is that work is an evil thing, a thing to be got over as quickly as possible. I thought of the servility of the English people in standing the bad system of working 8¾ hours a day in a putrid atmosphere for meagre wages and always feeling below par. I felt the queerness of a system that carefully preserved its property by painting it frequently and thought not at all about the health of its human work-people. Preservation of woodwork. Ruination of employee's health. The frequent five-minute stare of the painter allied to the fact that I was constantly on the go working hard, brought a feeling of resentment at the inequality of the distribution of work, and I remembered the poem by W. H. Davies:

> *A poor life this if full of care*
> *We have not time to stand and stare.*

I got the impression that the atmosphere, the electric lights burning all day (bad lights), everything combined had an effect on the temper of everyone, spinners, piecers, bobbin carriers etc. The feeling of futility was a constant one during this day (more so than usual) to see the people wasting their lives (mine in particular) at such an occupation. To know that every little piecer dislikes the life he leads at work, and to see how conditioned he has to become, he curses, rails and dreams, but he comes up every day for more. For more bad air. For more slow painful hours. For meagre wages. After work is over he jumps into a round of pleasure. Pictures, dancing, cards, anything as a reaction against work. At 11.30 the call of the pay is a marvellous brightening time for spinners. They become jovial human beings for a time. What a power money has. This was an uneventful day.[11]

Binks's eloquent reports on the drudgery of the daily round in Worktown brought together the two sides of Mass-Observation's work. As well as joining Madge's national panel of observers to write some vivid accounts of his days in Bolton, he also became a valued member of Harrisson's team of observers in the town. But shared experience like this was to become the exception rather than the rule. There was such great divergence in the founders' vision of the operation and their personalities were so different that conflict was inevitable. Madge remained, in so many ways, the opposite of Harrisson, being neat, organised, softly spoken and diffident. Harrisson was arrogant, swashbuckling, full of energy, often drunk and always deliberately outrageous; his all-consuming ego would soon lead to an early falling-out with the London end of the operation.

5

THE CORONATION

*'Britain and the Empire has the chance today of showing
the world that we can employ a moral force I find singularly
lacking in every country in the world except our own'*

The Vicar of Bolton. Coronation Day Service

While he was at Cobden Mill Harrisson learned about footings – feasts of the whole of one department for some special occasion like Christmas. They were unofficial, but the management turned a blind eye. They usually took place at the 3.30 rest break, which meant that little more work was done that day. The name came from the smaller-scale celebrations held when someone got married, with the bride or bridegroom 'footing' the bill. Harrisson reported that 'they are already collecting 6d from everyone in the weaving shed for the Coronation footing, so it must be on a fairly lavish scale. Even the looms are to be decorated.'

Prior to his abdication the Coronation of Edward VIII had been set for 12 May 1937. Although the new King, George VI, declared that he wanted time to settle in to his role, it was decided that the Coronation could not be postponed and George would be crowned on the date originally designated for his brother. It was to be a glorious celebration designed not just to honour the new King but also to wipe out the shame and humiliation felt by the Establishment over the abdication. In March the *Daily Telegraph* reported that the cost would be, '£454,000, a far greater sum than has been spent on any previous Coronation'.[1] For most workers, including Bolton's mill hands, the day was to be a holiday. According to the *Manchester Evening News*. 'Lancashire weaving operatives will, subject to the approval of employers' local associations, have a holiday on Coronation Day and receive 5s for it.' But this wasn't good news for most of the workers, as the story explained: 'This is less than an ordinary day's wage. Operatives under 18 will receive 2s 6d. Some operatives will lose several shillings on the day under these terms.'[2] It wasn't just the Lancashire workers who were going to suffer. In South Wales the *Daily*

Express reported, 'Two thousand workers, workmen of the Ocean Col-
liery, Treharris, decided today that as the coal-owners were not prepared
to give a day's holiday with pay on Coronation Day they would go to work
as usual. The men stated that they would be idling their time by taking
the day as holiday insomuch as there were no local celebrations.'[3] These
newspaper quotes are taken from a library of press cuttings that was built
up by Mass-Observation during the three months preceding Coronation
Day, which were later included in the organisation's first book, *May 12
1937: Mass-Observation Day-Survey*. Over this period about 5,000 cuttings
were taken from national and provincial newspapers and periodicals. 'In
making this collection, the observers themselves played an essential part;
they made cuttings from their own local newspapers, and were able to
keep us posted as to the preparations and incidents they observed in the
pre-Coronation months in their own localities.'[4]

At the beginning of April the *News Chronicle* carried the story: 'The King
has surprised and delighted four workpeople by personally inviting them
to be present at the Coronation service in Westminster Abbey on May
12. One is a Scotch woman weaver, another a South Wales steel works
foreman. Then there is a girl employed at the Birmingham electricity
works and a young pit worker at Chesterfield.'[5] Recording conversations
he heard at Cobden Mill Harrisson noted the interest aroused by this:
'There seemed to be little interest in external affairs, such as the Spanish
War, but there was excitement about the four workpeople chosen to
attend the Coronation, particularly the textile weaver.'

This was exactly the sort of detail Harrisson expected his observers to
pick up, impressing on them the need to write down absolutely everything
they saw and heard. 'You can't ignore who did and did not drop their tram
tickets into the litter bins,' he told them. 'And the pattern of saliva round
a spittoon cannot be dismissed as irrelevant.'[6] So one observer recorded,
'Two old men arrive [in a pub] . . . Their beer mugs are placed on the
edge of the bar counter, and they have to reach forward, half standing
up, to get at them . . . At regular intervals they shoot tiny gobs of spittle
across into the sawdust.' In another observation every action of a solitary
drinker is recorded. 'Sits with pint mug on table, at his elbow, and reads
newspaper. Puts it down, yawns, lights fag, sips half an inch of beer, rests
left elbow on table, picks nose and examines result on forefinger and
thumb, suddenly seizes beer in left hand, drains mug, gets up and goes
without saying anything.'[7]

Of all the places in Worktown it was the pub, with its elaborate social
rituals and animated conversations, that Harrisson saw as occupying a

central position in the lives of the people of the town. More people, he felt, 'spend more time in public houses than they do in any other buildings except private houses and workplaces. To say that they go there to drink is about as true as to say they go into private houses to sleep. Of the social institutions that mould men's lives between home and work in an industrial town such as Northtown,* the pub has more buildings, holds more people, takes more of their time and money, than church, cinema, dance hall and political organisations put together.'[8]

Harrisson began his own observations of Bolton's pubs in his new local, the Royal Hotel. On 4 April he went into the bar parlour at 9.30 p.m. with local observer Peter Jackson, whom he had got to know at the WEA class. Conversation, he reported, was 'of pretty prosperous types, centring on a trilby who is £7 a week Stevenson.' Of thirteen conversations heard that evening six were about business, two about people and their ages, one about a bitch who had lost three pups, one about a bus route, one about bowls and a pub and one about marriage. Peter Jackson said this was pretty typical of the parlour in every pub.[9] The parlour was the term used for the best room in a small pub, while lounge was applied to the best room of bigger pubs. Women were admitted to these rooms and beer cost a penny a pint more than in the much more basic, men only, vault and taproom. The vault was distinguished by a bar counter, while the taproom was much more of a club and games room.[10]

Never more at ease than when drinking in masculine company whether in Malekula or in Bolton, Harrisson was very happy to go out and do pub observations. In the early days Jackson was a regular drinking partner, and in the Good Samaritan with him one evening Harrisson was recognised by somebody he'd worked with when he first came to Bolton:

We in at 9.15 . . . At 9.30 in flow the mob from 'Pauls' overdressed young men several with sub-Fairbanks moustaches †. . . light coats (signature of spring), two with vivid blue ties against blue collars fixed to white shirts. One plays the piano and plays well across the whole gamut of sentiment . . . Among these is Alec of Steeles,‡ heavy, doltish . . . handkerchief of brown pseudosilk sticking from breast pocket. He hails me Tommy, at

---

* In the early stages of the project and in the first books Harrisson referred to Bolton as Northtown as well as Worktown.
† Popular Hollywood film star of the day who had a moustache.
‡ One of the places Harrisson worked during his early days in Bolton.

Steeles they wondered what happened to me . . . what am I doing now? I satisfy them. 'Why don't you come round?' (to Steeles).[11]

While closely observed reports like this formed the basis of the Bolton operation, in Blackheath Madge and Jennings were collecting observers' reports and an assortment of other material related to topics as diverse as dreams, church services and local council elections. As well as completing their day-survey diaries on the 12th of each month observers were also asked to comment or write reports on specific topics such as royalty and to complete regular questionnaires that were sent to them. The volunteers came from a wide variety of backgrounds, but young unmarried clerks and schoolteachers were particularly well represented. 'Mass-Observation's appeal', the historian Angus Calder has noted, 'was largely to much the same groups as congregated in the Left Book Club, supported Cripps' plans for a Popular Front, bought the new red and white Penguin Specials.'[12] Madge's house was soon swamped with their reports and diaries. Information poured in far more quickly than they could ever hope to process it. The main focus, though, was the nationwide effort to document the feelings of people about King Edward VIII's abdication four months earlier by collecting anecdotes, overheard comments and man-in-the-street interviews on or around the Coronation of George VI.

One of the things that surfaced was the number of rumours doing the rounds that the Coronation wouldn't take place. A newspaper vendor in Lewisham declared, 'There won't be no Coronation. The King will be dead by then. He's dying on his feet. They're keeping him alive artificially.' From Blackheath came a similar story: 'Daily woman reported in course of normal conversation that she had been told there would be no Coronation. She would at first give no reason but when pressed said it was because everybody wanted the Duke of Windsor back.' The proprietress of a stationer's shop in London said she had heard these stories : 'Oh yes, a good many people are saying so. I'm sure I don't know why. I expect they must be Communists.' There would, however, appear to have been some grounds for these rumours. 'At Lloyds one gathers,' to quote the *Daily Record* of 8 March, 'rather surprisingly high rates are being quoted for insurance against postponement of the Coronation, but there is no suggestion, of course, of any further sensational developments . . . The only other consideration is that the King, who, as has been mentioned before, is rather highly strung, might conceivably break down under the increasing strain as the ceremony draws nearer. But the week's rest he proposes to take beforehand should be sufficient safeguard.'

The rumours didn't put off the residents of Chesterton Road in Birmingham's Sparkbrook, and a woman whose house backed on to the street supplied details of their plans for the big day. 'The street will be barricaded at 7 a.m. and the men and boys will sweep and water the road and wash down the pavements. In the morning races for prizes will be run by the children. In the afternoon there will be a sit-down tea for the children and an open-air whist drive for the adults . . . Twelve pianos will be on the street – six each side. In the evening there will be bonfires, fireworks, singing, dancing and drinking.' In a Bolton cotton mill, however, the mood was a little more downbeat: 'I have asked several people what they planned to do on May 12. All these people had made no plans whatever for this particular day. They had no interest in it except that it was to be a holiday. They were glad of that part of it. Two boys, 17 years of age, were going out, one on his push-bike, the other tramping on the moors. But no one else had any plans prepared.'[13]

Madge and Jennings wanted to compare the experience of Coronation Day as recorded by their diarists with those of a normal day. Madge put in a lot of time and effort into training his recruits to the panel. To enhance their powers of observation he directed them to submit an account of the contents of their mantelpiece and those of their friends and relatives.[14] As the number of recruits to the national panel increased, the work involved in keeping contact with them and in reading and analysing their reports grew. Madge felt that the composition of his team of helpers in Blackheath should 'remain fluid until we can employ the best people for the job'.[15] Observers who lived in London would phone up or write and say they could help. At different times there were as many as twenty people who just turned up and worked for a day on some fairly mechanical job. One who came in to help was Bill Lee from Uxbridge, whose father was a retired teacher. He'd graduated from University College London and trained as a teacher of English, but when he left university in 1934 at the height of the Depression it was very difficult to get a job. He worked as a supply teacher, and an advertisement in the *New Statesman* drew him to a meeting addressed by Madge in Holborn in 1937. He visited Madge's house at his request to discuss possible work with Mass-Observation and remembers a small child playing with simple home-made toys. At the start of his involvement he was asked to comment on the day-surveys.[16]

Nineteen-year-old Priscilla Feare lived near Madge's house at Grotes Buildings and answered an advertisement for voluntary workers. She remembered 'going to an old house, perhaps Georgian, very tall and narrow, and seeing Kathleen floating through the gardens with a picture hat looking like a *Vogue* model. Madge himself was rumoured to be Secretary of the Lewisham Communist Party, and everybody around was fairly naturally left-wing – it was a radical kind of movement.' She worked on collating and typing and did some interviewing. Madge gave the impression of 'being rather languid, but of knowing what he was doing. He was most charming and wonderful to work for.' The Madges, she recalled, had hardly any furniture and they ran up bills with tradesmen which they could not always pay. She remembered being alone in the house, answering the door and finding the butcher there demanding his money. She herself drew no pay. She lived at home with her father who was a railway executive and her stepmother who ran a school. The M-O operation attracted a self-selecting group of radical young people among whom Priscilla felt very much at home, but, she said, 'My father scorned my long haired friends.' She recalled, in summer, delightful lunches out on the patio, which attracted the derision of Tom Harrisson, who went on about how tough life was for the observers in Bolton.[17]

Harrisson probably had good reason to deride the comforts of the London wing of Mass-Observation. His operation in Bolton was rough and ready. The Davenport Street house reeked of bad air, damp and cold. Everybody was a volunteer, but Harrisson still needed money for the project, if only to pay the household bills. He would occasionally get money by giving a talk or writing a newspaper article about his adventures, but was often not much better off than any of the observers, and whenever he did receive any money, none of it went into making Davenport Street more comfortable. Usually, in these early days, three or four observers lived there with him, enslaved by his charisma and his willingness to work sixteen hours a day. Madge didn't entirely approve of this communal existence, observing later in a memo to Harrisson: 'All private life was killed and M-O was the only thing anyone was allowed to think about from dawn till dream.' Harrisson countered by declaring of Madge, working away in Blackheath, 'there could be no doubt both through the material and through the evidence of observers, that he took the work much more leisurely and less intensively than I myself did, enjoying plenty of leisure and intellectual conversations, seeing much of his contemporary poets'.[18]

The work in Bolton was largely experimental and exploratory and Harrisson and his team had to find new ways of working, of collecting information, observing behaviour and recording attitudes. Harrisson instructed the observers to record all sorts of detail like hand movements, hats and clothing and to note everything they said. So in a restaurant an observer noted that everyone 'holds their knife as if it were a scalpel or pencil'. At another table two men 'agree there would be more chance of world peace if Hitler and Mussolini were off the map', and a woman thinks it's sad about somebody's baby being taken to the fever hospital: 'There's a lot of typhoid about just lately.' For Harrisson the ornithologist, the key to objective reporting was watching and listening, observing the masses as if they were birds. For him interviewing was not good. In his view it was almost designed to solicit what the respondent thought his interrogator wanted to hear, rather than his real private opinion. Real private opinions, he would often stress, came over in conversations, so there was a lot of listening in and noting what people were saying.

Observers were finding references to the abdication and the Coronation coming up in conversations they were recording as part of the pub survey. In one a ragsorter, who was getting a divorce, linked it with the Duke and Mrs Simpson, indicating the extent to which ordinary working people in Bolton were aware of the bias in the media that was such a central concern of Mass-Observation. 'Mine won't be broadcast,' she said. 'I won't see me photo in the paper.' Another woman remarked, 'It showed the press weren't free.' 'Aye, it did and all.' There's nowt in t'Coronation. I can see nowt in't,' declares another woman.[19] At a girls' school staff meeting the discussion was about the Coronation programme and how they might spend the 4½d per head allowed by the City Council for refreshments. There was also a suggestion that they might ask the children to bring in pennies to buy more decorations – balloons in red, white and blue and 'that crinkly paper which has such a nice blue. We could use it to decorate all the tables. Perhaps we might have a large Union Jack.' Another teacher then said, 'What about asking all the children to bring flags? Wouldn't they all enjoy themselves running around the playground and waving them about?'[20]

In London on Sunday 9 May, a final rehearsal was held for the Coronation pageant. After spending the night in the rain, half a million people saw the procession crawl from Buckingham Palace gates to Westminster Abbey – seventeen minutes late, its colour and glory hidden by mackintoshes and horse blankets.[21] That same morning a service presented by the Archbishops of Canterbury and York for use in churches on the Sunday before Coronation Day was held at Deane Parish Church in Bolton, which stood on the edge of the steep-sided ravine of Deane Clough. The purpose, observers reported, seemed to be that 'the people pray to God for his help in the dedication of the King and Queen, and that the people themselves will dedicate themselves anew to the service of God, just as their King is doing'.

In the churchyard before the service a crowd of about fifty people, mostly girls and young women, waited for the Mayor of Bolton to arrive.

The church stands back about 100 yards from the road and posted along the path were three sidemen, who were waiting anxiously for His Worship and ready to pass on the signal to the bell-ringers. As observer neared the church they passed the signal on, and the ringers in the belfry burst out into a loud peal. After the Mayor and his party arrived and took their places three Girl Guides took a union jack from the back of the church, advanced in step to the altar and laid it there. During the service the vicar gave a short address saying, 'We have in George VI a man who will follow closely in the steps of his father, a man loved, honoured and trusted by his people.' In the hymn after this short address a collection was taken for local charities. This was followed by God Save The King.

Referring to the Coronation in one of their manifestos, Madge and Harrisson explained that when George's brother Edward had abdicated in December, 'millions of people who passed their lives as the obedient automata of a system' were suddenly left to decide for themselves what they thought of its breakdown. The Coronation was designed to put to rest any anxiety they had by means of a grand show. But it was a delicate moment to be manipulating the British people – given the use that European fascists were making of nationalist spectacles at the time – and thus an ideal one for Mass-Observation. Forty-three day-surveys were collected, seventy-seven people answered written questionnaires and a squad of twelve observers covered the happenings in the streets of London from midnight on 11 May till after midnight the next day. They worked in shifts and kept in touch with M-O headquarters by telephone, like reporters with a newspaper office. While they were working they took notes almost continuously, and from their notes wrote up lengthy reports. On Coronation Day Jennings's own day-survey opens with an account of having slept through his 3 a.m. alarm and so missing the first train into town from Blackheath at 3.45. He spent the day photographing crowds in the Mall and writing detailed notes:

12. On the right the Abbey choir pours out across the park. On the left the Marine's bugle blows in the barracks. Down the centre stream thousands of people.

12.20. Evening newspapers with pictures of the procession are on sale in Buckingham Palace Road: 'Haven't they got them all ready quick?'

12.40. At Hyde Park Corner the sound reproduction was definitely not good . . . On the words 'His Majesty King George VI is acclaimed' the crowd cheers and the first gun goes off . . . Then someone up in Piccadilly gives a long single cheer . . .

Jennings's report ends in a pub near Piccadilly Circus where people are drinking port and champagne cocktails. Here he recorded fragments of conversation:

'We've had a marvellous day, Joe. Everything went as smooth as that.'
Waiter: 'It was a fine spectacle. I wouldn't have missed it.'[22]

In Bolton a line of bemedalled police stood in front of the gates of the parish church before the Coronation service that was being held there. In the church, all the right-side middle block of seats were filled with councillors and public officials. Many of the councillors were in morning clothes. Sitting on his own at the back was the Chief Constable of Bolton in his uniform of blue with trappings of silver, a tall man who tried to look important and stern, but instead looked pale and ill at ease. In the left middle block sat members of the general public and two rows from the back sat four Territorial Army officers complete with swords. Within this block were many Salvation Army lassies – some with ribbons corded in red, white and blue from the left shoulder to the waist; some also had red, white and blue handkerchiefs slipped under the epaulette on the left shoulder.

The Vicar appeared from the vestry and announced the first hymn, 'All people that on earth do dwell'; singing this, the choir of about sixteen boys and ten men appeared, followed by four clergy. From the pulpit the Vicar delivered the sermon, noting in jingoistic terms that 'Britain and the Empire has the chance today of showing the world that we can employ a moral force I find singularly lacking in every country in the world except our own.' He added that 'there are rumblings of wars and the possibility is not remote. It behoves us to look to the unity of our peoples: that is in essence the point of the Coronation of our King; there is a need for our dedicating ourselves anew to service unselfish and in unity.' During the singing of God Save the King nearly everybody stiffens and holds their arms straight down, but at the second verse most people take up the sheets to follow it as they don't know the words.

John Sommerfield did a round of pubs. From 2.30 until 3.15 he was in the Grapes on Water Street. 'Chaps all drinking pints in the vault,' he reported, 'four playing dominoes, no one drunk, but everyone had been drinking quite a lot. Loud singing and laughing from the lounge.' He went on to Yates's, which was 'full, but not packed out. The usual crowd, a few drunks, not much wine spilt on floor yet.' In the One Horseshoe he found the 'Lounge very full. Lots of old women wearing red, white and blue hats, singing drunkenly. All the regulars there. Lots of chaps having pints. Many women drinking mild.' At the Roebuck he found the lounge pretty full. In his report he described a conversation:

Very old woman. 'I'll say long live the king, but I don't know t'bugger.'
    Woman about 45. 'Aye. First they marry, then they have a separation and they marry again and you don't know where you are.'
    Man. 'They be suppin' cocktails and brandy now.'
    Very old woman. 'They can have all their cocks and the tails, but give me this.' (Points to her beer.)
    Man (referring to a wireless announcer, who is bawling incomprehensibly). 'I'll reckon he's knocked back a few pints by now.'
    Woman. 'Pints of whisky most like.'[23]

Just over a week after the Coronation there was another holiday in Bolton. At Whitsuntide, the annual walks began. These were a characteristic feature of springtime in the Lancashire mill towns. Processions would set off from different churches, each with its tall banners, and there would be a dramatic convergence in the town centre. Trinity Sunday was the day of the Roman Catholic processions. They were supposed to be a demonstration of faith, but for some they just provided an excuse for a day's drinking. Sommerfield, who was in the town centre with a group of observers, went into a pub with some of them at 2.45. 'Ask for drinks,' he reported. 'Publican laughs and says, "Do you know what time we close Sunday?" We say, "No." He says, "Two o'clock." Then adds, "Do we bloody 'ell! I'm going to make hay while the sun shines. And I'll tell you another thing. I'm not closing down for a while yet. It's the first time it's been 2 o'clock closing and scholars* walking at 2.30. It's a bloody shame.'

The town centre was alive. There were lemonade tables in the less crowded by-streets, ice-cream carts in every side-street. But rather strangely the Grapes in Victoria Square appeared to be shut. Several St

* School children.

John Ambulance men in uniform were at the side door. But Sommerfield noticed that there was a steady and noticeable stream towards the pub. 'We follow it through back door into yard,' he reported.

> There's a crowd there. Many are crowding men's and women's lavatories, but most are crushing towards the pub passage. A man's voice is heard: 'Make way there.' A second asks why? 'Because it's bloody full up. That's why' comes the answer, with a third voice adding, 'You can't stir in there.' Most of the crowd trying to push their way in are R.C.s or bandsmen. Members of some of the bands miss their places in the procession, and later in Mawdsley Street bandsmen are seen creeping in with their cornets while others run after their bands down Newport Street. There are lots of police about.[24]

Sommerfield's reports on the pubs he visited are always lively, and he was particularly good at recording the conversations he heard. 'A lot of perfectly normal ordinary pub conversation', he recalled, 'is a bit odd. But there's an awful lot we recorded that was really eccentric.' In a pub called the Dog and Partridge, for example, he found three women, seven men, all regulars, mostly market people, chatting to each other.

> A large tough guy with masses of hair held down by a hairnet sits at the table with a group of four, puts his head in his hands and complains of being tired. They talk about trade being bad. Hairnet suddenly takes a small live tortoise out of his overcoat pocket and threatens woman with it. She screams a little. 'What do you feed it on?' somebody asks. 'Milk.' 'How much?' A quiet thin man in a bowler sitting in another group leans forward and says quickly, 'Quart and a half.' Hairnet says, 'I give it a saucer full on Sunday.' Woman asks, 'How old is it?' 'Only thirty-six.' Conversation goes on about how you can't drown tortoises or suffocate them. The only way to kill them is to cut off their heads, but you can't get at their head![25]

The surrealistic element of a pub conversation like this appealed to Humphrey Jennings and in the early stages of the Worktown project he was among those who made the journey to Bolton. On arrival he immediately set to work taking photographs and painting townscapes. His time in the town was brief but it made a big impression on him. When he first stepped out of the station he saw more than Bolton. The vision of mill chimneys and the operatives' terraced houses introduced him to an

England he had not known before: the land of industry, of the factory, of the working class. It was a vision that was to stay with him and have a major influence on his later work as a documentary film-maker. On this visit he wrote home to his wife Cecily, 'Cotton seems to produce a desolation greater – more extended – than any other industry ... The desolation – the peculiar kind of human misery which it expresses comes I think from the fact that "Cotton" simply means work.'[26]

But Jennings didn't have the freedom to leave London for long periods. Apart from heeding the claims of family life, he also had his hands full helping to organise the Blackheath end of Mass-Observation. In any case, as Harrisson recalled, 'Humphrey was much more interested in the purely poetic side and soon it wasn't satisfying him.' Never one of nature's joiners and usually quick to develop heretical tendencies within any movement he did join, he was not destined to stay with Mass-Observation for very long, and it was the book on the Coronation that he was editing that was to bring matters to a head.

6

ACROSS THE CLASS DIVIDE

'I travelled north on the Manchester night train with all the
excitement of a true explorer en route for North Borneo'

Brian Barefoot

Harrisson's dictum that his observers should not conduct interviews does not appear to have lasted for very long. Throughout the spring and early summer young men with notebooks were to be seen regularly stopping people in the street to ask questions or counting the throng that poured into the market hall on a Saturday morning. Asked about weekend shopping a woman of fifty replied, 'I go shopping Friday night, get my butcher's meat for the weekend and pay everything, clubs and so. Saturday morning like any other morning; afternoon I have a lay down and in the evening we go to the pictures. Sunday: cooking dinner in the morning, afternoon to Sunday School, in the evening we go and have a walk or visit relations.' She also revealed that she was 'very fond of sweets. Chocolates too. I eat them when I am alone. Buy them myself, out of my housekeeping money. I look after my little self, nobody else does.' Talking about shopping another woman said, 'If we had to econo- mise we would eat fewer potatoes and more bread, margarine instead of butter, less meat and fish.'[1]

'Going to the pictures' came across in many interviews as a favourite pastime, so observers went into cinemas to record reactions to different types of films. Armed with stopwatches they went to comedies, timed the length of the audience's laughter and noted what made them laugh. Much of the humour, it appeared, was not very sophisticated. 'The pic- ture', one observer reported, 'was about two girls who went and spent ten days in a forest. Everyone roared at the dress of the two girls when they entered. One was dressed in a tiger's skin and the other an exaggerated Indian squaw dress. Also it caused lots of amusement when the blonde in the tiger's dress thumped her chest like Tarzan. She did this three times and there was loud laughter each time.'[2]

Market research and opinion polls were in their infancy. The British Market Research Bureau had only been set up in 1933 and the first opinion polls were run by British Gallup in 1937, just two years after its American forefather was founded. So Mass-Observation's experiments in this sort of day-to-day investigation were breaking important new ground. At Davenport Street there were long conversations into the night about the work. Harrisson would always press home his view that the privileged classes, of which he and most of the people he had attracted to the project were members, had a duty to lead. To do it well, leaders needed to be in active dialogue with the common people to learn about their hopes and fears and to teach them better ways of thinking about the world and coping with the challenges it threw up. Needless to say, the majority of his young volunteers agreed wholeheartedly with him. Getting to know the common people better was their *raison d'être* for being in this strange place.

For most of them the first ordinary working people they got to know were the locals who had got involved with the project – men like Eric Letchford, Tom Honeyford and Harry Gordon. It opened up a whole new world for them, but it worked both ways. Harry Gordon said later that the biggest thing he got from his involvement with Mass-Observation was the contact it gave him with these middle-class Southerners. 'I never knew a university student until I got to know Tom Harrisson's crowd,' he said, 'and when I got to know these people, I got to like them. I found them smashing. I were never dressed up when I went out with them, I never had any decent clothes, and I always had clogs on, but they never used to take exception to you. They didn't look down on you and they always addressed you by your first name. I found them people I liked just as well as my own type of person.'

For a local man like Gordon, life in Bolton was very different from that of the observers. 'I used to have to go and sign on at the dole,' he recalled, 'and possibly get a couple of days' work here, there and everywhere.' At the end of a day spent in their company he had a home to go to. 'I wanted to be home for five o'clock at the very latest,' he explained, 'the reason being I was unemployed and my wife was working. She used to arrive at our house somewhere about half-past five. My job was to get away from the team, arrive home and have the table ready. She used to bring the tea down from my mother's – I didn't do the cooking.' In spite of the differences Gordon found he had a lot in common with many of the observers. 'I were a member of the Communist Party; a member of the Anti-Fascist Committee and I were a Roman Catholic at the same time. But the main thing for me at that time was the politics. The main thing was to keep the Blackshirts away from the Town Hall steps and I found out that these fellows had the same inclinations to the same type of politics as me. We never had a difference of opinion about the politics.'

Like most of the people who got involved in Worktown Gordon never got paid for any of his work. He did it, though, because he firmly believed that Mass-Observation would change quite a lot of things. 'Anyway,' he reasoned somewhat unconvincingly, 'people like me who worked for Mass-Observation at that time were quite pleased not to get anything because possibly if you were on the dole and you were receiving money from anywhere and the authorities got to know they'd shove you in clink as soon as look at you.'[3] Harrisson made as big an impression on a local man like Gordon as he did on the middle-class Southerners he attracted to the project. 'I don't think I've ever met a fellow like Tom Harrisson,' Gordon enthused. 'He were fantastic. When he said he wanted something doing he wanted it doing. And when he wanted anything he wanted anything and everything. He wanted everything as could possibly be found out about any subject he'd asked anybody to investigate. One thing I didn't like about him was the fact that people like me when we used to meet the people we were going out with always used to have to stand outside. He wouldn't let you go in.' In spite of this Gordon had fond memories of working with the observers and found the time he spent with the team 'quite interesting'.

Another local who got involved in the project was the young future novelist and playwright Bill Naughton, the coalman who delivered to Davenport Street. He'd learned about the project from a newspaper article featuring Mass-Observation in which a coal-miner gave an account of his day.[4] For every local working-class observer like this, however, there always seemed to be two or three middle-class types up from the South. Many came to Bolton during breaks from study at Oxford and Cambridge, and for them the journey represented a chance to tell the 'truth' about everyday life for ordinary working people. One of them was Brian Barefoot, who fits the not quite accurate stereotype that a steady supply of unemployed, mostly Southern, university-educated youths took jobs or lived on subsistence pay as full-time observers.

Barefoot was unemployed and living at his parents' home in Ipswich but had been accepted for a medical course at Edinburgh University. In the meantime he needed a job, so he put an ad in the Personal Column of the *New Statesman* saying, 'Student desires vacation job. Proletarian employment preferred. Varied non-academic experience, travelled.' The one reply he got was from Harrisson. Scribbled in his almost illegible handwriting it read: 'There ain't no academia about here in this universal smokey cobbleclog, but if you don't mind the low pay and like the sound of the work, you can start as soon as you like.' It was such an unconventional letter that Barefoot's first thought was 'Crank!' and he nearly threw it away. But then he showed it to a friend who remarked, 'Evidently a man of tremendous vitality,' and advised him to follow it up.[5]

'I'd never had a proper job before,' Barefoot recalled,

but he did apparently want somebody like me, which seemed flattering, so after thinking about it for a few days I decided to go. I packed a rucksack and leather suitcase and travelled north on the Manchester night train with all the excitement of a true explorer en route for North Borneo. I'd never been to the North of England before and knew practically nothing about Lancashire except that it produced music-hall comedians, so everything about the adventure was new. I reached Bolton at breakfast time and my first meeting with the other experimenters was in the kitchen where they were having breakfast. I could tell at a glance that two of them were uni men and two working class. Tom Harrisson I met later in the morning – he always got up late *– and in a short chat he gave me a rough idea of what I should be expected to do, saying that it was necessary for him to be rather autocratic at times in order to keep the experiment going. It was clear that he had complete self-confidence, complete devotion to an idea that no one had had before, complete determination to work at that idea and pursue it to the finest detail. Compared to me (he was only three years older) he seemed to have led a remarkable life.

Barefoot's main job was to help Walter Hood with the political investigation, and on his first day he helped to canvass streets asking the inhabitants whether they voted and, if not, why they didn't. After dinner he helped count social groups on a busy street corner, then went to a Bolton Wanderers game, the first large-scale football match he had ever attended. The idea here was to observe conversations among the crowd, and comment on the game and the players. On the following day (Sunday), he went to a Catholic and a C of E service. His impression of

---

* Harrisson's hours were very irregular. According to many of the observers he had a habit of getting up late, but when the need arose he would also stay up all night working.

Bolton was that it was 'almost entirely a working-class town'. There were, he felt, few middle-class streets or organisations, and his impression was that the mill owners all lived outside the town.

Around the time of Barefoot's arrival Harrisson ceased working as a solo 'participant observer' and became more like a general, sending his troops out on information raids: eavesdropping on conversations in pubs and stores, visiting fortune tellers and football matches, compiling statistics on everything from the average time taken to consume a pint of bitter in a pub to the etiquette of queues.[6] Counts and timings were done everywhere. On the top deck of a tramcar one observer counted the number of passengers and recorded them at half-hourly intervals in the course of one evening. Starting at 6 p.m. we learn from him that there were seventeen, nine on the right hand side and eight on the left, while on the last tram at 11.30 p.m. there were nine, five of them on the right and four on the left. In a pub observers recorded the lengths of time spent there by the drinkers. Nearly half (thirteen out of twenty-eight) spent more than fifteen minutes but less than forty-five drinking and the greatest number came in between 8.30 and 9.30.[7] In chip shops, analysis by the team of six-penny portions of chips revealed an average number of twenty-five and one-sixth chips a portion.

The fundamental method for Mass-Observation work in Bolton was in-filtration of as many different groups as the experimenters could manage and observation of them without being observed. Walter Hood began to infiltrate Bolton's left-wing organisations. But within a few months of his arrival the 'unobserved' observer was already being recognised in these circles and when attending a garden party held by the Left Book Club he reported that 'owing to the fact that there were five people who knew what we are doing . . . it meant I was unable to make any elaborate notes'. Nevertheless, acting on Harrisson's instructions, when he got back to Davenport Street he remembered enough to be able to record that all the young men had been dressed in sports coats and flannels except one who was in blue blazer. Councillor Farringdon wore a grey flannel suit. At 7.30 a group of four men, including Farringdon, were playing bowls. A group of six led by Tom Binks were discussing anarchism and the class structure of society.

With their ability to become part of the groups they were observing, Hood and Sommerfield impressed the younger middle-class observers like Barefoot. Barefoot admired Hood because he was 'a worker who had climbed up to a middle-class standard and had yet never gone over to the "ruling-class" side . . .' Sommerfield – soldier, writer and social explorer from a middle-class background – was always popular, optimistic and sociable. He had, Barefoot perceived, 'an aura of toughness about him' – precisely the quality that Harrisson valued more than anything else. This toughness and their shared experience as upper-middle-class men prepared to rough it in working-class conditions made him the most trusted of all Harrisson's recruits and he was, Barefoot recalled, 'closer to Tom Harrisson's confidence than any of the rest of us'.

Barefoot talked to Sommerfield about Spain and the recent bombing of the small Basque market town of Guernica. It had been almost completely destroyed by bombs dropped by German and Italian planes and hundreds of innocent civilian had lost their lives. The atrocity of Guernica had seized the imagination of the British public as a symbol of the impact of war on defenceless citizens and stoked up fears about Germany's future intentions towards Britain. In spite of this, the British government adhered rigidly to a 'non-intervention' policy. Sommerfield told Barefoot about his recent experiences in Spain and said he couldn't imagine a greater contrast between his life there and Bolton. 'I wasn't involved in everyday working life in Spain; I was involved in places where people were shooting at me and anyway there's no drinkable beer in Spain. But it was a totally different world I was living in there. I was just trying to preserve my skin there, which I managed to do. Bolton is completely different. I'd never been in any of these small industrial Northern towns before and I didn't like the look of it at first. But I'm getting to like it because of the people here.'[8]

Sommerfield also talked about his writing and the benefits of being in Bolton and being part of the Worktown project. The people they were seeing had fascinating stories to tell. Learning how to observe the behaviour of people, how to see things as he hadn't seen them before; how to listen to what people actually said rather than what he or they thought they were saying was, he felt, of great value to him as a writer 'because when people say things I like to get the vocabulary right and the order in which they say things correct, that sort of thing'.

For Barefoot getting to know the place and the people involved walking round the town in the odd bits of spare time he had. In the valley at the back of Bolton Wanderers' football ground, Burnden Park, he came across a few old mills where kids from the terraced houses near by would go fishing in the lodges. 'Lodge', he learned, was a Lancashire word for mill pond, and the lodges provided water for the boilers in the mill's engine house. The Bolton branch of the Manchester–Bolton–Bury Canal ran alongside the River Croal in the valley, and one warm Sunday afternoon he walked along the canal towpath with local helper Tom Honeyford.

Bolton's earliest cotton mills had been built on the banks of the Croal when it was a small, clean stream. Now river and canal were little better than sewers: both were used as rubbish tips, and as they walked they came across small groups of lads dredging with ropes and iron hooks for plunder. The mills that lined the canal were long abandoned and derelict, but Barefoot was fascinated by them and the work that had gone on in them. Honeyford had spent most of his working life in mills working as a little piecer before being promoted to spinner. As they walked along the canal bank, he told Barefoot about his working life, and it soon became clear that a lot of his memories were not happy ones, particularly when it came to trying to get promotion from piecer to spinner. Returning from military service, he said, 'I was unlucky so had to become a piecer though I had a stronger claim to a position as spinner than most who got the jobs. I was pushed out by the scheming of people who got there, irrespective of any question of justice or fair play. I knew there was going to be a long wait in front of me as I was incapable of practising the sort of stunts which lead to success. So I began playing the piano in pubs to supplement my wage. Prospects started to improve when I got doing the job of spinner when any were off sick.'

Continuing along the towpath they came across the remains of Victorian coal-mining engineering, all made of wood, with inclined railways down the side of the banking, pit winding headgear and a huge boiler house at the bottom of a big chimney. Inside they could make out the old pit winding engine still *in situ* with gas lamps all around it. Further along the canal got wider and they passed a stretch that was full of sunken boats. Their prows and sterns were sticking out of the water and the rest of the barges could be made out under the water. They all had 'LMS' and 'Ladyshore Coal Company. Little Lever' written along their sides. By the side of the canal a handsome boat-building shed, which looked rather like a railway station, with beautifully cut timber boards, was still standing.

As they walked on towards Manchester, Honeyford continued with his story. He finally got to be a spinner when he was thirty-three, but the mill where he worked was:

one of the worst, never a successful mill, always on the verge of bankruptcy. This resulted in squeezing the last ounce out of the men. We had one of the worst types of boss, one who liked being played up to, giving favours to those who flattered, while torturing those who didn't show proper respect for his bloated importance. With the cunning of his low intelligence he used to make my life hell. I did my best but the writing was on the wall for me. A system of tyranny was practised. This involved finding fault with a spinner like me who wasn't sufficiently servile and dismissing him. The spinner would then be informed by one of the toadies that if he went and begged for his place back, he would get it. I'd seen this happen a few times and sure enough it came to my turn, I was manoeuvred into a position and dismissed. The toadies duly informed me that I'd get my job back if I went and asked, but the knowledge that I had been unjustly treated, that I was being broken to please the vanity of a foolish man kept me away. I could not sink to such depths of degradation, so I've been unemployed ever since with the added stigma of being sacked. I was forty-three when this happened, so I'd been a spinner for ten years and a piecer for twenty.[9]

Honeyford had become a member of the WEA class, where he first met Harrisson. 'Through contact with an able tutor,' he said, 'I am learning to exercise choice in thought and in literature. I have my music also, as an escape from everything and everybody, together with a happy home. The monotony of a plain diet is somewhat tiresome, but it is the penalty the lucky people impose on the unlucky.' With his high principles, his thirst for knowledge and the free time that came from unemployment Honeyford was very much the sort of local contact who proved to be invaluable to Mass-Observation in Bolton. Harrisson prized his services highly and described him as 'a constant helper'.[10]

For a middle-class Southerner like Barefoot, contact like this with a man who'd spent his life working in a cotton mill opened his eyes to a whole world of working-class industrial life previously unknown to him. One of the things that he and other well-educated young observers found a real eye-opener was that a working man like Honeyford, who'd left school at the age of fourteen, could be so well read and so appreciative of the finer things in life such as music. Another eye-opener for Barefoot was meeting and getting to know Bill Naughton. His first encounter with him was when they went out on an assignment together. They seemed to be getting on well, Barefoot recalled, and having a pleasant chat. He clearly felt that they had been getting on as equals so it came as a surprise when Naughton told him before leaving that it had been interesting to meet him, because one didn't often get the chance of talking to people of a different class. Generally, though, they got on well together and Naughton introduced him to aspects of Bolton life that were very new to him, like the all-in wrestling match he went to with him. Although he'd been to a boxing match, he'd never attended a wrestling match before and his feelings before going were influenced by highly coloured accounts of the sport provided by newspapers and acquaintances who had themselves been to it. 'I expected', he said, 'an entertainment which would probably involve a certain amount of blood-letting, possibly a broken arm or two, certainly sadistic yells from the tough onlookers. On the other hand the entertainment might be merely funny. I did not anticipate any particular display of skill, and I felt that whatever might happen I would not be bored. I, therefore, entered the stadium with something of the feeling I had when about to witness my first operation in Edinburgh Infirmary – apprehension but a determination to go through with it.'

The stadium, he reported, could crowd about 1,000 people into its wooden-floored and wooden-walled interior and that evening it was full. He noted an 'overwhelming preponderance of caps among men's headgear: trilbies and women very scanty. Reminded very much of a football crowd at the start of a match; the men discuss the local heroes and speculate on their chances in the forthcoming struggle. The ring, illuminated by floodlights, is in the centre of the floor.' The evening was started by the MC (evening dress, Southern accent) coming into the ring and announcing the names and qualifications of the first pair of wrestlers. At first sight they didn't look very tough. Barefoot thought the referee looked much bigger and tougher. 'The wrestlers get down to it,' he reported, 'and are soon interlocked on the floor. As they grapple there are shouts of "Pull his armpits in . . . give 'im the works . . . break his false teeth . . . make him shout mama." As one wrestler pulls his opponent's legs apart a woman shouts, "Go on. Pull 'em open . . . Put it on, Carroll lad." Can't tell which man is winning: both are of equal build and hair colour, one wearing dark blue shorts, the other black. Even when the fight was all over I had no idea which was the winner and which the loser.'

During the second fight Barefoot said he began to get interested for the first time. 'Both men were so far removed in appearance from the men one sees on the streets of Bolton that it was possible to detach one-self from them as individuals and think of them solely as animals.' At the interval he concluded: 'The difference between the gory tales spread about and the less thrilling reality is like the advertisement of a striptease show compared with the show itself.' The second half of the evening was, Barefoot felt, less interesting. 'In fact, after a couple of rounds I began to get very bored with the whole thing, and wondered why anyone would want to come and watch two sweating strangers sprawling together on a small open space. The whole entertainment lasted just over two hours, but I was quite glad when the last throw had been made and I could return to fresh air.'[11]

Of all the observers from a working-class background, Barefoot got on particularly well with Walter Hood and remembered him fondly as someone who was good to work with. 'I found him very unsubtle and easy to understand, completely honest and sincere, humorous and energetic; and I worked together with him quite a lot, since we were both in theory engaged on collecting material for the book on political behaviour. . . . He was typically extroverted and a good canvasser and interviewer; I was just the opposite; but we got on very well together.' For a young middle-class socialist like Barefoot, Walter Hood provided the introduction he was looking for into working-class culture and the struggle to 'better oneself'. His family, Barefoot learned, was very poor and he had a tough upbringing with memories of trips to the soup kitchen and his father talking of strikes, mining and death. He felt great solidarity, he explained, with the working class that he was part of and from an early age felt a sense of responsibility to make the lives of his people better. He had gained a scholarship to Ryhope Secondary School in Sunderland but had to leave after three years to work in a coal-mine as his father wasn't earning enough to maintain the scholarship. He soon began to feel the injustice of the terrible working conditions miners had to put up with. At the age of twenty, he became a member of the Labour Party and was elected Chairman of the County Labour League and representative for Durham in the National Labour League of Youth.

Hood talked a lot about the importance of education. He said that when he was a young miner he began to understand that it was only through education that he and the workers of his community could make a difference to their social situation, so it was a great thing for him when his village clubbed together to send him to college. That is when he went to Ruskin College in Oxford on a scholarship to study trade unionism. He was there from 1934 to 1936, during which time he was extremely active politically. He chaired many meetings, attended talks and protests and often came into conflict with the police.

It was while he was in Oxford, he explained, that he began to mix with left-wing public school boys, some of whom joined him during vacations at the Clarion Rural Campaign – a Labour Party offshoot – set up to preach socialism to agricultural workers. He also drew cartoons for the student newspaper *Isis*. Through this and his interest in art in general he got to know the Principal of Ruskin, Barrett Brown, who offered him an arts scholarship. Among his tutors were the artists Julian Trevelyan and William Coldstream. Around this time, he said, he began to look at how he could express working-class ideas in his paintings and drawings and started to depict ordinary working-class scenes – women washing their clothes, miners coming home from the pit and people drinking.

Down and out after he left Ruskin in 1936, he spent some time living off Trevelyan and his circle in London, before taking off for the summer to France with an Oxford student he had met on the Clarion Campaign who had come home with him 'to see how the miners lived'. The two friends planned to write a book on 'the English in the 1930s' which would focus on unemployment and the rights of workers. Looking for an advance to live on they went to Gollancz who put them in touch with Harrisson.[12]

Barefoot worked closely with Hood, assisting him with the politics fieldwork. One of the first meetings they attended together was a Left Book Club discussion of Clement Attlee's book *The Labour Party in Perspective*. Attlee, who went on to serve as Prime Minister from 1945 to 1951, was the leader of the Labour Party. After reversing Labour's previous policy of pacifism and appeasement, he became a strong critic of Prime Minister Neville Chamberlain's attempts at appeasement of Nazi Germany. Attlee's book crystallised the political concerns of the left in Britain in the late 1930s. It was strongly anti-fascist, at a time when many people in Britain were still ambivalent or ignorant of what was happening in Europe, and was concerned about the disunity on the left of British politics, wishing to encourage the formation of a Popular Front that would bring together different political groupings of the left and centre in a broad coalition. At the meeting there were seventeen men and nine women present, average age twenty-five. Typical of the detail that observers were expected to put into their reports, Barefoot wrote: 'Only one of the men wore a red tie. He was the local Communist leader.' The meeting went on for two and a half hours, at one stage getting very heated over discussion of armaments. Barefoot also noted: 'Man taking collection: "Sixpence is the minimum, and if you haven't got anything, don't put anything in."'[13]

At a Labour Party Crusade meeting a couple of weeks later Barefoot reported that evidently nearly all those present were party members or supporters. Two communists had come along in order to put forward their party line. There were about sixty people present, mostly men, the majority middle aged. Barefoot wasn't impressed by what he saw and heard, noting that 'anything less like a "Crusade" would be hard to discover. It was just an ordinary meeting with less enthusiasm than is exhibited in a Church Harvest Festival. The only time the meeting livened up was when the United Front was being discussed.' Barefoot recorded that he 'carried away a bad impression of the speaker, Burke, the Labour M.P. for Burnley. He was clearly of working-class origin, but was rapidly acquiring a Westminster presence. He used many outworn phrases – certainly did not talk the language of the people.' As a Crusade meeting it was not a great success. At the end of it the Chairman announced that he wanted to make an appeal to those who were not already members of the Labour Party to leave their names, but Barefoot didn't see anyone hand in his name. Nor, he noted, were any forms or pamphlets handed out, no posters were on the walls, no songs were sung, and no collection was taken.[14]

The feeling of the meeting was very definitely anti-communist and back at Davenport Street over a fish and chip supper there was further discussion about the defection of large numbers of Labour Party members to the Communist Party of Great Britain. This had come about because the British Labour Party had not responded to a call to join a Popular Front against fascism – a front that, it was argued, should cut across class divisions and include democratic political parties from across the spectrum. The whole question brought great discord to the left wing and this would be reflected in discussions around the kitchen table in Davenport Street.

Class divisions were certainly being cut across in the house. Barefoot found that, despite the difference in their backgrounds, he had much in common with Hood and Wilcock, and along with them he got involved in local fund-raising efforts for victims of the Spanish Civil War. As house-to-house collectors during Spain Week they were asked to record what was said to them by people at their doors. No attempt was made to start a conversation and the remarks quoted represented the unforced reaction of ordinary folk to the idea of Spanish relief. Many gave a simple answer of yes or no or 'Not tonight, thank you' and these were ignored. Of 118 who said more than this, 72.9 per cent would not give to the collection. These were not all hostile to the cause, and offered a variety of reasons for their refusal. Unemployment or poverty was a general plea (37.2 per cent) and was rivalled by lack of sympathy or definite hostility to the cause. Out of twenty-two unsympathetic persons, fourteen thought it was not our business to help foreigners. 'I don't believe in helping these foreigners. England always helps other countries – nobody would help us' was the

view of one man. 'These foreigners start these wars, let them get on with
it' and 'Help to fight among themselves? No, don't hold with it' were the
responses from two others. Some non-givers said they'd given before and
a third of the total number complained that too many collections came
round. Those who gave to the collection said little. About a third made
remarks of a political or semi-political nature. 'Anything I can do for you
I will. Franco must go' was one view, while another who was sympathetic
to the cause made a contribution with the reservation 'I hope they don't
use this for arms. I don't mind giving as you say it is for food and medical
supplies. There's been enough bloodshed as it is.'[15]

7

THE SECRET PHOTOGRAPHER

*'I always come back to the factor I was constantly being
faced with – the class distinction, the fact that I was somebody
from another planet, intruding on another kind of life'*

Humphrey Spender

Tom Harrisson was the project leader in Bolton and the prime mover behind everything that was done there, but there is another name that is more closely associated with the project than his – the photographer Humphrey Spender. Spender was a pioneer of the documentary photography style that suited Mass-Observation's methods of gathering information and he became a key member of the Worktown team. He was the brother of the poet Stephen Spender, but Harrisson knew about him through another brother, Michael, who had been the photographer on the Oxford expedition to the New Hebrides. It was here that he had first seen photography being used scientifically to collect anthropological data and he decided that 'the use of scientific instruments of precision, photography, film technique ... will provide a check on our observations'.[1] Spender was another upper-middle-class young man who felt it was his duty to make contact with and get to know the working class. He had a strong social conscience and realised that photographs could draw attention to inequalities in society. His photographs of unemployment and poverty in Jarrow and Stepney, published in the *Listener* (1934) and the *Left Review* (1936), were critical social documents at the beginning of the British documentary movement.[2]

Born in Hampstead, north London into what he described as 'a privileged background of frequently changing nannies and governesses and two devoted servants', Spender was the youngest of the four children of the liberal journalist Herbert Spender. As a twenty-one-year-old student at the Architectural Association School in London, he experimented with the possibilities offered by the technically advanced cameras and lenses manufactured in Germany, where he travelled during the summer months. Like his friend Christopher Isherwood, he saw the rise of Nazism at first hand on these visits and while there he also became aware of German illustrated newspapers and candid photography. He never practised as an architect. Instead he set up as a photographer and became one of the first British photographers to use what was at the time cutting-edge technology in the form of a small 35mm Leica camera. Cameras like this were making it possible for a photographer to be less obtrusive in public, allowing for more intimate social-documentary images. Spender wasn't going to earn a living from this sort of photography, however, so he opened a commercial photographic studio in the Strand with his fellow Architectural Association student and lover, Bill Edmiston. Although they were successful early on doing celebrity portraits, fashion and a bit of advertising, Spender soon got bored with producing slick, glossy, posed photographs and started to do the sort of work that interested him on a voluntary basis.

Spender had strong left-wing political views and a commitment to change.[3] 'There was much that horrified me,' he said: 'slums, the terrible standard of living of many people, unemployment.' One of his best friends was a probation officer, a woman called Clemence Paine, who worked for a very well-known magistrate Basil Henriques. Henriques sat in the juvenile courts dealing with East End children – Stepney, Mile End, the Docks, the Isle of Dogs – and Paine was always telling Spender horrific stories about the reasons why these children were committing petty crimes. She explained to him that the connection between bad housing and juvenile crime was very strong, and a lot of good would be done if public awareness of bad housing conditions could be raised. So Spender agreed to take a set of photographs of people living in poverty in the slums of Stepney.

He continued to do his studio work with Bill Edmiston, 'until one day the phone rang and it was the *Daily Mirror*. One of the directors, Guy Bartholomew, had come up with an idea for introducing a touch of "Art" into the paper. "Lensman" was to be the pseudonym for a roving photographer taking "artistic" photographs all over the country. For some unexplained reason they were inviting one of us to do the job. Bill Edmiston didn't want it, so I took it on, and the partnership with him gradually died.' When Spender accepted the job offer it was ostensibly to photograph 'candid' English life, the chance encounters of the city and the sort of slices of real life by which Spender was intrigued, but that was not how it turned out. 'Unfortunately,' he said,

Lensman was under the control of the resident art editor, H. Rider-Rider. From the moment he set eyes on me he absolutely loathed me. I was everything he disliked – a sort of posh-speaking upstart – so he tried to put me down from the word go. I started on the lines that Bartholomew had envisaged, cruising around the country in a car. But what the art editor thought was art was not what I thought was art. He insisted on staged and pastoral 'artistic' photographs of thatched cottages and rolling countryside.

Spender fought for the right to use his Leica camera, but Rider-Rider protested that the small negative produced by his miniature camera would not allow for the necessary retouching of reality. As this was anathema to Spender's photo aesthetic, his work for the *Mirror* was punctuated by a constant series of battles and disagreements. So, while staying on at the *Mirror*, which paid his wages, he volunteered to photograph the economic and social conditions of the working class for friends involved in projects exposing the plight of the unemployed.

Spender was in the vanguard of a new 'objective' documentary movement that used the camera as a recorder of everyday life. Photographers went into the coal mines, the steel and cotton mills and the slums of industrial towns hardest hit by the Depression. From this work, and set against a background of the international crises of the 1930s, the British documentary movement helped to forge a new social consciousness. Spender was commissioned by the *Left Review* to photograph the Jarrow hunger marchers and a rally of the British Union of Fascists in the Albert Hall, where physical threats by black-shirted Fascist thugs brought home the need to take seriously what was happening in Germany. Throughout this time he continued to travel around Europe, recording the social and political turmoil of the late 1930s. Describing his own political attachments he said, 'I was in sympathy rather naively with an idealised version of Communism. I did not align myself to the extent that [my brother] Stephen did, to the point of actually joining the party; but I was certainly sympathetic. Our family background was strongly Liberal, so that's where my sympathies lay – Liberalism and the left.'[4]

It was his growing commitment to the sociological study of the British people that led to his involvement with Mass-Observation. 'Tom Harrisson', he remembered,

was searching around for people who would work for nothing and somebody must have coughed up my name as an idiot who would be likely to do so. He knew I was very interested in photography and had probably seen some of my work for the *Daily Mirror* He came to my family house saying, 'You're a photographer, you've got exactly the right kind of equipment, one of the few people who is using an easily concealable camera, come down to join this team.' He was persuasive too. His argument went like this: 'To improve something you've got to be well informed. What could be a better way of being informed than to take photographs.' There wasn't any money, Tom just had no money. But I was very intrigued by him; he had that kind of magnetic personality.[5]

There were two sorts of reason why Spender said he accepted Harrisson's invitation to become involved in the Worktown project. 'On the one hand I thought what he was proposing would be useful ... I was in sympathy with a very strong line of his, that the mass-media misrepresented working-class life and public opinion generally. On the other hand, Tom was full of enthusiasm and get-up-and-go and he was very witty. I've always been the victim of anyone who could make me laugh and he had me rolling on the floor. By reducing me to a jelly of hysterical laughter, he had no difficulty in persuading me that, by joining his Worktown team, I could not fail to make the world a better place.' But there was another attraction. 'My kind of class', he explained, 'certainly came from a privileged background. There were always servants in the house and we were really protected from it [contact with the working class] ... so immediately that set up a peculiar attraction towards forbidden fruit, towards the common people.'[6] Spender saw the Worktown project as an extension of the work he had been doing on the Jarrow march and in Stepney, since Bolton had unemployment levels typical of many industrial areas at the time. Working for the *Mirror* had persuaded him that all press photography was propaganda, something he had first learned from seeing the work of Goebbels on visits to Christopher Isherwood in Berlin. It was to counter such claims that Mass-Observation had been founded, to 'study real life', and the Worktown photography was the biggest voluntary project he took on.

Arriving in Bolton for the first time he was struck by the colour of the brick – a very brackish dark red – and he found the landscape very mysterious. 'A hell of a lot of smog' was one of the first things he remembered. Harrisson took him to one of the local pubs and told him a bit more about his thinking. 'We are all studying the behaviour of what we think are simple and primitive peoples,' he said, 'when our own behaviour in our own country is, my goodness, just as peculiar, just as extraordinary if one stands outside it and watches how people behave.' He pointed to the sawdust on the floor and the spittoons which were standing around and he said, 'Who would think for instance that spitting is a kind of ritual in itself, spitting is a prepared-for ritual – look at the sawdust. Probably somewhere on the wall you will find a notice which says "Penalty for spitting 40 shillings".'[7]

Spender became the photo-documentarian for the project, capturing 'significant moments' in the daily flow of life in factories, pubs, parks, shops and markets and on the street, but Harrisson never gave him any written directives. Everything was chaotic. 'There was a daily session', Spender recalled, 'which usually took the form of Tom seizing about half a dozen national newspapers, reading the headlines, getting us laughing and interested, and quite on the spur of the moment, impulsively hitting on a theme that he thought would be productive. His sudden, mercurial ideas about possible topics for photographs were spontaneous, and usually came up at these daily informal breakfast gatherings.'[8] Harrisson would 'get wild enthusiasms like there are 70 religious denominations represented each by a different building in Bolton. He'd say, there's Total Immersion, Bethel Evangelical or Four Square . . . He'd go off into hysterical lists of things and get us all laughing . . . These things need photographing.'[9] Spender was encouraged by Harrisson to travel on the top decks of buses and trams because he thought this was where young couples got up to no good, and on one occasion in an upmarket café he suggested to him that he should try to capture a posh lady putting a spoon in her bag. 'Every day started with a kind of lead, and then you were working on your own. I took bus rides around, in a way killing time, letting things happen.'[10]

'I did sit and write [a list of] the sociological events that obviously had to be covered, not necessarily that I wanted to cover or thought would make good photographs. I used my own initiative after Tom's initial suggestions. Away from headquarters I was very much on my own, sometimes frightened, embarrassed, bored and depressed. To the working people of this town my manner of speaking was "la-de-fuckin-da". To me their language and accent were foreign. It rained a lot and the light was smoggy. The 35mm camera, in this place an almost sci-fi contraption, attracted suspicious interest, so the equipment had to be minimal.'[11] Spender worked on his own to explore Bolton with Harrisson's suggestions in mind, documenting daily living conditions and decaying environments. He took pictures of rainswept cobbled streets, small boys and girls playing in derelict wastelands and one boy peeing into a puddle. Always in the background were the familiar focal points of the community, the fish and chip shop, the corner shop, the pub and the market hall. One of the observed rituals was the scrubbing and stoning* of the front step and pavement. 'I saw this very downtrodden lady actually washing the paving stones', he recalled 'and being observed by a tiny tot whose stance and general appearance is just so very touching. She doesn't want to be separated from mum. It makes me want to cry every time I look at her.' For Spender the job involved 'an enormous amount of patience, of boredom, of waiting for things to happen, of knowing that if I waited long enough, what I wanted would happen, so it was quite a stressful situation at times.'

A camera was an unusual sight in 1930s Bolton, where Spender's Leica would have cost six months' wages for an ordinary workman. Wandering round Bolton with his camera concealed under his coat, it was not easy for him to remain anonymous, particularly as he was a striking figure. Spender was a handsome man and he was subjected to various types of wolf whistles and catcalls from the female workers at one mill he visited. He went to great lengths to try to make himself invisible. He used the smallest camera he could, his miniature 35mm Leica which he hid under his voluminous old mackintosh. But, he recalled, 'the Leica I was using at the start of the M-O work was stolen, and I bought a Zeiss Contax 35. This means that most of the M-O work was taken with a very remarkable wide-angle lens called a Biogon, which fitted the Contax. The Biogon had a remarkable depth of focus and my normal practice was to leave it set with as great a depth of focus as possible. A lot of the interior photography depended on that particular lens.' The camera itself was small and had a very quiet shutter action. Using a noisier camera would have drawn attention to him – something he expressly wanted to avoid.

What I found actually doing the job were a lot of practical difficulties, a lot of coping with my own reactions, of trying not to be embarrassed, at the same time as trying not to drop my camera or lose my films or take photographs with no film in the camera. I'm not a totally well-organised person, so I was quite preoccupied with that kind of thing, together with getting exposures right and so on. I always come back to the factor I was constantly being faced with – the class distinction, the fact that I was somebody from another planet, intruding on another kind of life. And, of

---

* The stone steps at the front of a house were cleaned by scrubbing or 'stoning' them with a type of scouring block known as a donkey stone.

course when something difficult or embarrassing occurred, one tended to revert to stereotype.[12]

To this middle-class Southerner, the Northern mill town with its dark skies, choking smog and poverty came as a shock. He found it rather menacing and alarming.

> I felt very much a foreigner ... I've got no sense of direction and I was always getting lost: quite often if I asked for directions, it was difficult to understand what people were saying. And the whole townscape was severe and made me apprehensive. There was a particular kind of dark red brick ... a particular dark green to the grass, from the pollution; and the height of the factory chimneys, with smoke belching from them – these were alarming. In general, the experience was alarming – and depressing, because of the evident poverty, or at least the lack of anything that could be called luxury. People tended to look preoccupied, if not actually unhappy – though when you were in a pub there was a kind of community feeling, the feeling of a lot of people who knew each other, and who were happy to know each other.

A significant influence on the work in Bolton came from the surrealist movement, with which Madge and Jennings were so closely associated. Incorporating the notion that popular culture was as valid as high art, it tied in with the Mass-Observation idea that popular art forms and people's responses to them were a way to get to the truth about human experience. It meant that the Worktown project became a melting pot for different ideas about society, providing an opportunity for a diverse group with a wide range of interests and talents to work together in a new and creative way. Artists and poets influenced by surrealism and socialist ideologies were attracted to the organisation to work alongside sociologists and anthropologists. 'People who came up', Spender remembered, 'tended to do all kinds of things which they weren't normally doing, so people who never wrote started to write and people who never painted started to paint and so on.'

While most of his time was now being taken up by Mass-Observation, Jennings didn't entirely abandon his surrealist activities. His poems, essays and other writings continued to appear in surrealist journals. The spring 1937 issue of *Contemporary Poetry and Prose* included his report on the Industrial Revolution: 'The material transformer of the world has just been born. It was trotted out in its skeleton, to the music of a mineral train from the black country, with heart and lungs and muscles exposed to view in complex hideosity. It once ranged wild in the marshy forests of the Netherlands, where the electrical phenomenon and the pale blue eyes connected it with apparitions, demons, wizards and divinities.' That was not the sort of description that Harrisson would have encouraged his observers to write, but he did have an interest in bringing surrealism to Bolton, and one of the artists who developed a close association with Worktown was the surrealist Julian Trevelyan.

Trevelyan had been a friend of Jennings at Trinity College, Cambridge. He left before completing his studies and moved to Paris where he took up art, studying alongside Picasso and Max Ernst. He first visited Bolton in June 1937 and made several visits later. 'Tom asked me up to Bolton first of all to paint it,' he recalled in his autobiography *Indigo Days*, 'and I set out with him from London one night at ten o'clock to drive there, with Bill Empson in the back. Along the great trunk road we drove, past the streams of lorries, their lights flashing and dipping in the secret language known only to their drivers. At last, about five in the morning, Bill became restless, and we had to stop in a cafe so that he should not see the dawn that upset him strangely.' When they arrived they found 'a house like any other in Bolton, it contained a few beds and office desks, and an old crone who cooked us bacon and eggs and tea on a smoky grate'.[13]

Empson was a noted poet and influential literary critic and Harrisson had just the job for him. He was sent out to report on the contents of sweetshop windows, while Trevelyan was sent out to make a collage of a Bolton streetscape from newspaper reports of the Coronation. One Boltonian commented, 'This gives me the worker versus royalty feeling.' At night, Trevelyan said, he drank beer 'in various pubs and watched an all-in wrestling match in a foundry rather reminiscent of some prison of Piranesi, with chains and ladders and pieces of rusty machinery'. But he said he felt 'aware of the gulf of education, language, accent and social behaviour' separating him from Bolton's inhabitants.[14] Out on the streets he made further collages of what he saw out of newspapers, copies of *Picture Post*, old catalogues and bits of coloured paper which blew about in the wind as he tried to gum them on to paper while sitting out in the open air watched by inquisitive and suspicious Boltonians.[15] Walter Hood, who was an accomplished, self-taught artist and proud of his achievements, also did some drawing. He believed passionately in the capacity of working people to produce their own poetry, literature and, in his case, drawing and painting. He recalled that he 'had long talks with

Julian Trevelyan and I did enjoy his company. He did some very good paintings of Bolton but he didn't put a worker in the streets, and that annoyed me like blazes.'[16]

The painter and photographer Michael Wickham also came up from London and set up his easel in the street. Wickham was a larger-than-life character, a great raconteur and bon vivant, who drove around Bolton in a large Bentley. It was through Charles Madge that he got involved with Mass-Observation. 'He was a friend of mine', he said, 'long before I knew Tom. I was very much the sort of young man on the fringe of all that Bloomsbury Group* at that time and Charles also had some connection there. Julian Trevelyan and I went up there together with Humphrey Spender. We were taking photographs and painting around the place. We painted in the streets. The idea being that we would get public comments and you would actually have a relationship between the artist and the people.'[17]

Wickham's memory of Spender was that he was a very neurotic and nervous chap. 'He was a very nice man but he and his brother were both highly strung fellows.' Coming from the other end of the social spectrum, Harry Gordon had a very similar view. 'Spender were a left-winger, although he were very, very shy and very reluctant and he had a very bad memory. He couldn't remember what day it were.' Wickham again: 'He felt embarrassed often at taking photos of people, because it was done so much less in those days. It was a pretty rare thing to have anybody try to take photos in pubs and places of that sort. Even in churches and chapels we used to try to take photographs. Occasionally one fell foul of the minister who said you mustn't do it in here. It was very difficult trying to do really natural, realistic photographs in pubs, because as soon as you started to do it, they all realised and they all put on their photographing faces.'

Wickham knew Sommerfield well, having first met him in London in somewhat unusual circumstances. 'I met John originally through getting off with his wife. It was an extraordinary occasion. He had a marvellous girl called Stella, beautiful woman, and I met her at a party, not knowing anything about her at all. She was just a girl at a party. And we got off together and went back to her flat. And in the morning she said would you like to meet my husband, he's in the next room. And there was dear

* An influential group of writers, intellectuals and artists who worked together near Bloomsbury in central London. Among its best-known members were Virginia Woolf, E. M. Forster and Lytton Strachey.

John, and we've never looked back. And we've been friends ever since.'
Visitors like Wickham were always welcome. Harrisson had so many
subjects he wanted to follow, he needed help from as many observers as
he could get for nothing and so he called on his friends. He had merely
to ask, as Spender explained: 'The effect Tom had on me was absolutely
magnetic, charismatic. He had this mysterious capacity . . . that one could
simply become his slave and he had only to suggest something and off
you went. People said to me, "You are an absolute idiot to be doing this
for nothing. One just doesn't work for nothing. There must be some
money available." And Tom would say, "There isn't any money so if you
are going to do it, you will do it for nothing."'

Spender was fortunate in having a well-paid job with the *Mirror*, and
between his stints in Bolton he recalled 'cruising round the country in
an open two-seater Alvis 12/50 with dickey wire wheels and constantly
failing brakes, on a lonely search for the Art Editor's dream pictures – the
old mill wheel, the village green with smithy or game of cricket, pretty
girl on galloping horse on windswept downs, hair blowing against a background of scudding clouds'.[18] There couldn't have been a greater contrast
to the back streets and factories he was shooting in Bolton. Because he
wanted to remain as invisible as he could to those he was photographing,
Spender ruled out almost entirely taking pictures in the home or on the
factory floor. There were some exceptions, but to do this meant getting
permission, the scene would have to be set up and there would be no
chance of capturing the naturalness and spontaneity he was looking for.
One of the few photographs that he set up shows a baby being bathed in
front of a roaring fire. 'The family didn't mind – as long as their home was
not made to look impoverished. There had to be a fire burning to show
they had enough money to buy coal.'

Generally he avoided the set-up shot as much as he could because he
believed a photograph was ruined if the subject became aware of him
and looked directly into his lens. While he was at the *Mirror* Spender
had developed a great dislike of such shots. His experience in Bolton
reinforced this as he found that families who let him into their homes
would do anything in an attempt to conceal their poverty. One house he
went into didn't have electricity, but when they knew he was coming
they bought an electric Hoover and when he arrived to take his pictures
the parts were proudly displayed on the mantelpiece in the front parlour. Although deeply conscious of the difference between himself, an
upper-class Londoner, and his working-class subjects, Spender never
condescended either to caricaturing them or to dealing with them on any

but the most compassionate terms. One of his most notable sequences of photographs is the funeral of John Shaw of Davenport Street. Nothing is known about the man other than the fact that he was a neighbour, but Spender's photographs of his funeral are among the best known of his Worktown photographs. As he recalled, 'Tom Harrisson believed that everyday life in Bolton was very rich in ritual, which in his view was parallel to the rituals of primitive tribes. And one of the things that he was particularly involved with was funerals and so he got me on to tracing the whole procedure through one particular funeral.'[19] Spender followed John Shaw's cortège from his home to Heaton Cemetery, taking a memorable set of photographs along the way. Brian Barefoot, who was waiting at the cemetery, described the scene there:

> The grave was one row back from the main path, but had a smaller path leading right to it. It was covered with two planks and a mound of earth excavated from the grave was heaped on one side. Two gravediggers dressed in floppy felt hats, brown overalls and thick trousers, leggings and clogs of wood stood near. A third workman in the same dress but without overall stood at the bottom of the main path and supervised the carrying of the coffin to the grave. The cortège arrived just after two o'clock, it consisted of the motor hearse, with wreaths of flowers on the roof, then three hired and one private car, then another hired car with flowers on the roof, then six more hired cars. They all stopped at the bottom of the footpath leading to the graves. The mourners got out of the cars and formed a procession four abreast as they came up the hill. First came the gravedigger, then the coffin, borne by six men, then the mourners, twenty-one men and three women. All wore black or navy blue suits, black ties. The coffin was carried to the grave and lowered in. Each of the mourners was given a white chrysanthemum by one of the gravediggers. The ceremony consisted of an address read by a middle-aged man, which was original and moving, and well delivered. Most of the men had tears in their eyes; one or two had obviously been weeping a great deal previous to the funeral.[20]

At such a sensitive time and with so much emotion on display it is not surprising that the hypersensitive Spender was not comfortable with what he was doing. 'Taking pictures of a funeral was one of the times when my own super-respectable conventional attitudes of respect for people in states of sorrow intervened very much. I hated doing it. This was a kind of exploitation of grief to the extent that things were very

difficult, particularly in the churchyard. The great problem to me was
that I am a very easily embarrassed person in public situations, and essen-
tially the whole activity was fraught with anxiety and embarrassment and
danger. In many kinds of ways it was torture.' But it wasn't only taking
pictures of a funeral that brought terrors for him. When asked if he ever
talked to men in a pub he said, 'No. I would have been terrified. The
whole difficulty for me, there, was what happens when you talk to them.
They are total foreigners, it was acutely embarrassing.'[21] Harrisson did
show some understanding of the difficulties Spender faced: 'Humphrey
Spender's photographs are those of the unobserved observer, participat-
ing, accepted, unnoticed in living situations. This is a difficult role at the
best of times, requiring nerve and sensitivity; it was especially difficult in
those days when photographic equipment was much less sophisticated.
Film emulsions were much slower. There was no automatic calculation
of exposure. Flashbulbs of enormous size could be used only as a last
resort and inevitably upset the whole balance of the human situation.
The camera, like the writing hand, must not be in evidence.'

Although he was very clear about his own social status and that of
many members of his team Harrisson would, according to Spender, state
quite often that 'class was never a problem as far as he was concerned,
that basically following anthropological law, if you came from another
valley, you were a foreigner, therefore all foreigners were the same'.
But Spender wasn't certain about that. 'People in Bolton', he observed,
'would still tend to call one "Sir" if one had a middle-class accent. I think
they were very much aware that we were a different breed of people and
it took quite a long time to establish confidence.' Harrisson was genuinely interested in everything that went on around him in working-class
settings. Spender recalled being asked to find out 'how people hold their
hands, the number of sugar lumps that people pop into their mouths
. . . how much people stole things like teaspoons in restaurants, matches,
bits of paper'. Harrisson was also very observant himself. 'Every single
feature of a pub room would be significant,' Spender said, 'the aspidistra,
the obscured glass, the music on the piano, the wallpaper pattern, the
style of the stools – whereas the ordinary person who hadn't travelled
and seen primitive peoples would not have noticed. Tom noticed all
the woodwork; the snob screen, which is a class division; saloon* bar as
opposed to the bar where the darts go on.'

While Harrisson and Spender were both anxious to work incognito,

---

* Like lounge or parlour. Another name for the best room in a pub.

Madge needed as much publicity as he could get and it was only by advertising the project that he would be able to recruit more volunteers and widen the social and political range of the panel. Articles in the national press helped to broaden the base and the widespread press coverage that followed the publication in June 1937 of the Mass-Observation pamphlet outlining the organisation's aims brought in a flood of new offers of help. By this time Madge and Jennings were trying to cope with an increasingly unwieldy avalanche of directive and diary material arriving by post every month from hundreds of volunteers who reported on their own views, dreams, tastes in clothing and daily activities. Madge noted that observers' reports were showing a marked increase in accuracy and control of the subjective elements.

Madge and Harrisson were both keen to gather endorsements from the great and the good, and with this in mind they set up an advisory committee which included H. G. Wells, J. B. Priestley and Julian Huxley, who was Britain's best-known scientist. In spite of the backing of such distinguished figures, however, many academics were critical of Mass-Observation and its methods. Right from the start Madge and Harrisson had declared, 'Our first concern is to collect data, not interpret it.'[22] One of the main objections that social scientists had to the organisation stemmed from this; M-O was accused of collecting lots of data without first developing a theoretical framework and then deciding what data would be relevant. The problem then arose of how to handle the flood of material that came in without narrowing the field and limiting the kind of data to be considered. It was one that never went away and it would become critical when it came to trying to analyse and collate the material for the Gollancz books.

8

A DAY IN THE LIFE

'As far as money was concerned, there wasn't much being passed around. We got accommodation, grub and I had to have beer money, a lot of it, that was occupational, that wasn't for pleasure'

John Sommerfield

Throughout the summer of 1937, Harrisson continued to attract a wide range of young, leftward-leaning artists, intellectuals and would-be politicians to join him in Bolton. There was always a welcome for anyone who was interested in his social experiment and willing to help, and 85 Davenport Street was always full. 'On one occasion,' Brian Barefoot recalled, 'it accommodated twelve observers, every room a bedroom at night except the kitchen. It was typically working class, with a back yard as the only recreation ground, apart from the tiny patch of front garden, left to run to weed, and not, as is the case of every other house in the street, cultivated as assiduously as an aspidistra.' Inside it was spartan with just a table, a few old chairs and a desk in the front room. The kitchen was always filthy with dirty pots piled up in the porcelain sink and the whole place stank of fish and chips. Absolutely ghastly was the way Spender described it: 'the food was awful and it was a rickety old house and people were smoking the whole time, so it was absolutely full of cigarette smoke and in fact the whole place caught fire on one occasion.' 'Small and a bit congested and possibly people might say a bit slummy' was how John Sommerfield remembered it. 'I was lucky. There was one tiny little room which I had as a bedroom of my own, but a lot of people had to share bedrooms.'

Louie Davies and her husband ran the left-wing Workers' Bookshop on Dean Road and she got to know the residents when she was delivering papers – the *Daily Worker*, the *Daily Herald* and the *Manchester Guardian*. She remembered the house as 'a real dump. When I used to call you opened a door and went down the lobby and you saw this big room where they were all sat with these completely littered desks with cups of tea that had been there for nearly a week. They'd have all the walls decorated with every bit and piece they'd cut out of the papers. They'd nobody to keep it tidy for them. And they was brewing pots of tea and talking; they'd typewriters, they'd duplicators and they did a lot of conferring with one another, all the notes they'd made in the walkabouts the night before and they were all telling their tales about what they thought about it all.' She remembers them as 'generous with the booze when they went drinking. But I didn't care for them a lot, cos they was drinking too much. Some was quite good politically. They came to our meetings on the square – Communist Party meetings. A lot of them was fairly friendly, but I didn't like them because a lot of the things they did I didn't approve of. And I didn't like the way they put women down.'[1]

The people in the house were constantly changing. Spender recalled that 'if I was there one week and the next occasion would be say four weeks from then I would go up again and there would be a different lot of people'. Harrisson lived in the house himself, and Walter Hood remembered that he always had the best room.

> He was a funny lad in some ways. He would get up late and, unwashed and unshaven, he would go straight to work in the front room, writing letters and articles, with papers strewn all over the floor. Some days he would stop in bed all day and just read, and let his beard grow. He had an awful habit of having one friend near him, a young student – Woodrow Wyatt – and his job was turning the bloody handle of the gramophone, and time and time again it was George Formby, 'When I'm Cleaning Windows'. This was to help him sleep; he wanted background music. This and Gracie Fields, 'The Biggest Aspidistra in the World'. He'd have this played for hour after hour while I was in the 'kitchen room' writing up notes and searching through every pocket time and time again for a fag-end I knew wasn't there.

'Our Gracie', the 'Lancashire lass' from nearby Rochdale, and the singer and comedian Formby from Wigan were two of the biggest music-hall and recording stars of the day. Hood said he never did learn what solace they gave Harrisson or 'if he thought it was atuning him to Lancashire working people. But it sickened me for ever for these Lancashire songsters – and that's a pity.'

There was never any dispute about who was in charge. Harrison made it clear to everybody that he was the boss, and as Brian Barefoot recalled:

> He would sack people without hesitation who were critical of him. He

would demand of us more work than we were capable of giving, even though we tried to emulate his own overpowering devotion to work, and then he became enraged if we made small mistakes. He was selfish concerning his employee's right to a little free time; and at one time or another he must have quarrelled with nearly everyone at Davenport Street. Indifferent to personal hygiene – shaving irregularly, his longish black hair was not too often washed or cut and indeed he did not take a bath all that often, which made him not particularly nice to be near. But none of this prevented him from being a constant source of inspiration to those who joined the Worktown experiment under his autocratic leadership. He had the charisma that every expedition member expects his leader to have. He knew all the really top people – newspaper magnates, leading industrialists, the high men at the BBC – and I think we may not have appreciated at the time the enormous efforts he must have made to raise funds for the project and the constant stress that running it more or less single handed must have entailed. Madge was an intellectual, ideal for running the 'introvert' side of M-O, but he would certainly never have had the drive to organise the Bolton team, browbeat the BBC, raise the money, sustain the publicity and all the other things that Tom did so well.

More than any other factor it was Harrisson's drive and enthusiasm and the sheer force of his personality that drew the volunteers in. It might have looked, as Angus Calder has pointed out, 'like a topical cultural fad ... a not very political way of expressing social concern', within a context of 'general unease about where modern society was heading, as Hitler, Franco and Mussolini strode on'.[2] But as Michael Wickham explained: 'It was quite incredible how he [Harrisson] managed to get us all to go out and do what fundamentally was fairly boring. Going out and bringing back and writing all these reports and stuffing them in file boxes. Michael Foot, Harold Wilson and Dick Crossman* came up. It was

* Michael Foot. Joined the Labour Party and fought his first parliamentary election in 1935. Associated with the Labour left for most of his career. Member of Parliament from 1945 to 1955 and from 1960 until 1992. Cabinet Minister in Harold Wilson's government and Labour leader at 1983 general election.
  Harold Wilson. Labour Party politician. One of the youngest ever Oxford University dons in 1937 at the age of 21. Entered parliament in 1945. Elected leader of the Labour Party in 1963. Narrowly won 1964 election, going on to win increased majority in 1966. Prime Minister from 1964 to 1970 and 1974 to 1976.
  Richard Crossman. Labour Party politician and author. Taught philosophy at Oxford and in 1935 became head of the Labour group on Oxford City Council. Entered the House of Commons in 1945. Cabinet minister in Harold Wilson's government.

a constant flood of people coming in and out the whole time. I remember very well Harold Wilson – what a boring little man he was, we couldn't stand Harold because he was so dull and he always had all the facts but never had any of the ideas. Totally dotty little man. Tom and I couldn't stand him.'[3]

Despite differences in personality, beliefs and social background, the observers got on remarkably well. Walter Hood described it as an 'early commune'. But, as with later communes in the 1960s and 1970s, life at Davenport Street for the observers was chaotic and there was never enough money. Harrisson paid the rent and the daily help but that was about all. He ran up debts with tradesmen and Bill Rigby, an unemployed ex-miner in his sixties who did odd jobs around the house, complained that he was hardly ever paid for his work. When funds ran low Harrisson dispensed with the services of the daily help, providing, when reminded, cash for food instead.[4] Hood recalled, 'Tom used to get so involved with his writing and what he was doing, he never bothered at all whether there was anything for us to eat . . . so it was my job to have a word with him and say, "Look Tom, what about it? I mean there's not even a bloody tin of bully beef for us to have a go at." And Tom would fork out a couple of quid and I would go around and do a bit of shopping.'[5] At odd, late hours, Harrisson treated the staff to fish and chips from the shop on the corner and there was frequent debate over their fish suppers. Was Mass-Observation giving existing elites the knowledge of the masses necessary to rule them effectively or empowering the masses to overthrow those elites was one of the questions that was frequently discussed. But after supper there was always more work to follow. Harrisson insisted on immediate recording of the day's observations, 'not four or eight hours later', Hood said, 'even if this meant stopping up all night'.[6]

Observers were given their board and keep, but there was no regular pay. Hood was promised a pound a week when he was recruited, but he never once received it, although cash would be found for emergencies, to buy books or, as Hood recalled with some bitterness, for taxi rides when Harrisson went into Manchester to do a broadcast or meet a potential funder.[7] Sommerfield didn't fare any better. 'As far as money was concerned,' he observed, 'there wasn't much being passed around. We got accommodation, grub and I had to have beer money, a lot of it, that was occupational, that wasn't for pleasure. But if Victor Gollancz hadn't coughed up what was then a lot of money for all these books in advance, I don't think we could have carried on.'[8]

For Hood and Sommerfield there were real problems if they didn't receive the pay they had been promised. For others of more independent means money didn't matter. They were on a mission. 'We sought to fully penetrate the society we were studying,' one of the early observers said, 'to live in it as effective members of it and to percolate into every corner of every day and every night of industrial life.' Living in the society they were studying meant that between half-past six and seven o'clock every morning the team would be woken by the sound of clog irons* on the paving stones as the workers tramped up to the mills. All would be hustle and bustle and the noise would reach a great crescendo about ten minutes before work was due to start. Once a week on a Monday every street had its lines of washing hanging out and the coalman with his horse and cart would be in trouble from all the housewives if he had a delivery to make up their street. Washday for most housewives was a day of drudgery with the posser,† the washboard and the mangle. Women would wear the same drab coats every day and go shopping with a shawl or headscarf covering their heads.

Cheap, affordable terraced houses for the working classes were the norm for most employed in the cotton industry – 'two up and two down' with two bedrooms, a front room or parlour which came directly off the street and a living room at the back. The front room was the best room, but it would invariably be sparsely furnished with maybe a small sideboard, a two-seater couch and a peg rug‡ in front of the fireplace. The living room's main focal point was the cast-iron fireplace with hob and oven that gleamed with regular polishing and blackleading. Built on to the back of the living room was a small scullery. Here the sink with its one cold-water tap overlooked a small stone-flagged yard. Cooking would be done on a small gas ring with food stored in a metal-grilled meat safe. Dominating the scullery would be a large wooden mangle used for wringing out the washing with the dolly tub§ and posser standing next to it. A back door from the scullery opened on to the yard with the house's only toilet standing at the bottom of it.

Women spent a lot of time keeping up appearances. Despite the soot and grime, curtains were spotlessly clean and at the front the steps

---

* U-shaped strips of iron, nailed under the sole of clogs at toe and heel.
† Posser. A tool used for hand washing of laundry. Washing was put in water in a large tub and pounded with the posser using up and down movements. Also known as a ponch.
‡ Peg rug. Floor covering made from scraps of old rags cut into strips and hooked onto a canvas web. Better known as rag rugs.
§ Tub that was filled with hot water for washing clothes.

to the door were donkey-stoned to a pure white or brilliant yellow by housewives dressed in uniform pinnies. They had usually got the stone from the rag and bone man when he swapped it for some of their old rags or junk. For the women washday was a very regular event. Spender said, 'The more I got to know about Bolton, the more I knew that certain weekly events were regularly programmed, and in walking round I noticed it (washday) happening in the narrow streets where the houses were back to back and I decided that this was not only a typical event in Bolton but would also make a marvellous photograph if I waited for the correct wind conditions and the lighting conditions.'⁹ The result was one of Spender's best-known Worktown photographs.

Most houses had an ash pit next to the toilet at the bottom of the yard with an ornate cast- iron door in the back-street wall. Narrow passages ran along the back of the yards, in between another row of terraced houses. On ash-pit day men would come along here with their wagon and shovels to remove the ashes. This whole area was a breeding ground for rats and many a rat would be killed with a swing of the ash man's shovel. In these crowded streets there was very little greenery or fresh air, no beauty in their surroundings, but there was a feeling of warmth and friendliness and a real sense of community. On warm summer evenings all the kids would be out playing, inventing their own forms of amusement. The girls would throw their skipping ropes around the gas lamps to make swings; the lads would kick a tennis ball against the gable end of a house and women sat on the doorsteps with cups of tea, chatting with neighbours, catching up on gossip.

Harrisson decided that a typical street was needed for a proposed 'Day in the Life of a Street' report. The idea was to make a complete survey of every observable event that occurred in a particular street from 5 a.m. to midnight on one particular day in summer. From this it was hoped there would emerge a composite picture of the Worktowner's daily routine, and perhaps also some conclusions as to the significance of rush-hours, the fashionableness of certain clothes or colours and the kinds of activities that people pursued in the street, as distinct from in the privacy of their own homes. There was one very obvious choice for the street to be studied, as Brian Barefoot explained in his memoir.

It was only practicable to carry out such a survey from our own headquarters in Davenport Street, which was typical of streets in the area in that it had a front and back street. Davenport Street was the traffic artery, lined by front doors; Back Davenport Street was a long narrow alley, frequented by children and animals. The back door of each house opened on to a concrete yard, at the end of which was a wooden door giving on to the back. Three observers, working in shifts of two at a time, recorded every activity throughout the day. Fundamentally what we were recording was the activity of the street (front and back) in terms of groups (man alone, woman alone, couple, two men and one woman and so on); position (near or far side, entering or emerging from a house, standing on doorstep or in garden), clothes (type, colour, headgear), action, burden (carrying or not carrying something), animals, traffic (man or woman driver, motor car, cycle, van).

The survey recorded that the first hour was very quiet.

Lights are switched on, one by one, in the dark houses, the roar of a tram-car is heard in the distance, a lamplighter passes, then a tramway man on his way to work. Chimneys begin to smoke. A few men wearing caps and raincoats pass down the street. A newsboy delivers the morning papers. In the back street is heard the sound of clogs; the mills will soon be starting work for the day. Down the front street a single car passes. A bird sings. The hour from six to seven is also quiet; a woman puts out empty milk bottles; several men pass carrying their lunch wrapped in red kerchiefs or paper bags. At 6.52 the first man wearing a trilby hat is observed; the sound of clogs continues in the back street.

Between 7 and 8 a.m., thirteen cyclists, five vans, one horse-drawn cart and just one car were observed; but the tedium experienced by one observer is revealed in him recording 'black cat without tail going mad in distance'. Around eight o'clock 'the postman comes on his round. More people come out of their front doors. Coal is being shovelled in the back yards. A lavatory plug is pulled.' Then just before nine the children were on their way to school: 'The children do not linger. One or two play with a ball, but otherwise they go straight to school.' The quietest time of the day was between 9 and 11 in the morning.

No doubt all the women who were not working were engaged in house-work; the men (except the unemployed) had gone off to work; the children were at school. The corner shop gets a few customers; the shopkeeper cleans the front . . . In the back street a woman is seen washing clothes in her yard. A middle-aged man puts a ladder against a lamp post and does some repairs to the lamp. He moves to another lamp and repeats the operation . . . A few small children play in the back street. But nothing of great interest happens during these two hours. There are still more men wearing coats than not wearing them, although this is June.

During the 'shopping period' a car with a learner's 'L' card passed up the street; a telegraph boy called at no. 85 (M-Os headquarters); an ice-cream tricycle came by; the local midwife came up the street, in her blue uniform; a man tried to part the dogs who were starting to fight. The rag and bone man came along, crying out: 'Any rags?' – he got no customers. Between 1 and 2 p.m. there were more single individuals in the street than at any other time: 'presumably people coming home from work for their dinner.' The back street was now very quiet but between 2 and 3 p.m. there was more action. Path-sweeping, gate-painting and dog-exercising were now observed activities. At 2.40 the most interesting event of the day took place. Eight aeroplanes flew over – a rare sight in Worktown, which is nowhere near a military airport and some distance from a civil one. 'Two men in the garden of no. 84 shout to attract the attention of two women. Young woman points and says, "Look at them!" Other woman says, "That's war!" and laughs. The butcher at the Co-op shop and the landlord of the Royal pub come out to see.'

As the teatime rush-hour was starting, there was a window-cleaner in the street, whistling 'Country Cousin of Mine'. About a quarter past five there were more young women in the front street: the mills had closed for the day. One of the mill girls, returning home, still had cotton waste in her hair. The busiest half-hour was between 5.30 and 6, when seventy people passed. A gang of three window-cleaners pushed their cart up the street, and children clustered round the window of the little local shop. Although the street was fairly quiet between seven and eight in the evening, the half-hour between eight and eight-thirty produced the biggest rush of the day, in which women predominated. The 'evening out' had started. After that the street gradually became quieter. From nine o'clock onwards the lights began to be switched on in the houses, the first drunks came wandering home, and the latecomers came back one by one.

'Between 10.30 and 11.00 seven people go into front doors of local houses for every one who comes out. At eleven there are candles lit upstairs at nos. 92 and 98. In the back street a group of adolescents, stand and talk at the corner for over half an hour. They sing and talk loudly

. . . lights go on and off in houses . . . At a quarter-past eleven the street lamps are turned off. There are still a few lights on in the houses, both front and back, and a few stragglers have still to come home. It is eleven minutes past midnight before the last man goes down the street, a car passes, and all lights are extinguished, except for candle lights in nos. 90 and 92 . . . Finally at 12.30 p.m. the street is dark and silent. The day is over.'

Reviewing the events of the day as a whole, observers found that the most popular form of headgear among the men was the flat cap, though there was a tendency among the young men to wear no headgear at all. Most women put on a hat when they went out in the evening, and berets were very popular among schoolgirls. The mill girls never wore hats to or from work. As regards traffic, bicycles predominated when men were going to and from work, and were not much used for other purposes. Motor cars easily outnumbered other forms of transport in the middle of the day, and showed minor peaks at times when middle-class men were starting and finishing work. Surprisingly, only four motorcycles were noted during the whole day. Altogether, 1,245 people were observed in the street, 682 men and 563 women. Blue was the most popular clothing colour, closely followed by black.[10]

The activities of the residents of Davenport Street and the streets surrounding it were constantly put under the microscope. Walking along nearby Vernon Street one morning, local observer Eric Letchford came across an altercation.

Observer was passing 39 Vernon Street at 11.10 a.m. On the pavement was a typical navvy with a shopping bag in his hand. He went up to the front door and kicked at the panel several times and shouted, 'Come down here you Irish bastard, an' I'll string you on this bloody woodbine tin. I'll give 'im bloody Paddy.' He then walked a few strides away and came back to repeat the kicking of the door, saying, 'I'll give him bloody Paddy, the bloody Irish Swine,' and all the time Paddy is look-ing through the bedroom window with a look of fear on his face. This was repeated several times until the tenant, (Paddy) a little man, came out and said, 'I'm going to fetch a policeman,' and walked towards Chorley Old Road with the navvy following him and trying to explain himself.[11]

One place he would have found a policeman was at the junction of Deansgate and Bradshawgate, where horse-drawn vehicles competed for space with lorries, cars, double-decker buses and the trams that clanked along the middle of the road. Here a policeman used to stand on a small wooden platform to control the traffic flow. This sort of police activity was another aspect of Worktown life to be observed and noted, and Humphrey Pease was the man to do it. Pease was a keen amateur ornithologist, but during his time in Bolton he turned his talents to secret observation of the police. Starting on Deansgate at 2.35 one afternoon he noted: 'P.C. standing by traffic lights outside Woolworth's. Looks right and left at traffic as pedestrians cross. At 2.37 he walks slowly along to traffic lights opposite Bradshawgate.' Pease followed the policeman around all afternoon, reporting his every movement until 'On approaching the cross roads – Manor St, Bow St, Fold Road – he puts his right hand in his overcoat pocket and pulls out a pair of white sleeves and slips them on as he goes to centre of crossing and begins point duty.'[12]

As well as these everyday comings and goings on the street, the Worktown project was also gathering accounts of the daily routine in individual households. Mrs Duckworth was a working-class housewife who got up each morning at about quarter past seven. 'Mind,' she told an observer, 'I don't come down dressed but get bread and butter for Ernest (husband).' While Ernest lights the fire before going to work she goes back to bed to give the baby his feed. Then she has to get her daughter Sheila up for school.

I'm left by myself at 10 minutes to nine. I tidy up and make the beds – I clean the windows on Thursdays. If I go out it's just to get something for the dinner – the butchers or some shop like that. We always have a cooked dinner except on Monday when we have cold meat from Sunday – There's always a puddin' – then a cup of tea. I'm busy giving Thomas (the baby) his dinner until one – Then I have a look at the paper until two. Sometimes I wash up sometimes I leave it for Sheila. Then I have a smoke . . . I couldn't tell you when I had a new frock. It must be three years. Sometimes I go into town – I generally now go into Queen's Park. I go about 3.30. You see Tommy has his bottle about 3 o'clock – I get back about 5.30. Tea is at six. We all get it with Father – Sheila gets the tea ready an' does the washin' up. Tommy goes to bed at 7 o'clock. Sheila goes to bed early an' we have supper any time between 10.30 and 12 o'clock. We have a good feed – fish and chips – boiled onions – tripe something like that. I feed the baby after supper – an' he's got to go on the jerry – We get to bed around 12 or 12.30 . . .

Mrs Duckworth's daily routine never varies very much, and week in week out there is very little variety for her. People like her living on the poverty line, whether as a result of unemployment or simply low wages, had a dreary existence. She does all the mending on Thursday and she very rarely goes out in the evening. Ernest, she says, never goes out and she has only been out three times since Thomas was born. She clearly has very few clothes and makes the point that she changes her skirt when she goes out and wears a brown coat with a fur collar. 'In summer,' she says, 'a blue coat which she has had two summers . . . no different clothes for Sunday.' Money is tight and Mrs Duckworth says that 'the house takes £1 a week before they begin to eat. What with rent – coal & light.' They are buying their house through a building society. She laughs and says, 'It will be ours when we're 90.'[13]

In never going out, Ernest appears to have been something of an exception. After work and tea a worker's time was his own. In one street, an observer noted,

one man will surely leave his home between 6.30 and 7.00 p.m. in the summer months and walk at a peculiarly leisurely gait to the Merchall Park bowling green. He will just as surely stroll at the same speed around 9.00 p.m. to the Alexandria Hotel in Stewart Street for a pint or two and a game of dominoes. Another neighbour can be depended upon to stand either at his home front door or at the street corner for long periods during the fine weather, steadily puffing his pipe, sometimes for hours on end, with an occasional nod to an acquaintance, but very seldom speaking. The wives of these men appeared never to go out on week nights (except perhaps on Mondays, to the cinema), but the whole ritual of both the men and the women had a definiteness about it . . . In the colder weather much the same thing occurred except the times for going out were later and the immediate objective was the pub.

At 85 Davenport Street the observers had their own daily routine. Brian Barefoot remembered working 'late into the night so breakfast was never very early. It took place between nine and ten and normally consisted of tea, bread and jam, and nearly always one fried egg, lying in solitary grandeur on a plate. There were few organised events to report in the mornings, but we were kept busy just the same. There were "street-counts" to do in various parts of the town, shops to study, and from 11.30 to 12 the pubs would be open – though there were very few customers in the smaller pubs during the midday opening time.' At one o'clock

A view of Bolton taken from the roof of Mere Hall Art Gallery in April 1938. All over town, mill chimneys towered over rows of terraced houses.

While reading a copy of the *New Statesman* at Bolton Library, Tom Harrisson saw the letter from Charles Madge that led to them setting up Mass-Observation.

Women talking on a street corner on Deansgate in the town centre. Instructing his volunteers on how their anthropological fieldwork should be done, Tom Harrisson emphasised how much could be learned just from watching a group like this.

The corner of Bank Street and Church Street in Bolton's bustling town centre.

Gray Street, with Albert Mill in the background. Bolton's landscape was dominated by smoke-blackened mills, factories and endless rows of terraced houses.

Women checking towelling fabric in a mill. Line shafting, which transmitted power to all the machinery, ran the whole length of the mill floor and could be as long as 200 feet.

Ladies taking tea in a busy town centre café. On one occasion, in an upmarket café, Tom Harrisson suggested to Humphrey Spender that he should try to photograph a posh lady putting a spoon in her bag.

Observers were encouraged by Harrisson to travel on the top decks of buses and trams and listen in to conversations.

Planning observations at 85 Davenport Street. There was a daily session which usually took the form of Harrisson seizing about half a dozen national newspapers, reading the headlines and hitting on a theme that he thought would be productive. (*Left to right:* Walter Hood, Tom Harrisson, John Sommerfield and an unknown observer)

Children joining in with a rally for Labour candidate George Tomlinson on the day of the Farnworth by-election, 27 January 1938.

Canvassers at work in the Conservative Club rooms during the by-election. One observer infiltrated this group to get an inside view of the Conservative election machine.

they were back at Davenport Street. 'For dinner there was always a good blow-out. The woman who "did" for us cooked almost the same midday dinner every day – steak pudding, sausages and boiled cod – all of her repertoire that I can remember. The next break was at five, for tea, which was similar to breakfast except that instead of the fried egg, there was usually a slice of cake. That completed the diet provided by the management, but if we could personally afford it we could buy fish and chips later from the shop down the road. I often had a fruitcake sent from home and, being vitamin conscious, I could buy oranges from time to time and share them out. We also from time to time drank half-pints of beer in the pubs in the evening, when we could afford it. Beer was about sixpence a pint.'[14]

Hood recalled that they 'had a lady who came in every morning and she used to clean up. Mind you it was an awful job with all the papers and that, and we had very little furniture in the sense of anything worthwhile polishing. But she used to wash up all the dirty dishes and things like that, then she would go shopping for us if we had any money. And she used to do our washing; she was always complaining about how dirty the towels were. She used to use green carbolic soap, because I used to slip down to the shop at the bottom of the street to get a couple of those bars for the washing and that's what we used for washing ourselves.' He went on:

There was a toilet outside in the yard and there was also a bath inside the house but there was little time to bathe when we were working hard; and Tom Harrisson set us a tremendous example by working solidly for weeks on end. I can remember one occasion when he had a long report to complete. He sat at a table on the first floor behind a typewriter, and worked away at it for something like fourteen hours non-stop, without breaking off for any rest or sleep. A plate of fish and chips or a pot of tea was brought to him from time to time. No one dared interrupt until the effort was over and he would again be fit to crack a joke and speak politely to his subordinates. At the end of this long slog he was surrounded by a little cloud of halitosis and bad air; but the report was finished and presumably the experiment could continue. He would not do this occasionally but quite often if the situation demanded and we respected him for it.

It wasn't just Harrisson who worked long hours. He expected the same from his volunteers. 'Talk about the forty-hour week and the rights of the workers!' Barefoot declared. 'If anyone needed a trade union it was the Mass-Observers.'

Throughout their time in Bolton the market was always a focal point for observers. Harry Gordon recalled how groups of them would go there when it was a bad day. 'This is where they could enjoy themselves having a chinwag with different people. Another reason they enjoyed it, it was quite close to Davenport Street and they were under cover here, they weren't out in the rain.'[15] The market was always busy and, because of its significance in the life of Worktown, a team of observers led by John Sommerfield reported on its activities from first thing in the morning until all the stalls closed down at night. In the first hour vans kept arriving, coming down the aisles between the stalls. Stallholders were unpacking these vans and setting up their stalls. On several stalls were baskets, boxes or an enormous bundle covered in tarpaulin, awaiting the owners. 'To observer's right', Sommerfield noted, 'was the Jewish clothes merchant: opposite was a woman setting out shirts, blouses, household linen etc. A van stood in the aisle, and from this two women were unpacking rolls of material and setting up the next stall beyond. The nearer woman, stout, cheerful, about 40, was singing hymns to herself as she worked.'

On one stall a man was selling mandrake root. On another a stocking salesman's pitch was 'These have all been washed thirty times. You can get correct sizes – they're all knitted to fit, there's no ankle bagginess.' At a toffee stall, 'Ah've t'best toffee in t'town, toffee made wi' real butter, homemade toffee.' Walking further through the market an observer spots a man auctioning china. He is 'twenty-five, flashy cut light suit, but very dirty, has very brilliantined hair, gestures a lot, speaks semi-cockney. He holds up the china on a board covered with black velvet. 'It's something new and original; it's quality, two and six.'

At 6 p.m. the observer reported: 'the market is at a low ebb, many parts being almost deserted, and the barkers resting their voices. By seven it has filled up again, and from seven to eight there is a real "last hour". It is during this last hour that many young people, particularly mill girls, come in and stroll around. The whole place is full of a hum of talk and there is a continual overtone of the barkers shouting like the talk in a full pub and the calling of the orders by the waiters on.' In the observer's opinion the market cannot just be regarded as a place for buying and selling, any more than a pub can. 'People meet each other, chat, stroll about looking at and fingering, and above all, in the open market, they listen to the wonderful talk of the barkers, particularly those selling herbs, cures, or dealing in magic. It is the barkers of these stalls who are the most fluent, cheerful, give the best show. It is very difficult to estimate the number of people who use the market. At a crowded time in the evening (7.45) during fifteen minutes 110 people passed down one aisle (vegetables). There are seven of these aisles, some more and some less crowded, as well as two transverse alleys. These figures suggest that at a rush-hour period not much less than 1,000 people walk through.' At 8 o'clock a bell is rung for about thirty seconds and all selling is supposed to stop. However it goes on for about five or ten minutes later – depending, said a chap, on where the cops are. The gates take some time to shut and all the time there is a flow of people coming out. A big green motor van comes for all the clothes-stall chaps and takes their stuff back to Cheetham Hill (Manchester). People stand around the open market watching the chaps pack their stuff up. The market is teeming with life right up to the last moment.[16]

In Blackheath as well as in Bolton, reports, diaries and observations piled up. The Coronation Day reports had all come in along with the twelve main texts written by observers on the day and the library of about 5,000 press cuttings that had been collected dealing with preparations for the day. The result of this was a plethora of material to be sorted, indexed and filed, and then the mammoth task of editing it down to book length. Madge regarded himself as combining anthropology and social psychology in his handling of the material and, writing for the *Left Review*, he described these two sciences as 'potentially the foremost allies of revolution'.[17] It fell to Jennings and Madge, with the help of William Empson and Kathleen Raine, to cut and shape the reports into a narrative mosaic.

For Jennings there were other things to distract him. Although ostensibly happily married, with his wife Cecily very much part of his Blackheath circle of friends, he began a short-lived affair with the thirty-nine-year-old American heiress Peggy Guggenheim. They had met through a former lover of his, Emily Coleman. Jennings had gone down to her house at Petersfield and Guggenheim recorded, 'Emily was there, and as she had finished with him, she offered him to me as though he were a sort of object she no longer required and I went to his room and took him in the same spirit.' Guggenheim's account of their affair begins with the observation that Humphrey was 'a sort of genius, and looked like Donald Duck'. When she went to Paris to stay with her mother Jennings followed her and they took a room in a small hotel on the Left Bank. Jennings was extremely vain and Guggenheim said that 'he was very pleased with his ugly, emaciated body' and kept jumping about the bed declaiming: 'Look at me! Don't you like me? Don't you think I'm beautiful?' Guggenheim had no desire to spend the weekend in bed with him so insisted on going to the Paris Exposition. She also took him to see Marcel Duchamp, whom he wanted to meet, and in return he introduced her to André Breton.[18]

Along with Madge, Jennings was now claiming that Mass-Observation was creating a new kind of literature and this highlighted growing differences between the two of them and Harrisson. Julian Trevelyan was close to all three and he could see at first hand the tensions within the organisation arising from the different views each of them had about it. In his autobiography *Indigo Days* he summarised these differences.

> M-O was really the product of three minds, each seeking from it something different. To Humphrey Jennings it was an extension of his Surrealist vision of Industrial England; the cotton workers of Bolton were the descendants of Stephenson and Watt, the dwellers in Blake's dark Satanic mills reborn into a world of greyhound racing and Marks and Spencer . . . His interest was intense but not long lived. To Charles Madge, Mass-Observation was a new kind of poetry. It was chiefly he who collated the 'reports' sent in each month by voluntary observers all over the country; who would choose out a description of five minutes in a country bus by a working girl and hold it up for all the world to see, to savour the poetic overtones in those few casual words . . . Tom, however, was the man of action, the anthropologist with the notebook. Not for Tom the eighteenth-century house in Blackheath, but rather the working-class house in Worktown, anonymous, and like those on either side of it.[19]

The three were so different that something had to give and Jennings was the first to go. The catalyst was Mass-Observation's first book *May 12 1937: Mass-Observation Day-Survey*. The style of the book was influenced largely by Jennings, who intended it to carry on in prose the experiments being made with documentary film, cutting from account to account, from shot to shot, building up an overall picture of Coronation Day. Images and events were set side by side in montage sequences that painted a picture of what was happening on the day. The material was to speak for itself, guided minimally by the hand of the producer. But the book, which was published in September 1937, was not a success and it was to be Jennings's first and last major job for Mass-Observation. The evocative juxtaposition of images that Jennings did so brilliantly in film worked less well in book form. It was widely reviewed, but most of the reviews were dismissive. The *Spectator* said, 'Scientifically they [the reports] are about as valuable as a chimpanzee's tea-party at the zoo,' while another critic complained: 'The facts simply multiply like maggots in a cheese.' It was a disaster. *May 12* sold only 800 copies, partly because it was not aimed with any precision at its intended target readership. A contemporary letter from someone describing himself as 'a working man' complained at the price. How could he be expected to afford a book costing 12/6d when a miner's wage was about £2 a week?[20] But, worse than this, the book turned Mass-Observation into a subject for ridicule and music-hall jokes. A review in the *New Statesman* projected the image of Mass-Observers under the bed, or at least observing which side of the bed people got out of in the morning. It summed up the book and the movement as 'a perfect study for a Marx Brothers film'.

Harrisson was enraged. He thought Madge had been crazy to give Jennings free rein to edit the material and deplored the picture it painted of Mass-Observation's work. As he looked on he believed that what he had to offer to the Mass-Observation movement was something much more tangible – a structure built around the observation of what people really did, not what they wrote about in their diaries. Madge apologized for Jennings's use of documentary techniques designed to appeal on a poetic and emotional level, saying that M-O was 'more than journalism or film documentary because it has the aim not only of presenting, but of classifying and analysing the immediate human world'. He also recorded, however, that Jennings 'shied away from what he felt to be a banal streak in Tom's expressionist quasi-anthropology. I too', he added, 'had some difficulty in reconciling myself to Tom's showmanship and the excessive claims he tended to make for his work. But his energy and magnetism were irresistible.'[21]

Jennings thought Harrisson was a philistine and over the next few months he began to distance himself from the organisation he had been involved in founding. Instead he went back to the art world and helped to launch Peggy Guggenheim on her career as one of the twentieth century's great art collectors. Their affair didn't last for long but it came at a turning point in Guggenheim's life, when she was energetically seeking to learn all she could about contemporary art. Inspired by the ground-breaking surrealism exhibition at the New Burlington Galleries in 1936, which Jennings had been involved in organising, she hit upon the idea of starting a gallery dealing exclusively in modern artists. Helped by Jennings she began to look for a suitable space. They fixed on 30 Cork Street, and the gallery, which she called Guggenheim Jeune, opened

there in January 1938.[22] Although he didn't make a formal break with
Mass-Observation until later in 1938, Jennings was now back in a world
where he was much more comfortable and he had very little further involvement with Madge, Harrisson and what was becoming increasingly
an experiment in social anthropology.

9

HEALTH, HOUSING AND POLITICS

'There are not enough nurses and the whole hospital is understaffed'

Steward at Townley's Hospital

The last Saturday afternoon in August 1937 was warm and sunny with not a cloud in the sky. Tom Harrisson set off from Davenport Street to tour the countryside in his car to see where people spent a lovely Saturday afternoon like this. 'Its 4.30,' he recorded, 'and Blackburn Road is crowded with shoppers. At Eagley there are a few people on the cricket ground where a match is in progress. There are fourteen spectators on seats around and twelve in the two pavilions. One man is fishing in the adjacent reservoir.' Driving further out of town towards the moors he found at Egerton there was a funeral. A party of mourners in black were coming away from the church and slowly walking up the pavement. One girl with head sunk on chest, the rest chatting. Beyond Egerton on the road to Blackburn he spotted three people on top of the moors to the right of the road and a man and woman in a field on the left. Further up on a side road another man and woman in shorts walked towards the main road. All around, he noted, 'lovely green country with sheep, without wire or notices, untrod today by humans'.

On a side road to Belmont he saw 'a motorbike just off the main road with a man in goggles necking a woman in a green overcoat and green beret, leaning against bike right by roadside. They ignore observer's car passing. Two boys with bikes sit on them against a stone wall and look into a field. A young man in shorts, with mac rolled in strap on back, walks towards Belmont with a woman; they stop to lean over a bridge and look at small stream. Do not touch each other. No one in fields, extensively visible both sides of road.' On this warm summer afternoon all is still, and Harrisson's description as he stops and climbs a wall is highly evocative.

In the distance four shots are fired, rapidly; a kestrel rises from a wall. Seven women loosely together walk towards Belmont on the left hand side of the road; several have paper parcels (food?). Some wear hats and heavyish overcoats more suitable for shopping. A car is parked on the left-hand side of the road going to Walmsley; three women sit on a rug by it, on the edge of the road, eating from papers. At a branch in the road, a lorry has smashed into a wall, without serious damage to wall or lorry. Seven cars are drawn up near and there are many people around. Two other lorries are there and three police. Just up the hill from this accident and road junction, there are a number of people sitting by the side of the road in grassland on the left, in groups, apparently picnickers. All are within 200 yards of the main road – on this long lovely stretch of road with extensive fields on either side. In one, just by a gate, five Brownies in uniform with a Guide mistress in uniform play cricket with a soft ball and no stumps, laughing and having fun. At Rotary Camp Clough there are a number of people in this lovely glade, noise and laughter, a child calls, fern and heather collected.[1]

On the face of it Harrisson's account of his Saturday afternoon drive is not very different from the *May 12* book he hated so much. What was different was the way he was intending to use all the observations that were piling up in Bolton in the planned Gollancz books. Not for him the documentary montage; his idea was for much more structured analysis with extracts from the reports used to illustrate specific points. After the catastrophe of *May 12* he insisted that in future M-O should publish nothing of that sort again except in conjunction with intensive, whole-time research into objective aspects of the subject. Madge accepted this and told his observers that their September day-surveys, which fell on a Sunday, would be used as part of a big book on religion and its role in social life – that is, one of the books that Harrisson was planning for Gollancz.[2]

For the observers in Bolton this emphasis on research and analysis meant a lot more work. Not only did they have to go out, make the observations and then write them up; they were also involved in a lot of the analytical work required for the books. After a weekend out observing, Brian Barefoot recalled that 'on Monday we did indoor theoretical work, sorting out all the political material we had collected, and trying to sift it into appropriate sections; e.g. Political Meetings, Elections, Non-Voters etc. On the other days Tom would decide on an event to be covered; he would draft a "directive" indicating the points on which information was needed and would then send as many of us as were available to cover the event in the way that newspaper reporters would cover a meeting. Each paragraph in our report would answer a question in the directive.'[3]

This can be seen in a report by Barefoot on a Labour Party Crusade meeting in which he had a number of specific headings, and noted the speaker's references to them. The first of these was 'Entertainment, Culture'. Under this heading he reported that the speaker mentioned municipal art collections and libraries, saying that rich people didn't need these things. 'This has been a very sound investment for the working class.' The observer didn't like the way the speaker showed off about having been to Italy. 'I was in Rome. I was in Naples. I was in the Isle of Capri.' Under 'Science and Planning' he referred to a complete planning and reorganisation of industrial life under socialism. The next heading was 'Sex', to which there was no reference in the meeting. Next 'Violence': the speaker stated that he believed in backing an idea with force if necessary. Reference to wars in China and Spain. 'Women' was the next heading. The speaker said, 'Every woman knows that the cost of living has gone up by 2 per cent.' Three women murmured, 'Hear, hear.' Under the last heading 'Work and Play', Barefoot reported that the first half of the speaker's address was a history of the British working class and about the vast pool of unemployment that had been in existence for seventeen years. He also mentioned self-help as a desirable quality in a Labour supporter.[4] Nationally 1937 saw unemployment drop below one and a half million, to a large extent due to the threat of war and the need to rearm. In Lancashire, however, the decline of the textile industry that had begun after the First World War continued. Over a five-month period from late 1937 to early 1938 unemployment in the Lancashire cotton trade rose from 39,153 to 88,164, prompting a demand for more assistance from the government for the industry.[5]

Apart from short reports, Barefoot also wrote three long pieces of research while he was in Bolton. His first was an analysis of the political attitudes of the people in the town. It took over a fortnight to complete, though he was working hard every day; and it was, he commented, 'the first piece of research that I ever attempted. I am in fact rather proud of it and consider that there are many original thoughts in it; and the other observers who read it also liked it. In particular, I valued Tom Harrisson's approval, because I think something of him as a writer.' Barefoot's report presents a vivid picture of political life in Bolton. He described conditions in the town's industries as very bad, and felt there was a stubborn opposition to them among the working people, which did not find expression in trade union or even political action. He was of the opinion that 'the picture of Bolton from a political angle shows a town depending on industry for its livelihood, but in which the working class has to live in very poor conditions, and does very little on its own initiative to better those conditions'.

'In Lancashire,' he asserted, 'it is the working class who seem to care least about what happens in the council chamber and in Parliament. The county returns far more Conservative than Labour members of Parliament and has more Conservative than Labour town councils. The history of the working class in Lancashire made them thoroughly bourgeois and respectable.' It was a picture that was reflected nationally with strong working-class support for the Conservative-dominated National Government led by Stanley Baldwin. Since the end of the First World War the Tories had been making increasing inroads into working-class areas, meeting the challenge of Labour and the trade unions and standing up to what was seen by many as the increased threat of Communism. It meant that throughout the 1930s they commanded well over 50 per cent of the vote and dominated national office. Despite persistent high unemployment and the fact that Baldwin made deep cuts in spending he wasn't punished by the electorate because living standards rose for the majority of the population who had a job. This was partly due to a fall in prices. The cost of essentials like food and rent fell 15 per cent during the decade, so for most people life was reasonably comfortable.

In Bolton the Conservative Party, supported by large numbers of working-class votes, was firmly in control of the council. All of those involved in the Worktown politics project were socialists. During his short stay in Bolton Barefoot had got to know a lot of the leading figures in the Labour Party and didn't have a very high opinion of them: 'The Labour Party people themselves worship at the shrines which their party is pledged to overthrow – their aim is to make money, to be popular among the real middle class, to lead a sober and safe life – the pie-and-chips respectability that is worse than the other, because it is so lacking in imagination. One of the Labour leaders in Bolton affects a pseudo-Oxford accent and talks about the Leadah of the Labah group.'

He felt that all three parties had lost touch with the people they were supposed to represent. The elected councillors, he wrote, 'hardly ever visit their supporters between elections. To the ordinary voter the town councillor is simply someone who comes round at election time, is elected and never heard of again till the next election. Time after time we have heard the phrase "They're all alike; they're only out for themselves"'

– This was, Barefoot suggested, what most people, who hardly ever saw their councillors or had a chance to explain their grievances, thought about them. 'These men, who the ordinary voter had trusted to put things right, were all mere careerists. It made people lose faith in politics and was one of the prime causes of apathy . . . It is no wonder that the average elector, confronted with the rival appeals of two men who represent certain political parties, but who may be no better men for being connected with one party or the other, lumps them together as self-seekers. "They all shit in the same pot" said one man being canvassed.'

After listing the efforts of the political parties to organise social events for their members and to attract younger members Barefoot concluded that 'Only the Left Book Club and the Peace Pledge Union [which had been campaigning for a warless world since 1934] have no cause to complain that young people seem to take no interest in politics nowadays.' Indeed the Peace Pledge Union had a membership of over 118,000, described by one of their number as 'an amorphous mass of ordinary well-meaning but fluffy peace lovers'.[6] Membership of the Left Book Club was going from strength to strength, and by the end of 1937 there were 730 local discussion groups with a total average fortnightly attendance of 12,000. They discussed books, distributed leaflets, organised political meetings, walks, sports events and weekend schools and raised funding for medical aid for Spain.

Membership of both organisations, Barefoot explained in his report, 'is primarily youthful, and the members have a very real enthusiasm and a faith in what they are trying to do. This is probably because these organisations are new and not imbued with pre-war traditionalism. Young folk find it easier to see through the cant and hypocrisy, the self-seeking careerism that are found in the old parties. For this reason they see no object in taking up political activity. The amount of their weekly wages, the cinema, holidays, taking girls out, all seem far more important than the everlasting argument and voting which is all that political democracy gives them.' Barefoot's views, especially those about voting, were of particular interest to Harrisson, for whom the study of the non-voter formed a central plank of the Worktown politics project. He wanted to find answers to the question of why politicians were unable to connect effectively with Bolton's workers, and with local council elections due in November he would have the perfect opportunity to investigate.

Barefoot's second report was on public health in the town where the cotton workers went home to overcrowded and insanitary houses, lacking in sunlight and blackened with soot. Quoting from a housing report, he wrote: 'In one house an unfortunate mother was nursing her baby in a room – kept beautifully clean – which had once been a scullery. A dismal procession of men and women passed through to the common sanitary convenience which constituted the entire outlook of the room ... In another case a stream of liquid, resulting from the overflow of defective pails, reached to the door of the house and settled there. Sometimes the sanitary conveniences could only be reached through dark entries, where rubbish accumulated. Pail closets were not, in many cases, emptied nearly often enough. We have seen houses overrun with vermin, and heard pitiable stories of weekly expenditure upon disinfectants, which meant deprivation of food. In one such house we saw a child seriously ill with pneumonia in a bed in the kitchen, through the wainscoting of which rats made a nightly invasion ... The lives of these people are robbed of decency, dignity and privacy even in the sacred intimacies of birth and death, yet their heroism is marvellous.'[7]

'To the credit of the town', Barefoot reported, 'it must be added that as a result of this survey a great number of houses in East Ward were demolished; but the fact of overcrowding and lack of sanitary conveniences still persists in many parts of Worktown.' There were still many appalling Victorian slums in the town and large pockets of inadequate, overcrowded houses. Many of these dwellings lacked any hot-water supply, an inside toilet or a bath. The extent of bug infestation in the town, Mass-Observation reported, 'was sufficient to ensure that every Mass-Observer was bitten during the first six months of our observations. Our headquarters started crawling in spring. We estimate that 20 per cent of all working-class houses are definitely bug infested and the owners ready to admit it.'

A slum-clearance programme had started to replace some of the worst of the Victorian housing with bright new council houses on the edge of town with hot water, inside toilets and bathrooms and above all gardens. In Bolton, as in the rest of the country, most of the Victorian slum properties were rented from private landlords, but during the inter-war years government policy pegging rents to their pre-war level meant there was no incentive for private developers to build low-cost housing for uneconomic rents, particularly as building costs were rising. The result was that the private landlord's role in housing the poor was gradually taken over by local authorities. In the 1920s and 1930s of all new houses built 31.5 per cent were council houses.[8] These houses were of a much higher standard than most tenants who were rehoused had been used to, with bathrooms, inside toilets and fitted kitchens – but in many cases without a front parlour. This went right against the working-class tradition of having a 'best room' for family gatherings and entertaining, leading to the conclusion in a Mass-Observation survey that 'since people had a strong aversion to eating in what they regarded as their "best room", the new houses built between the wars have proved themselves much less in accordance with the needs of the people who live in them than the old houses of the nineteenth century'.[9]

On Bolton's new Top o'th'Brow housing estate, Mass-Observation reported, 'In regard to gardens, there is an unspoken resentment against the man who allows his plot to run to weeds. The brotherhood of gardeners regards with scowls and mutterings the expanse of chicken weed, sorrel, dandelion etc. of their own non-gardening neighbours ... Among the gardeners themselves, the spirit is really friendly at most times; help between each other and gifts of plants etc. being manifestations of this spirit ... the competitions are popular, and real efforts are made towards prizewinning.' The result was some very pretty gardens. 'The popular conception of certain sections of the public that working-class tenants of estates do not prevail [sic] themselves of their new amenities is erroneous. It has been said that coal has been stored in the bath, etc., but this is totally untrue of the large majority of estate tenants. With very isolated exceptions, a pride in living and appearance is adopted, that in the previous house, flat, or rooms, had no room for expression.'[10]

But, in spite of the huge improvements the new council houses brought to the quality of life of Bolton's residents, a lot of the older inner-city dwellers were reluctant to move out to these green pastures. On one street a woman of about fifty-five was sitting outside her house on a chair on the pavement. She was, an observer noted, very fat and was wearing a silk frock, blue with white flowers. Along the street were spaces where houses had been pulled down for slum clearance. The observer introduced himself as a foreigner who was interested in housing estates and would like to know what English housewives think about them. She told him: 'A lot of fuss is made about this slum clearance. These houses are not so bad. What do you think? This street is not bad and the co-op houses are much too expensive ... three shillings, no four shillings more rent. Who can afford this?... And in winter they need three times as much coal as we do, the walls are very thin and probably wet too and the rooms are bigger. Yes, a bath is alright but you must heat it if you want it. Who can afford it?... I have three daughters going to the mill. They are quite near so they come home for dinner. If I would live in a co-op house they would have to go by tram and would have to have their dinner in town. It would cost me (calculates a while) about one shilling more a week as it does now. I could not afford it.'[11]

On the new housing estates there were no pubs. An ex-landlord who lived on one revealed that some 50 per cent of the men drank. 'They make tracks to their own localities.' But he pointed out they could afford to do this only at weekends. An unemployed man who had been moved out to an estate in a slum-clearance programme revealed the difference living on an estate made. 'Whilst it is fairly common for the male street dweller to have a "mate" or "boozing partner" living in or close to his own street, the average estate man who takes a drink, apparently prefers his own company, or relies on meeting friends in his perambulations in the town. The estate man completely changes his social activities on removing from the street to the estate, sometimes breaking down the habits of a lifetime. To my knowledge a man may have for years frequented a particular pub five, six or seven nights a week, but living on the estate his jaunts are restricted to weekends.'

'The estate', the same man continued,

> seems to develop along the lines of 'communal life' . . . the 'village' atmosphere where 'everybody knows everybody else', is very noticeable . . . the transport facilities of the tenants is a good instance of this unusual joviality. The conductors are invariably on intimate terms with most of their fares . . . he, the conductor, knows a large number of the passengers almost as personal friends, and most journeys to and from the town are enlivened by the wisecracks passed between him and his friends . . . It is particularly marked on the late Saturday-night buses . . . The jollity, although very noisy, is never wranglesome. Sheer drunkenness is rare. I have seen no instances where people have been more than fuddled . . . the bus appears to be the connecting link between two worlds as typified by the town and the estate, and is the scene of more exchanged intimacies than any other place. In this respect it particularly takes the place of the absent pub. It is the meeting place of the estate, and the bus stop at the shopping centre becomes to a limited degree the centre around which the estate revolves.[12]

At a time when many of the older terraced houses did not have baths, public baths and wash houses were still a feature of most British towns. Humphrey Pease, an old Etonian and former art student at the Slade, reported on his use of the slipper baths at Bridgeman Street Swimming

Baths. Not being familiar with them and never having used one, the first thing he did was to ask the woman in the office at the turnstile gate what a slipper bath was. She explained that it was just an ordinary hot bath and did he want first or second class. He paid fourpence for a second-class bath, was given a piece of soap and two towels and passed through the gate. On the wall a poster showing one boy sponging himself under a shower bath while another swam in the water displayed the message: 'A Good Wash before using the swimming bath helps everyone to be healthier.' Another notice said, 'Bathers using the swimming baths will please note that no bather can be guaranteed the exclusive use of a dressing cubicle. Bathers are strongly advised to leave money and other valuables at the ticket office.'

Pease entered the second-class slipper baths, which were a series of cubicles, about ten on either side of a passage leading to the swing doors giving on to the swimming bath. An unseen man called out 'Number 2', so he took cubicle number two. The cubicle contained, beside the bath, a small duckboard, a wooden stool, a small wall mirror, a row of pegs for hanging clothes, and two scrubbing brushes, one with a long handle. After bathing he entered the swimming bath and found it empty. The bath had a wooden gallery, in need of repainting, running round three sides of it. In the middle of one side of this was a large notice reading 'Males Only on this side of the bath' and a similar one reading 'Females Only' on the opposite side. In answer to a question from the observer the attendant said that people did not use the bath much so early in the year, except for the schools. Two schoolboys were the only people to use the bath while the observer was present.[13]

As a medical student, Barefoot was particularly interested in health provision in Bolton, so the main focus of his public health report was on the town's hospitals. Health care in Britain was made up of a patchwork of institutions which were not always accessible according to need. A system of National Health Insurance, established by Lloyd George in 1911, offered benefits to contributors below a certain level of income but this did not cover dependants. Contributions were paid at a flat rate – approximately half by the employer and half by the employee. Contributors received cash payments for sickness, accident and disability. They also had the right to free, but limited, care from a doctor on a local list, but were only entitled to hospital treatment when suffering from tuberculosis. The main deficiencies of this system were lack of hospital care and lack of health care for dependants of working men and women. As a result an illness could cause serious financial problems. The other major system was that of the voluntary hospitals, most of which were supported by donations.

Barefoot recorded: 'The town's main hospital – the Royal Infirmary – with its £3000 deficit exhibits many defects of the voluntary system, i.e. supported by subscriptions from well-off people and tuppence a week contributions from the patients. It has 226 beds and deals with 6,000 in-patients and 12,000 new out-patients every year. Every day over a hundred casualties are treated.' An observer who secured permission to visit the infirmary in September 1937 first saw the out-patients block, 'where patients come who are able to be treated on the spot'. Before they could be treated they had to bring with them a note from their doctor, and a certificate to say that their contributions of 2d a week towards the hospital's contributory scheme had been paid through their employer, or alternatively, if they were individual members of the scheme, their contributory card. Hospital treatment was not covered by health insurance, and at a voluntary hospital like the Infirmary those on low incomes had a right to treatment if they or, if they were lucky, their employer paid a few pence a week. Alternatively they might be charged whatever the hospital almoner thought they could afford. It wasn't a good system. The hospitals were permanently short of money and were dependent on bequests, flag days and fund-raising events such as garden parties.

Leading out of the out-patient block at the Infirmary were special departments for dental treatment, massage, electricity and muscular re-education. The observer was told that the waiting list for the aural departments, which held only about ten patients, was very long – people often had to wait twelve months before they could be admitted. The waiting list numbered about 400 altogether. Next the observer was taken to the pathological block, and shown the pathological museum, the bacteriological and biochemical laboratories and the mortuary. The mortuary attendant was very proud of his refrigerators where the corpses were kept 'like frozen beef'. The hospital was well maintained and clearly very efficient. 'It is hard to realise', the observer noted, 'that one is inside the building that looks so very dingy and ugly from outside. The colour scheme of buff and green must be restful to illness-weary eyes, and the rubber floors everywhere ensure a quiet that is too often absent from hospitals.' The defects of the Infirmary, he went on, were the same as other voluntary hospitals, including piecemeal additions to the building resulting in immense corridor length, a long waiting list and protracted waits in the out-patients department.

The Infirmary was one of five hospitals in Worktown. If it occupied the top rung of the ladder or top place in the league table of hospitals, Barefoot wrote, the bottom rung was occupied by the hospital which 'receives mentally deficient and insane people from Worktown and other districts'. An observer who visited it was informed that . . . it had been condemned twenty-five years ago and that it was not a mental hospital but mainly used as a place to keep people who were weak-minded through age or illness, and who were a nuisance to keep elsewhere – while mixed with such cases were a number of insane people, who were getting no treatment for their trouble. In the eight months since the start of the year there had been twenty-four deaths in the mental block out of 141 patients – as compared with the normal rate in mental hospitals of six in 1,000 . . . The wards were completely bare. All the walls in the block were simply brick painted dark red or green. The main corridor was open at one end, with a grille of iron bars as a door.

'The extremely unpleasant nightmare quality of everything could only be acquired by age,' the observer concluded. All the floors were worn, all the metal was rusted and corroded, and the woodwork mouldering. He described two padded cells: 'floor and walls to eight feet upholstered in white rubberoid substance. Strong electric light above, enclosed in wire cage. Gutter running round wall to collect urine, special bolt on door over a foot long, all oiled and polished, which closes door irrevocably when it is slammed to after the probably struggling violent patient has been thrown in. These cells are however the only places where a mental patient has any chance of getting away from the others; though the sensation of being in one, combined with rubber smell, is like that stage of anaesthetic when the world is closing in on one in waves. Observer left feeling slightly sick.'

Barefoot's reports on Bolton's hospitals reveal behaviour and attitudes among some of the patients that would be familiar to hospital staff today. 'Nowadays anyone comes to hospital for anything,' the steward at Townley's Hospital reported, 'whereas in the old days people who came in were ill, now when you go out to meet an ambulance, likely as not the patient will hop out and scamper into the hospital. Often as not when you see the ambulance go clanking down the street, bell clearing all traffic, there'll be a man inside with a bunion.' The same steward was of the opinion that nurses' conditions were very unsatisfactory, that something ought to be done about it, and that the government shelving their claims for an inquiry was not good. 'There are not enough nurses,' he concluded, 'and the whole hospital is understaffed.'

These reports were written towards the end of Barefoot's first stay in

Bolton. Before leaving, however, he had long discussions with Walter Hood about the findings of the politics survey up to this stage. 'We have a great amount of material', he said, 'on the public and private lives of all the councillors, what committees they are on, their private occupations, their weaknesses and antecedents, most of it unprintable in its present form, because of libel laws. But it is also worthwhile trying to find out if a councillor's own business increases when he is elected, that is, if the Town Council becomes little more than a Chamber of Commerce, as seems to be the case in the more backward parts of the USA.'

Hood said he was thinking in terms of the book that Tom was sure would be published quite soon to be called 'Politics and the Non-Voter'. 'You see the significance?' he asked. 'Not Politics and the Voter or Politics and Working People, but the *Non*-voter – the man that didn't worry about it.' Barefoot agreed that they were concerned with the question why people don't vote, but an equally interesting question, he felt, was why people do vote. 'Is it', he wondered, 'because they have a political philosophy of their own, and support the man who most nearly represents their own views, or is it for quite trivial reasons – because one candidate has a nice face, or is a nearby neighbour, or a Roman Catholic, or wears the same sort of hat as the voter himself?'

Propaganda, they both acknowledged, was the key issue. Barefoot voiced the opinion that 'the propaganda the politicians use stands no chance in a world which has got used to huge posters advertising cinema programmes, or the radio station at Luxembourg* advertising Horlicks Malted Milk. There is no colour in their campaigns.' He added, 'Politicians are still mostly of the old rationalist school which will not admit that people are more likely to be encouraged to vote by means of a gaudily dressed lie rather than a sober truth. Propaganda is carried out by personal canvassing, by the candidate for election or by his helpers, by broadcasts and public meetings, and by pamphlets and addresses.'

For the local council elections coming up in November it was planned that the whole Worktown team should get involved in canvassing for the Labour candidate in one ward, to produce election material and to monitor the effects of their intervention. Barefoot would have left to take up his university studies by then, but he felt that ample scope would be afforded to study the problem of effective propaganda and canvassing by this proposed 'controlled' election. It ought to be possible, he suggested,

* Commercial radio station set up in 1933 to broadcast in English from Luxembourg.

'to divide the ward into sections, and discover by sending out different forms of election address to each section, and finding how each section voted on polling day, which sort of election appeal is most effective. And people's opinions could be collected on which of these three methods of propaganda was the most effective.'[14]

About the end of September Barefoot returned home to Ipswich, and then went up to Edinburgh to start his medical studies. At university he enthusiastically recommended Mass-Observation to fellow students as 'the finest plan yet invented for bringing the remote intellectual into contact with real life'. Just before leaving Bolton he wrote cheerfully in his diary: 'To think that I was dubious about going on the Clarion Campaign and about coming to Bolton! I thought both experiences would demand of me more than I possess, but they have both been thrilling and encouraging, and I have made several real friends in each place – for an introvert like myself with an unhappy adolescence, that is indeed an achievement . . . This is the last day in Bolton, and I carry away with me the memory of a really happy month, plenty of congenial work, and friendly companions. I hope to see them again before long.'[15]

It was not going to be long before Barefoot did see them again and this was the work pattern for most of the observers – short periods of time in Bolton interspersed with longer periods when they returned to their normal life. For Humphrey Spender, short visits to Bolton punctuated the job that continued to provide his income. It meant, he reflected, that 'I couldn't spend nearly enough time there, I had a job with the *Mirror*, I was very much at the command of the art editor who was highly suspicious of my other activities. I suppose I went up about once every six weeks or so and spent anything up to ten days there, but normally about five days.'

Michael Wickham was another who made several short visits . 'I came back to the South of England', he said, 'because I was married and I had a wife there. I suppose I was never there for more than a couple of months at a time but over a couple of years. What one was doing was very mundane. One was told to go off and attend, say, a funeral service and make a note of what people did . . . I was interested in people and Tom probably realised that, though extremely middle class, I was sympathetic to the sort of people he wanted to examine. He managed to get me into a coal-mine once. Even with high unemployment in the coal industry, he got me into the Weedon Coal Corporation's mine in Wigan as an assistant check weighman to discover what miners said when they were actually in the mine. Of course they actually said very little except "Where's the fucking spanner?" You know the sort of thing, cursing about the whole beastly job.'[16]

After Barefoot had left, Wilcock and Hood continued to be involved in efforts to raise funds for Spanish relief, and at the beginning of October Wilcock reported on a sale of work at the home of Miss Barlow, in Edgeworth, to support the work of the Spanish Medical Aid Committee. In it he described some Basque children who were going around selling 1d and 2d bars of chocolate. These children attracted the buyers with their slow count of the change and their quaint expressions when asking people to buy, 'Oonlee two', putting up two fingers to express the price. Later on in the evening he described an entertainment by the Basque children in the library.[17]

The children were refugees from the Spanish Civil War who were living at Watermillock, a large country house on Crompton Way near the edge of Bolton. Following the bombing of Guernica, the British government had agreed to accept 4,000 children, aged from five to fifteen, with the proviso that they were not to be a cost to the taxpayer, but were to be the financial responsibility of those who brought them. In Bolton a fund had been started to bring a group to the town and maintain them during their stay until it was possible to send them home again once hostilities had ceased. Wilcock and Hood both became actively involved in fund-raising activities for the Watermillock children and the Spanish Medical Aid Fund. In Spain Franco's Nationalists were gaining the upper hand. His armies, which had begun the year in control of half of Spain, had gradually extended their grip on the country, capturing the major cities of Bilbao and Santander. With the fall of Gijon in October the Republicans lost their last remaining stronghold in the north. The fighting and continuing atrocities by both sides created floods of refugees and the conflict was beginning to escalate further with attacks on neutral shipping in the Mediterranean. The fascist threat was growing as a Nazi Party was formed in Hungary, Sudeten Nazis rioted in Czechoslovakia and Germany was believed to be spending £1,000 million a year on arms. There was no doubt much discussion of the worsening international situation, but for the Worktown team in the autumn of 1937, with council elections coming up, the focus was on local politics.

10

POLITICS AND THE NON-VOTER

*'For the first time in my life I was looking at politics, I was looking
at socialism, I was looking at trade unionism, I was looking at the
Labour Party as it really was, not what I romantically thought it was'*

Walter Hood

With its classical pillars and portico, its decorative stonework, its great
flight of steps and soaring clock tower, Bolton Town Hall was a symbol
of the sense of glory which the civic controllers of Worktown felt about
themselves. The tower rose 200 feet above the ground. It was taller
than the tallest of the factory chimneys. At night its illuminated clock
face was visible and conspicuous from far and wide over the town. In
this £1,000,000 civic centre, whose upkeep alone cost £9,000 a year,
the business of Worktown government was carried on.[1] Thus began a
Mass-Observation report on municipal politics. It went on to describe the
activities of Bolton's councillors.

> On the first Monday in every month, the Alderman and councillors arrive,
> some in cars, many on foot, for the Council meeting, held in the Council
> Chamber on the second floor. They gather inside, chatting and talking
> until, promptly at 10.02, the Mayor arrives, and the session begins. They
> go in through the side entrance, [where Walter Hood, leading a team of
> observers, met Alderman B. (Liberal) and four others he saw later on the
> Conservative benches]. They greet each other effusively and one of them
> puts his right arm round B.'s shoulder. The lift comes down and they all
> get in. Outside the council chamber there is a hubbub of chatter, a cloud
> of smoke. A youngish man hails Hood: 'Hello Brother! How are you?'

Walter Hood was now established as an activist in local Labour Party
circles and was well known to most of the Labour councillors. Like him,
most of those involved in the politics project were socialists, and they
quickly established close working relations with the local Labour Party

as well as with the communists, the Left Book Club and other left-wing organisations in the town.[2] Local communists and political activists had no difficulty working with fellow communists like the Spanish Civil War veteran Sommerfield or with nationally known Labour activists like Hood. In fact local Labour campaigns were run from 85 Davenport Street and investigations into methods for enticing non-voters to vote were indirectly aimed at making them vote Labour.[3] It was easier to investigate the Labour Party than any other: it was better organised, it was naturally stronger in an industrial town like Bolton and, because most of the observers were themselves socialists, they could work honestly with the Labour Party.

Although religion was his main area, Joe Wilcock was one of those involved in the politics project and contributed to the report on the Council meeting along with Walter Hood and Frank Cawson. Cawson was another middle-class socialist who was employed by Harrisson for a short time. His father was an accountant and when he got involved with Mass-Observation he had just come down from Oxford. 'My father sent me for a Dip Ed* to Liverpool,' he explained, 'because he had rather hoped to improve the family fortunes by sending me to Oxford, and when I came back a socialist, he thought he wasn't going to send good money after bad, so I went to Liverpool. And it was while I was at Liverpool, I saw a letter about Mass-Observation in the *New Statesman* which interested me.' On his first visit to Bolton he met a woman 'from the marketing side of Boots who was rather horrified about it all. She thought it was a bit sordid and unsystematic.' When his studies were completed Cawson went to Bolton to work as a full-time observer, where his first job was to help compile a report on municipal politics.

As the local council elections came round in November 1937, the pursuit of the non-voter was central to the Worktown team's agenda. Harrisson took a campaigning stance on this. The politicians, he felt, had to take a lot of the blame; their electioneering and the election material they produced were archaic. They fostered popular indifference to politics by continuing to present their message in formal language which advertisers, film producers and newspaper sub-editors had long since rejected. Harrisson wanted to demonstrate that the language and techniques of these new media entrepreneurs could be utilised to stimulate the non-voter into active citizenship.[4] Walter Hood was closely involved with Harrisson in this work. 'Tom realised very quickly', he said, 'that the

* Diploma of Education: postgraduate qualification for those wishing to teach.

prosaic ordinary leaflet that the Labour Party wards got out, didn't have much effect on working people. So he developed a composite leaflet, similar to a football-pools coupon. We distributed this to a certain section of one ward to see whether the people there voted more, or voted better, or were more interested in local politics, than people who received no leaflets at all.'[5] Monitoring the voting, the team found that the 3,000 people in households that received the leaflets were 10 to 15 per cent more likely to vote than their unleafleted neighbours.[6]

In the Great Lever ward they took things a stage further by running the whole Labour campaign in an experiment designed to see what, in Harrisson's words, 'pep and vigour and militancy would do in local politics'. There was no hope at all of winning the seat. There had never been a Labour man in for Great Lever, and in the previous ten years the highest poll was less than a thousand for Labour. It was a very large ward with no permanent Labour organisation at all. The candidate had only a few helpers and on the Saturday, nine days before polling, had only just begun to deliver election addresses and had not canvassed any-where. He had no chance of canvassing most of the ward. 'Great Lever', Harrisson declared, 'was suitable for our experiment not only because it was large and low polled, but also because it was without any adequate organisation, so that all help was welcome, and there was nothing to be lost whatever the result.'[7]

Mass-Observation had a team of more than twenty working in the ward which included, alongside its regular observers, five women from Man-chester University and a number of local residents. Davenport Street was bursting at the seams as volunteers flooded north to knock on the doors of the Great Lever ward. One who responded to the call to help with the campaign was Zita Baker. Her divorce had been finalised in August and it was clear, as Harrisson now realised, that she was going to marry Dick Crossman. She was evidently ambitious and Crossman offered better prospects than the impecunious Harrisson. Her future husband was widely recognised as one of the most brilliant men of his generation, but it was Zita who was pushing him forward in his political career, proposing him as a Labour candidate for Oxford City Council before he was even a member of the party. Dick was the rising celebrity and she was his most powerful supporter. Thanks to her efforts he was on the bottom rung of a political career that would lead to him becoming a Labour cabinet minister.[8]

Another who came north to help with the campaign was Barbara Phil-lipson, who had first heard about Mass-Observation through Madge's friend Guy Hunter. She was a freelance artist who periodically had gaps between jobs. Guy Hunter thought the work on the election campaign in Bolton would interest her, so he took her to Blackheath to meet Madge and Kathleen Raine and then she was 'pushed off to Bolton for this by-election'. Her impressions of the town were very different from those of most of the observers up from the South. 'I loved Bolton,' she declared. 'I thought it was an absolutely darling little town. Not that first time because I arrived in fog and I had to take a taxi from the station right across Bolton to Tom's house and then I was told I couldn't stay there. I'd have to go back to the station and stay at the Station Hotel, which made me a bit peeved. But one of them came with me and carried my suitcase. I was fascinated with the Lancashire people because I couldn't understand a word they said at first, but I got used to that. It was just like a foreign language – broad Lancashire.'[9]

The Worktown team in Great Lever quickly picked up on an air of despondency among the few Labour activists there and a general lack of enthusiasm. This came over at election meetings, as Zita Baker found at one she attended at a local school. There was, she saw, 'no noticeable effect on the audience from any of the speakers, though all were very different. They did not seem to fidget or clap more for one speaker than another.' But Walter Hood, who was himself one of the speakers, had a different opinion, saying that he definitely could feel if an audience was responding or not and he got the impression that a response came during speeches of Alderman McCall, Councillor Bull and his own. After the showing of a short film, *Your Bolton*, the candidate Bill Hadley spoke: 'I hope I can justify the honour and trust that my fellow citizens have put in me. Our present representation on the town council is far from satisfactory and now I beg to place myself as your representative . . . I appeal to you to support me on November 1st so that I may play my part in making Bolton a brighter and happier town.' Baker estimated that out of the fifty-five present 'quite 80 per cent were regular habitués of this type of meeting. They gave the impression of knowing all the speakers quite well. The audience seemed bored and unenthusiastic until the very end when the speeches of Councillor Bull and Walter Hood stirred them and they clapped long and heartily. Even the candidate didn't evoke any real response.'[10]

Harrisson urged his team to look beyond the world of the activists, who would attend a meeting like this, to the world with which they were trying to engage. 'You've got to put aside your conventional socialist condemnation of the apathetic masses,' he said, 'and start from the assumption that the non-voter is every bit as much a human being with hopes and fears and social feelings as the voter and often has as good a reason for not voting as the voter has for using his vote.' But the team didn't see very much of Harrisson, and Phillipson remembered him spending most of his time at the Labour headquarters. He 'didn't appear very much until the last day and we just had to go around asking questionnaires. Well, I'd never done any electioneering and I thought this was a rotten way of doing it because if they're not going to vote Labour they'll slam the door in your face, and if they are, they'll do it anyhow. You won't persuade them so what is the point of doing this? I couldn't see it at all.'

In their attempts to reach the non-voters and persuade them to come out to support their candidate the team distributed their own colloquially phrased leaflets and made election tours with the support of a loudspeaker van, a device hitherto little used in political campaigning. One observer, Sheila Fox, had a sports car and this was also fitted with a loudspeaker and mike. One of its principal uses was to follow up the larger speaker van and play the game 'knock, knock'. This involved somebody in the van saying 'Knock, knock' to which the reply came from the car, 'Who's there? Connie. Connie who? The Connie-servey-tivvy Party who want to get control of our Council. Don't let them do it.' This last answer was made in an affected upper-class voice. Four of these 'knock, knocks' were played in sequence. The second was 'Mark. Mark who? Mark your ballot paper Labour on Monday.' The other two involved plays on the names of the candidates, Harding the Conservative and Hadley the Labour candidate. 'Hard. Hard who? Harding. Hard to get in but darned easy to get out again.' Followed by 'Had. Had who? Hadley. The Labour candidate for Great Lever. Had you that time. Yes, but he won't have you when he's on the Council. He'll serve you well.'

It was, Harrisson recorded in his report on the campaign, necessary to drive very slowly to get these messages across. This sort of thing was very new. 'There is no doubt that propaganda in this way has an almost magical effect in so far as the sound itself stops so many people in their tracks and seems to bewilder them for several seconds. Horses are particularly affected, and repeatedly it was necessary to stop speaking, while two horses were caused to bolt. There is no doubt that the van had a very large effect and evoked hostility, especially after 8 p.m., so in general after the first evening it was not used after 8.30. The voting returns suggest that this hostility came mainly from or entirely from Tories or uninterested persons. The van spoke to the people as they came out of Harding's meeting on the general line of 'Let's have change and give

Labour a chance. You've heard what Mr Harding has to say and I don't think he's said anything definite. Let's give him a rest for three years and put the Labour man Bill Hadley on the Council.'

Kids were fascinated by the van. 'In many streets', Harrisson wrote,

when we arrived the kids would boo the Labour van and say 'Vote for Harding', but as soon as we had played George Formby, 'Cleaning Windows', which became the local theme song of the election, and then put the mike through the window for one or two to shout into, it was 'Vote for Hadley'. At first they were frightened of the microphone but when one small boy with glasses had sung and another had given a mouth-organ solo, others were ready to do so. The children were heard in various parts of the area later at night and also next morning singing 'Cleaning Windows', saying 'Vote Labour', and one record *sic* of 'Six on the backside for Harding'. They were attracted to the campaign by the van and some became invaluable helpers. They distributed a good deal of our literature.

Brian Barefoot was particularly keen to get involved in the campaign. For a twenty-three-year-old middle-class socialist the project could not have suited him better in his quest for contact with working-class life. In November he had a long-weekend holiday so, travelling by bus from Edinburgh to Preston and then on to Bolton, he found himself in the thick of the campaign. 'On Friday morning,' he wrote in his memoir, 'I was doing routine election work in the committee room, marking cards and so on; in the afternoon I and three others were putting pamphlets into envelopes behind locked doors in Davenport Street. In the evening there was a mass canvass. The loudspeaker van went round a selected group of streets, playing tunes on the gramophone and giving out, via Tom at the microphone, appropriate propaganda; while the rest of us knocked up the people and asked them to vote Labour.'

Saturday was the fullest day for Barefoot, and also by then he was no longer tired.

In the morning went out with Sheila [Fox] in her car (a loudspeaker fixed to the outside) together with a man from the *March of Time* newsreel, who was filming us: we woke up the street by going down it several times with me speaking through the mike, then stopped for *March of Time* to film it. We enlisted the help of the kids, who spoke and sang into the mike while they were being filmed. Then in the afternoon I was again 'broadcasting' – this time giving out appropriate propaganda before the

Wanderers' football match: 'You've got a first-rate football team in Bolton; why not have a first-rate local government?' In the evening we had the job of distributing leaflets, myself again in Sheila's car repeating slowly through the mike: 'Sensational news! Startling disclosures! Read this!' while the others handed out the leaflets. The local children were wildly on our side, and sang 'Vote, vote, vote for Mr Hadley!' everywhere. But the adults seemed less interested by the propaganda.

In fact the Mass-Observation tactics did not go down very well with everybody. As Barefoot reported, 'People were not yet ready for loud-speaker vans and colloquially phrased leaflets; the older people and party members resented what they thought of as the vulgarity of the campaign. They still preferred the old-fashioned way: the canvassers at the door; the sober, conventional leaflet.' Barefoot had to return to Edinburgh on Sunday, the day before polling day, but he'd found the few days he spent in Bolton very useful and felt he'd learned a lot. 'It was a chance', he explained, 'to use our newly developed techniques to find out what people really felt about the issues, which candidate they were likely to support and how many of them would really vote at all.'[11]

On election day itself the campaign team had the van out early. It had three loudspeakers, which could be heard over half a mile and easily blasted out the one-speaker Conservative van. 'Whenever the Conservative van entered the ward,' Harrisson recalled, 'we drowned it and chased it out. Noticeable was the disinclination of Conservatives to engage in repartee. When we drowned their van one time, the speaker began to shout, "Vote for Conservative and the rights of free speech." The Labour van's superior equipment and volume, undoubtedly made some impression on people but more than anything else it infuriated the Conservatives.'

Four other cars were put into service on polling day – one to bring in the snatcher cards* from the polling stations. This belonged to Penelope Barlow, the daughter of Sir Thomas Barlow, the Bolton-born royal physician who had provided some of the financial support for the Worktown project. Michael Wickham's Bentley was principally utilized to drive hordes of kids around singing 'Vote for Hadley'. Two others

---

* I cannot find a definition for this but from the context it would appear that they are the cards on which tellers outside the polling stations record the elector number of people who have voted. By identifying electors who have not voted the party can contact them and encourage them to vote.

were brought out for short periods to take voters to the polling stations, although, as it was a fine day, many preferred to walk. Kids were also employed on polling day and were perfectly reliable in bringing in returns from the polling stations. 'They were also recruited', Harrisson reported, 'to knock on the doors of houses which had not been canvassed because we could never find the people in. The kids simply said, "I have come on behalf of Mr Bill Hadley, the Labour candidate. I hope you will vote today."'[12]

When the polls closed at 8 o'clock Harrisson went to the Town Hall, where the votes were being counted. When he arrived there were half a dozen police at the entrance. Inside printed notices directed those attending the count to committee rooms, stating which wards were being counted in which. The Great Lever count was on the first floor. At the door into the room where this was taking place a detective took Harrisson's card which gave him access. When he entered he found himself in a large hall with about seventy people, the majority male, sitting at seven tables or round the four sides of a rectangle facing inwards on to an open blank space.[13] While the count was going on at the Town Hall, John Sommerfield went to the Labour Club. He went into the billiard room which was packed – 'so full', he reported, 'there is a shortage of seats and a waiter brings beer boxes for people to sit on. There is a terrific noise of talk, not only of a lot of people talking, but all talking very loudly. Nearly everyone in the room is wearing election colours. There are all age groups and about a third of the crowd is female. A man is knocking hell out of the piano. Some girls scream now and then. A middle-aged woman, drinking mild, holds a baby in her lap. Later she undoes her blouse and gives it a meal. No one appears to take any notice of this, the woman herself least of all. Observer recognises plenty of election workers around. No one appears drunk yet, but all very cheerful. Some people go out and come back with newspaper parcels of fish and chips, which they hand round to friends.'[14]

When the results were declared the Conservative, Harding, held the seat as expected, but the team's campaign was regarded as a success. Mass-Observation's intervention increased the Labour vote by several hundred and it was the highest ever recorded for Great Lever. Harrisson was pleased. 'The election as conducted by us in Great Lever', he declared, 'set a new standard in local elections, one of fierce attack. It made the Conservative candidate, the Conservative agent and others really angry and stirred up many in the area. As one man said, "They've never seen a bit of showmanship before." Many got sick of the loudspeakers, but the combined use of a Formby record and observer's voice never failed to open a third or so of the doors.'[15]

At the end of the campaign many of the volunteers who had swelled the Mass-Observation ranks went home. Before they left, Barbara Phillipson remembered, 'Tom asked us to sing the Red Flag* when he threw a party at the end of the weekend, and they all started singing, very very badly, a sort of miserable wail. I'd never heard it before and I didn't know the words so I didn't sing and then somebody said, "Why aren't you singing?" and I said, "Well, I don't know the words." "Well, never mind, just sing the tune," and I said, "But it's such a nasty tune, isn't it?", so they shut up and I was allowed not to sing it.† They were all Commies, of course, or very left wing. It was the fashion then for people who believed they were intelligentsia to be Communists. Everybody was. I wasn't because I hate politics.'[16]

Two days after the municipal elections Harrisson attended a Delegate Meeting of Bolton Labour Party. 'Observer's party', he reported, 'enter the meeting at 7.35. McCall, in the chair, sets the tone of the meeting with "We've got to face the facts, unpleasant as they may be . . . What we've got to do is try and look at ourselves and ask ourselves and see if we have done our share." Much of the meeting was then devoted to Labour's poor showing in the elections, with McCall appealing to the delegates to "keep as cool as they can".' In spite of this the meeting became heated and there was a protest from a man sitting in front of Harrisson that the floor was being given to councillors and executive committee members and that this wasn't fair to the ordinary people who only get this opportunity of speaking.

After the meeting Harrisson had a discussion with Jack Fagan in the Royal Arms over five gills of mild. Harrisson had known him from his very earliest days in Bolton. A one-time communist and Secretary of the local Unemployed Workers' Movement, Fagan was one of the ten members of Bolton's Labour Executive and he placed himself unconditionally at Harrisson's disposal, guaranteeing fifteen to twenty persons all over the town to start political-observer training immediately. They then discussed Walter Hood and the disquiet in some circles about his participant-observer role – infiltrating the local party when some people didn't have any knowledge of his involvement with Mass-Observation.

---

* Song associated with left-wing politics. Semi-official anthem of the Labour party.
† Barbara Phillipson refers to the original tune of the 'Red Flag' before the words were put to the tune of 'Tannenbaum, mein Tannenbaum'.

'No one suggested until quite recently', Fagan said, 'that Walter was engaged in any type of research in Bolton. When they did realise it, the avalanche broke.'[17]

Harrisson himself had, by this time, become so closely associated with the Labour Party that there was a proposal to nominate him for the local executive and another for the formation of a Labour Research Group under his direction. He described this relationship as a 'community of interest between our Mass-Observation work and the Labour movement'.[18] Observers attending Labour Party meetings would find that he was often the subject of discussion. Barefoot went to the inaugural meeting of a proposed Central Labour Guild. He reported that 'Those present talked till 8.25, first of all on the Delegate meeting the previous night, which all condemned as "dog-fighting", saying that it was a pity that there was so much quarrelling between groups and so much personal animosity. One man referred to a speech Harrisson had made. "Harrisson is a clever fellow, but all this stuff about asking people to come round to his house on Saturday to meet a statistician . . . Statistics! What good are statistics to me? I want to get the people out to vote."'

Harrisson's role with Mass-Observation in Bolton and his Worktown project was changing. As the observers' reports were written up he would read them and make comments on some of them in his near-illegible handwriting, but as the project progressed and moved towards its second year fewer observations were made by him. His observation on Remembrance Sunday in Bolton on 7 November 1937 was an exception, undertaken as a contribution to a nationwide survey for which Panel volunteers were mobilised. At 7.57 he recorded that he was passing Victoria Hall. 'The crowd outside swelled on to the tram lines. In less than a minute a procession of some 300, closely packed fours and sixes, forms up outside the Market Hall. It walks briskly, nearly as fast as the observer's normal pace. There is another 200 round the Cenotaph. A policeman clears a lane through them, "Keep back there, please, keep back." Hannah (the vicar of Bolton) walks briskly up to it and without ceremony places wreath at foot of it. With hat off he stands on the step and says, "Let us sing a brief couple of verses of a well-known hymn that we all know."'

In his broad Scottish accent Hannah proclaimed the first verse of 'Abide with Me' and all sing it. On the Town Hall steps at the Library end another 'Scotch' voice was talking about the workers in Spain under the red banner of the NUWM (National Unemployed Workers' Movement), which had been set up in 1921 to mobilise unemployed discontent. At the end of the brief ceremony Hannah gave the blessing and said, 'Shall we disperse as quickly as we can and help the officers?' Three lads walked away saying, 'Hello, let's go and listen to these now.' And many apparently thought the same for the NUWM had the largest audience yet seen. As Harrisson walked past, the speaker was saying that the workers who had died in Spain died for a real ideal, those who died in the Great War not so real. 'We believe also that a million British working people were deluded by the British upper class, were deluded into doing so [going to war]. There can be no question whatever but that they went to France believing that they were helping to bring an end to militarism, to bring an end to Imperialistic wars, on the part of the Kaiser.'[19]

Germany no longer had a Kaiser, but the Great War certainly hadn't brought an end to the country's militarism. With Hitler as Chancellor, Germany was on the march again. Following his annexation of the Rhineland his next target was Austria, but the National government in London didn't want to get involved. Stanley Baldwin had resigned as Prime Minister in May 1937 and Neville Chamberlain had taken over. Chamberlain's policy was one of making political concessions towards Nazi Germany and his commitment to an active, positive pursuit of a working accommodation with the fascist dictators confirmed a growing mood of non-involvement in European affairs. Generally the concessions he was making were widely seen as positive. Many on the right saw Russia and the spread of Communism as a greater threat to Britain than the Nazis, and there were some who went as far as declaring that there was common ground between Great Britain and Hitler's Germany, bound together by Teutonic racial origins and anti-Communism. On the left some said that Chamberlain looked forward to a war between Germany and Russia, and the Labour leader Clement Attlee claimed that the National government had connived at German rearmament because of its hatred of Russia.

On the domestic front, following the local council elections the Worktown team continued to work actively for the Bolton Labour Party. This was real 'participant observation' in action. The next month there was a parliamentary by-election in the Tonge constituency. There were three polling stations, and Harrisson and Hood were put in charge of one of them, Tonge Moor Council School. The committee rooms were at 132 Tonge Moor Road, about 200 yards from the school. On the day of the by-election Hood arrived at 7.55. The front door was open and there was a woman in the kitchen. 'She came into the front room,' Hood reported, 'and asked if I had any brown paper for the floor as the Labour Party generally brought it. Having none, the woman brought in lots of newspapers, which she helped to put down. She pointed out that there was plenty of coal and left.'

The floor of the committee room was covered with newspapers, and twice during the day a housewife came in and laid more down to protect the carpet. Harrisson took over manning the committee room from Hood at 10.30. A small boy, aged about thirteen, was helping by getting returns from polling stations. His name was Tomlinson and he said his father had told him to help. At 10.50 somebody came in a car to deliver a yellow 'Labour Committee Room' notice. The boy stuck it in the window after buying a pennyworth of drawing pins. Various people came in saying where cars were wanted to bring people out to vote. One woman, Mrs Noblett, went out to see someone up the road. 'It may mean two votes,' she said. At 11.55 a Tory van drove slowly past broadcasting the injunction 'Be sure to use your vote today for a young and capable man, Dr Chadderton, who lives and works in Tonge Ward.' A pale-faced lad of about twenty-one arrived. He was a League of Youth member and said he had come to help. But when Harrisson asked him to go and stir up Denvale Street, he said he would not go alone because he didn't know his way round there. He would wait till someone else could go with him.

So it went on for the rest of the day, with people coming and going and asking for cars to get people out to vote. In the middle of the afternoon Hood returned to take over from Harrisson. He talked to the boy who had been helping throughout the day. 'We talk about all-in wrestling,' Hood recalled, 'on which, like his father, he is very keen. Then tells of his ambition to be a stonemason, a sculptor, he says. Asked if anyone wants to go in the mill, he rejects the idea with scorn. He tells how his family managed somehow on the dole. Now better; father working; working nights, disorganises home a bit. But we manage somehow.'

Around four a fattish man of about forty-five arrived in a saloon car. He went into the committee rooms and asked if it was busy there. Then he agreed rather reluctantly to take his car to Denville Avenue. Hood later learned that he was Alderman Cheadle, who did not absolutely appreciate the way he told him to do something without acknowledging his position. But he did what he was told. '4.40,' Hood reported, 'Mrs Noblett back and fusses about Darbyshire kid getting his tea; then about his wet feet. Observer says, "He's alright! I'm looking after him. His father is a special friend of mine. He'll get his tea. I haven't even had my breakfast yet, you know."'[20]

Weather-wise November was generally the worst time in Bolton, and this year was no exception. Thick smogs enveloped the town for days on end, and from the edge of the moors just above the town you couldn't see the place because it was completely covered in a thick greenish-yellow blanket. All was dark and depressing and for observers who were not familiar with the town it made it doubly difficult to find their way round. Trying to return home to Davenport Street from a meeting or a visit to the cinema in the evening they would get lost. But the awful weather didn't dampen the observers' enthusiasm, and for a political activist like Hood there couldn't have been a better job. He developed new methods of monitoring public opinion, learnt how people listened and about their attention spans and was shown by Harrisson methods of presenting results and how writing up notes straight away helped them avoid becoming biased.[21] It was an exciting time for him and he learned to look at the political life he was familiar with in new ways, mapping where people chose to sit at meetings – 'the distance between people . . . the whole problem of the physical reactions of one person to another' – or trying to classify the language of gesture employed by platform speakers.[22] 'For the first time in my life since I was a boy of 16 or 17,' he recalled, 'I was looking at politics, I was looking at socialism, I was looking at trade unionism, I was looking at the Labour Party as it really was, not what I romantically thought it was . . . Now I was wanting to know what people thought, why they thought the way they did and how they thought about politics, and that was . . . really fascinating.'[23]

11

THE PUB AND THE PEOPLE

'I took very great trouble not to be visibly writing anything down.
If I had anything complicated to write down I went in the lavatory and did it'

John Sommerfield

On the night of the local council elections John Sommerfield was busy doing a round of some of the town centre pubs. At 10.30 he found the large vault at the Black Horse was almost empty, while the lobby was crowded. 'Lots of drunks and some women standing there who look like whores,' he wrote. 'In room at the back there is sound of loud singing and piano playing. No one is wearing election colours.' Sommerfield thought it looked like any pub before closing time on Saturday. Next stop at 11 was the Lord Nelson. 'Not very full. Groups of youthful drunks, but no noisy behaviour. No one wears election colours and observer doesn't hear any references to the election.' At 11.15 he was in a large Tetley pub. 'Lounge three-quarters full. A middle-aged man is playing the cornet in the lobby. Then he comes into the lounge and stands in front of the fire. He says he will play his favourite tune, which he does with much pathos and loud and soft. Everyone looks serious and is quiet. At end they clap him. No election colours or reference here either. But in all these pubs there was so much noise that it was very hard to hear what people were saying.'[1]

There were over 300 pubs in a town with a population of 180,000 – places where, at the end of a long working day, men, and it was usually men, could relax with their mates. Because of its importance to the social and economic life of the town, the pub, along with politics and religion, was one of the major focuses for the Worktown team. John Sommerfield was the leader and main observer for the project, and at the outset he and Harrisson set out guidelines for pub observers and the things they should make a note of. These included: types of pub; number and names of rooms; seating; tables; bars; spittoons, arrangement and usage; pictures, aspidistras and decoration generally; drinks bought and who buys which;

who the people are in a pub and what they wear; who sits and who stands; any distinguishing characteristics of drinkers peculiar to certain rooms and/or certain pubs; behaviour on entering, ordering, leaving; standing drinks and drinking; subjects of conversations and swearing; who smokes, who doesn't, when and where; whores, amateur and professional; activities of bookmakers and betting generally; hawkers, what they sell and how they are received by drinkers; beggars; what games are played and how they are played, who plays them and in what rooms; are they played for beer, for money or for nothing; is there any organisation for them both within the pub and inter-pub?; music, singing, piano, etc.; who provides it and what is provided; social activities, picnics and outings; weekend drinking compared to weekday drinking; watch out for drinkers changing to different pubs or different rooms for the weekend; statistical observations; pick on a few 'control' pubs and get counts throughout the week, and hour by hour when possible; also time taken to drink a gill on different nights; how much drunk, how long stayed; try to get a map to show where regulars come from to a certain pub. With regard to games there was a note that it was important for observers to join in the games where possible and record all the rules of play.[2]

It was a tall order and, in the line of duty, Sommerfield would visit several pubs in a day. One Friday he started his round in the vault of the St George at 7.30 p.m., where he noted that there were 'spittoons, but no loose sawdust'. This was exactly the sort of detail that Harrisson wanted. A few dim middle-aged chaps, he reported, were in sipping mild. A little man with cap and dungarees came in and had a bottle of pale ale. He said he had looked in between going to his union meeting and leaving work, then started talking about running and the personalities of past great runners. The talk got round to pubs and there was a story about some pub that used to serve 'chickens' and the crowds that gathered to sample them. Chickens, Sommerfield explained in his report, were small glasses of strong ale.

From the George he moved on to the One Horseshoe where he went into the parlour. In there he found half a dozen old Irish men and women, the women with shawls over their heads. They were, he observed, 'sitting around talking like characters in a phoney Irish play. One old tough guy with corduroy trousers, rather tight, was having backchat with his sister about who was paying for the drinks. A very old woman came in, hobbling, bent, and covered with a black shawl. She only had half of her face; the rest had gone for syphilis. A drunk got up and sang a very long, pathetic song called "Vanity Fair", in a loud voice. The syphilitic old lady joined in sometimes with horrible effect. Some people clapped when it was all over. The drunk hopped about from one leg to another looking very pleased with himself, and then sat down.' When Sommerfield left everyone said, 'God bless.'

At 9.30 he moved on to Yates's Wine Lodge. 'Packed', he reported, 'more than yesterday, but less people drunk. A number of middle-aged tarts circulating. Lavatory very busy.' By 9.50 he'd seen enough and moved on to the Grapes, where he stayed until 10.15. The small lounge he was in was full up. 'Some middle-aged women drinking Guinness, barmaid knocking back Guinness. The big lounge packed full, no room to sit down. Not much fuss at closing time.' When he left at 10.15 there were plenty staying on, some still drinking. That evening he'd been drinking in five different pubs. The general impression, he recorded, was that the pubs were more crowded and people drinking more quickly than on the last few nights, but very few people were really drunk.[3] Fewer women than men spent time in the pubs. The team estimated that only 16 per cent of Bolton's drinkers were women – a figure that was reflected in traditional working-class pubs around the country – and they would be barred from the vault and tap room where the men drank and consigned to the parlour or best room.

There was, in Mass-Observation's view, 'something of the gent's lavatory and structure in a vault, which is almost always long and thin, and stone floored (in the older pubs). The vault is nothing like home. It is an exclusively male gathering. And the males who come to it come singly. They know that they will meet company there. There are seldom pictures or decorations of any sort ... very seldom aspidistras.' It was a place where men went to meet other men and relax and it had its own code of conduct: 'You may spit on the floor or burn the bar with a cigarette, and the barmaid won't reprove you. Indeed, as one pub-goer remarked: "You can do almost anything you bloody well like in the vault, short of shitting on the place."' In the vault drinkers stood at the bar. The tap room differed in that it was a sitting room with wooden benches around the walls, wooden stools and unpolished wooden tables. Other than that the same people went in and prices were the same as the vault. On week nights men wore caps, scarves knotted round the neck and coat, trousers and waistcoats of dark materials that often belonged to different suits. Some drank in their working clothes – dungarees of various kinds and bib-and-brace overalls were often seen, as well as corduroys and old trousers or coats that were stained with earth or plaster according to the wearer's occupation.

In the lounge there were padded seats and chairs, a piano and no standing. 'Aspidistras or other plants in 75 per cent; pictures on the wall, or modern wall decor; never stone floored, but lino or rubbercloth. Generally a hearthrug . . . And always someone to bring your drinks on a tray . . . In brief, the lounge is a large, comfortable room with decorations such as may be found in any Worktown home on a middle-class level of comfort.' Unlike the vault, the lounge was not a place you went to on your own. 'If you do,' M-O reported, 'you are conspicuous. You come to the lounge with your social group, ready made, and sit at a table . . . There is no sex division in the lounge. Each table tends to be a hetero-sexual group.' On average close to 45 per cent of the people in the lounge were women. A lot of people, however, looked down on women who frequented pubs, which may account for Sommerfield's disparaging reference to 'middle-aged tarts' in Yates's Wine Bar.

Singing and music, usually impromptu, like the drunk with his 'Vanity Fair' song, were a feature of pub life. In the parlours of most pubs there was a piano and all customers were welcome to play it and sing along with it. In the Grapes the following Saturday Sommerfield came across more impromptu music. A small old man was playing the violin, standing up, stamping heavily to keep time, making a revolting noise with his instrument. No one cared about it, and when his back was turned people made derisive gestures. Then a pedlar came in, a fellow of about forty, very shabbily dressed. He had bootlaces, razor blades and copies of *Old Moore's Almanack*. He sold a pair of bootlaces to one chap for a penny and collected two other pennies for nothing.[4] Many hawkers and pedlars like this had regular rounds and times of arrival. Usually their relationship with the landlord was friendly. A lot of them sold food, particularly pies, but this wasn't the only thing. One drinker the team knew got all his 'contraceptive machinery' from a man who also sold razor blades and 'novelties' such as joke cigars. The hawkers differed from other pub-goers in that they were permitted to come in and go out again without having a drink. A pub near the market was a special hangout for many of them.[5]

Harrisson's aim was 'to make an objective, unbiased appraisal of the pub, and especially of how the pub works out in human terms of everyday and every-night life, among the hundreds of thousands of people who find in it one of their principal life interests'. The object of the studies in Worktown, he stated, was 'to take the whole structure of the place and analyse it out'.[6] This involved collating the mass of observations that were made, taking extracts from them and sorting them under different headings. In the case of the pub, these headings included

'Drink', 'Drinkers', 'Sports', 'Games and Gambling', 'Drinking', 'Singers and Pianists', 'Bookies' and 'Prostitutes', each of which drew on extracts from dozens of reports. Under the heading 'Drink Servers', a further sub-section of the material assessed the importance of personality. This was recorded in *The Pub and the People*: 'It is difficult to assess the importance of the landlord's personality. Customers' remarks such as: "He's a coarse fellow, in his shirt sleeves always, he looks as if he's just got out of bed" and "He's alright, he's been a working man round 'ere 'imself, not like some other landlords, everybody speaks well of him." These comments do not correlate with the amount of pub custom. (The latter, for instance, only does a small business.) "We don't consider the landlord. Any bloody bugger'll do. It's the company that matters," is another view.' There was a report of a conversation with the landlord of the pub where the last remark was made: 'He says that 50 per cent of the goodwill of his sort of pub depended on the popularity of the landlord . . . gave as an example of his own success that he dare not have a fixed night off, as his customers would start making it a night of non-attendance. He himself had to be good at cards, dominoes, and an authority on all sporting matters, he had also purposely to lose at these games sometimes. He had to be many-sided to agree with all and sundry, and often left the room when he was going to find himself in direct contradiction with them.'

In one of the most successful of the smaller town-centre pubs the land-lord is unpopular with his staff and own wife even: 'Landlady drinking with female regular, and the barmaid, who looks up, sees into the lobby where the landlord has just arrived, and says, "Here he comes – with his black face," and the landlady repeats to her friend, "Charlie's just come in, with his black face." Two of the barmaids here, daughters of Charlie, are both attractive, with well-conditioned reflex smile to all customers. The pub is always full of youthful customers. Barmaids with sex-appeal are a great draw.' Two young men play quoits with the barmaid, who is, thinks the observer,

attractive in a coarse way. She is good at quoits anyway and wins. One player leaves. She plays again with the other, winning again. This chap, young, red faced, blonde, healthy looking, unshaved, cap on one side of his head, face washed but hands dirty, is apparently on fumbling relations with the barmaid. When they have finished their game he talks friendly to the observer . . . then goes out to the lavatory. The barmaid takes his pint pot and hides it in the front parlour, which is empty and unlit. He doesn't notice its absence till he has been back for about three minutes, then has byplay with her, both eventually departing to the parlour to fetch the beer. They didn't come back for the rest of the evening, and the lights didn't come on either. Later the landlord comes in, says he has been to the Old Soldier, and that there had only been three people in, though it is usually full. He has been round some other pubs too, and they're all the same, things are very slack.

It is quite common for landlords to drink in each other's pubs and go round drinking in each other's company. Recently one fell dead in another's pub. The news that he drank there surprised many friends. The Old Soldier, referred to above, is well known as a publican's drinking place. Conversation about landlords in the tap room. B.C. tells a story about a widow landlady, who got herself a 'fancy man', a young chap who lived at the pub and was drunk all the time. He came to a sad end, tottered off to sleep one night in a condition of near-coma, fell into bed on one side and out of it the other, with his head jammed into the chamber-pot. He lay there, unconscious, and died, 'drowned' says B.C.[7]

Sommerfield's reports are full of detailed observation. He noticed that 'Time Gentlemen please!' was always called with the same distinctive intonation, explained what makes drunk talk sound drunk and showed that classier pubs had fewer spittoons. He was also a master at 'blending in'. He interviewed no one formally, but merely drank, watched and listened, and he became a master of the art of 'swiggling'. This was something that several observers had remarked on after detailed observation of what was done with a glass of beer while it was being drunk. They noted that most drinkers fiddled with it, often in a rhythmical way and some people had a habit of what they came to call 'swiggling' their glasses, which consisted in moving them round and round in circles, either on the bar counter or table top, or in the air so that the beer eddies round and round.[8]

Sommerfield soon started to be recognised in a lot of the pubs he visited. 'I spent a lot of time in a lot of pubs,' he recalled. 'I got to know a lot of people and you can't help getting involved. But the whole thing was to try to see it as if I wasn't involved. It's hard to know if people knew we were observing them. I don't think they did. I think they thought it was very funny having a South of England foreigner sitting in their pub and drinking there. I took very great trouble not to be visibly writing anything down. If I had anything to write down complicated I went in the lavatory and did it. But in the end I suppose some people knew but nobody seemed to mind very much.'[9]

Not only did people not seem to mind too much, in a lot of the pubs he visited Sommerfield was accepted by the regulars. He was brought into their conversations and games and, as was the case at the One Horseshoe on Bank Street, shared a few jokes with them. When he went into the lounge at the back one Monday night there were about twenty people in. 'Around the rather shabby tables and benches were seven women, five oldish men, wearing caps and scarves, two youths, seventeen – eighteen, cheap smart, Vaseline hair, watch chains. There were also four women over fifty with shawls, one with clogs. The majority were Irish, rather drunk, singing a lot. The old men sang Irish miserable songs, different individuals starting them and others taking them up. The youths sang jazz songs, one with a terrific high tenor, was applauded by everyone. While he sang his pal did a kind of Charleston in the middle of the room, very fast, movements well controlled but not much to do with the time of the song. Some of the older men joined in the songs, the women didn't sing at all.' Everyone there was very friendly, with different groups shouting across the room to each other. 'Youths were playing the comedian, plenty of patter. One rather drunk youth of seventeen, smart suit, bright tie, Vaselined hair began talking to me and telling me dirty stories. "Little Audrey went to heaven and St Peter said, 'She can come in, she's a virgin.' And she laughed and laughed because she knew she had been screwed in her coffin." He told me another little Audrey story about her being up a tree, but owing to the noise and him being drunk I couldn't get the point. He also gave me cigarette card folded to make dirty pictures.'[10]

Another pub Sommerfield visited regularly was the Dog and Partridge near the market. On one occasion he went into the lounge, but the proprietor, after he had served him, said, 'Why don't you come in here?' Sommerfield followed him into a little parlour, where a huge old man was sitting, drinking a pint. The place was, he said, 'ordinary type of comfortable-shabby little parlour'. In it there was a hair dartboard and dominoes and the proprietor started taking practice shots. Sommerfield reported, 'I remarked on the dartboard, what a good one it was, and a conversation started about games. The proprietor said that darts were coming back now. He thought shove ha'penny would too. He and the old man got talking about piggy and how they used to play it. They kept on saying it was good exercise – the sort you played with an iron 7lb ring. "Uses every muscle in your body," the proprietor said. Talk then got on to personalities, then football. They asked me if I would like to play dominoes, but I was going, so the two of them settled down to play.'[11]

On his next visit he played dominoes with an old man who was drinking a gill. 'I won fairly consistently,' he reported. 'It was interesting to see the old chap's reactions about standing drinks after each game. After I had won twice I suggested that I should pay for the next round of drinks; he agreed, looking slightly uncomfortable, but relieved. Some men from the market came in, very tough, very loud and cheerful. One chap who seemed to be a leading figure (short, red faced, thick neck, enormous arms, no coat, sleeves rolled up, collar open at neck) immediately stood drinks all around, including me and the old man. There was a lot of talk about dogs, also darts. Two of them played round the board. They placed the darts very well indeed, but they were standing only about six feet from the board.'[12]

Sommerfield was a novelist with an eye for character and an ear for dialogue, which he reveals in his report on an evening's drinking which he started at the Great Birthday Night, held at Yates's Wine Lodge every Thursday. He went in about 7.35 p.m. There were, he reported, 'approx 80 people, trade brisk, barmen skipping about like mad. Large skinny black dog running about getting under people's feet and being patted. Great barrels being rolled around. Cheerful air, conversation loud. Mostly working-class people, men and women. The Birthday Port going like mad, toothglasses half full for 5d. I had one; it was thick, sweet, goose-berryish. While I was there another barrel of it was being heaved and shoved into position, the first one being almost empty, tilted down very far. Everything very brisk, very animated. Barmen grinning and standing in a straight row behind the bar as if waiting for heavy work.'

At around 8.15 p.m. it was time for a change of scene and Sommer-field moved on to the George on Great Moor Street opposite the railway station. 'It was a shabby place,' he thought, 'with the bar in a passage by the lounge, from which you could see and hear into the saloon. One man standing in passage bar drinking hot rum, cap, blue coat, slightly shabby, alcoholic's face. Tough in cap and scarf in saloon drinking pint of mild. Working-class girl popped in at side of bar, held out an empty rum bottle to the barmaid, who took it and filled it up without anything having been said. Someone in the lounge starts to knock the hell out of a piano. Kid of about five in the kitchen starts howling. Appearance of mother carrying him in her arms up to bed, the kid yelling like a pig being picked up by its tail. Door marked PRIVATE slams behind them and sound recedes upstairs. Piano wins. Little drunk in passage bar orders another and stands the barmaid one with lemonade in it.'

Going back to Yates's Wine Lodge at 9.45 p.m. he found the place was packed, at least 200 people.

Terrific din of conversations. Stuff spilt all over the floor, a few drunk, mostly women, but the majority cheerful only. Women cackling. Some people were having a bottle of champagne. The barrels of the birthday port all gone. Lots drinking hot rum with lemon in it. Manager standing behind the bar like a general directing his troops. Crowds of women were drinking Guinness and were very fat. A lot were powdered and had dirty fingernails. I had a whisky; it was 7d, a penny more than in many places, which is excessive, especially as it was their own brand and very watery. At ten to ten a brass bell was rung, warning people of closing time. At ten it was rung again; no one took much notice; the chucker out – a chap of about 45, rather miserable and inefficient looking, in a faded blue uniform and peaked cap, shouted 'time' but not very loudly. At five past the barmen began to shout; by ten past about half the people had left, a few still had drinks. The doors leading into the main road were locked. People went out by the side. A few hung around in groups, most went off quite briskly. Round the corner the big sergeant of police with his walking stick was lurking.[13]

Harrisson was himself a lively writer and encouraged his observers to write up their reports as vividly as possible. Local observer Eric Letchford was one who took this advice to heart. Though he entered fully into the 'scientific' aims of Mass-Observation – zealously counting, for instance, how many matches, 'spits' and cigarette ends landed in the spittoons in the Crofter's Hotel vault one night, and trying to render Lancashire speech as directly as possible – his accounts are sometimes highly personal.[14]

I entered the Saddle Hotel at 7.5 p.m. New barmaid being taught to pump beer and check sales. The landlady Mrs Smith was not too keen when the new barmaid was pumping the beer, but every time she went to the till Mrs Smith was all eyes down look in. Mrs Smith was then asked to have a game of dominoes so she called the other barmaid and warned her to look after the new one every time she went to the till. There were only seven men in vault. I watched a group of three men have a round of drinks taking 7–7–9 minutes respectively. I then followed them out at 7.30 p.m. as far as Great Moor Street where they caught a tram to the Greyhound Track, Manchester Road. One of the three men was telling a story about the Duke of Windsor but owing to his voice being low all that I could hear was something about the place where they have gone for their honeymoon being called Jubilee Fucking Corner. One man also commented on new barmaid, he said, 'Somebody'll open her legs for her before she's been here long.'[15]

After drinking in three more pubs that evening he reported that when he was leaving the last and walking along Bradshawgate, 'I passed observers John Sommerfield and Warbrick near Rimmers Outfitters. I shouted twice to J.S. and nearly all Bradshawgate heard me, but because he was with the new observer he didn't want anything to do with me (The Cunt). In future I do all my own observing on my (Tod Sloane).'[16] Not much love lost there, but Letchford was a willing observer and with around 300 pubs to get round in Bolton, he had plenty of opportunity to indulge in his predilection for consuming large quantities of beer. One night he consumed, between 7.45 and 9.30, fourteen half-pints of seven different beers in fourteen different hostelries before meeting Harrisson in the Man and Scythe. His report ends rather proudly, 'Total Beer Drunk 8½ pints.'[17]

Among the other members of the unit which carried out the pub investigation were the eighteen-year-old Oxford student Woodrow Wyatt and Blackpool-born Herbert Howarth, who had been recruited by Madge in Oxford. Wyatt recalled going to the pub with Harrisson. 'Instead of being an ordinary visit to an ordinary pub it would become infused with the sense of significance which Tom spread around.' Harrisson himself had the skills that were needed for the pub observations. Alert to body language, he would discreetly eye a group of pub regulars and pick out who were friends with whom and who deferred to whom. Everything the observers saw in the pubs was recorded – conversations, relationships, fights and arguments like this:

Two men in vault, one woman hawker sits between them. Men pay for drinks in turn for all three. Gills, one in ten minutes. One of the men has been sacked and paid up, same morning. They soon get to the stage of telling each other what fine chaps they are, what they did in the past etc. This reminiscing is rudely disturbed by the voice of a woman. She open the door and shouts in, 'Come on out of it you dirty stop out all night' – bounces out, to patrol the street opposite. She is the wife of the man sacked. He betrays uneasiness, which he pretends to laugh off by grinning. Wife comes back to the attack. Another woman asks her to come and have a drink. Wife refuses, shouting at her husband, confused words of temper. She goes away again to patrol the street. The two men peep over the window to see if she is gone – wife sees them – dashes in again, says, 'What, you'll laugh at me' (Kicks husband and thumps him) makes growling noises while doing so . . . Husband does not retaliate, merely grins – woman becomes more infuriated, kick again – both go out in the street – landlady of pub says, 'Don't hurt her, she's only doing what's right' – Wife out in street gives all out – takes off a clog – cracks husband on head with it – husband finally hits her – she goes away at this. They, the two men and the woman hawker, stay on till pub shuts. Hawker attempts to get on with erring husband, but he doesn't bite – the men leave for unknown destination.[18]

There was a lot of domestic drama like this being played out in front of the observers in Bolton's pubs. A lot of the observation, however, was much more mundane. One of the things the team wanted to find out was the average number of drinkers in a particular pub on each night of the week. They also counted the number of pints consumed in an evening at the pub, and techniques were developed to record things like the speed at which groups of drinkers finished their beer; 'it takes two, or preferably three trained observers, one watching, one timing, one writing down and checking to secure 40 or 50 timings a night'. Writing at a time when 'mild' was five pence a pint they found that the regular pub-goer was drinking between fifteen and twenty pints a week. But it wasn't just the Bolton locals who were putting away large amounts of beer. 'We wish to record our gratitude to several brewers,' the report on the first year's work stated. 'Maybe we can blame bits of this book on the beer, for one of us alone drank 800 pints in collecting observational material; all the observers who helped have between them paid the local beer sellers some seventy pounds for their liquid.'[19] One volunteer, it was recorded, began his evening's observations at the Commercial Hotel at 7.45 and finished at the Man and Scythe at 10.45. In between he drank: two half-pints mild beer; one Hamers; one Cornbrook; five Magees; two Walkers; two Draught Bass; one Swales – a grand total of fourteen and a half pints.

Most men, it was found, confined their drinking to Friday and Saturday evenings. Many would 'wait for the last hour'. 'Never mind what time you open or what time you close. It's all they've got money for,' one barmaid remarked. The democracy of drinking manifested itself both in the merging of individuals into groups and in the basic ritual of drinking, that of standing rounds. This, the most fundamental and regular of all the pub rituals, was based on an assumption that all the members of the drinking group had the same amount of money to spend. A barman noted that this was 'a firmly established custom . . . Missing your turn would cause social stigma, anyone so behaving would be called mean, a sponger etc.' Most pubs ran a slate so that a man could get his drinks on credit and pay when he had the funds. There were rarely defaulters and observers found some pubs where the landlord did not need to note what his patrons owed him; they kept a small notebook and jotted it down themselves.

Fish and chips from the shop just down the street was one of the staples of the observers' diet and they would often go there after a night in the pub. One evening Sommerfield went out to get the fish and chips and recorded the conversation he had there: 'Myself, proprietor and working-class man of about forty. Conversation arose out of discussion about rules and regulations. Singing in pubs had been stopped in Bolton. "Done the town a lot of harm." "Taking the money out of Bolton." People go outside to where they are less fussy. But the singing got to be a bit of a scandal. "They were advertising for auditions in the pubs and girls came along got up as if they were going on the stage. There was a girl who used to do a comic number and when they clapped her she used to pull out her tit and clap on it. She had fine big ones too (indicative sketching gesture with both hands)."'[20]

The problem about the singing ban came up a few weeks later when Sommerfield was having a lunchtime drink with another observer. After talking about pub games – dominoes, darts and cards – the landlord proclaimed that he 'was pretty indignant about the chief constable's prohibition of singing and music. "It's taking thousands of pounds out of Bolton. People are taking a tram ride out to places like Moses Gate and going to the pubs there. They are packed out every night of the week."'[21] It was a Friday and that evening Sommerfield decided to take the tram to Moses Gate, which was just outside Bolton on the road to Manchester. When he got there he found there were three big pubs at a crossroads around a triangular traffic island with a public lavatory in the middle. Sommerfield didn't find any evidence of music being played in the first two pubs he visited but the landlord in the third told him he had a pianist two nights a week and a singer on Saturdays. Singing in pubs being stopped in Bolton had made a big difference to him. While he was there Sommerfield timed a group of ten men who came in around eight o'clock and ordered their first drinks. One took five minutes to finish his, one took six, two took eight, one took eleven, one took twelve and three took fourteen. The tendency in drinking was to leave the glass standing untouched for about a minute, take one or two good gulps, leave it again, then take sips until the last third, then finish it off with one or two gulps again. Whatever else the observer was there to look at, timings like this were done in every pub they visited. 'We have timed about a thousand drinkers. It is very difficult laborious work,' according to the Mass-Observation study *The Pub and the People*, and '63.8 per cent of all times were between 6 and 10 minutes, the day's average being 9.7 minutes. Only 9.6 per cent of the times were under 6 minutes, and 26.6 per cent were above 10 minutes.'

The last of the Moses Gate pubs Sommerfield visited that Friday night was the Railway Hotel. Between 8.30 and 9.30 p.m. he was in the big oblong lounge, with its old leather-covered benches and tables and its dog-dish spittoons. The oblong wooden tables that filled the room had iron legs. The piano started up at 8.35, singing at 8.45. The singer was 'a young man of about 35, with concealed baldness, a tweed jacket, flannel trousers, no chin, bags under his eyes and a heavy sophisticated manner'. Sommerfield thought he was 'dissipated looking' and reported that 'he sang songs about love in a loud bollocky baritone that fairly made the glasses ring'. When he came to the chorus he held out the song sheet so that everyone could see the title. Some of the women joined in rather weakly.

At 9.35 p.m. Sommerfield went to the Walkers Arms where he went into the main lounge. It was a big room with a carpet, round tables, benches and chairs, and there was a big fire burning. There were eleven men and thirteen women in the room and a man playing the piano, Victorian music-hall songs. Women were joining in the choruses. Few people, he reported, were noticeably drunk, but there was a cheerful alcoholic atmosphere. A young working-class chap got up and sang songs in a very weak voice. No one took much notice except when there was a chorus to join in. The proprietor called time at ten; no one took any notice. At 10.20 there was still a big crowd. The potman said Bolton people came out here, mostly on Saturdays. When Sommerfield went out of the pub at 10.30, however, there was no one waiting for the Bolton tram.[22]

Sommerfield fitted in well, but for some of the observers visits to pubs could be a problem. Harry Gordon said it was the dialect that made the customers very suspicious of these people with their 'posh talk'. 'They were looked upon', he said, 'as snoopers for Debt Collectors or from the Assistance Board or the Dole Office. Many of the town-centre pubs had characters all their own and to have a stranger watching them sup their beer was annoying to the regulars. Also to see the observers booking down this. As well as how many puffs at a cigarette and how many times it was lit, used to aggravate them.' There was a lot of suspicion about the motives behind the Worktown project and about Mass-Observation in general, and it would lead to difficulties for some of the observers and for Humphrey Spender in particular, who was not welcome with his camera in a lot of places.

SNOOPERS

'We were called spies, pryers, mass-eavesdroppers,
nosey-parkers, peeping-toms, lopers, snoopers, envelope-steamers,
keyhole artists, sex maniacs, sissies, society playboys'

Humphrey Spender

Press hostility to Mass-Observation and particularly to the organisation's presence in Bolton began early on. A leader in the *Bolton Evening News* in June 1937 called the project 'an unequalled opportunity for the pettifogging, the malicious, the cranky, the interfering and the mildly dotty'. In the *News Chronicle* a Labour MP threatened: 'If I catch anybody mass-observing me, there's going to be trouble.'[1] The idea that they were a bunch of busybodies began to be voiced in many quarters, together with a growing feeling that this was the upper-middle classes using the lower-middle classes to spy on the working classes. Louie Davies, who delivered newspapers to Davenport Street, said, 'People didn't like them because they were asking things that they didn't like answering. And they thought they was snobbish. But some did like them. Some were prepared to tell them things. They were talking to them but they thought, "Nosey bugger he is."'

Spender in particular experienced negative reactions from people who objected to being photographed. Years after the project had finished he said, 'We were called spies, pryers, mass-eavesdroppers, nosey-parkers, peeping-toms, lopers, snoopers, envelope-steamers, keyhole artists, sex maniacs, sissies, society playboys.' He was a sensitive character and felt uncomfortable with all of this, especially as he did himself believe that he was intruding on people's privacy.

Stealth was important. Speaking of the way he worked, Spender explained:

If you were a stranger in a place where people knew each other, such as a pub, you were immediately a focus of interest. They would eye you closely and see you had a camera, and then you would try various forms of deception – like just fiddling with the camera, twisting the settings, taking the lens out, putting it back, committing awful crimes like blowing into it, or rather pretending to blow into it, cleaning the viewfinder. People merely looked at you, thought 'Oh, there's a bloke with a camera, he's cleaning it up.' And then got on with whatever they were doing and you became part of the landscape. It was all a matter of trickery – deceit. The great objective was usually to avoid suspicion because people looking suspicious are people looking unnatural. There was the obvious technique of concealing the camera, hung from your neck on a piece of string, and allowing the lens to emerge from a very shabby raincoat, or similar garment. In order to work the camera I had a hole in my right hand pocket – or in both pockets. Another technique was to do a continuous pan, starting from a point exactly opposite your subject, shooting at the moment you arrived at the subject and then continuing the swing right round: nobody quite knew what you were up to – you were simply experimenting with your camera.

For a while he used a right-angled lens which enabled him to face in one direction while taking photographs in another. He also discovered that if he put his camera on a pub table, tilted it with a bit of screwed up paper or matchsticks, and used a wide-angle lens, he could get pictures of people at other tables without them noticing. Another trick he used was the old one of just loafing around, focusing on something equidistant from the person – but in the opposite direction. 'Then', he explained, 'you suddenly turn, shoot at once and get away as quickly as you can. Quite a lot were done without looking through the viewfinder – by just aiming the camera from, say, waist height, or with the camera resting on a table at which I was sitting. That would be after having done test shots, to discover correct angles for any particular lens. Other occasions came under the category of the patient method, where you settled down for anything up to an hour or an hour and a half, and became part of the scenery. When people were no longer taking any notice, then you produced your camera and started operating.' He found that this was especially necessary in streets. 'You could just be leaning against a lamppost, or waiting for a bus. And there is a whole series of pictures of people window-shopping: I can remember hanging round in shop entrances, and sometimes when the shop was on a corner, shooting through two layers of glass on to a person round the corner.'[2] Even using all these tricks and armed with the most minimal equipment, detached observation was often an intrusive and uncomfortable task and he sometimes ran into trouble for photographing people without their permission. One publican was so incensed that he punched him in the stomach. 'I learned later that there were customers in the pub who were on benefits and didn't want to be seen drinking. But it was very difficult to conceal oneself and I found that once I was noticed, once you became the object of everybody's attention you'd finish. I had to be an invisible spy – an impossibility which I didn't particularly enjoy trying to achieve.'

Spender was constantly wrestling not only with the problems of being unobserved but with the ethics of surreptitious photography. His intentions were honourable, recognising that a large part of the population was living in poor conditions while another social stratum was oblivious to it and uncaring. Nevertheless he found the experience of taking the photographs stressful and disliked the intrusiveness of his work. One occasion when he ran into difficulties was when he was photographing at the Saddle Hotel. He was standing at a counter which gave a view on to a long row of drinkers standing at an opposite counter. The pub was very crowded and those serving drinks were sufficiently busy to keep them from paying much attention to what their customers were doing. Then he recalled, 'My viewfinder was suddenly blocked by a large blue waistcoat and an aggressive voice said, "What do you think you're doing.? My customers don't want any photographs taken in here, nor do I. It's usual to ask the manager's permission."'

Spender asked if he could have permission to take a picture of the barman. 'I shan't', he added, 'include any of your customers.'

But the manager was intransigent: 'I've said before I won't have any photographs taken in here; my customers don't want it. What's more, before you leave you're going to destroy the films you've already taken.'

Spender put a protective hand over his camera and said, 'It's a pity I'll have to go without buying another drink.'

'I wouldn't serve you,' came the reply. 'Come on, destroy those films or I'll fetch a policeman.'

'Oh, is there any law in England which prevents me taking photographs in public houses?'

'You needn't talk in that semi-educated way. You won't go until I've fetched a policeman,' and he walked with me to the door, which he blocked, saying, 'Destroy those films'.

'Well, let's fetch a policeman and see what the English law has to say about it.'

The manager then went out and started beckoning for a policeman, who arrived in about three minutes, a sympathetic long-faced man who was completely dazed by the complaint and obviously didn't know the answer to my question – does the English law forbid me to take photographs inside a public house?

The manager blustered, talked about forcing Spender to destroy the films and called him semi-educated again, to which Spender responded that his education on English law seemed sounder than his. The policeman asked him why he was photographing, to which Spender replied that he was photographing life in an industrial town entirely for his own pleasure. The manager then realised he was losing valuable time and went back to scenes of righteous indignation inside his pub. The policeman laughed and jerked his thumb into the pub, saying the manager was a queer customer.[3]

Spender said later that his rather pompous reaction to the publican must have been pretty insufferable. 'However much I tried, though, I could not hide characteristics of myself that I would have preferred to keep hidden.'[4] But he said, 'for me to go into a North Country pub, and really speaking a completely different language, to be a kind of "hail fellow, well met" person was very embarrassing, as it was for me to be questioned as having taken someone's photograph, "What the hell are you taking it for?" which often happened.'[5] He put up with it, however. 'People like me were accused of being spies and snoopers. And it really was a kind of spying. But since Tom continued to make me laugh the whole time I found it, not exactly laughable in Bolton, because it was in fact from time to time very depressing, but certainly Tom with his enthusiasm kept the whole thing going, and as far as I was concerned I became committed to it.'[6]

While Harrisson liked to ignore the matter of class difference, often proclaiming his ability to get along fine with working-class folk, Spender was the opposite. He never overcame his acute class-consciousness and sense of embarrassment in prying and intruding into the lives of others and he always felt threatened. In one of his pub photographs a man in a cloth cap standing at the bar appears to be waving a sign of greeting, but the reality was that he was making an offensive gesture telling Spender to get lost. 'This was a threat,' Spender recalled of that occasion. 'This was "Get out!" I probably felt nervous. By that time I had made the exposure and probably went.' The man with the raised arm was unemployed and on assistance relief; if he were identified in a pub his payments would have been stopped. Spender was breaking a taboo of privacy which might have threatened the man's financial wellbeing.[7]

Out of deference to people's vulnerability, Spender could not always venture where the Mass-Observers with pad and pencil could go more freely. But even a pad and pencil could be a problem for an observer in a pub, because, as Brian Barefoot recalled, 'a Lancashire pub in the 1930s was definitely not the place to write your letters, do your accounts, or indeed indicate in any way at all that you were even able to write. Although I had taken notes unobserved at all kinds of places – in churches, at meetings, at sports events – I can still remember the sudden hush that spread around the bar in a small Bolton pub where I was doing a "count". I looked up. The landlord and several customers were regarding me closely. "Doing your homework, then?" enquired the landlord in a tone devoid of any sympathy. I soon left and did no more counts in that pub.'[8]

For a middle-class Southerner like Barefoot, fitting in and trying to hide the real reason for his presence at an event was always difficult and often involved a certain level of subterfuge. When he went to observe the Albert Place Methodist Bazaar, as soon as he produced his notebook from his pocket and started to make notes, the minister came up to him and said: 'Excuse me. Are you the reporter?' Barefoot came out with his usual line that he was from the *Citizen*. This was the official organ of the Bolton Labour Party which Harrisson had virtually taken over by this time.[9] The minister asked how often the paper came out, and said that he had noticed Barefoot at the bazaar he'd attended the previous Friday evening. He then talked about North Country local pride, how they looked on Southerners with suspicion (he himself came from London).

In spite of the opposition, it wasn't all antagonistic and confrontational. Many local people began to lose their suspicions of the Worktown project and there were occasions when people invited observers into their houses and took them into their confidence to reveal details of their private lives. One report tells how an observer was talking to a woman who was sitting on a chair on the pavement outside her house when another woman with a newborn baby on her arm came by. She stopped and joined in the conversation, telling the observer that she would describe to him what living conditions were like in the old housing round there if he went with her. She went round the corner, he reported, 'to an awful hole. There she takes me to the kitchen where the cot of the baby is, and brings two other children to bed. The house is rather dirty, very poorly furnished, the chairs are rather shaky. I stayed with her for about two hours, because she told me a lot of her personal troubles, rather a sad story.' She went on to talk about a new housing estate: '"I would like to move. It is so nice up there; there is a garden for the children and a bath. You know I have heard they take all the furniture and disinfect it. You can't help it here, you get bugs, they come from all the houses. And then I think if he (the husband) would be there away from the bad company perhaps he would stop drinking, if he had a nice garden and the children would be nice and healthier, perhaps he would take to me again" . . . Man works in a mill, she does not know what he earns. She has to fight for her household money. He drinks and goes about with other women. And only when he is drunk he comes to her and produces another baby.'[10]

For the observers going into people's houses and reporting on what they saw and what they were told wasn't a problem, but for Spender, with his camera, it was. 'Domestic interiors', he said,

> was something that we did very much discuss. The moment you start thinking about them, you're involved in quite a lot of planning and organisation, finding a willing family: and clearly you can't go into some-body's house and remain unnoticed, so immediately you're up against the possibilities of play-acting, a kind of falsity. And you're under suspicion. 'Why do you want to come and photograph me?' You might find that the husband and wife, faced with the possibility, might have a conversation beginning along the lines, 'Can't let him see the dirty old carpet, must wash the curtains, the dog's absolutely filthy, get him washed, must iron Mary's dress,' and so on. You are then going into a false situation. We talked about this and decided against it . . . Tom was preoccupied with the likelihood of influencing, disturbing the details of people's habitual behaviour, and literally giving a false picture.[11]

Going into factories was also a problem for Spender. 'Although there was the possibility of easy access through Tom's industrial benefactors, it's very difficult to go unnoticed in factories. You have to get permission, clearly; and from the word go, you've got a foreman or deputy manager or some functionary asking himself, "Is there anything we don't want to be publicised? Are we breaking any regulations? Could these photographs be used in evidence against us?" So immediately people are very wary and on their best behaviour. The occasional factory visits we made were very much prearranged. You were always taken around and it bored me to be trailed around. Everything had to be set up. I had to ask someone to do a certain thing or stand in a certain position. "Stand like this, don't look at the camera, let the camera see the thing you're holding." I was much more interested in the secret photograph.'[12]

In his book *Lensman* Spender wrote, 'Mass-Observation was committed to "study real life" and for this purpose the concealed prying camera was essential . . . At our disgusting breakfasts in the smelly parlour of our headquarters house, Tom Harrisson would talk me into taking my camera to christenings, Holy Communions, pubs, railway stations, public lavatories. I was obliged to take photographs of everyday scenes, of people everywhere. Tom literally did say go into public lavatories and take pictures of people peeing. That I didn't quite have the courage to do.' Harrisson, however, had no scruples and didn't expect his observers to have any. Public lavatories, he believed, were fertile ground for his anthropological investigations. He was particularly interested in graffiti and he would send observers out with their notebooks to record everything that was written and drawn on the walls.

John Sommerfield appears to have had no qualms about snooping around in public lavatories and to have been particularly assiduous in the search for bog graffiti, or graphiti as he always referred to it in his reports. He saw plenty of it in the toilets of the many pubs he visited, nearly all of it crude, predictable and repetitive. But there were other places to look and nowhere was left unvisited in his search. At Heaton Cemetery he diligently reported: 'Visited the above cemetery and examined the urinals attached to the various chapels in the cemetery. Each urinal is of similar design, and in every case is situated in the N.W. corner of the chapel. They are constructed of rough stone, and are about seven foot long and three feet wide. The only swear words marked on any of the lavs was the following which was found on the Roman Catholic Chapel lav: "Fuck God". There is a lavatory by the entrance of the cemetery. This has sit-down cubicles – four in number. The walls are all whitewashed. There was only one writing on one of the walls in a cubicle viz: "I like to watch girls coming off a bus and coming downstairs to see their knickers. And sometimes their twats when they don't wear knickers." Somebody had added beneath the above: "Poor Fool."' Whether Sommerfield found anything or not he would always write up a short report: 'Gentleman's Public Lavatory Bridge Street. Observer entered every one of the lavatories in this convenience, and examined all walls etc. for writing and/or drawings, but was unable to find any markings of any description. This convenience is of recent construction and all the walls are glazed brick.'[13]

This interest in public lavatories led one member of the team at least into increasingly scatalogical areas of investigation. 'Inspired by a conversation with Joe Wilcock,' he declared, 'this is an attempt to give some kind of scientific explanation of piss and shit after a week's observation of urinals in Bolton.' He claims in his four-page report on the subject, 'I can prove by the aid of my wife, who has spent several years in a cotton mill, that a great number of Bolton mill girls owe their beautiful complexion to the application of piss to their skin. It is also a fact that navvies, although accustomed to their job, are apt to be unfortunate in getting a new spade, this of course makes the hands rather tender and the first thing the navvy does is to piss on his hands this taking the soreness away. It is also a fact that people who develop chilblains are often advised that the best thing to do is to put their feet in the chamber before retiring, the piss stopping all irritation.'[14] The author is not identified but, in its forthright approach, it has all the hallmarks of local observer Eric Letchford – and not many others had wives who had 'spent several years in a cotton mill'.

There were times when the Mass-Observation reports resembled the late *News of the World* – all human life was there. Even if it appeared to be a little indelicate, there was a duty to record it. Overall the general brief was to produce information about people's behaviour in all kinds of situations – bus queues, football crowds, dance halls, restaurants, pubs, church, in the streets, people talking to each other, people not talking to each other, what they were wearing, whether they wore hats, what they wore on their feet – the list was endless, and a great mixture.[15] Nothing was regarded as too trivial. At a dance at the Aspin Hall we learn that six blondes wore turquoise-blue dresses and four wore pink, while five of the brunettes favoured flowered dresses and four wore green. In a pub a group of four men 'who had won a lot of money on a horse were drinking heavily. The drunkest was a Napoleonic little man wearing a bowler hat, who sat at a table and held forth in a loud voice, with wide gestures, often using long words, carefully enunciating them, in the manner of a stage drunk . . . "A man only counts from the chin up," he said, and pushed his bowler hat right to the back of his head. The others laughed and seemed to think he was being funny.'

'Many people who come here', Harrisson commented, 'are rather overwhelmed by the amount of apparently trivial observation and record we are collecting. But it is the trivial of today that may prove significant tomorrow. The observer or photographer must shed preconceptions about what is good to observe and what is bad to observe; and shed all habitual frames of reference which may inhibit fresh observation and obscure the unexpected. Everything that men, women and children do should be recorded with the discipline of natural science and human wonder.'[16] So in a fish and chip shop it was noted: 'Anything with fish was eaten with one fork (waitress only served one fork). Knife and fork served for meat.' At a church service 'a man of Navy type, dressed in a blue suit, after kneeling, begins to finger his moustache and twiddle the points'. At a Salvation Army meeting it was reported that 'A woman announces hymn 164 and reads the first verse after which the band plays the tune and then sing the words without music.'

Much of what was recorded appears to be pure whimsy, but something original was born out of this mass of surveys. Harrisson's great central tenet was observation and thanks to his habit of demanding information on anything, no matter how trivial, there is a wealth of minute detail. On one day in October 1937, for example, we know that out of nine conversations monitored (or eavesdropped on?) in the town centre between 4.30 p.m. and 5.15 p.m., four were about sport, two were about money, one was about the weather, one about hobbies and one involved three workmen telling dirty jokes while they were waiting for a tram. Getting this sort of information involved a lot of hanging around and looking as unobtrusive as possible. Michael Wickham recalled, 'When John [Sommerfield] and I were researching characteristics of conversation in pubs, we used to go to the same pub over and over again and just kind of drink and potter and play darts and that sort of thing. So that finally one established that one was perfectly all right, in spite of the fact that one spoke with an Oxford accent. We dressed exactly like everybody else. We were rather particular about that, to wear slightly scruffy old lounge suits and cloth caps.'[17]

There was clearly a lot of listening in to other people's conversations, but also, it would appear, a certain amount of speculation about some of the pubs' customers and their relationships, as this report indicates. 'Tall girl, blonde, short fur coat, dark well-cut tweed skirt, handsome, powdered but little lipstick or rouge, wearing good silk stockings and expensive shoes, comes in with a chap of about twenty-five, mackintosh, scarf, but no hat, flannel trousers. They sit very close together, very affectionate, especially the girl. An observer suggests that it is the chauffeur and daughter of the house having an underground affair. Others agree that it is a situation of this kind. They drink three rounds of mild, then the man has a fourth, and the girl takes a gin and lime. She pays every time.'[18]

In the introduction to *The Pub and the People* Harrisson claimed that 'for the first two years we were practically unnoticed, and investigators penetrated every part of local life, joined political, cultural organisations of all sorts, worked in a wide range of jobs and made a great circle of friends and acquaintances at every level of the town structure'. But 'practically unnoticed' was hardly the case. Walter Hood had become well known locally as a Labour activist, and his friends and acquaintances in the party knew why he was in Bolton. Likewise with Wilcock; drafting an appeal to churchgoers to write about the 'part religion plays in personal life', he wrote, 'You probably know that a number of people have been making a special study of Christian churches in Bolton.' When working on the pub survey, going to the same pubs meant observers came to be accepted by the locals and many progressed from listening in to other people's conversations to getting into conversation with them. When they did they were able to steer the chat round to pick up all sorts of local information, like the details Eric Letchford obtained from a regular he got to know in the Prince William about the activities of prostitutes there.

I received some very interesting conversation during my stay there. I got in touch with a man who spends on an average six nights per week [there] and spends as much as a pound per week on drink for himself and lady friends. This man pointed out all the prostitutes as they came in and their methods of operation. In the first place he gave me to understand that a great deal of jealousy attached to this particular pub owing to the fact that where you find a dozen prostitutes in a particular place at one time they watch one another for stealing their clients. They also observe what clients their rivals pick up. To give an instance of this he tells a story about himself and two prostitutes that attended there regularly and he says I always took the same one home and she often asked him why he did not take her pal home and he replied that he did not fancy her. But the climax came when she got into trouble and she said, 'I'll go away to Blackpool to get rid of it but I won't blame you because I like you too much.' And he goes on to tell me that when she returned she wanted to know whether he had been with Gloria and he said, 'No.' She then said, 'I'm glad to hear that because she's got a dose.' Different types of prostitutes attend there. He pointed out a mother and daughter and 'there's Ginger over there. You can do her on the doorstep for 2/6d. But', he says, 'I think there's something wrong with her.'

A conversation I overheard between Dolly and her pal was about a man whom both had been with and he always makes arrangements to meet them at one particular time 4.00 p.m. and when he went to Dolly's house he had her parading around in the bedroom in the nude and with different garments on and in the end, Dolly said, 'I got bloody fed up with him.

I don't think he could get the horn so I had to be satisfied with a pound.' Dolly then says, 'I can get eight in a night.' An elderly prostitute then entered with a client. When I asked him how much they usually charge he replied that there are types that will do it for free drink. Those are the type who are married or receiving some income from elsewhere. Then there are those who manage to scrape enough together by back-street methods, prices varying from 2/- to 5/-. But the real professional type that take their clients home usually charge from 10/- to any price according to what they think a client can pay.[19]

The early Worktown team members were, as James Hinton pointed out in his history of the Mass-Observers, all men and it was with working-class masculinity that they empathised. Women, when they were discussed at all, were usually cast as objects of predatory male desire (including that of the observers).[20] Sommerfield in particular showed what has been described as a 'fascinating disgust at the conduct of "dirty girls" flirting in the pub'.[21] At the Grapes, a rather scruffy, small place near Bank Street, he found: 'Some of the women in there were young, not exactly whores,' he decided rather judgementally, 'but getting on for it.' Many of the men were under twenty-five. 'A blonde barmaid, daughter of the house, with a lecherous eye, flirting about; her mother kept popping in and giving her a dirty look.'[22] Sommerfield reveals a thinly disguised contempt for the women he sees in pubs in his sometimes derogatory descriptions of them. The women in one pub he says were 'all over forty except for one little tart with colleague of about thirty-five both standing with frozen smiles in one place not drinking'. In another the 'barmaid about thirty-five, made up, hairnet, green blouse, vicious face. Leered at me in a sexy way all the time.' Sommerfield, wrote the artist Graham Bell, led the field in constant smutty talk about women, copulation and so on, much to the disgust of more sensitive souls like Spender,[23] and to the discomfort of the few women who took up residence at Davenport Street to work on the project.

13

WORKTOWN WOMEN

*'The best of this job is that you needn't think about it.
I've sorted out all sorts of problems while working at it'*

Lilian, mill girl

The vast majority of the observers were men, but the Mass-Observation study was particularly interested in the large number of working women in Bolton. The saying 'a woman's place is in the home' was still current, but mill-working families needed more than one income to survive even when the husband was in work, and at the time 44 per cent of the town's adult women earned their own or their family's living. A wife would generally carry on at work until her husband was promoted or until childcare made work impossible. With young children times were often hard – the family budget improving only when children were old enough to go to work in the mill. Family income would then increase as the children got older, since they remained at home until marriage, paying their earnings to their mother and receiving only a few shillings back as pocket money.

To find out more about the working life of a Bolton mill girl, Penelope Barlow, the daughter of local M-O benefactor, Sir Thomas Barlow, who had been educated at Cheltenham Ladies' College and Newnham College, Cambridge, was recruited by Harrisson to work for a few weeks in one of the mills owned by Musgrave Spinning Company. Despite the clear difference in social status she got on well with the mill girls she was working with. She was quickly taken into their confidence and within days of starting at the mill she was able to report: 'Hilda said – quite spontaneously – "I wish I could get out of this mill. I'd like to work in a shop. Marks and Spencer's best, but I wouldn't really mind. It's clean and quiet and interesting."'[1] Shop work was another major area of employment for women. Nationally shop assistants, particularly in the big department stores, were predominantly female with around 400,000 women employees in the retail industry, 90 per cent of whom were single.

Soon after starting at Musgrave's, Penelope asked Joe, who was one of the overlookers, how it was there was so little interest in the union among the women in the card room where she was working. He said that the union was the Card, Ring and Blowing Rooms Union and that the subscription for women was one shilling. The benefits were ten to twelve shillings and this would be paid for up to six weeks of the year. Conditions in Musgrave's, and in fact in Bolton as a whole, were good, so that the women did not need the collective-bargaining strength of the union to get them better conditions as was the case in such places as Rochdale, where female membership was much higher. In particular the people here, Joe explained, had security of tenure. No one was dismissed unless it was absolutely necessary, and he himself regarded dismissal as a personal failure. Given security, and standard hours and wages, then, the women consider that the sick benefits aren't worth a shilling a week.

For the first two weeks at the mill Penelope worked in the card room and she learned from the girls she was working with that for some reason it had an undoubted reputation as a bad place for the younger girls to work in. The welfare supervisor in a weaving mill, she was told, often had mothers coming in with children to their first interview and saying, 'I don't want her to go in the card room.' A twenty-year-old tenter* she was working with pointed out some of the bad influences a young girl could be subjected to. 'There's a friend of ours', she confided, 'goes out with a married man. She's only sixteen and of course her mother doesn't know anything about it. He's twenty-eight. It was a forced marriage and the wife's a silly little thing, but that doesn't make it any better. He promises her all sorts of things, but she ought to have more sense than to think she'll get anything out of it. Disgusting, I call it.' Generally, however, Penelope found that, although there was much talk of lads, there was rarely any suggestion of anything improper, and most of the girls were easily shocked at any suggestion of anything like a forced marriage. One said, 'Yes, I know whom you're talking about, but I never see her. Mother doesn't like me to go with her – she says she's not nice to know.'

Each night, after a long shift at the mill, Penelope put all these comments from the girls she was working with into her report. During her first week much of what she recorded was conversations between the girls themselves that she had overheard without being part of. Some of the girls, she said, were planning a party the following Sunday. Beatty, Jessie and Mabel, who were all going out with three railway boys, and also Celia (a comber) and her husband. They were planning what games

---

* General term for someone who tends machinery.

to play, all of which seemed to include some combination of turning out the lights, pairing off with one of the boys and kissing. There was Postman's Knock, Film Stars and Spin the Bottle. For the mill workers Friday pay-night, with its economic and leisure release for the weekend, was the high point of the week. Towards the end of the week Penelope reported, 'One of the men said, "Another day gone and tomorrow's Friday when we get our pennies from heaven." Mabel gets 22/11d a week without overtime. She said, "We all queue up for wages outside the watch-house, there's an awful squash. The engine goes on running, but the machines can go to hell when it's payday."'

On the way to work one morning Mabel and Beatty were talking about Armistice Day. Neither was wearing a poppy, but both said they had them at home. They said that the two minutes' silence was kept in the mill, but the engines weren't stopped. On Armistice Day everyone seemed to stop work about five to eleven and where possible leaned against a wall or machine. The best indications of the beginning and end of the two minutes were the slowing down and restarting of the machines. Everyone was very still; only one man by the door kept looking at his watch. When the machines started again, everyone went peacefully back to work without comment.

While Penelope Barlow observed Armistice morning at work, Zita Baker reported on the way it was observed in the town centre. She walked down Knowsley Street and along to the post office, passing two girls and one man all busy selling poppies. Baker bought one off a girl who was standing in front of Dolcis shoe shop. 'Girl selling', she noted, 'age twenty tall dark lipstick. Another girl buying dressed in brick red. The seller said, "It don't go very well do it, love? But you must have a poppy. 'Ere, let me pin it for you." A good many men were hurrying in the direction of the cenotaph with rows of medals pinned on them. Some were accompanied by their wives. A few groups chatting at street corners – all men mostly wearing caps and scarves.' Baker couldn't hear what they were saying, and at 10.45 she went into Marks and Spencer's.

Only three customers [she reported], two girls at the shoe counter were checking over shoes together and two girls leaning over the watch counter looking out at the few people passing in the street outside. Otherwise all the girls were singly standing in their own counters and very quietly folding and straightening things. At 11.00 whistles were heard outside and an alarm went off at far end of shop. Everyone immediately stood still. A girl at the stocking counter looked down with her eyes fixed on the stockings, hands at her sides . . . A girl at one door stood to attention, eyes shut; a girl near the other door stood with head bent and arms folded. Girl inside clock counter sobbed loudly and blew her nose three times. Girl at food counter cried quietly and wiped her eyes. Outside there were only three people in sight. A woman opposite was looking into the window of a jeweller and at the sound of the whistles faced the street and stood with her head bent. The shopkeeper came to the doorway and stood with legs apart, hands behind his back, staring straight in front of him. About thirty seconds before the end of the silence, a hooter sounded, the alarm at end of shop went off and everyone stirred. The sobbing girl wiped her eyes and smiled at the girls at the watch counter.[2]

Harrisson's old flame was still a frequent visitor to Davenport Street. Her marriage to Crossman was now fixed, but she was still drawn to Harrisson and was happy to come and stay with him and work as an observer. Crossman does not appear to have been too worried about her frequent trips to Bolton. He explained: 'We have got to non-possessiveness as Zita and Dick, two modern Oxford unconventionals, and we have within the present social structure attained the relationship which is aesthetically the most satisfying.' For Harrisson, apart from the still very obvious attraction Zita held for him, having a woman on the team, even for the short periods she came to stay, made it possible to report on things that a woman would have been more at home with than the male observers. . Not many of the men on the team would have been too keen to spend their day looking at ladies underwear but Zita was able to deliver this report on 'magnificent window displays of corsets in five shops just off and around Deansgate. They are all, without exception, pink. In one window fifty-seven pairs, then forty-five, thirty-eight, twenty-five and fifteen. They are mostly exceedingly complicated with bones running vertically and slopingly and intricate lacing. Some are for very fat women indeed. Most of the corsets are made of strong cotton material with elastic insets but some of brocade, artificial silk and artificial satin. The prices range from 1/11 to 2/11 in three shops; in one shop there was a pair of corsets price 5/11 and in another three pairs at 3/11.'

When she went into one of the shops, the assistant said that a lot of quite young women bought them but mostly the stoutish ones. Most of their customers, however, were over thirty. Some customers were very rough on their corsets and had to get a pair at least every three months, while others took great care of them and then they might last two years. But they ought to be washed fairly often and that wore them out. Kershaws of

Farnworth, she discovered, produced most corset material – latex. Bolton market sold odd bits of latex – obviously sub-standard bits. These were bought by women to patch up their old corsets or to make new ones.[3]

Baker's presence also made it possible to cover women's meetings. One that she reported on was the Bolton Women Citizens' Association. The meeting took place in a comfortably furnished room about eighteen feet square with large gas fire and chairs placed round the walls. There was a table in the middle with mixed chrysanthemums and a little table by an easy chair in a corner by the large window. There were seventeen women present, mostly aged about fifty. The majority were dressed in dark coats with fur collars. Five women had on fur coats, which were an essential part of any smart, well-to-do woman's wardrobe. Baker was not able to take notes as it was an informal discussion meeting. The subject was 'Pensions for Spinsters' – or, more to the point, the lack of them. In 1936 there were 175,000 women between fifty-five and sixty-five who were single, and it was for them that Florence White, a spinster who ran a small confectioner's shop in Bradford, founded the National Spinsters' Pension Association. White wanted to draw public attention to the plight of unmarried women on low incomes who had no pension entitlement. Taking the slogan 'Equity with the Widow', because widows received a pension of ten shillings a week providing her husband had contributed to the National Insurance Scheme, the Association campaigned for pensions for spinsters at fifty-five.[4]

At the Bolton meeting a chairwoman for the afternoon was informally elected, a Miss Taylor, 'a large pleasant looking woman of about forty'. The meeting began with the Secretary reading out a foolscap typewritten document of about five pages which had been sent from the Ministry of Pensions stating the whole position with arguments for and against. The discussion was opened by a tall gaunt spinster of sixty-five who said that she was ten years too late to get a spinster's pension at fifty-five, but that she had worked in a mill all her life and had determined to do all that she could to see that other spinsters got this pension at fifty-five. She spoke, Baker thought, 'very movingly of the hardship of going out to work when old, specially stating the case of two or three old unmarried sisters who all had to go out and they could never afford to have anyone at home to cook a decent meal for them, or to keep the house nice. "What sort of a life is that?" she said.'

Baker continued to report in some detail on the discussions that took place. A married woman aged about sixty dwelt on how dreadfully sad was the lot of the aged spinster who had never known a real home or a man's love and went to her grave working hard and unloved. Many women took their handkerchiefs out of their bags and wiped their eyes. One woman had tears running right down her face because she couldn't find her handkerchief immediately. There was a good deal of discussion about widows getting pensions so easily, and there seemed to be a slight grudge about that. The argument that a pension of ten shillings would allow spinsters to compete in the labour markets for less wages and thus lower the wage level was discussed for longer than any other point. One exceptionally well-dressed woman (aged fifty) with an unattractive face said that this pension might make it possible for people to take into their homes elderly women who would do a little work for them and they would just be paid a little. Thus they would get a good home instead of living a lonely old age.

The Chairwoman was the only person who expressed any diffidence about the scheme, saying that she did not like this creation of a new section in the pensions scheme; and that in her opinion all workers in industry should be pensioned off at fifty, men and women alike. The meeting broke up informally and little tables were carried into the room on which places were arranged for tea. At teatime the discussion still went on privately and at the observer's table the discussion got on to working-class homes, very high rents, malnutrition, councillors not knowing what goes on or how the poor live and trade unions. Baker left shaking hands with women at her table and receiving many invitations to come again.[5]

Throughout November 1937 Baker stayed at Davenport Street and reported on a wide range of events. One of them was the Enterprise Bazaar at St Bartholomew's School. When she arrived outside on the pavement there were ten women, five children, three prams. There were six placards tied on the railings saying 'Cotton Queen* Opens Bazaar'. The school hall where the bazaar was being held was arranged with rows of school benches. The audience was composed of about 150 women. Many had babies on their laps. Baker sat next to a woman who was suckling a baby dressed in a bright-red knitted suit. 'It was suckling very noisily,' she noted. At 3.25 the Cotton Queen entered at the back of the room and there were slight claps. She was wearing a cheap-looking tiara on her smooth brown hair. Over an embroidered white cotton frock she

---

* Competition that operated between 1930 and 1939 to find Britain's Cotton Queen. The aim was to improve the fortunes of the ailing cotton industry through the selection of a beautiful young woman as the representative of the industry.

wore a blue cotton velvet evening wrap with dirty white rabbit collar
and cuffs. She looked, Baker commented, 'very healthy and plump and
smiled all the time. She wore no powder or lipstick. Following her were
three other women, the Chairman and the Vicar. Once they had arranged
themselves on the platform the Vicar said a short prayer asking God to
bless the bazaar and make it a success. Then followed the Lord's Prayer.
On sitting down the baby in red started howling, and observer held baby
while mother fished about for her other breast which she seemed to have
some difficulty in finding. The baby was returned and put to it. It gave a
big sigh.' After the Chairman had made his opening remarks the Cotton
Queen stood and made a speech about it being a great honour to have
been asked to open this bazaar and how as long as she was Cotton Queen
she would do all she could to boost cotton. After this all trooped off the
platform and everyone else stood up and moved off towards the stalls.[6]

On her visits to Bolton Baker, like everyone else, had to put up with
the dank, drab squalor of Davenport Street. 'Right awful mess that place
was,' Michael Wickham recalled. 'It was incredible really, the sort of dis-
order, the kind of casualness of it all. But somehow there was someone
there who could do it. There was a girl called Sheila – Watson I think.
The secretary girl. She kept us in order and put the thing into some kind
of shape when she could. Then later in '37 Sheila Fox was a member of
the team. A tall dark girl with a slim figure – full of life . . . imperious and
uppish. Seducing us all . . . quite an attractive girl. She was notable for two
things. She was a Trotskyite and she had a car. Very few people in those
days were Trotskyites and few women had cars. She was one person who
was not afraid to quarrel with Tom; as a result she was sacked.' Wickham
claimed to have spent several months working with Mass-Observation
and sleeping with most of the women in Bolton. 'There weren't many
rooms,' he observed. 'It's quite incredible how many people we got into
that house. We used to sleep toe to head in the beds – and with anybody,
women and all . . . Yes it was horrors to the local vicar if he'd known
what we were doing. Zita Crossman was there. I remember her very well
indeed . . . I fucked her once . . . everybody was fucking everybody in
those days.'[7]

Horrors to the local vicar if he'd known and probably horrors to Lady
Barlow if she'd known more about the company her daughter Penelope
was keeping and their bohemian existence. Baker encountered Penelope's mother at a bazaar in aid of the Girls' Moral Welfare Association.
When she arrived a speaker was saying, 'The association brings happiness and joy to their lives by teaching them to live in a happier Christian

way. We are very fortunate in having such an association in Bolton, whose committee works unseen and quietly.' She then went on to say a lot of complimentary things about the Barlow family and how famous they were in Bolton and how kind it was of Lady Barlow to come this afternoon. Lady Barlow then got up to speak. 'It used to be thought', she said, 'that our work for these fallen girls was ended when we had taught them laundry or domestic work, but now we know that we must do much more and really find out what has caused their fall. So often it is bad home conditions – a father and mother who don't get on or a step-parent. And not only do we need to care for these girls when they have fallen, but we must protect them where there is danger and if possible remove them from danger.'[8]

Lady Barlow's daughter, Penelope, was still working at Musgrave's Mill. After two weeks there she had been given a job in the winding room. On the morning she was due to start there she asked in the watch-house for Cliff Talbot, as she had been instructed. He led her into the mill and up to the top floor. As they went up, he said, 'I hear you've never done any winding before. I've decided you should learn with Lilian Greenhalgh and her sister.' Then he handed her over to them. Lilian took her dinner, mug and towel and showed her a peg for her coat. Penelope started to learn the art of winding on one of Lilian's winders, and occasionally, 'more by good luck than good management, succeeded, but generally failed'. Most of the time Lilian left her alone. Sometimes she came and made encouraging noises. Lilian and her sister worked on two adjacent winders. The sister called Penelope 'Love' throughout the day. About 9.30 Lilian said, 'Do you like tea?' and Penelope replied, 'Very much.' So they put tea in their pots, which were fetched and filled by a girl from downstairs. 'Lilian', Penelope recalled, 'had a bottle of condensed milk, which she offered to me, but I declined it. She gave me some wedding cake, which she said was from Emily further up the room. At dinnertime my tea was again made. The majority of people dashed off at 12.18.' The Greenhalghs stayed at the mill for their lunch and they asked Penelope if she wanted to join them. Lilian produced a spare copy of *Woman and Beauty* and they settled down to eat and read in silence. Another girl joined them and started to talk about films – *The Prince and the Pauper** particularly, and criticised it intelligently on historical grounds, that Edward VI was too weak to have been the tough lad he was made out to be in the film.

---

* 1937 film starring Errol Flynn based on Mark Twain novel about Edward VI.

Penelope went across to see Mabel in the card room. As she was going the winding-room girls said to her, 'Have you worked in the card room?', 'How long?' 'Is it very dirty?' None of them had worked there; only one of the three had ever set foot inside it. When she got back they were talking about keep-fit classes on Monday evenings, and were joined by several other people. Lilian was knitting. They talked about jumper patterns. One of the other girls said that she had heard of a school where all the boys were taught knitting, and had seen a photograph of them. This so amused Lilian that she exploded into her tea, upsetting it. After dinner Penelope reported that she pieced up* for the sister.

I gradually got better and by the end of the afternoon could do it with-out a hitch, though not at standard speed. The sister said at intervals, 'That's champion,' 'You're getting on fine,' and, as she sat on a skip for a few minutes, 'I've got a labourer this afternoon.' Towards the end she went to look at the time and came skipping back, saying that it was a quarter-past five. So we changed our shoes, and combed our hair in front of a mirror hung on a pillar. At 5.25 we put on our coats, but continued working right up to the last minute, though everyone stopped punctually with the engine. Just as we were ready to go Lilian said, 'How have you enjoyed it?' I said, 'Very much so far, how did you enjoy it?' She said, 'Not at all.' She used to like it, but she was bored with it now. She was now twenty-four and she'd been at it eight years.

For the rest of her time at Musgrave's Penelope worked in the wind-ing room and became friends with Lilian. She found out that she was the youngest of seven children and the only one now at home. She had been a winder since leaving school, but had not worked all that time at Musgrave's. She had been voted Bolton's Personality Girl No. 1 and was engaged to an engineer, who had gone to Australia (for good) at Easter. She was supposed to follow in six months, but didn't expect to go until some time the next year. 'Is not in any hurry, as she doesn't want to leave her family. Wears no engagement ring. Meanwhile she leads a gay life in Bolton and in particular with a boy called Frank. She says that he is a nice boy but too attractive and good looking and conceited as all the girls run after him. So she has adopted him and is trying to get him to think, and to read a bit. They often dance, sometimes at the Palais; the other night at the Co-op.'

* Repairing yarn breakages.

As the days went by Penelope began to find out more about Lilian. When young she had elocution lessons and was very ambitious; she won a Shakespeare competition, and a Personality Competition once at the Palais de Danse. After it she was feted all round, but simply hated it and disliked the people she met – 'Your class', she called them to Penelope. The result was that she lost all ambition, and was pleased to live peacefully at home again. Penelope reported all her conversations with Lilian about her life and ambitions, her boyfriend, her attitude to work and leisure time, and a dinnertime conversation about their reading habits which brought some surprises.

As it seems to be the thing to take something to read at dinnertime I took Penguin *Short History of the World*. Lilian said to me, 'Are you a Wells fan too? I'm just getting to the end of the *Science of Life*. It's taken me nine months to read. Fortunately I found a friend to lend it to me – I haven't got it of course, it's too expensive.' Later she said, 'Have you ever read any D. H. Lawrence?' We both had, but not the same. She said, 'I used to like him: now I'm not quite sure. But he does make you think. It's the same with Galsworthy. When I read the *Forsyte Saga* I thought it was the best book I ever read, but now I think all the people are too good. Yes, they may be stupid, but I do like a bit of real wickedness now and again.' Later 'Have you read any Bertrand Russell? I read an article not long ago, and I'd like to read something else by him.'

The fact that a mill girl like Lilian was so well read should not have come as a surprise. In the days before television, when money for other forms of entertainment was scarce, reading was popular and public libraries were well frequented. At the mill, dinner was a particularly good time for Penelope to find out more about the lives of the girls. On one occasion Lilian said, 'I'm sick of working here. What's civilisation brought us to if we wind and wind all day and lots of people sit and do nothing. There's one good thing Hitler's done – make everyone do some work for once in their lives. He was an idealist when he started, and on the whole I think he's done more good than harm. Now Mussolini I haven't got a good word for; I'd have him shot tomorrow.'

Part of Penelope Barlow's brief was to find out about wages. 'Not long ago,' Lilian told her, 'wages were lowered. You used to be able to earn 35/- a week on winders without undue effort.' A batch of people came up from the card room and worked so hard that they earned 45/- a week. 'Thoroughly greedy,' said Lilian. The management thought this wage unduly high, and reduced rates, 'so that now you have to work very hard to get 35/- a week'. The winding room were on piecework. Booking-in day* was Wednesday and on Thursday each operative was given a small slip of paper with her wage on it. She had a record of her work done in a small notebook, and was expected to check up to see that her wage was correct. If it was not, she complained to the overlooker and the matter was investigated and adjusted by wage-time on Friday. Payment was made on Friday afternoon about 3 p.m. A clerk from the accounting office came with the wages in tins. Cliff, the overlooker, stood by and read out the number of each person. They filed past in the order of the frames, the whole proceedings taking only about five minutes. Most people didn't look at their wages until they got back to their frames.

Penelope found that there was much more of a winding-room spirit than there was in the card room. For one thing, the former room was smaller, the girls worked near to each other, and there was less variation in their ages. For another thing they all had the same status, and there was no one job better than another. Winding was the top job in the spinning mill. No one was waiting to get a move somewhere else, as in the card room; nor was there anyone obviously anxious to get into other jobs, such as shops. On the other hand there was nothing to look forward to – no improvement of position or earnings. One winder, aged about thirty, said, 'No, I don't like it, but one's got to earn one's living.' Lilian was of the opinion that 'The best of this job is that you needn't think about it. I've sorted out all sorts of problems while working at it.'

Penelope had started her work experience at Musgrave's in early November and was due to leave at the end of the first week in December. Before she left she revealed to Lilian the real reason she had been there. 'I told Lilian Greenhalgh that I was going on Saturday; that I only came for a month to get a practical background to a theoretical education, and to see how another class of people lived and worked and thought. I might one day do the sort of work Miss Weetman is doing. [Personnel] She said of course she knew from the first moment that I was not an ordinary new winder, and wondered how long I would be staying. She thought perhaps I had been training to take Miss Weetman's place or become her assistant. Everyone had been wondering about me, and some had pestered her, but of course she knew nothing and had said so. And they, being an

---

* Day the workers on piece work handed in their record of the work they had done so that their wage could be calculated.

exceedingly decent lot of girls, hadn't bothered me. She wouldn't tell anyone until I went. She said, "I didn't think you'd stay very long; you're too intelligent."[9]

Having fitted in so well at the mill, Penelope Barlow was clearly adaptable. For Harrisson this was one of the prime attributes his observers had to possess. 'To be able to operate in our way,' he said, 'we have to become assimilated into the society and into all of its parts. So our observers have joined each of the political parties, every pub, club, society, corner organisation and gang existing at every level of Worktown life. They are trained to observe and record on the spot without being noticed so that life continues as if there were no strangers. The observer is not a stranger, merely a participant, reporting continuously back to headquarters.'[10] For some observers this meant getting involved with groups with which they felt distinctly uncomfortable. In Zita Baker's case it meant attending a British Union of Fascists meeting. Since the Battle of Cable Street and the passing of the Public Order Act 1936, which required police consent for political marches and forbade the wearing of political uniforms in public, the influence of the BUF had declined, but it still had a presence on the political scene and Mass-Observation wanted to record its activities in Bolton. When she arrived at the meeting Baker found that she wasn't the only infiltrator there, reporting that at the start of the meeting there were fourteen men present and seven women, including three Labour Party members. Four men came in late greeted by the doorkeeper in a whisper, 'Hello, I'm glad you could come.' The speaker was dressed in a dark-brown dress and coat, brown shoes, brown felt hat, bright yellow scarf, and she was wearing a Fascist badge. She had, Zita felt, a charming voice, clearly, conversationally spoken. She stood behind a table displaying posters and photographs of Oswald Mosley and began her address with an attack on democracy, saying that we had had it for years and years and there was absolutely nothing to show for it. There followed an account of the career of the Leader. She said that the great attack on Mosley from the press and other sources was because they thought he intended to imitate Hitler and Mussolini and to smash the trade unions. But that wasn't the case. Mosley, she said, knew that the people of England would never stand for a dictator.

The speaker went on to talk about the National Socialists' economic policies and how they would benefit the Lancashire cotton industry and about the completely apathetic political outlook in England today when 60 per cent don't vote. She ended with a plea that people should not

believe the lies they hear and read about Mosley but should read *Action*[*]
for themselves and think and wake up before it was too late and they
were betrayed again. There was complete silence during the speech,
and as it went on those members of the Labour Party who were present
started to show a growing interest. One of them began to take notes and
was eagerly watched by a presumed Fascist.

At the end of the speech the applause lasted for fourteen seconds
and the Chairman made an appeal for funds: 'Our organisation is not
so wealthy as some people think, and as we have this room to pay for I
would be most grateful if you would contribute.' She then went round
with a collection box. Everybody dropped coppers in except Zita and the
members of the Labour Party. The meeting then opened for questions.
Among the questions from the floor was one asking what the Fascists
would do about the House of Lords, one about the colonies and several
about the Spanish Civil War. One man said, 'You have made a slash-
ing attack on democracy but you haven't said anything at all about the
concrete things you intend to do when elected.' After the questions the
organiser said, 'We will now end our meeting in the usual manner.' She
stood stiffly at attention, raised her hand in a Hitler salute and said in a
loud voice, 'British First: God Save the King.' Twenty-two others quickly
rose to their feet and gave the salute.[11]

Within a few days Baker was back in the sort of company she was
more at home with when she attended an aid meeting to raise funds for
dependants of men fallen and fighting in Spain. About eighty were present. They were 'mostly very poor, wearing dirty shabby clothes, caps,
scarves and clogs. Behind the observer there were two middle-aged men
who might have been parsons and had Oxford voices. The Chairwoman
was a woman Baker had seen speak at a Left Book Club meeting. With
her on the platform were two men who had fought with the International
Brigades, introduced as Comrade Jock Cunningham and Comrade
Aitken. Both spoke for an hour each about their experiences in Spain.
After they'd spoken the Chairwoman said, 'Now we have to do our part
for the fight in Spain and so there will be a Bazaar and Social on November 20. The collection came to 35/1d.' Comrade Aitken responded
to this: 'Though I think thirty-five shillings is very good for a meeting
of this kind, we have got to raise seven hundred a week and this won't
go very far. There is going to be a hat out at the door and if you have

---

[*] First published on 21 February 1936, this weekly newspaper became the official organ
of the BUF.

another bob, even if it means sacrifice, put it in.' To Baker the effect of the meeting was:

> lamentable, pathetic and miserable. It was a meeting to raise money for Spain and it was obvious that a meeting to raise money for the audience of this meeting would have been just as profitable. They could ill afford to give but observer saw none refuse though one man in front gave the men on either side a penny to put in the bowler hat. The audience appeared to be used to Communist lectures and clapped at the usual Communist remarks. The collection in aid of the dependants of those fighting and killed in Spain was taken by three men all of which observer had previously seen at Left Book Club meetings. Judging from the noise it all sounded like coppers. Observer tried to look in but failed. There was a lot of digging deep into overcoats to find the money to give. After the meeting broke up the audience dispersed slowly as if loath to leave the nice warm hall for the outside bitter cold. Observer left gloves in Hall and had to dash up stairs again to collect them. Passing a lot of the audience still making their way down various remarks were thrown out at her, 'Good night, lovey,' 'Looking for a sweetie, darling.'[12]

This was to be Zita Baker's final visit to Bolton. Soon after leaving Bolton for the last time, on 18 December she married Richard Crossman. Whatever their relationship was when she visited Bolton, her passionate affair with Harrisson was long past. In her presence, though, he recognised what he had lost. 'It is easy for anyone who knew them both' – his biographer Judith Heimann believed – 'to feel a pang of regret that it was not possible for these two extraordinary people to build a life together. Her kindness and fundamental honesty would have been so good for him; his making no allowances for her femininity, treating her like the tough, energetic and adventurous person she was would have been so good for her.'[13]

14

PINCH THE SERMON

*'There's a lot of good people in the world, but people that call themselves Christians
are the sort that go to church and put "No Hawkers. No Circulars. Keep Out"
on their gate and wouldn't do a kindness to anybody under the sun'*

Mass-Observation interview

The day after Zita Baker married Richard Crossman, Tom Harrisson
attended the nativity play at St George's Road Congregational Church.
The service, he reported, started with a hymn, followed by the Lord's
Prayer and two Bible readings relevant to the play. The Vicar then announced that the play had been written by a congregational minister and
was being acted by church members. It was to be taken not as a dramatic
show, he insisted, but as an act of worship in which the players asked
all to participate. In Act One Joseph and Mary were on stage, talking
about going to Bethlehem for a census. Act Two found them on their
way to Bethlehem and in Act Three, Harrisson wrote, 'we see Romans,
a rabbi, the landlord and maids in the inn at Bethlehem. Act Four – the
shepherds in the fields see vision and in Act Five the infant Jesus is in
Mary's arms adored by the shepherds.'

The performance was not very sophisticated. There were delays
between each of the acts of between five and twelve minutes. During
these breaks the organ was played and in one a hymn was sung. Twice
men in suits were visible trying to slip about unseen and twice during
intervals something fell down. Torches were flashed about during the
intervals because the whole church was in darkness and apparently the
actors had a lot of trouble finding whatever they were trying to find.
The pub scene included 'a loose woman singing a loose song, which the
boss of the centurions called a ribald tune; two junior centurions played
dice throughout. Senior centurion has pretty left-wing anti-Caesar conversation with a rabbi who thinks about the long-anticipated coming
of the Messiah. The revelation to the shepherds in Act Four is in the
form of a white light by the organ loft, which goes out again suddenly

after voice announces peace and good will on earth. Lights come on in unexpected places several times, including one time several people titter when they don't seem to be able to get it right. There are only three mistakes noted, including one when the leader of the shepherds appears through the curtain, forgets his cue and leans back so a second shepherd can whisper it to him. This shepherd is wearing glasses. After Act Five all came on to the stage to sing a hymn with the congregation. Mostly older people present.'[1]

Along with the pub and politics, religion was one of the mainstays of Mass-Observation's work in Bolton and over 400 reports on church services were amassed. From the Church of England and the Roman Catholics to obscure groups and sects like the Mazdaznans, Primitive Methodists, Unitarians, Christian Scientists and members of the Pentecostal League of Prayer, every religion that was practised in Bolton was reported on. Counts were made of people going into church and of the amount of money received in collections. Observers were instructed to count hatpins, list the hymns sung in church and 'any other dope you can get hold of', and try and pinch a copy of the sermon' while they were at it. Confirmation services, Lord Mayor's services, funerals and memorial services were all covered, along with special services for groups of people as diverse as busmen, sportsmen and old women. The object was to find out 'how religion works or doesn't in a large industrial town'.

With 204 churches of every known or imagined denomination, Bolton was an ideal place for the work, but Mass-Observation believed that the implications of the study went far beyond the town. In 1930s Britain most of the population would have professed to be Christian in that they were baptised and generally subscribed to what was regarded as Christian morality, but only a minority were actual churchgoers. In much the same way as he was concerned with the non-voter in the politics survey, Harrisson wanted to find out more about the non-churchgoer and finding out why people did go to church might give some clues. From the outset, though, he recognised that 'one difficulty in getting a clear picture of religion in Northtown[*] is that any one set of religious beliefs is only held by a minority. The position is of official tolerance and equality of beliefs, with a much weakened state religion in the form of the "Established" Anglican Church.' Religion was, he believed, the 'oldest and most familiar, though also most puzzling, of social institutions in Worktown. Religion

---

[*] Throughout the project Harrisson continued to refer to Bolton as both Worktown and Northtown.

unlike pub-going, claims to be a whole-time, not part-time, institution. It claims its part in every activity. Yet as things are today its organised hold is weakening. Does this mean that it is dying out, or is there some universal and inescapable human need for religion, which will create new and parallel forms even if the old ones perish?'

Not surprisingly Mass-Observation never found any real answers to a question as big and wide ranging as this, but there were certainly clear signs that religion may have been dying out. In December Harrisson and other members of the team were working on a report entitled 'Christmas is Coming to Worktown'. It recorded that 'over the past week, on their walks round the town, they have observed a striking change of atmosphere. The Christmas season is in full swing; the shops, showing special displays are crowded; and over all smiles the bearded benevolent face of Father Christmas. He – and not the Christ child or his mother – is the central cult figure.'[2] The fact that the religious significance of Christmas was largely ignored or overlooked is unsurprising. Easter, Christmas and Whitsun, Mass-Observation reported, were days that to the majority of Worktowners 'no longer have any more conscious religious significance than does Sunday, other than as days of release from the factory routine'.[3] In Bolton, as in the rest of the country, church attendance in the 1930s was in decline. It was a decade, as Juliet Gardiner puts it in *The Thirties*, 'during which the Church's authority was tested by social and legal changes, its doctrines were challenged, its importance in many people's lives diminished, and its role of giving a clear spiritual and moral lead to the nation was reduced not only by its own divisions in the face of shifting social and moral attitudes, but also by the confusion and volatility of domestic and international politics'.[4]

There were clear signs of hostility to the Church in interviews conducted by Mass-Observation. 'There's a lot of good people in the world, but people that call themselves Christians are the sort that go to church and put "No Hawkers. No Circulars. Keep Out" on their gate and wouldn't do a kindness to anybody under the sun' was the sort of comment that summed up the attitude of many people to the Church. The decline of churchgoing and of the influence of religion was seen by Mass-Observation as part of a wider trend, as reported in *The Pub and the People*:

All the older institutions are declining. It is a main feature of the contemporary scene. The Church in recent years has suffered, numerically and thus economically, far more than the pub. The political machine has equally suffered from an increasing apathy . . . The pub, the church, the political party, are answers to questions of living that were vital long before Worktown became a town. The questions why are we here, where are we going, what is it all for, is life worth living, what else can I do? – are still here. But the actual factual answers are not necessarily the same. There are now a number of alternative answers. The football pools, the cinema, the radio and the *Daily Mirror* give alternative answers to the question, Is life worth living? A hundred years ago the main answers were in a man's own heart, his wife's body, the parish church or the local pub.[5]

The decline in the influence of the Church was a cause of concern to many, and Joe Wilcock reported on a teacher's views on encouraging the churchgoing habit in her pupils: 'I've said before and I say it now, if we are going to do anything to catch the children, we shall have to do something about getting them to come to church. It's not enough to say "Oh let them please themselves." If we don't get them now, we shall lose a whole generation of them.'[6] But in spite of concerns like this the Church still played an important part in the life of the town, even though its influence wasn't always immediately obvious. 'It would be easy', the report went on, 'to spend a year in Worktown and, if you didn't go to church, think that the Church was less important than the tram or the political party. But its leaders are also leaders of politics, police, magistrates' benches, local press and businessmen.'

The place of the church in the civic life of the town was demonstrated at the funeral service of the Town Clerk at St George's. The funeral had drawn quite a crowd keen to pay their respects to somebody who had given distinguished service to the town. In his sermon the Vicar of Bolton referred to the service the Town Clerk had rendered to Bolton. Though he had met him seldom, his opinion was a high one. This service was neither the time nor the occasion for many words. He desired to express on behalf of many citizens of this town and the Christian Church their deep sense of loss. His acquaintance with him had been almost wholly official. But in his contacts with him he gained an impression of a man 'as honest as the day, kindly and understanding and sincerely devoted to the duties of his office. His service for the town was valuable, efficient and always devoted.'[7]

At the outset Harrisson discussed strategy with Wilcock. Key to their approach was getting the Rev. Davidson, the Vicar of Bolton, involved and on their side. Harrisson reported that he had already put to Davidson two areas they wanted to concentrate on. The first was the social activity of the Churches, including their influence on politics, business, crime, prisons and relief of the sick. The second was the influence of Christianity on the individual, with special reference to the most important stages of life and life problems, for example guidance or teaching of the Church at adolescence, at marriage, in questions affecting career, over births and deaths. He was also interested in the general educational influence of the Church. Wilcock was a devout Christian and one of the things on his mind was the fear that Mass-Observation would make some blasphemous use of material gathered for the religion survey. Some of his colleagues, who didn't share his religious convictions, thought he was over-sensitive in this respect, but it was clear to everybody that he inspired trust and confidence in the world of Bolton Christianity.

This confidence was essential if Mass-Observation were to get anywhere with the religion survey, as many of the town's clerics were suspicious and there was some distrust of the organisation and its motives. 'What have you come about? Religion? What qualifications has the observer? Do you call yourself a Christian?' was the sort of questioning that was directed at observers. 'Very good,' one cleric replied when the answer was in the affirmative. 'Then keep it up. Don't lose faith. Science and enquiry can never hurt the everlasting truth. I welcome every enquiry undertaken in the spirit you seem to have; never forget that science cannot explain God or the conduct of those who know him.'

Although he'd brought Wilcock in to lead the team, Harrisson himself kept in close contact with the Church of England. His view was that 'Davidson and his friends must be got on our side by every whim, lie and persuasion, since they are the clue to Joe's peace of mind, and since a review of Christianity in Bolton cannot possibly omit what they have to offer in the way of information.' Commitment to a religion was, for Harrisson, a key issue, so he went to observe a service that was all about commitment – a Church of England confirmation service. There were just short of a hundred candidates and a congregation of 240. The procession at the start of the service was headed by four choirboys in white, then fourteen women in long black cloaks with white, starched collars, white pastoral ties and black undergraduate caps. Following them came a parson with a crucifix raised, then the Vicar, then two men in lounge suits, each bearing an eight-foot ebony cane with a silver knob on top, and, following them at about three yards' distance, the Bishop in glasses, middle aged, dour looking, wearing a red hood. The Bishop gave an address about confirmation and left two thoughts with the candidates: 'Oh God, give me Thy Holy Spirit' and then 'God accept my heart this day.' After everybody had come forward to the Bishop to be confirmed, there was a prayer which he read out of an enormous book, then taking two steps forward he raised his right hand and delivered the blessing. In a further address the Bishop used an analogy about climbing a mountain to talk about what young people setting off in life would like to achieve.[8]

For the purpose of the inquiry Wilcock became a regular attender at churches of all denominations. Bolton, like most of the North-west, had a substantial Catholic population, and at St Mary's Roman Catholic Church he described the ritual of the 11 o'clock sung Mass. He arrived early and Father Lawless, the parish priest, was walking about the church, talking to people as they passed him. 'Many', Wilcock noted, 'were very poor, stained and well worn.' By three minutes to eleven there were approximately 150 people in the church. An altar boy came into the sanctuary and lit one candle each side of the tabernacle. At eleven the priest came to the altar, 'wearing a large sort of surplice which reached to his ankles with a purple scarf at the shoulders'. He was carrying the chalice, over which there was a purple cloth. He and the altar boy went to the altar steps and genuflected together. He put the chalice down and opened the service book as the organ played. He put his glasses on and read for thirty seconds, then moved to the centre and nodded slowly to the altar. As the choir sang a chant the priest was handed a brush with a brass handle. The altar boy and the priest began to walk round the church. The priest dipped the brush into the water that the altar boy was carrying, raised it to the level of his head and splashed it on to the congregation. He was speaking as he did every splash and everybody was standing as he moved around the church.

By this time the Mass had hardly started, but Harrisson was particularly interested in ritual so Wilcock continued to describe the actions of the priest in this level of detail for the rest of the service. The report is handwritten and goes on for page after page, as do most of the reports on church services, but it is debatable how much they tell us about the bigger issues that Harrisson wanted to address in the religion survey. On a social level perhaps the most telling point in the report is the record of collections that are taken from what is predominantly a poor congregation. As he came into the church Wilcock reported that 'Near one of the three entrances there is a man with a plate. He is taking over from another man who evidently was the collector at the last Mass. He is counting the money there. The people who come in sometimes have their money ready and put it on the plate, then turn to the Holy Water font which is fastened to the wall.' As he waited for the Mass to start he mentioned the 'constant rattle of coins from the direction of the doors'. After the sermon the people all stood and the choir 'begin to sing. The men begin to go round the church for the collection. They use heavy brass plates. The money rattles as they collect and the choir sings.' At the end of the Mass 'there are men at the door collecting again. This makes three collections for this service. Observer watches the people giving. Five out of every six are putting coins on the plate which is held out to them. Single pennies are the most usual.'[9]

Two weeks later Wilcock went to the Catholic Mission at the Grand Theatre, organised by the Bolton branch of the Knights of St Columba.* It started with replies to questions which had been handed in. These included 'Why does the Catholic Church not believe in cremation?' and why do Catholics only allow the laity to take Communion in one kind? In reply to a question about the Bible it was stated that there were 2,000 mistakes in the English Bible. It had, it was claimed, been deliberately altered in translation to suit the needs of the Reformation. Dr Hampson, who answered the questions, smiled very often and caused much laughter at some of the questions.

After the questions the Chairman rose to announce the other speaker, Father Dempster. This priest, about fifteen stone and six foot tall, had silver hair and a round face. He spoke for about thirty minutes, all of which, Wilcock thought, was a 'magnificent peroration'. He mentioned that the Church did not care for the dictators, then made out that salvation could come only from the Church. He referred to England as 'Mary's Dower'. After he had finished the Chairman could not get order as a result of the clapping . . . They finished the meeting with the singing of 'Faith of Our Fathers'. The observer was standing at the back for this where a theatre attendant said to him, 'By gum. I wish we could get so many in every neet. It's funny how they can get them to come to a meeting like this.'[10] It was perhaps not surprising, though, that it was a Catholic meeting that attracted such large numbers. As church attendance in general declined, only the Roman Catholic numbers were sustained throughout the 1930s, partly because of a rapid expansion of the clergy and a major church-building programme, but also because of the influx of Irish Catholic working-class immigrants with a high birth rate.

It wasn't just the mainstream religions like the Catholics and Anglicans that were observed. Bolton had many small sects such as the

---

* A Catholic men's organisation, founded in Glasgow in 1919, dedicated to the principles of charity, unity and fraternity.

fundamentalist Beulah Hall group, who had their impoverished-looking little meeting room over a row of lodging houses and shops on Bank Street. To get to the service hall Wilcock wandered through a passage which was painted bright yellow. This colour was carried right through the whole of the church. Entering the meeting hall he found a group of people sitting round an open stove – three men, about eight women and three children. He recorded that his impression was 'that of going into one of the Wild West churches of the middle nineteenth century'. Rough and ready it might have been, but the members of the church were welcoming. The men rose and, smiling, said, 'Good evening, Brother.' One of them came up to Wilcock and held out his hand, saying, 'Good evening, won't you come nearer to the front here.'

Wilcock described the meeting room in great detail: the platform at the far end; the wooden rail which rises above the platform; the entrances at each end of the platform; the old harmonium; the picture of Christ raising a man from the waters; the table from which communion is distributed; the simple straight-backed chairs with plywood bottoms; the stove with its circular flue zigzagging to the roof; the six bare electric lights; the walls covered with tongue-and-grooved wood; the four windows on each side; the dirty, unscrubbed floor with red, green and yellow coconut matting running down the centre. The whole place had a feeling of poverty.

The women sat near the iron stove and began to talk. They asked one of their number who was wearing old and greasy clothes why she had not been lately. She replied that she had been working. Asked what she did she said that she worked at the Bee-Hive Spinning Co. Wilcock recognised the name. It was a place he had worked at some twelve years previously. After more talk about the dole a woman who had spent most of her time turning over the leaves of the Bible and making notes went to the platform and from there she started the service. 'We'll commence the service by singing hymn 81,' she announced. After the hymn the woman read the fifth chapter of the Book of First Thessalonians. She read, Wilcock noted, rather well, better than say an Anglican parson, intelligent and clear. During the reading there were several times when someone broke in with 'Amen'. The service continued in this fashion with more hymns and readings and a time of prayer, during which everybody knelt on the floor. Throughout the service there were many 'Hallelujahs' and 'Praise the Lords'. When it had finished everybody congregated round the fire. Two of the women went into the vestry and brought out cups of tea with two biscuits on each of the saucers. They all sat and talked

Monday was washing day and, although soot and smoke filled the air, the washing always had to be hung out to dry in the back entry.

Despite the soot and grime, front steps and the pavements outside peoples' houses were donkey stoned to a pure white or brilliant yellow by housewives dressed in uniform pinnies.

Men playing dominoes in a pub. Harrisson believed that the pub, more than anywhere else, occupied a central position in the lives of the people of Worktown.

In pubs and cafés the observers' brief was to note down conversations and watch people's behaviour, documenting like 'cameras' everything that was seen.

The landlord of this pub, the Saddle Hotel, spotted Humphrey Spender taking this photograph and it resulted in an angry confrontation during which he demanded for Spender to destroy the film.

This photograph of workers hemming towels was taken during an organised visit to a mill. Spender felt that this sort of shot was too staged.

Up to forty thousand people watched Bolton Wanderers on a Saturday afternoon: it was the largest focus of a mass of people, about a fifth of the town's population, but strangely Mass-Observation didn't report on any of the matches.

The Grapes Hotel, 20 Water Street. In 1936 there were 304 pubs in Bolton, one on nearly every street corner.

n dance halls young men and women were freed from parental supervision; there was little doubt in the eyes of observers that the dance hall was saturated in sexual significance.

The Bolton Odeon opened in August 1937, only a month before this photograph was taken. In the 1930s between 600 and 750 new films were released annually in Britain, and streamlined art deco dream palaces like the Odeon were built in towns and cities throughout the country.

LEFT
Mass-Observer, ex-miner and Labour activist Walter Hood, dressed up in a woman's hat and coat, drinking a bottle of beer. Young writers, artists and intellectuals were attracted to the bohemian lifestyle of the Worktown project.

BELOW
Tom Harrisson playing an old piano in a photograph possibly taken at the Mass-Observers' base at 85 Davenport Street.

William Coldstream's painting on the roof of Mere Hall Art Gallery. Coldstream and his friend Graham Bell were members of the Euston Road realist group of painters. Harrisson invited them to Bolton to record Worktown on canvas.

Graham Bell (*left*) with Humphrey Spender (*right*) on the roof of Mere Hall Art Gallery.

Children peeping through a gap in a railway bridge fence. Spender took a sequence of photographs of children playing on this railway bridge.

over their tea and biscuits. As Wilcock left the hall they called out, 'Good night and God bless you, Brother.'[11]

The Beulah Methodists were a small church, but many of the town's fringe cults and religions were even more obscure and Harrisson insisted that they should all be investigated. One of these was the Mazdaznans – a body that had arrived in Lancashire from America. Similar to Christian Science, it combined the appeal of church and health club and seemed to have been supported financially by selling health foods to its members.[12] Joe Wilcock attended one of its meetings. Dr Jessie Anthony of San Francisco and Manchester, a doctor of medicine and a 'dietician', was the main speaker. Wilcock had never before seen anybody remotely like this addressing or conducting a religious service. To the rather pious lay preacher she clearly seemed to be a rather exotic creature. 'This lady', he reported,

> is an amazing person in stature; she is about 5' 10" in height and has a perfect figure that is the comment of all present. She is dressed in a dark purple evening gown, covering in skintight fashion her bosom and posterior; long flowing sleeves and all the seams of the gown go in a V shape to the 'vagina' that is obvious to anyone. She is Eton-cropped and the hair in front comes down over the forehead, flat. An oval face slightly powdered, and a long mouth uncoloured giving the impression of an Egyptian Princess reincarnated. She wears silver evening shoes. She sits there pleasant faced, but stiff and straight, hand laid across her solar plexus, palms upward. When she rises you fear that her gown may split at the thigh seams, but no it only sweeps the floor.

The meeting opened with a piece of classical music, then Miss Simons, who was chairing the meeting, rose to announce that they would sing the hymn or song on the sheet first. While doing this she exhorted the congregation to add an exercise of circular motion by the fingertips on the hollow bone below the centre of the ribs. This wasn't religion as Brother Joe knew it. 'Dr Jessie', he recorded, 'rises figure erect and hands, palms upwards laid across the upper part of her stomach and except for about 10 seconds they remain there for all her lecture, "How to be happier than we are". "There is always a means to this end, and we have come here to tell you how it is attained."' Wilcock went on to report in detail the content of Dr Jessie's talk. It was all about the vibrations of proper breathing touching the brain and this helping us to have faith to do our Saviour's bidding, which will bring happiness. He reported that during the singing of the hymns they went through several exercises. The first was breathing and at the same time massaging the gland under the centre of the ribs, near the solar plexus. Next he reported 'taking deep breaths (and to music), on release of breath, you hum the music played'. He went on to detail a whole programme of similar exercises. Most of the people present did the exercises, the report went on, after which, he wrote, 'An old woman of fifty-eight – sixty said, "I have faith in this new movement, if it can do so much for Dr Jessie Anthony, then I want it for myself." The woman was grey and suffering from muscular trouble, probably rheumatism, stiff in the neck. Another woman just said, "I know now that I have found the truth . . . This is what I have been waiting for!"'[13]

Although religion was primarily the province of Joe Wilcock, there were so many different religious groups and services to be covered that many other observers were involved. One of them was Brian Barefoot. Although his main area of work was with Walter Hood on the politics survey, he recalled that 'we were not restricted to our own specialised interests as regards the preliminary reporting. We were all considered to be trained observers and, therefore, able to record objectively the events, people and ideas that came to our notice. The Pentecostal League of Prayer tea-party was certainly one of the odder events I reported. Twenty-six women and ten men, mostly lower-middle class and undistinguished in appearance or clothes, had mostly come it seemed for the free tea.' There were also two seventeen-year-old boys who:

caused amusement and laughter by eating all the food they could possibly get; but otherwise the table was very quiet. Half the people never spoke at all, and the remainder only spoke at intervals. Most of the people seemed to know one another, but there were no warm greetings. One felt that they were all kind-hearted people at bottom, but their temperament made it impossible for them to show it openly. The woman in charge was about forty, wearing mannish clothes, the only one who was at all cheerful. Such conversation as there was was non-religious and non-intellectual. The tea itself was liberal, and it was as much appreciated by the observer as anyone. There was a liberal balance of good solid fare – white and brown bread and butter, teacakes, jam sandwiches, meat-paste sandwiches, fruitcake and Christmas cake. Everyone tucked in and the table was clear in a quarter of an hour. As soon as a plate was emptied, one of the helpers took it out of the room, filled it and brought it back. In fact, there was as much to eat as anybody wanted, and there was no charge for it.

After tea the leading woman got up and said she'd had difficulty in finding someone to address them this afternoon but she had eventually got Pastor B. Lipschutz to speak. The Pastor got up on a small platform. He was a rotund friendly Jew, aged about sixty, who came from Lithuania. He first led the hymn-singing, said a long prayer and read from the Book of Jeremiah. He then gave his talk, speaking very sincerely and unselfconsciously in very good English, gesturing now and then with his arms. He started by referring to the meaning of joy, then went on to the question of God's chosen people. He talked about the union of Jewish and Christian communities to murmurs of assent from the audience and about his own Jewish congregation in Manchester. Barefoot reported that he 'was greatly impressed by the personality of Pastor Lipschutz and came away with the strong impression of having heard a very unusual and outstanding man. Although some of his ideas seem narrow and fantastic, yet he gave the sense of having through suffering learned the meaning of courage and love. One could see by the look in his eye that "love" for him meant something strong and not weakly sentimental, and it was the foundation of his whole being.'[14]

Barefoot began to get to know Wilcock well as he worked with him. He was, he recalled, 'introverted and sensitive, and yet has led a very hard life and knows how to talk to people in such a way as to gain their confidence. He is not an intellectual, and finds it hard to write; but he has a great deal of intelligence, and is the nearest thing I have met to a true Christian.'[15] Wilcock was clearly the right man to lead the religion investigation, but Harrisson remained very hands-on in issuing directives and was very specific in his instructions. 'Go to Bank Street Unitarian Chapel. Record exact attitudes of prayer of as many people as possible, and of one person also throughout the service as a control. Study the behaviour of the choir all through, the attention they pay as compared with the congregation, their prayer attitudes, stance, sermon behaviour. Make plan of their position, and also any notes you can on the organist. Concentrate on behaviour. Follow a group out, mid-aged, and home noting all you can all the way and timing them from time they start from church till time they arrive the other end, noting exact route so that afterwards we can work out speed they travelled at. Note this just the same if they take a tram.'[16]

A February 1938 directive on 'Sunday behaviour' included the injunction 'You know some of the times at which church bells will ring. Can you send out observers to get as much information as possible? Do people notice; do they walk faster or slower; do they look up; do they hum; do they notice when hymn tunes are played?' In response Walter Hood went out and described what he heard on a street corner the next Sunday morning:

> It is 9.50 by the Anglican church clock opposite. Three men stand by the pillarbox talking. I can hear a bell about a quarter of a mile away ringing quickly on one high note, thirteen during ten seconds on the watch. At 9.55 two men join in the group already there. The distant bell is now of a lower pitch, and not audible when a car passes. At 9.57 a big clock some-where in the town centre chimes and strikes ten, and at 9.59 (according to its own clock) the church here also chimes and strikes ten, with a stroke every two seconds. Now begins a peal of eight bells ringing changes. This is somewhere in the centre of the town and cannot be heard when traffic is passing. Now from the church opposite comes a deep one-note rung irregularly for about half a minute; this is followed by a bell of higher pitch for forty seconds; then a thirty-second pause: a three-note peal of higher pitch.

Hood's report goes on to describe in great detail every ring of the bell, its pitch, how many times it is repeated and how it is combined with other peals. But what effect did the bells have on the behaviour of passers-by? 'During the next eleven minutes the observer watches twenty-five people passing down the street and can see no perceptible alteration in their walk or behaviour until the bell stops. Then a man about forty, bowler hat, blue suit, limping, stops abruptly, dives into right-hand waistcoat pocket, takes out watch, looks at it, does not look at church clock, replaces watch and limps on past the church entrance. The bell starts again at 10.21. There are five people in sight when this happens ... Bells stop at 10.30. Forty-one people have passed while they were ringing. Observer noted nothing in their behaviour or movements that indicated the effect of the bells on them, except the cases mentioned.'[17]

Not everybody liked the church bells or approved of them, especially if they rang out for too long, as this conversation in the Savoy Supper Bar fish and chip shop between John Sommerfield, the proprietor and a working-class man of about forty, reveals. 'Proprietor complained about noise of bells on Saturday. They had broken a record ringing some blasted peal for seven hours. Nearly broken his head. Other man said, apropos of stopping sales of fish and chips on Sundays, "If they want to stop something on Sundays why don't they stop church bell ringing?"

Very indignant about it. Proprietor said they had rehearsed on Thursday night for three hours. It was shocking. Man muttered something about "wringing their necks instead of bells".[18]

Forever looking to broaden the study, Harrisson's attention turned to popular superstition. Bill Lee, who had been involved with the Blackheath end of Mass-Observation, was told to post observers close to ladders with detailed instructions on what to look for, or to watch for children attempting to avoid stepping on the cracks between the paving stones; 'choose a good crack and stand by it . . . or follow children in turn over a fixed stretch'. Helpful hints followed on how, using dried peas and several pockets, one could simultaneously count both the number of cracks and the number stepped upon. 'If this yields anything,' Harrisson concluded, 'further and more detailed directives can be sent, including one on conversation while crack-stepping.'[19]

Lee was typical of many of the volunteers who came up to Bolton. He described himself as not very political, though he was 'definitely left-wing'. He went up to Bolton more than once, but did not stay for very long on any occasion. He had been in Lancashire briefly before – his father was from Birkenhead. But 'Bolton was like a foreign country to me.' He remembered sitting in public gardens watching people passing by and noting the groupings of people at different times, and studying the ways in which young men picked up girls. But his main work was on the religion survey. He had been brought up as a member of the Church of England, but was agnostic by this time. He visited large numbers of different services of different denominations. 'I was extremely skilful at writing in my pocket.' Occasionally there were suspicious eyes cast. He studied the different postures in which people prayed – standing, sitting, leaning forward, kneeling. To establish the catchment areas of churches, people were followed to their homes. On two or three occasions he posed as a *Bolton Evening News* reporter at such functions as church fetes. Harrisson, he recalled, wanted him to go and lodge with a really rough working-class family and write reports on them. Although he needed the money he turned this down.

The religion survey was carried out against a background of public debate about the morality of war and conflicting political ideologies, and observers' reports make some reference to views expressed from Bolton's pulpits. During a sermon at St Mary's Roman Catholic Church the parish priest, Father Lawless, spoke about the threat of socialist and communist propaganda. Discussing the prospect of war another priest declared, 'I feel sure you are right that we must be done with war. I know that Jesus would have none of it. I am hurt when I think of Spain; I am inclined to think that Franco could do little else, no one could say that Communism would allow the Church to live, that means the children of God would suffer the fetters like Russia. But I know that Fascism and German Hitlerism is probably a greater potential enemy.'

Comments like this reflected the ambivalence of the Churches on the growing international tension. The Spanish Civil War was particularly divisive, with an official Catholic Bishops' Fund for aid to the Nationalists and the Catholic newspaper the *Tablet* giving its support to Franco. Other church groups were equally committed to the Republicans and many expressed disquiet at the rise of Nazism without having the courage to stand up and say so. The Church of England was divided, with the Bishop of Gloucester, who chaired the Church of England Council on Foreign Affairs, incensing many of his fellow bishops with his pro-Nazi pronouncements – praising them for their self-discipline and self-sacrifice. At the other end of the political spectrum the Dean of Canterbury's pro-Soviet rhetoric earned him the nickname 'the Red Dean'.

Of all the religious groups and denominations that Mass-Observation reported on in Bolton, it was the Society of Friends, with its commitment to peace, human rights and social justice, that was probably more in tune with the social and political sensibilities of many of the observers than any of the others. Joe Wilcock got to know many of Bolton's Quakers through their involvement with organisations that he had become closely involved in like the Peace Pledge Union and the Spanish Relief Committee, so he reported on several of their meetings. At one there was a notice on the wall saying 'The Sec is prepared to accept the offerings of the members towards the work of the Society in Spain.' There was also a letter from the Chairman of the hostel at Watermillock thanking them for the help given. On the calendar there was a note in the date space for the three meetings that month of the Peace Pledge Union.

Wilcock found the meeting itself hard going. It started at 11 o'clock with one of the women who was present speaking briefly. 'Then', Wilcock reported,

> there is quiet again till 11.15 when she speaks briefly again about the 23rd Psalm. Not one of the congregation rises or kneels during the whole of the service. During the service, some of them have their eyes closed. Most of the time they sit in silence. And the ticking of the clock is dominant. This can be heard the whole time. To the observer the silence is tortuous.

At 11.28 the woman turns to the man beside her. She is smiling; she puts out her hand and they both smile; they shake hands; the service is over. In a discussion at the end it is suggested that they meet once a week to talk and to pray about the world situation – 'to understand', one man says, 'God's will in this dark International Crisis'. A man suggests they discuss the whole pacifist position. The meeting finished at 11.50. Two members came to observer to shake hands. One of them took his address and promised to write, 'I know what it's for. You are from the survey people, I suppose. I will be glad to get this information to you.'[20]

Just as Walter Hood and Harrisson himself had become well known within Bolton Labour Party circles and were recognised in the groups they were observing, so Wilcock was beginning to be known in church circles. At the end of one Mass at St Mary's, Father Lawless said to him, 'Are you a convert? Oh I see. What parish are you in? Well, I am glad to see you. Come again, will you?' Trying to fit in, trying to become a part of a group, whether church, political or pub, without giving away their true identity was a challenge, and it was to lead some observers into compromising situations.

15

COMPROMISED

'Money. We haven't had nearly enough. Three times we've had our
morning charladies leave because we couldn't pay the butcher's bill'

Tom Harrisson and Charles Madge, Report on First Year's Work

January 1938 was bitterly cold. Brian Barefoot, on vacation from his medical studies at Edinburgh University, came to Bolton to do some more
work on the political survey. But living in Davenport Street at that time
of the year was, he recalled, a lot harder than it had been in the summer.
'There was the ordeal of lighting the fire each morning, working in stuffy
rooms inadequately heated, and going out for short walks merely in order
to get warm.' During this stay, which lasted a fortnight, Barefoot reported
that 'Tom Harrisson was in a bad mood; nothing could be done to his
satisfaction, so that finally I was glad to leave for Edinburgh.' Like so
many other observers, however, Barefoot was prepared to put up with
Harrisson's moods because he thought he was a genius. 'Everything in
him,' he said, 'his unconventionality, his emotional imbalance, the fact
that he's "difficult to live with", the fact that he does not give a damn
for the fame or criticisms of others, the very newness of his idea Mass-
Observation – they all go to prove this . . . It is a curious emotional power
that men of genius have – they don't seem to say things in any different
way, and yet one is compelled to listen and agree.'[1]

'The most perfect living example of disordered "genius", perhaps
starting a new type, that of Bohemian scientist,' was the way Madge
described Harrisson, and he certainly had some bizarre ideas. He would
sometimes fantasise, for example, about setting up museums of sounds,
smells, food and recorded dialect to enable observers to familiarise themselves with the local culture before going into the field, or about a field
wardrobe from which they could borrow the necessary outfit for effective
assimilation. He was, in Spender's view, 'a sort of scatter-brained intellectual. He was a brilliant fellow and he was a genius at getting money
out of people, Tom Barlow, people like that, that he managed to get to

put up a lot of money on the grounds that it would be useful to industry to know what people want.'

No one found it easy to be around such a genius, but it didn't deter them. Julian Trevelyan was one who was enslaved by Harrisson's manner, and he was a frequent visitor to Bolton. He remembers him as 'lean and serious and talking in a dead-pan voice, yet saying extremely funny things. He complained to me that he could not really sleep unless he could feel through the wall the people next door going to bed; could not work unless the radio was turned on full blast. Tom went out for his material to the pubs, to the dogs, to the dance halls. He sent a band of willing workers flying round making reports on anything, from the contents of a chemist's shop window to an account of a service in a spiritualist church. For Tom had an almost hypnotic power over those who worked for him, he would ask the most impossible things of us and we would willingly do them.'[2]

Throughout the winter the volunteer observers continued to flood in. Harrisson always impressed on new arrivals his belief that, as in bird-watching, academic training was not essential to a good Mass-Observer. All they needed, he told them, was the will to do it, an ability to make themselves inconspicuous and a lot of practice. But for most of them winter in Bolton was not a pleasant experience as a Mass-Observation report, *Industrial Spring*, highlighted. 'Of forty-two Southerners who came up to work with us in winter, thirty-nine found Worktown "ugly", "awful", often intolerable.'[3] One of the new recruits was Frank Cawson. He was asked to work with Walter Hood on the 'Politics and the Non-Voter' book, but soon found, like all the other observers, that he was involved in a much wider range of activities and observations. 'It was like a small store,' he recalled, 'and everybody had a hand in everything. I went on pub surveys, religious surveys and so forth. I remember once there was a Unitarian clergyman who was rather a friend of Tom's and he upbraided him for the fact that halfway through the service, two of the congregation got up and went away. He said to Tom, "I bet they're a couple of your chaps." There was one occasion when I was with Spender when he took photographs of people in a pub and he was rounded on by the landlord and he said, "Well, I wasn't doing any harm," and the landlord said, "Well, there might be someone here with someone else's wife. What right have you to be photographing here?"'[4]

Cawson, who felt a great sense of guilt about not being working class, said, 'What I was doing was discovering how working-class people lived – very fascinating. There were what you called the "backs", a sort of alleyway which ran between the back doors of the houses to the road and in which people made love. Most of us were young and unmarried at the time and I remember one chap, another observer, giving me a desperate account of how he was trying to make a girl. It was raining. There was a drip of water in the brim of his hat and he was terribly careful because he had to avoid jerking his hat so that the water might spill down her neck which he thought would have a counterproductive effect.'

For young, single male observers, making it with a local girl was almost part of the job. After all, picking up a local girl for a kiss and cuddle in the back row of the cinema or a 'knee-trembler' in a back alley could be seen as real participant observation. Walter Hood's report on a chance encounter he had with a Bolton girl shows that Mass-Observation work wasn't all hard work and no fun. He passed the girl in Knowsley Street – 'she looked at me hard so I turned back and made her acquaintance . . . She must have walked by slowly because she was only about three yards ahead of me . . . I asked her where she was going in the rain – "Oh! Just taking a stroll," then she suggested we might go to the pictures. She was about twenty, dressed in cloche hat and a brown tweed coat, brown high heel shoes. We went to the Embassy . . . When we went inside she went into back seat . . . (In this picture house the seats at the back are for two.) Naturally I followed. She sat quiet, for ten minutes, then I offered her a cigarette – She took off her hat . . . loosened her coat . . . took off her gloves – and took the cigarette.'

At this point Hood managed to combine a bit of business with pleasure, asking his new friend a few questions about the sort of films she liked, which he would use for a cinema survey that had been started by M-O. The big picture was George Raft as a band conductor. Hood asked his new friend if she liked this picture. Yes. 'But it's not a good part for George Raft – he's a tough guy.' Her favourite film-star, she told him, was John Loder; the best film which she had really enjoyed *The Ghost Goes West*. She didn't like thrillers, but enjoyed films with good singing and something to laugh at – or a good story (love). She knew lots of film stars that Hood had never heard of. They continued to talk about films until a wild-looking man came on the screen and this, Hood explained, 'gave her an opportunity to appear afraid. She got hold of my hand and I put my left arm around her. She slightly lifted her right arm – so I put my hand around her breast. I messed around. During the Raft picture she left go of my hand and started to rub her hand up and down my thigh – I then began to feel the breasts of the girl with my now disengaged hand but she stopped my hand straying too far. We also did some kissing.'

After the show they took a Great Lever bus. It was still raining when they got off just before the terminus. 'She took me to a shop door-way – with a street-lamp shining in,' Hood recalled. 'I tried to persuade her to move along to her home. "No" – she said, "I always stay here with a chap, at least for the first time." She wanted to see me again . . . She was a pretty girl too.'[5]

Whether Hood saw the girl again is not recorded, but it is clear that, for the young men from Davenport Street, Worktown had its attractions. But Cawson recalled, 'We were all very hard up. Sometimes I think Tom Harrisson didn't know where to go for the next penny. We once had a very exciting day when Ernest Simon visited and the great idea was to get some money out of him. Tom said, "Now he's coming this morning. Now when he comes I want everyone to bash their typewriter like crazy, there must be an absolute hive of activity." He came in and was whisked around and I was briefly introduced to him. I think he left £50 because I know we went out and had a meal on it.'

Going out and having a meal on it probably meant fish and chips, which was part of the staple diet not just for Boltonians but also for the Worktown team. Many fish and chip shops had a small café attached. One of them, the Palace on Newport Street, was described by John Sommerfield. He did not observe the front part where the food was handed over the counter but went up four steps into the backroom. It had worn yellow lino, brown-painted woodwork and new patterned wallpaper in browns and yellows. It was a small room with just one table in the centre and two shelf tables built out from the wall. 'Clean white tablecloths with coloured edging', Sommerfield reported. 'Open fire, with kettles and small copper boiler. Everything very clean and plain, characterless. Waitress was woman about 40 wearing clean white overall, slightly starched. Man in white jacket and apron passed backwards and forwards from front shop to door at back with plates. Menu listed: Fish, chips, peas, steak and kidney pie, steak pudding, meat and potato pie, ditto pasty. Single dishes and combinations with chips, peas or chips and peas were priced. Also pork pie (cold only), minerals, Oxo, Ovaltine, malted milk hot or cold. Tea in cups, in pot a penny extra. Tea was made by waitress in aluminium pots from boiler on fire.'

When Sommerfield went in, there was a couple of about forty with two boys at the centre table. They had fish, chips, peas and cups of tea. A youth of about twenty came in and sat at the shelf next to Sommerfield. He ordered steak pie in a confidential voice and subsequently ordered a cup of tea. He ate and drank quickly and left after about ten minutes without saying anything. Sommerfield himself had fish, chips, peas and a cup of tea, price 7d. 'Waitress', he recorded, 'was amiable. Almost inaudible conversation about football going on in back pantry, people at central table took slight interest; wife commented to waitress, "They're always on about it." Soon they left, saying "Goodnight" in a cordial tone.' Sommerfield's general observations on the place were that 'as the room was small, people's avoidance of taking notice of one another was self-conscious, a little strained'. He also noticed that there was a tendency for people to mumble when they ordered 'as if they didn't want to be overheard'.[6]

Sommerfield appears to have had as much of an appetite for fish and chips as he had for beer, and two nights later he was at the Savoy Supper Bar on Churchgate where he got into conversation with the proprietor, who told him that trade was best after ten. 'When they've had their beer they all come here.' He said that they came after the entertainments, and that he got people from the theatre opposite. A working-class man of about forty-five, good blue suit, rather shabby, old cloth cap, came in and ordered a plate of chips. 'Conversation with proprietor and myself about church bell ringing then got on to new act coming into operation on May 1st which would mean fish and chip shops closing on Sundays. Man said, "Bloody rules and regulations." Proprietor said Sunday was his best time in the summer, got people in cars in the evenings. Said he wouldn't mind so much if everyone was stopped from selling fish and chips, but the cafés would go on doing it. They gave you about six chips for threepence and they weren't good as they didn't have the proper facilities for cooking them.'

Soon after Cawson arrived in Bolton there was a parliamentary by-election in the Farnworth constituency. It was the custom for there to be about four or five ward meetings in a single night, and there'd be about four speakers and the candidate himself would speak at each of them. Walter Hood and Cawson went round to all the meetings and crept into the back. 'Obviously,' he said, 'the candidate was very aware that we were there and was rather put out that every time he had to make a speech, the same chaps were there, listening and making notes. What we tried to do was to analyse his speech under two heads, whether it was putting forward a policy or whether it was attacking the policy of the opposition. I remember having a red pencil and a blue pencil. When it was positive I marked it on a time scale in red and when it was negative, I marked it in blue. The interesting thing was that as the night wore on it became more and more negative and less and less time was given to positive objectives. People are more interested in hearing attack than in hearing a straightforward exposition and as the evening wears on, you play to the gallery.'

The causes of non-voting still provided the main focus and observers were particularly concerned about the reliability of canvass returns. So it was a matter of checking what people told the canvasser about their voting intentions against what the total figures were in the election. In order to do this Mass-Observation needed access to the canvass returns of the two main parties. Cawson and Hood discussed their tactics with Harrisson and decided that it would be a good idea if one of them identified completely with the Labour Party and one identified with the Conservative Party. Because Harrisson and Hood were already closely linked with the Labour Party and Cawson was a new face in town it was decided that he would be the one to identify with the Conservatives. 'So', he recalled, 'I went along and joined the Conservative Party and I told them that I was temporarily unemployed and I was interested in helping the cause. So I worked for the Conservative Party Committee in one particular ward and Walter Hood worked for the Labour Party in the same ward. There was one awful circumstance where I thought one good way of getting information would be to chum up with a young girl worker. She was a terribly plain girl and I don't know whether anybody had ever asked her out before and I asked her out and quizzed her about this and that. Then afterwards she discovered and was terribly upset and said, "You only asked me out for what you could get out of me."'

Harrisson and Hood had no difficulty getting the Labour canvass returns. The Labour Party had, in fact, taken them to Davenport Street and the team were able to work on them at leisure. But how were they going to get the Conservative returns? Cawson had the answer. 'I'll pinch them,' he declared. So he found out where they were put and what happened and on one particular night, he said, 'I went in with a mackintosh which had a very big pocket. I went into the Committee Rooms at a time when I knew there was nobody else there and put the returns into the inside pocket and walked out. I brought them back to Davenport Street and about four of us worked all through the night, collating the figures. I did this genuinely out of a belief that I was helping to get a picture of reality.' On the day of the by-election itself Cawson was able to move with ease between the Labour and the Conservative committee rooms. At the Central Conservative Club he found eight women in the room, working. One had a loose-leaf book with an entry for every street and, against these, two columns for the names of the people who did the first canvass and the second canvass. His name was entered for the cards he took out. Then he recalls meeting Hood 'and we changed notes in one of the public lavatories where we were unobserved'.

After the Farnworth by-election Cawson continued to work with Walter Hood. He saw Hood as a key figure in Mass-Observation's Bolton operation. 'I think Tom Harrisson would have been much less ready to quarrel with Walter Hood than anybody else just because he felt it very important to keep the respect and support of him. Walter had a great advantage, it seemed to me, of having very close links or sympathy and support for the Labour Movement.'[7] Cawson often went with Hood to meetings right across the spectrum of left-wing politics. One of these was a communist meeting held at the Co-operative Hall. 'Community singing led by a singer and pianist from 7.20 to 7.40 preceding the speeches', he reported. 'The majority were moving their lips, very few were singing with abandon.' During the singing, a sixty-year-old man turned to Walter Hood and said, 'This is what the Labour Party has lost. It's forgotten how to sing. They're too respectable.'[8]

Throughout this time Cawson was able to keep a foot in both the Labour and Conservative camps, attending in March the inaugural meeting of the Junior Imperial League. A precursor of the Young Conservatives, the Junior Imperial and Constitutional League was intended to encourage practical political work and organisation among young people in Britain. Junior Associations were set up in each parliamentary constituency, co-operating closely with the Conservative and Unionist Associations with the aim of creating imperial unity and furthering the Conservative and Unionist cause. 'By kind permission of the members of the Derby Ward Club,' Cawson reported, 'the meeting was held in the upper room of the club premises free of charge. A hotpot supper was given by Councillor Ratcliffe of Derby Ward and prepared by the Women's Association.'

Cawson arrived shortly before eight o'clock to find some sixty girls and twenty boys present. The room was furnished at one end with long trestle tables covered with cloths. Opposite these in the centre was a table draped with the Union Jack and two posters in red, white and blue. 'JOIN THE IMPS'. It held some literature together with a box of IMP badges. With some coaxing, when the women in charge said the hotpots were getting cold, the young people were persuaded to take their seats. It was remarkable, Cawson observed, 'how the girls sat solidly at the back and the boys to the tables forward'. After the meal there was a break, while the speakers arranged themselves round the table. Dr Taylor took the chair and Miss Farrow, the IMPS national organiser who had travelled up from London for the meeting, made a very competent speech about it being their duty and privilege to take part in government and politics. Cawson was unable to take notes and found it difficult to pay attention, as he was seriously worried about what he could say himself. After the meeting he was told by Miss Farrow that some sixty names had been enrolled for membership, which she thought was good.[9]

Speaking about his time in Bolton, Cawson said one of the feelings he had about working there was that he was under a sort of pressure to get results, to get something which would show as interesting and worthy of writing up. 'It is this sense that you had at the back of your mind that, if I'm going to earn my keep or if this is going to continue, we've got to find interesting things.' One idea he had was 'that we get kids to write and to draw a picture of what they thought a rich man looked like and a poor man looked like. We had various teachers around, who were teaching in primary schools, and they got their classes to do this. And they were very interesting. The rich men all had top hats on, which were obviously stereotypes.' Another thing Cawson said was, 'Why don't I walk in the streets round Davenport Street every fifteen minutes through the day and compare what's happened from time to time, what people are doing, whether they're single or in groups. I was very interested in what groups people were in; whether it was a man–woman group or two-men group or two-women group, or whether they were large groups. I remember walking round and doing this all day. It was a pretty stressful day because I was on my feet most of the time. Two things emerged – the extent to which people went shopping before the meal, that is to say half an hour before dinnertime or teatime they'd be out on the streets buying a loaf or some fish paste, and the constant going to the corner shop for milk.'[10]

As Cawson walked round the streets of Bolton militarism was increasing across Europe and the threat of war was growing greater. From the beginning of his career in politics Hitler had stated that he would attempt a union of the country of his birth, Austria, with Germany, by any means possible and by force if necessary. By early 1938 he had consolidated his power in Germany and was ready to implement this long-held plan. At the end of February Herbert Morrison addressed the Bolton Labour Party. Morrison was a leading light in the Labour Party who had challenged Attlee for the leadership. 'This has been an exciting week,' he proclaimed, 'an exciting fortnight in politics and foreign affairs . . . First Austria is told by Hitler that he wanted a particular man or men to enter the Government . . . We said that it must be a shocking humiliation even for a little nation like Austria to have its government settled for it. Thank goodness we Britons, Sons of the Bulldog Breed, Sons of John Bull, had our Government . . . What a pity Austria is in such a situation.'[11]

In February the Foreign Secretary, Anthony Eden, resigned over the differences between him and Chamberlain 'in respect of the international problems of the day and as to the methods we seek to resolve them'. Eden's popularity made his resignation a sensational story, reaching through to sections of the population not usually touched by politics. This was apparent when, of people all over the country asked by M-O if they were following the news, 82 per cent said they were. The Eden crisis was also surveyed in Bolton. On 21 February when his resignation was announced in headlines everywhere, people questioned were unanimous in saying they had followed the news, but only one in fifteen believed all that was in the papers. Analysis of 15,000 conversations recorded in Bolton established that on an ordinary day only 0.3 per cent of the conversations were about politics; but on 21 February this rose to 4 per cent, a tribute not just to Eden's popularity but to a growing sense of crisis.[12]

In Austria the Nazis enjoyed a lot of popular support, and on 11 March Hitler sent an ultimatum to Chancellor Kurt Schuschnigg demanding that he hand over all power to the Austrian Nazis or face an invasion. Schuschnigg, realising that neither France nor Britain would actively support him, resigned in favour of his pro-Nazi Interior Minister Arthur Seyss-Inquart. On 12 March the German army crossed the Austrian border and Austria became the German province of Ostmark. Two days later an attempt was made to find out what the people of Worktown thought of the situation. The survey comprised two lines of approach: first to overhear what people were talking about in the streets and the pubs; and second to stimulate thought on the subject by asking questions of strangers. The Austrian situation formed just 4 per cent of the total conversation observed on that day. These casual references included a wide variety of opinion. In two cases the news was approved of; in six cases it was considered bad; in the remaining four no opinion was given. A man in a pub gave a long garden-story analogy to show that Austria was a small country belonging by rights to Germany. Another man was of the opinion that 'this country and Germany are sister and brother'. The barmaid said her father was saying yesterday there would be a war very soon and making her shake with alarm. On the main street a man said, 'This government wants to do something. Hitler's a bugger.' When questioned about the likelihood of war many were very aware of the situation, foretelling what would be decisive: 'Will in the end. He'll go for Czechoslovakia next . . . then we'll get involved.' The great majority of those questioned answered readily and at length. They had both opinions and knowledge.[13]

The general impression obtained from the survey was that most people understood the situation and that they all had some idea of what war meant.[14] The very real possibility that Britain would need to respond to German aggression some time in the future was now beginning to be debated not just among politicians, intellectuals and people in the media, but among a much wider general public. Not all of the debate, however, was at a very high level, and the following month Cawson reported, 'When the Austrian *Anschluss** happened, I went out asking people what they thought about it. I went outside the gates of a cotton mill asking the question "What do you think about the Austrian *Anschluss?*" One chap came out and looked me in the face and said "Fucking 'orrible, mate. Fucking 'orrible."' When another observer asked a barmaid the same question all she had to say was "Oh, I'm not fussy."'

To get all this material Harrisson needed a constant flow of volunteers, so Davenport Street was as overcrowded as ever and recruits were kept ceaselessly busy. 'All observers will record conversations in public lavatories at 5.30' was the sort of edict he would issue. So Bolton's public lavatories would be full of young men snooping around, notebook in hand, listening in to conversations. Harrisson was something of a control-freak and Woodrow Wyatt, fresh out of Oxford, remembered what it was like working with him: 'He had an abundant energy which he combined with great rudeness and an evident lack of fear for anyone . . . he had great effrontery and never minded tackling anyone, however eminent, for funds or support. Tom's method of work was novel to me. He would rarely shave but would plunge out of bed unwashed into the front room and begin to write emphatic letters and articles. In his letters everything was said at a shout, and he was nearly always rude to and about other people.'[15]

With such a forceful, uncompromising character heading the operation there were bound to be clashes of ego, especially when an observer arrived who was his match. One such was Dick Crossman. Although he was now married to the ambitious Zita, who was doing all she could to launch him on a political career, it didn't deter him from coming up to Bolton to share a house with his wife's ex-lover. Crossman was one of those men who had a finger in every pie – budding poet, journalist, politician

* Germany's annexation of Austria. March 1938

– a larger-than-life character who enjoyed living life to the full. That he enjoyed confrontation and argument and had a taste for adventure inevitably meant that his relationship with Harrisson would be combustible. 'Harrisson', Frank Cawson remembered, 'was extremely jealous of Crossman. It was a very interesting relationship. The one person who seems to have been as overbearing and impossible in personal relationships as Harrisson was Dick Crossman. Talk about two bears in a den. The notion of these two in a room together is astonishing.'[16]

Observation without being observed was still the staple of the work in Bolton, particularly infiltration of groups as participant observers. There was an uncomfortable element of spying in all this and all sorts of accusations were still being made in the national press about a whole lot of spies being active. But a great deal of Worktown evidence was gathered in this way, from Penelope Barlow's participant observation in the cotton mill to Frank Cawson's infiltration of the local Conservative Party. Some took it a stage further, forming friendships with the people they were observing. One of these was Barbara Phillipson, who was instructed by Harrisson to try to infiltrate the Mazdaznan sect and find out as much as she could about them. Joe Wilcock, she said, provided her with a contact. 'He knew someone called Mrs Farrimond and she had taken to this new religion, so he said that Mrs Farrimond would be able to introduce me to it. He took me round to tea with her and she took me to a service. You had to massage the back of your head while singing one of their little songs. I was jolly good at it and they liked me and so they asked me to tea again and I felt the most dreadful fake. Dear little Mrs Farrimond explained how she had tried all the religious sects and she had never found one that quite suited her. This one was just right and she had given her whole heart and soul to it.'

Barbara Phillipson was one of the few observers from the South of England who appeared to like Bolton. She found the people 'were very kind, they're very hospitable and they make you awfully welcome and always call you "love" – "Ee love, you feeling sickly?" when I was feeling sickly. "Come in and lie down." They really were terribly nice people. Awfully friendly. Sort of warm. Big hearted. Everybody was very devout and everybody went to church or chapel or some place on Sundays and the trams didn't start running till one o'clock. It was much more like Victorian England than London which was very sophisticated and godless and gay.' A similar view was expressed by another observer who commented that, had it not been for the vehicles, it looked for the entire world like the murky back streets of Dickensian London. There was certainly a feeling among a lot of the observers that Bolton hadn't moved with the times, but Phillipson said she thought this was lovely.[17] One of the reasons for this may have been that she got to know the Farrimond family very well and came to regard them as friends.

The services in Bolton were all in the evening. Before them Phillipson would always go to the Farrimonds for tea. On one particular occasion she reported that she arrived at 6.10 p.m. and was shown into the kitchen at the back, where tea was ready. Items eaten in order were a slice of herb and nut cake made by the hostess, a dish of green salad, a trifle, bread and butter and a plate of cakes, followed by a pot of tea. Phillipson was pleased to have salad. It was, she told Mrs Farrimond, the first time she'd had it since coming to Bolton. But she wondered, in view of the strict diet they had to observe, whether her Mazdaznan friends used to get very hungry. They were all vegetarians to start with and in Lent they had to cleanse their system. They had to give up all dairy food – no milk, no butter, no eggs. Just salad and unleavened bread that was rather like Ryvita crispbread. They lived on this for six weeks, and Phillipson asked: '"Don't you get awfully thin and weak? I couldn't imagine myself living on that." Her son was a great hefty lad who worked on the railway and she said, "Oh! He lives on it and he's strong enough," and I thought I wonder if he does or if he goes and has a steak and kidney pudding on the side sometimes when she's not looking. I couldn't believe anyone could work on lettuce and matzo bread.'

But this closeness not just to the Farrimonds but to the whole Maz-daznan group they were part of put Phillipson in some tricky situations as she tried to maintain the subterfuge. After one meeting, they waited about, as if loath to say goodnight, and Mrs Farrimond asked her which way she was going back. Phillipson was still trying to hide from them the fact that she was a member of the Mass-Observation team and the previous week she had taken the tram to Davenport Street with the story that she was staying with friends in Powell Street. This time she said vaguely she thought a 10 bus would do for her. 'Why, where do ee want to get to then?' a small thin man asked. 'St George's Road,' Phillipson replied cautiously. Others joined in the conversation. 'Ee, a noomber 10 boos won't du. Yer want ter tek an N tram, or an O tram,' one old lady said. It seemed that, unfortunately, the small thin man lived that way himself, and would show her how to get home. Goodbyes were said and the man escorted Phillipson to the tram stop, remarking that either an O or an N tram would do for him. As only the former was at all good for the observer she sincerely hoped that it would come first. It did and she boarded the tram with some relief. Conversation on the journey was about Mazdaznan most of the way. The small man thought it was a very wonderful thing, because it told you how to live all of the time, and most religions did not bother with your health. It was so practical. Conversation was also about Mrs Farrimond. 'One of the nicest ladies he had ever met.'

At the Crofters pub, the man stood up to get off. Phillipson said she thought the next stop was hers. To her horror, he sat down again and said it would do for him, too. So they got off at the next stop. He then asked where she lived. She was terrified, thinking that the game would be up, but she said Bertrand Road. Oh, yes, he knew it well. He lived just along on the other side. She ought to have gone on several stops further. Observer said feebly, how stupid of her, but then, she wasn't used to Bolton, and always lost her way. As they walked along the road the man said he had to get his supper. He lived all alone since his mother passed away two years ago. When he got opposite his house, he said that he would just run in and put his bag away and then would walk home with Phillipson. She protested that he would be taken too much out of his way, and would be late for his supper. But he insisted. On the way he told her about how he lived and did for himself, and how he loved cooking and washing up, and did not have a housekeeper, because he really loved to do housework. He worked in the town, and got up and did all his housework before he went; he could not bear a mess. It was raining quite heavily now, but he said he liked to feel the rain in his face. To her relief he asked no questions about what she was doing in Bolton, but was interested to hear she came from London. He said he knew all about London; they lived in restaurants, and never did any housework. When they reached the end of Bertrand Road, Phillipson was afraid that he would want to come all the way to the fictitious house with her. But though he lingered, talking for about ten minutes, he did not come any nearer to the house, so at last she was able to say goodbye, safely.[18]

Barbara Phillipson's cover had almost been blown, but she got away with it and her new friends did not find out, or even suspect, that they had a Mass-Observation 'spy' in their midst. But infiltration of groups like this was not easy, and some of the smaller, more obscure sects were always suspicious when a stranger appeared, as she found out when she attended a service at Hebron Hall. When she went in a man in a blue serge suit, waiting just inside the door, shook her hand. Phillipson whispered, 'I'm on a visit to Bolton. May I come in?'

The man replied, 'Do you go to meetin' where ye coom from?'

Phillipson said she did and the man asked, 'Where do ye coom from?'
'London,' she said.

But the man continued to quiz her: 'Which meetin' do ye go to?'

'Well, I come from North London,' she answered.

'Who's the brethren at your meetin'?'

'Well, it's not quite the same as this,' Phillipson said somewhat defensively.

'No, it'll be alright; come in,' the man said.[19]

Phillipson explained how she tried to fit in and make herself inconspicuous at meetings and services. 'I used to get a hymn book or a prayer book from the place of worship and put a piece of paper inside and be sort of looking at it in my lap and all the time I was taking notes about how many people were there, how many men, how many women, and the order of the service and what they sang. I did it rather well because having been brought up to go to church twice a Sunday, since I could toddle, I could recognise the hymns and I didn't have to write them out. I just put the first line and then I knew what the hymn was, or Moody and Sankey* and that kind of thing. Sort of shorthand references, which the heathen comrades were all unable to do because they had never been to church in their life.'[20]

As the reports piled up in Bolton, Madge continued to oversee the Mass-Observation operation in Blackheath. By this time he was describing the disastrous *May 12* book as representing a stage that Mass-Observation had now left behind. Right from the start the relationship between Harrisson's anthropological approach and the more 'poetic' approach espoused by Madge and Jennings had been antagonistic. Now, although M-O continued to be involved in the nationwide surveys, the Worktown project had become the main focus for the organisation. This didn't suit Humphrey Jennings, who quit early in 1938, leaving the movement to be run by Madge and Harrisson. Madge explained in his autobiography that 'This was to some extent because he [Jennings] was absorbed in his own painting, photography and documentary film-making, but more, I think, because he was out of sympathy with the direction taken by Mass-Observation as a result of Tom's own initiatives or those which I took in an attempt to adapt my own initial approach to that of Tom.'[21]

When Jennings left he returned to the GPO Film Unit, where they continued to make documentaries celebrating the skills of the working

---

* Nineteenth-century evangelists who wrote and published books of hymns.

man. The 'creative treatments of actuality' that the unit specialised in included a number about the GPO, the most famous of which was *Night Mail*. To a score by Benjamin Britten and verse by W. H. Auden, the film followed the progress of a letter posted in London to its arrival in Glasgow the next morning. Jennings was returning to the unit in order to make 'a surrealist vision of industrial England'. The film's working title was *British Workers*, but after filming scenes in Bolton, Manchester, Sheffield and Pontypridd – men drinking in a pub, playing billiards, releasing pigeons and walking dogs, a ballroom slowly filling with dancers and a kazoo band playing 'If You Knew Susie' – he changed the title to *Spare Time*.[22] It is a Mass-Observation film in its method of looking, observation and poetic nature. It reveals the beginnings of Humphrey Jennings's style as a film-maker. Jennings also began to collect descriptions, in poetry and prose, of machines and the changes they had wrought in human life throughout history. He called the descriptions 'Images', and, as he assembled them, he came to believe that they could be read as 'a continuous narrative or film on the Industrial Revolution', much as he had meant *May 12* to be read as a film of the Coronation. He carried the clippings, which eventually filled twelve notebooks, in a weather-beaten suitcase. When a surrealist friend asked what was inside, Jennings answered, 'Pandemonium.' It provided the material that was later built into *Pandaemonium*, the book that, more than seventy years later, became the biggest single inspiration for Danny Boyle's Olympic Games Opening Ceremony.

The artistic side of Mass-Observation didn't come to an end with Jennings's departure. Early in 1938 Harrisson was discussing with Julian Trevelyan plans for an exhibition to coincide with the anticipated publication of *The Pub and the People*. Alongside photos and paintings they would have reconstructions of a bit of a pub, part of a street, the graffiti on one lavatory wall and a mock-up of a mantelpiece. There would be Bolton smells, 'fish and chips frying continuously and soot falling constantly. Typical meals would be served to the visitors.'[23] The book itself would be very different to *May 12*, which Harrisson disliked so intensely. Harrisson remarked that 'Madge and myself now work on a common programme and are no longer concerned with literature – he got rid of that in the Coronation book.' In spite of this it helped that the principal writer of the *The Pub and the People*, John Sommerfield, was a novelist with an eye for character and an ear for dialogue.

Frank Cawson recognised this. 'I thought John Sommerfield was a fantastic character,' he said. 'I was twenty-two, I'd done a degree in English, and here was not only a writer working in the place, but here was a writer in the new wave of proletarian writing. He had an aura of toughness about him, heavily built and slightly rugged with a rugged method of speaking.' Harrisson was different and Cawson had some reservations about him: 'You couldn't really talk to Tom Harrisson, not very well. I found him an engaging, remarkable sort of charisma, but he was explosive, irascible and not in any way a good manager of people. He was wonderful at firing people with his ideas and enthusiasm. He could take an idea, and out of nothing build it up to something rather exciting. He would fantasticate it and embroider it and put dynamism into it, but he couldn't discuss things. When Charles Madge came up – Charles Madge sat me down and we talked. This was when I'd expressed some reservations I had about the whole set-up.'[24]

But Madge didn't come up to Bolton very often. There was too much to be done in Blackheath. By the end of the first year the day-reports amounted to 2.3 million words. There were now about 600 observers, three-quarters of them recruited via the *New Statesman*. The panel was overwhelmingly middle class – teachers, scientists, businessmen, clerks and shopkeepers. No more than 10 per cent were in working-class oc-cupations. The sheer volume of material they produced was growing at an alarming rate, and all of it needed to be processed. For a small under-funded organisation this was proving to be difficult. It is unlikely that Madge had the resources to employ anyone on a full-time basis. Much of the work was done by himself and Kathleen Raine, aided by a fluctuating body of volunteers drawn mainly from observers resident in London.[25]

In the report on their first year's work, Harrisson and Madge wrote, 'Money. We haven't had nearly enough. Three times we've had our morning charladies leave because we couldn't pay the butcher's bill.' This constant shortage of money led to Harrisson compromising Mass-Observation's independence in a way that justified some of the reservations Cawson had always held about the set-up. A few weeks after the Farnworth by-election, where he'd employed such subterfuge to obtain the Conservative canvass results, Cawson was horrified to learn that Humphrey Jennings, who had remained in contact with Harrisson and Madge despite his split with the organisation, had sold the pirated canvass returns to his contacts at Transport House Research Depart-ment. Cawson said he realised this put him in a bad situation, but 'I never challenged him on this. I think I made some sort of noises when I heard about this, but I never said anything. It wasn't easy to do. Tom

Harrisson was a very forceful character – maybe I didn't have the guts; maybe I thought it would be unnecessary; maybe I just thought I would go quiet and I did, in fact, from that moment, apply for jobs. I worked full time in Bolton for four months then I left and took a job at Beverley Grammar School in the summer term of '38.'[26]

16

A NIGHT ON THE TOWN

*'To them the dance is temporary freedom from hard work and
worries – Let's enjoy ourselves today for tomorrow . . .'*

Observer Report

On a cold and foggy Sunday evening towards the end of winter the
sound of a brass band could be heard coming up Bradshawgate in the
town centre from the direction of Deansgate. It was the Salvation
Army. As they marched down the road, Frank Cawson stood watching
the parade go by. Right at the front was the Sergeant Major in a long
dark-blue coat and army officer's hat. Next came the flag-bearers. On
the flags were the name of the corps and the symbol of the Salvation
Army. Round it the words 'Blood and Fire'. Next came the band, five
rows of them followed by women carrying tambourines. Most of them
were wearing long dark-blue uniform coats, a bonnet with a net front
and on the red tape round the front the words 'Salvation Army' in
yellow letters. People on Bradshawgate, most with smiles on their faces,
stopped and watched as the band went past them playing marching
tunes. When the band got to the corner of Bradshawgate and Great
Moor Street they stopped playing at the traffic lights, but once on the
move they started playing again for the last forty yards to the Hall.
Here they stopped, took off their hats, placed them on their chests and
prayed for ten seconds with their heads bowed before walking into the
Hall.[1]

Later Cawson, still out on Bradshawgate, noted that there was much
standing in shop fronts of unisex groups, principally male, who were
interested mainly in passers-by of the opposite sex. But, he reported,
there was a scarcity of pick-ups. Only two cases of attempted pick-up
were observed. There was saluting of and talking with acquaintances.
Some girls were parading for two hours. The girl couple appeared to be
the most common grouping. There was a great deal of talking, continuously, among the girl friends, who linked arms and who were busied to

such an extent as not to notice the eye of the observer. The pick-up was not observed between complete strangers, but between acquaintances, semi-acquaintances and friends of acquaintances.

> 10.25 At Nelson Square two girls are talking to a man. The girls I have seen before three times in the course of the evening. And also last night. On both occasions they returned my glance. There is one girl in a green coat, with a face lacking in proportion and clarity of complexion. The other, maroon coat, straggling hair, bold bright carriage, gap toothed, large eyes, 'a lusty wench'. These two were talking to a man. The green one wanted to pull the other away but she stayed. After a couple of minutes they parted, the man going in an out-of-town direction and raising his hat and saying 'Goodnight' . . . The observer had the impression that the maroon-coated one was unusually well known and attractive. After going up Deansgate for ten yards they turned round somewhat abruptly and made a similar return. They met three men, who appeared to be well known to them. After some talking one man disappeared and they continued down Great Moor Street as a four. The girl in green had some time ago spotted the observer and frequently looked behind and spoke to the other [girl] who took no notice. On one occasion the one in green said, 'He's still following,' after which observer removed his hat, tried to camouflage his mackintosh and crossed quickly to the other side of the road. A few minutes later the maroon one looked round again, directly behind her, failed to notice observer. They then split up into two twos and linked arms. They went down a side street, passed through to the bus station and went upstairs on a 17 bus to Daubhill.[2]

Another observer reported on a group of five girls of eighteen to twenty smoking and laughing on a corner. On this occasion the pick-up is much more direct. 'Three young men of eighteen to twenty come out of the pub and talk to the girls; they begin to kiss them to the screams of the girls – laughing screams. One of the youths gets hold of the girl and bends her right back, making him bend over her; all the time kissing her; when finished he says: "God she's bloody hot." Girl: "You're not so bloody cold yourself." The young men go inside and bring out two bottles wrapped in light-brown tissue paper; they give these to the girls. They bring out two more young men, one of whom says: "Which is her?" They all ten go off down the alley.'[3]

The pick-up was a prime subject for observations, and nowhere was better for seeing it than the dance hall. Dance halls provided a space in which young men and women were freed from parental supervision, and there was little doubt that in the eyes of observers the dance hall was saturated in sexual significance. 'Plenty of sex in the air tonight,' one observer reported. 'Observer would estimate about a third were here to pick up or be picked.' Sex was found in a complex array of cultural signifiers – verbal, physical and facial expressions, clothing, make-up, dance steps, music tempo, atmosphere and even song lyrics. The word 'sex' referred to a wide range of interactions perceived as indicative of sexual intent, such as close-up dancing, hand-holding, hugging, flirting, petting, kissing and the phenomenon of 'picking up'.[4] In one report of a dance at the Spinners' Hall the observer devotes three and a half pages, entitled 'Necking', to the description of one female patron's apparently indiscriminate kissing encounters with various males and makes continual reference to the fascination of onlookers.

A dance-hall manager said: '"The point is where can the young people meet unless they get to the places where they can dance . . . I used to be a solo singer and my wife was a Methodist. I used to meet lots of the young folks who went to the Methodists and used to come here. I can't stand the people who say the dance halls are the places where they go wrong. They are no better and no worse than the youngsters who go to church. The galleries there are filled with young people who go because they are interested in the opposite sex, then they take the others for a walk, just like they do here. We aren't to blame for what happens after." One reason for the popularity of dancing here is that most of them do not have very bright lives and here is brighter than the homes they come from.' 'All present are working-class people,' one observer wrote, 'nearly all are workers in the mills and factories. To them the dance is temporary freedom from hard work and worries – Let's enjoy ourselves today for tomorrow . . .'

The whole atmosphere of the ballroom – sensuous and relaxing – contrasts with the greyness of Worktown, and the explanation that the dancers use the hall as an escape from their drab existence is a convincing one. A Mass-Observation report on the Worktown Dance Hall explains how the management cater accordingly: 'The public like subdued lighting. Not that this is a spooning ground. There isn't much of that. Our lights are on the dim side. We keep changing them. They like the latest of everything, so we put in tubular lights on the wall and lights in the ceiling – there used to be chandeliers before. They are very keen on everything such as the floor. The floor went off last June. We shut one night and with forty-eight hours' work we had a new maple floor in place of the old oak one. If the floor is getting too slippery or too fast they soon let you know about it.'

Observers were on a mission to hunt out romantic and sexual interactions. In the lounge at the Palais de Danse Walter Hood overheard the declaration 'I have been on the beer. Now I want to be on the women.' But it wasn't just in the dance halls with their subdued lighting. At a St Patrick's Eve Dance one observer gave a clear impression of the uncontrolled sexuality of the atmosphere. A woman grabbed hold of him and moved on to the dance floor, immediately enquiring if he was married prior to any other conversation. In close succession, the observer noted a priest 'jovially clap a young woman on the arse', several young couples 'necking at the bar' and a young woman assisting her mother into a taxi as her mother resisted and kissed two forty-year-old women. And all that was at a church dance.

Walter Hood did a lot of the dance-hall reports. During the interval of a dance in the Co-op Hall he went out for a drink. Two men he'd seen at the dance were in the pub. Sitting on the other side of the bar were two girls who had also been at the dance. The barman went up to the two girls and said, 'The chaps across there want to know what you are going to have.' One of the girls immediately said, 'Two ports' – although they both had three-quarters of a glass of beer beside them. The chaps did not even smile or show any sign at all of recognition, but talked together and laughed. The girls drank the port – neither side acknowledging the other – but when the girls moved out one of them said, 'Thanks,' with a smile. Hood noticed later in the evening that the two were paired up with the boys, but did not take them home.[5] More often than not the observers didn't find the romantic and sexual interactions they were looking for, as Brian Barefoot noted when he went to the 'Harlem Night' at the Aspin Hall. 'At least ten pairs of girls danced with each other the whole time, scarcely waiting at the beginning of the dance for a man to pick them up. One of these girls said to observer, "I'm a man-hater . . . I come here for the dancing, not to meet men," and this represents what observer felt about the whole affair – that all the chaps and girls were here because they enjoyed dancing for its own sake, and did not use the dance as an avenue in the process of getting off with one another.'[6]

In some places observers stepped into the action and became part of their own reports, indulging their own sexual desires. Walter Hood went to a dance at Bright Street Labour Club. It was late when he got there and he noted that it was 'a dirty dingy place' with 'a very poor type there', but this was not going to hold him back. He noticed two girls drinking beer, they 'took the bottle and had a swig' – not very refined. It was the last waltz and he danced with 'a poor type of girl dressed in black. I did no arranging to get any young girl home – so Jack Brough, an unemployed young fellow, went up to three girls, put his arms around two of them and arranged the whole thing.' One of the girls asked if Hood was a decent fellow, to which Jack Brough replied, 'Yes. I'll vouch for that.' Hood went off with Brough and two of the girls. 'We walked to the street where the girl lived (behind the station),' Hood disclosed. 'We stopped against a back lane. I made as if to walk down. She stopped two doors down and stood close to me (asking to be petted) – I kissed her – then she said, "Ee! It's late. I'll have to go home."'

On occasions like this an observer would have to walk back to Davenport Street, often from the other side of town, because they'd missed the last bus. Walking down Manchester Road, all would be still and quiet. Looking down one of the alleyways running off the road they would see the signal box on the main railway line from Manchester. On a moonlit night they would hear the whistle sound in the distance as a steam locomotive approached. Standing to watch they would see it bash across the end of the alleyway with its fire-hole door open. There would be a big shaft of fire in the sky and they would just be able to make out the driver and fireman crouched in position on the footplate. The carriages would rattle across the end of the alleyway and with another screech of its whistle as it hurtled through Trinity Street station it would be on its way into the night. Getting closer to Davenport Street another observer 'walked through a number of back streets but found them nearly empty; a few occasional pedestrians (chiefly male and chiefly alone); a few mixed groups at corners where the street lamp was lit. No couples embracing were seen. Lovers seemed to choose the semi-lit streets and shop doorways and other openings off the main thoroughfares.'[7]

It wasn't just dancing that gave the observers late nights out. Along with the dance hall, the cinema was of particular interest to Harrisson. The 1930s was a great decade of cinema-going. Between 600 and 750 new films were released annually in Britain between 1930 and 1939 and streamlined art deco dream palaces were built in towns and cities throughout the country. The number of cinemas multiplied to cater for an ever expanding audience, and by 1939 an average of nearly twenty million cinema tickets were being sold every week. Bolton was part of this boom. During Mass-Observation's first year there two new cinemas opened. The Odeon on Ashburner Street was the first. Seating over 2,500 people, at prices ranging from 6d to 1/6d, it had a weekly change of programme, continuous shows from Monday to Friday and three separate houses on Saturday. The staff of forty-one included pageboys, chocolate girls, usherettes, doormen and a resident organist. Harrisson was there for the grand opening. 'At 7.15,' he reported ,'scarlet bandsmen on top of steps of the new cinema. Playing vigorously and fair crowd with queue of fifty yards for shilling seats. Officers in green, cinema officials, one in green with three stripes. One cries, "All 'ave your tickets ready please." The scarlet bandsmen fanfare and then turn sharply in line and march into the cinema in file. The queue files through the cinemas left-hand door. It enters, gold paint, flowers, air of luxury. "Doesn't it look lovely when it's new," a woman says . . . Good organisation inside, usherettes and a man in evening dress shows observer to seat. At 7.30 the downstairs is half full. People look around a fair amount at the luxurious interior.'

With so much interest in the cinema it is no wonder that Harrisson declared, 'We were film-minded,' and in early 1938 he set up a grandly titled Cinema Research Unit, which seems to have consisted of a single researcher, John Martin Jones. He was a documentary film-maker and photographer who, in addition to his cinema research, took photographs of churches in Bolton. According to Harrisson he was a fascist.[8] How he got on with the predominantly left-wing, anti-fascist residents of Daven-port Street is not recorded, but it must have led to some interesting, if not heated, debate around the kitchen table. Harrisson produced an outline of the proposed research and Mass-Observation devised a competition, seeking information from the patrons of three Bolton cinemas on their cinema-going habits. A total of 559 replies were received, giving a unique insight into the cinema-going preferences of a single town in 1938. The three were chosen to represent three different types of cinema. The Odeon was top of the range. The Crompton, opened, like the Odeon, in 1937, was a middle-range cinema with seating for 1,200 at prices ranging from 3d to 1/3d. It had twice-weekly programme changes and continu-ous evening performances. The third cinema, the Palladium, was more down-market, indeed it was a local 'fleapit'. Opened on Christmas Day 1919, it had shown Bolton's first talkie in 1929, but since then it had gone down in the world. It had seating capacity for 1,238, at prices ranging from 4d to a shilling, twice-weekly programme changes, afternoon mat-inees and continuous evening performances.

Reasons for going to the cinema given by people who entered the competition were all variations of entertainment, amusement, relaxa-tion, to be taken out of themselves, to escape the cares of the world and everyday life. Some also mentioned that they valued films as a source of education, inspiration and knowledge. One of the things that came out very strongly was that people preferred American to British films because they were much slicker, more polished, fast-moving and often spectacular. Interviewed by Jones, Mr Hull, the manager of the Embassy Cinema, disclosed that he'd spoken to several of his patrons, all working class, and they didn't think they'd been anywhere if they hadn't been to the cinema twice a week. 'Business is better this year than last,' he went on.

If business is bad, the cinema is bad. You take any dispute concerning working people, in any mill or foundry in Bolton. During that dispute your evening takings drop, but your afternoon goes up. It proves that however hard up they are they still want the cinema, so they take the cheaper seats in the afternoon. Week in week out I get 6,000 people who come here regularly twice a week. They won't only go once, but two or even three times to a good musical. Musical pictures in Lancashire go the best of any . . . Another thing they like is old melodrama, especially in the cheap seats . . . They don't want hidden humour. They're working all day, and they come up here at night all dressed up like dandies. They think they're on top of the Earth, you've got to make them think that they are. If there's anything crude they like it. Think it's a smasher.

Broadening out the research, observers found that in Bolton, which they described as 'a mecca for the film fanatic', there were 'forty-seven cinemas of varying size, quality and character' within a five-mile radius of the centre of town. The average price to go to see a film was sixpence. Like the dance hall, the cinema provided a short escape from the drudgery of everyday life and, not surprisingly, the most popular films for men as well as women were musical romances, closely followed by 'drama and tragedy'. Women liked historical films whereas men went for crime. Cowboy films were also popular, particularly with the fleapits' male patrons. The observers found that most of the films people went to see were not British. Denis McDermott, a fourteen-year-old who went to the cinema in Bolton at least six times a month, said, 'American films are . . . 100 per cent better than British ones. They are far superior to British on every point: action, direction, humour, yes everything!'[9]

There were, however, some notable exceptions. In Bolton's cinemas film-goers would often see the stars they had previously watched in the music halls. The greatest Lancashire stars were George Formby and Gracie Fields. 'Our Gracie', as she was known to everyone, starred in a number of Northern working-class films. Not particularly young or beautiful when she made her screen debut, it was her personality, her singing voice, her comic timing and above all her naturalness and ordinariness that made her popular. The comedian Formby, with his ukulele and his mix of child-like innocence and smutty double-entendre in songs like 'My Little Stick of Blackpool Rock' and 'When I'm Cleaning Windows', which was banned by the BBC, was signed up by Ealing Studios for popular working-class-hero roles. But the appeal of both went way beyond Lancashire. They were national stars, appealing to working-class audiences across the country. Formby was the top British male star at the cinema box office from 1937 to 1943 and Fields was the top female star from 1936 to 1940. Their immense popularity stemmed in large part from the qualities they shared that were at a premium during the years of Depression and looming war – optimism, cheerfulness and indomitability.

Entertainment was the mainstay of the cinema but, if the commercial cinema did not appeal, there was a whole alternative radical film culture, and in February the New Royal turned to more serious matters. *Spanish Earth* was previewed in the *Bolton Citizen* as 'the best film not only this week, but this month. Grim, beautiful, and at times tragic, it is always gripping in its intensity. This is the finest film I have seen for years. It shows the Spanish people in their struggle for freedom against the Fascist invaders. Throughout the comments of Ernest Hemingway are vivid and interesting, and the whole production is a masterpiece, and should certainly not be missed.' The *Bolton Citizen*, it should be noted, was published by the Bolton Labour Party and left-wing opinion was very anti-Franco and pro-Republican.

During the week the film was showing at the New Royal, collections were held outside the cinema for the Basque children at Watermillock and for Spanish Medical Aid. Frank Cawson attended the first house on one of the nights. Arriving at the cinema he found two women standing outside with collecting tins. One of them said they had not been doing very well. She had been outside for four hours on the last two nights and it had been very cold indeed. When Cawson went into the cinema, it was less than a quarter full. At the start of the film one of the first comments he heard was 'Is this news?' Evidence suggests that this type of film only attracted the already committed rather than the mass audience, and this was very much the case here. The film was not well supported and the collection raised only 34s 0½d.[10] In a Mass-Observation interview the cinema manager admitted that 'business had been notably bad'. He wanted to have handbills all over town, but at the last moment the owner stopped this. Things were not helped by a lack of dialogue between the two organisations that the money was being raised for. Harrisson, who conducted the interview, noted the reason for this was that Mr Freeman of the Watermillock House Committee and Mrs Lockwood of Spanish Medical Aid were at loggerheads. 'Mrs Lockwood', he explained, 'was compelled to resign from the Watermillock committee, on to which she forced herself, because of her communist political activities among the kids. Spanish Medical Aid and Spanish Relief have constantly been nearly at war in the town, and there is apparently no satisfactory liaison between them.'[11]

In Spain itself the real war had entered its last full year, with the Nationalist forces of General Franco making sweeping gains. The Republicans mounted a brief counter-offensive in June, but with the withdrawal of Soviet and French aid it was clear that they would not be able to hold out much longer. In Austria Hitler's invasion was followed by attacks on Jewish property throughout the county as anti-Semitic laws were imposed. Jewish judges and state attorneys were forced out of their jobs, and Jews were forbidden to leave the country. In Vienna Nazi strormtroopers stood by and laughed at elderly Jews as they were forced to scrub the streets. There were half a million Jews in Germany, where Hitler had now taken over as War Minister, and millions more suffering from anti-Semitism in other European countries as local Nazis gained control. Since 1933 around 11,000 refugees had arrived in Britain from Germany and Austria – of whom 85 to 90 per cent were Jewish, but few, it would appear, found their way to Bolton.

Mass-Observation's second book, a report on their *First Year's Work*, was published in early 1938 and drew on material from the team in Bolton and from the national panel of volunteers. During the second half of 1937, members of the national panel had received questionnaires, known as directives, asking them about their social lives, their smoking and drinking habits, their reading preferences and what they kept on their mantelpieces. Attitudes to smokers revealed in the report were a world away from how they are regarded today. In fact, to be seen as a man, smoking was de rigueur, as one observer confessed: 'I notice I sometimes find myself inclined to "look down" on non-smokers. This may be quite unreasonable; but on the other hand I have noticed in many cases that there is something "queer" about men who are non-smokers. That is, they quite frequently have eccentricities, and even unpleasant traits, which are not noticeable in smokers.' Another went even further with her view: 'I always feel there's a milky babies' breath smell about a man who doesn't smoke; he seems to me not quite a *man*. He repels me in somewhat the same way as does a scoutmaster. Quite unreasonable of me, I know, but there it is – if a man hasn't the smell of tobacco about him, he doesn't seem to me quite wholesome.'

As well as the material submitted by the panel, the book drew on some of the findings of John Sommerfield's pub research. One of the main findings was that there was a distinct variation in the number of drinkers from day to day and from hour to hour. Just as the weekend peak is the dominating feature of the weekly cycle, so is the last-hour peak that of the daily cycle. Landlords, when questioned by observers, used identical words to describe this. They all said that their best custom was 'in the last hour'. The Friday and Saturday last hour is nearly three times as great as that of week nights, while the Sunday rise, though high, is spread over a longer period.

The key to the weekly routine for Worktowners was shortage of leisure time and of money. The high spots of the week were payday (Friday) and, with the mills working in the morning, Saturday afternoon – the beginning of the weekend – a time for rest and pleasure. For many going out at night depended very much on how many nights it was after payday. A sampling of 569 homes on weekday evenings revealed 73 per cent of families were at home. How many people went out depended entirely on the amount of money left from Friday. On Wednesday night the 304 pubs are empty, but on Saturday night they are crowded with around 20,000 pub regulars. But, in spite of the fact that there appeared to be one on every corner in the town centre, the pub, Mass-Observation recorded, was in decline. The popular press, football pools, cinema, radio and the dance hall were all making inroads into the dominance of the pub in working-class culture, 'shifting the emphasis of people's leisure from active and communal forms to those that are passive and individual'. The pub 'stresses the fact that you are living among your fellow men, that the issues of life . . . are not solitary but communal. The Church and the political party say the same thing in a different way. The films and pools do not . . . they emphasize the separateness of the individual and they do not ask him to know anyone. They do not suggest he has a duty to help anyone else but himself and maybe his wife and kids and old sick mother.'[12]

The football pools, in particular, played an important part in the lives of many Worktowners. Working in factories and trying to infiltrate working-class institutions, observers found a knowledge of football pools and their special language was as essential as smoking and swearing if they were to be accepted as ordinary. In the 1930s it was estimated that around a quarter of the adult population of Britain did the pools regularly. In Bolton, Mass-Observation recorded in *First Year's Work*,

> Up to forty thousand watch the Saturday football match at the Northtown Stadium. It is the largest focus of a mass of people, about a fifth of the town's population. But a much larger number of Northtowners are less directly but more intimately associated with the game that is played there, and other games all over the country. As a Northtowner put it: 'Now if it was a case of which would you have, Northtown to win and me to lose, or Northtown to lose and me to win, I'd say me to win of course.' The 'me' in this case, as in many millions of others, means his Football Pool coupon. On Saturday evenings the streets are loud with the cries of special paper-sellers. The *Northtown Evening News* brings out a special subsidiary paper, the *Buff*, announcing the results of all matches. Monday has gained a new significance for those who have 'come up', [won] for its newspapers announce the Pool 'dividends'.

So popular were the pools that special postmen were employed two or three days a week to deliver the coupons. 'Taking the number of packets taken out in a day as round about a thousand a man,' M-O estimated, 'we have the number of clients in all the pools. This cannot be less than sixty thousand, a third of the town's population.' The report went on to record some typical remarks in pubs. Among them: 'I like a bet an' this pools business gives you the best deal. Besides, look what it means if theau comes up wi' a big win. Finish workin' fer thi livin'.' Another said he was just 'a poor chap, who is out to get a bit mooar in the present world, bar actually stealing'. Others talked of knowing somebody who had won: 'Tom Sadler won o'er hundred quid un 'ee marked 'is coupon eaut i' this tap room. What is there to stop anybody else fra doin' t' same?' In another pub one Saturday night, the observer asked a sad-looking man what was the matter and got the answer: 'Ah've two bloody lines gone deawn through one club. Fancy one club lerrin' mi deawn o' t' seven results. Pool! It's enoof ta make a bloody fellah commit suicide!' Asking another chap if he thought it was a mug's game going in for the pools, he was told, 'Well, aye, but what con t' do when they show thi their photos does Littlewood's every wik: ah mean t' big prize winners. When theau sees them theau art itchin' t'ave another do, un thi resolution goes tu t' winds.'

Nationally the figures widely quoted as an average weekly 'investment' by 'Poolites' was 2/6d to 3/-. In Bolton observers found that the average was not so high, and a great many people were sixpenny backers. Just under a quarter of the people, it was found, had not won once, but 14 per cent had won more than ten times. These numerous small wins were an important feature of pools. In a sample of sixty people who had been 'in pools' for three years, 85 per cent had won something. The highest total winnings were twenty pounds, won by one man on a single occasion. Another man had won on twenty-eight separate occasions during the same period. 'The wins', the report went on, 'are called "Dividends", the stakes are "Investments". Each entry is a "line", and the term "Hard lines!" has now a new significance. To win is to "come up", and you can only do that if teams don't "let you down". Another basic expression for success occurs in the phrase, "If only we could hit Littlewood's."'

Littlewood's, set up by John Moores, a Liverpool telegraphist, in 1923, was the largest of the pools companies. Very few people changed from Littlewood's to other pools and few, the report went on, 'give up the pools altogether, once started as regulars. People liken it to smoking or drinking, many name it as an alternative or say that it has caused them to give up their beer or cigarettes. "It is the only way an out-of-work, down-and-out ex-soldier and too-old-at-forty-six can expect to get rich quick and end all his troubles, so I have to be without my old friend Mr Woodbine and what a pal!" Another says the pools are like a drug. "Somehow these pools are like a sort of growth that eat into one; once you start, unless you've very strong will-power, you can't stop. Every week when the postman drops the well-known envelope through the letter box, I feel I hate it . . ."'

The commonest way of starting, and continuing, was through one's friends. Not surprisingly, Mass-Observation reported, '95 per cent of poolites state that all or nearly all of their friends go in for pools, too. "I'll bust the bank yet, lad, just see if I don't. I've 'ad plenty o 'ard lines. One o' my owd pals won o'er five thousand two seasons since, an if 'ee con do it, so con I." People see the way the pools has changed the lives of friends and workmates. "One mon ut our 'shop' won a couple o' hundred, un ee's opened a little shop eaut on it, so's 'is wife con make a bit to help 'is wage. I durn't see why I corn't go on an' win same as 'im." Another reflects on the way a pools win would change his life. "I reckon one o' these days I'll touch 'em, and then it's the south of England for me. Theau never knows thi luck, that's it."'

The standard evening for filling in coupons, it was found, was Thursday, with the majority, 67 per cent, saying they spent less than an hour on the coupon. A great many spent only a few minutes, a typical comment being 'About ten minutes filling coupon. I never study the teams playing. I just jot down 1, 2 or X as they come in my mind. It is not the time you spend. I believe it is all luck.' The major motive, the report found, not unexpectedly, was money, but correlated with it were some significant subsidiaries of thrill, dream, time, competition and spiritual hope: 'What is more fascinating than choosing out your lines with the hopes of taking you to Dreamland via Paradise, or opening your Green Final on Saturday evening with a bumping heart?' Another looks at filling in his pools coupon in the context of his hopes and fears in life: 'I have reached the age of realisation that my youthful dreams of easy money will never materialise. I have no family expectation and employment is a fickle jade. Therefore I try my luck while I am still employed, in the hope that it will remove the fear of unemployment. Someday I may come up, then the terrors of illness, poverty, unemployment, my helplessness to help others, will be less terrible, and the little world in which I move may be a degree happier.'

Doing the pools was all about dreams and aspirations. 'In every working-class Northtowner,' the report went on, 'there is the wish to get out of the rut he or she lives in and for which at present the only other physical outlet is the week's holiday. And the dreary winter weeks are made easier by the coupon interest on Thursday, the results interest on Saturday, and (if you have come up) the dividend interest on Monday. It is no exaggeration to say that the pools have changed the traditional trajectory of the week: "Can we couponers imagine a winter evening minus our Littlewood's? That Saturday night's fascination of scrutinising the football results and eagerly looking whether such and such a club has 'let you down' or have I really 'come up'? We working lads couldn't miss that." Another speaks of the "little gamble and a little thrill at weekends, when the Green Final comes round, and, of course, the hope that some day that little dream business of mine come true. But win or lose I always look forward to Saturday and the Green Final."'[13]

This report on football pools was included in *First Year's Work*. By the time it was published most of the observations and reports had been completed for the books on the pub, religion and politics, but analysing the material, organising it and drawing conclusions from it was proving to be difficult. Charles Madge acknowledged that 'both Wilcock and Walter Hood collected an immense amount of very interesting useful material and Gollancz was promised books on the political aspect and the religious aspect, neither of which ever materialized. This was because there was no one there capable of systematic sifting of this very diverse material and turning it into a book. I think only Tom Harrisson could have done it and he was so engrossed in other things that he never got round to it.'[14] Sommerfield was a different case. Like Hood and Wilcock he had collected a vast amount of material, but he was an accomplished writer and by the late spring of 1938 he was spending most of his time back in London writing up his report on the pub fieldwork. 'I didn't leave M-O,' he said, 'I gradually receded from it, simply because I had done all the fieldwork. Then I had to spend a long time writing it which I could do better at home in London.'[15]

Like Sommerfield, many of the original stalwarts were beginning to withdraw from the Bolton operation, and there were signs that some of the early zeal was beginning to dissipate. Throughout the late spring and early summer of 1938 Harrisson continued to lead the team in Bolton, but his own enthusiasm for the project was beginning to wane. More and more of his time was spent away from Davenport Street, and Frank Cawson recalled that once in a while when Bolton became a little too much to take, Harrisson would drive down to London on a Friday afternoon and take off for Paris for a weekend with a friend of his from Argentina, Fredi Guthmann, a wealthy poet. Of those trips Harrisson reflected, 'Freddie and I had some very wild times. I was on Pernod in those days. Once in Paris we went along to an avant-garde play. After a while it got boring so we got up and sat down with the actors on the stage and tried to become part of the play. They had quite a job getting us out – Freddie was an enormous man of about six foot five, but, however wild the weekend, I was always back in Bolton on Monday and no one knew where I had been.'[16] And Harrisson was not finished with Bolton just yet. He might have been losing some of his early enthusiasm but there was still one more grand experiment he wanted to carry out there. He was, he declared, 'fed up with hearing well-off people say that "the man in the street can't appreciate art". Time to test out the statement, see if it is true.'

17

ART AND THE ORDINARY CHAP

'I want you to paint pictures of this town, the honest,
unvarnished scenery of soot and factory, cobbled
street and washing hung out at the back'

Tom Harrisson's instructions to visiting artists

On a fine spring afternoon in 1938 Tom Harrisson went up on to the moors around Belmont to the north of Bolton accompanied by two visitors to the town. His companions were both leading artists of the day, William Coldstream and Graham Bell, members of the Euston Road realist group of painters. From their vantage point, high above the town, the mill chimneys towered above everything like tall grass in a meadow, and they watched the shadows of the chimneys from up there on the moors as they moved slowly, like the hands of a clock, over the streets and houses of the grimy town. Harrisson told his companions that he wanted to see how an artist might react to Bolton and how the town's inhabitants might react to their art. By facilitating this kind of dialogue between worker and artist, he explained, he was looking for a way to rescue the former from aesthetic deprivation and the latter from ivory-tower isolation.

In the spring sunshine Harrisson set out his ideas about art and the working class. One of the things that impressed him, he observed, was the capacity of the working man or woman to adjust expectations to circumstances. 'Modesty of desire' was the way he put it. It was not, he insisted, that working people lacked the capacity to appreciate life's richer pleasures. 'You only need to study working-class gardens to know that however poor, ignorant or apathetic, most men and women have the sensibility for the appreciation of anything beautiful.'[1] But their circumstances gave them very little opportunity to develop these sensibilities. Any desire they had for beautiful things was shattered by the reality of their unavailability.

'Working-class people', Harrisson postulated, 'recognise the boundaries of their lives, set by the atmosphere of smoke, the horizon of factories and the future of doubtful employment. But this doesn't mean they are miserable. Well-off Southern visitors like you might find it impossible to imagine anyone being happy living in Worktown's appalling conditions, but in fact the great majority of Boltonians are not only incomprehensibly proud of their home town, they also claim to be happy here. "Make the best of what you've got" is their philosophy.'[2] There was, he went on to explain, 'a tendency for the man in the street to complain of art that it is not useful to him . . . yet every ornament on his mantelpiece is a proof that he has aesthetic needs . . . Mass-Observation is going to try to find out what this need is and then if possible to get the artists to satisfy it.' This, he told them, 'is where you come in. I want you to paint pictures of this town, the honest, unvarnished scenery of soot and factory, cobbled street and washing hung out at the back.'[3]

Harrisson wanted Coldstream and Bell to put on canvas their visions of Bolton in the severe realism for which they were known. But he was interested in surrealism and impressionism as well as realism and regarded them as three very different ways of seeing. So Julian Trevelyan and Michael Wickham were asked to come back to Bolton to join the realists. Trevelyan was instructed to set up his easel in the middle of the street again with people looking on while he made bright-coloured collages of the town. Wickham was to give his impressionistic view of the town. As Harrisson told them, 'It is because we distrust the value of mere words that we are keen to employ artists and photographers.'

Trevelyan and Wickham were already familiar with the town, having made several previous visits, but to Coldstream and Bell it was an exciting, if not challenging, new experience. Coldstream had trained as a painter, but the slump had made him aware of the social problems that Britain faced. He decided that film was a better medium for him to communicate his social concerns, so he joined the GPO Film Unit. It was the time of two major new directions in British art – abstraction and surrealism – and in 1936 there were major exhibitions of both in London. Coldstream was one of a number of artists and critics who felt that with these movements art had lost its way. Surrealists and abstractionists were, he felt, a small clique of artists who had cut themselves off from the general public and he was anxious to reconnect. He became convinced that art ought to be directed at a wider public. 'It seemed to me important that the broken communication between the artists and the public should be built up again and this most probably implied a move towards realism.' South-African-born Graham Bell was a friend of Coldstream's and together they devised 'A Plan for Artists' which proposed a new movement to 'combat the influence of Paris' (in abstract and surrealistic art) with a return to putting on canvas what the painter saw in the real world around him. Out of this grew the Euston Road School, a group of artists who were committed to making their art accessible to the 'man in the street'.

Coldstream's first contact with Mass-Observation came in 1937 when, 'at the request of Stephen Spender, I painted the wife he had recently married, Inez. It was at that time I first met Charles Madge, whom Inez later married as her second husband. I painted this portrait in a room which I rented on the first floor of a house just off Charlotte Street W.1, where the Post Office Tower [today called the BT Tower] now stands. I had the front room and Graham Bell worked in the back room which opened off it. Graham and I were at that time doing figurative painting ("straight" painting done direct from nature) and we regarded this activity as something of a breakaway from prevalent forms of avant-garde art. We probably thought and implied that our work in this style would be more accessible to large numbers of people than abstract or surrealist painting. I myself never joined any political party but, together with most of my contemporaries, I certainly felt strong sympathies for the left. It was, therefore, natural that when we met Tom Harrisson we should have been attracted by his social concerns with a mainly working-class area. I did not know the North, though I was born in Northumberland, so I thought that it would be a good idea to go to Bolton.'[4]

Coldstream's objective in joining the project was to use the organisation as a means to re-establish a link between the artist and society. He had become disillusioned with the art world and believed that artists had increasingly imposed a distance between the average individual and their understanding of a work of art. He accepted Harrisson's invitation in an effort to amend this situation. 'Graham and I', he recalled, 'got permission to paint from the roof of the Art Gallery. Bolton was very impressive from there with views over the town of the mills and their smoking chimneys.' Every morning Coldstream and Bell would go up on to the roof of the Art Gallery and set to work, sitting back to back on either side of a chimney stack painting in opposite directions. They got to know the doorkeeper, who had been in the navy, and in the evening, Coldstream remembered, 'We used to go and sit in the balcony of the local palais de danse and we used to sketch the Lancashire lads and lasses below. I made a lot of sketches which I never subsequently used. Nothing we ever did got used. I think we were rather a disappointment to Tom Harrisson. We saw him from time to time and I think he came up on to the roof once to see what we were doing. Humphrey Spender was taking photographs of Graham and me painting. I never got to know Tom Harrisson well. He was a young man of very great energy and magnetic personality. He seemed to me to be a romantic; not so much an engaging man, more a magnetic personality – a powerful man with more than a trace of theatricality. He appalled me when I first saw him in Bolton, sprawled on his large bed strewn with papers and issuing orders in all directions.' Coldstream said that Harrisson 'liked to look tough – a curiously popular form of romanticism common at that time, especially among the left wing. He had the manner of the hard man, the detective, a figure like Edward G. Robinson.'[5]

As for the rest of the observers, Coldstream felt that the Davenport Street staff had 'a ridiculous persecution mania. They believe that fascist roughs and other lawless elements are continually hoping to break in and bust up the house. Consequently the house is locked and barred, and every room has its padlock, and everyone in the house locks his room religiously as he comes out of it.' What Coldstream didn't know was that they had some grounds for this. As Harrisson wrote, 'One Saturday evening some persons burgled the house and destroyed a considerable part of the results of the non-political (i.e. non-voter) part of the work, some of which cannot be replaced. Of course we expect this type of opposition, everyone who is trying to report truly and accurately what happens in modern life must expect that sort of thing. £300 went down the drain that burgle.'

Coldstream and Bell had arrived in Bolton looking forward to their time there, but their initial enthusiasm soon deserted them and they began to dislike everything about the place. Davenport Street and the whole Mass-Observation set-up was a particular problem for them. All the time they were in Bolton they complained bitterly about the food, the filth and what they saw as the slovenly disorganisation of everyday life there. 'The food was terrible,' Coldstream said, 'all out of cans and no fresh vegetables.'[6] And the lingering smell of fish and chips never left the house. One day Bell threw open all the windows while the others slept. He claimed to have reduced the smell of the house by half – 'i.e. we banished stale sweat, and about half the smell of onions and vinegar. We were powerless against the drains.'

Bell recorded their trials in daily letters he sent to his girlfriend in London. When they arrived in Bolton, after a pretty awful journey, he told her, they found Harrisson in bed 'surrounded by incredible squalor, filthy defunct meals, pieces of paper in a ruin of a house as sordid as anything; conspiratorial atmosphere. Harrisson acts the leader all the time and the rest play up splendidly.' Fortunately Davenport Street was full, so they didn't have to stay there. Instead they stayed in 'an extraordinary little house, theatrical lodgings'. But it wasn't very good: 'everything even making the beds is of a standard of incompetence you wouldn't believe. And as for the bedclothes I have one sheet, an under-blanket, various knitted garments and a cot eiderdown on my bed. Bill and I sat in our room last night writing poems about Bolton. At about ten the landlady came in and asked if we wanted some tea. We said yes. She came in gave us some tea and took the teapot. "Thank you very much," I said. 'Goodnight.' 'Aw ahve not finished with you yet,' she exclaimed in menacing tones, and a moment later returned with one chamber pot.'

The town itself they found no better, 'more undistinguished than words can describe, small and squalid but utterly unspectacular. The smallness of everything is rather noticeable. When you wake in the morning here the transition from the minor unpleasantness of the dream world is to this real nightmare. The smell is inescapable, the inhabitants smoke hard all the time.' One consolation was that 'the people are all very nice but their stupidity is fantastic. When I hear them talking I simply bury my head in my hands.' On their first afternoon in the town, Bell wrote, 'We trudged all round the outskirts, and about 5 o'clock we could be seen in a huge canyon surrounded by rubbish dumps of great height by the sewage system of the town, standing between a cemetery and a squalid little river full of old tins and dead things. There was nowhere to go. An old man leaning over the cemetery wall looked at us for some time and then said, "You can't cross brook and you can't go on this way. You maun go back way you came." What with the smell and the thought of possible lodgings and the difficulty of doing any painting and the poverty of the people and the expensiveness of life and the extraordinary behaviour of the Mass-Observers and the fact that all the newspapers up here have a strong flavouring of special Bolton news we were pretty depressed.'

On 21 April they started painting on the Art Gallery roof. 'The place is in the middle of a dreadful slum,' noted Bell,

and the only people who ever go in are the wives of men who are playing bowls in the park. Bill is doing a 36 × 28 of the view – a sandy children's playground with rows and rows of little dirty red houses swathed in smoke behind it. My picture is smaller, 24 × 20, of the grimy little park with cotton mills and smoke and the inevitable slums. Bill's is very good, mine rather poor so far. It is very cold on the roof, but we are not much observed, which in Bill's opinion has compensated for everything. He suffers considerably going about the streets of Bolton with me. The caretaker and his wife at the Art Gallery are very nice people who give us cups of tea. We had our lunch up here yesterday – as far as I have seen the only decent thing to eat in this part of the world are little buns that you can buy in bake shops. We painted for five hours. At the end we were hungry and tired but oh dear me what a depressing sight our 'tea' was when it came, plate covered in a mountain of cotton wool-like potato, itself anointed with a cold glue-like fluid and botulous-looking sausages nosing indecently about. We just managed to eat some, but the body went into some newspaper to be put in a litter can today. I may say there isn't even a Lyons* in this town and I miss them.

As time went on things got worse. Replying to one of his girlfriend's letters Bell wrote: 'Darling Angel, it was nice to get your letter. I found it lying among the intolerable squalor of Big Black Carstairs Harrisson's camp. Several of the beavers sat around on their haunches chewing beetle nut and saying how hard they have to work, although of course no one ever does a thing except add to the confusion.' Their own work he said was going well: 'We had a good day on the roof, not so cold.' But then, 'unable to face our landlady's horrid handiwork, we dined out with Stephen's brother, Humphrey, who is up here taking photographs for M-O and not getting paid for it. We spent the whole evening gossiping about the great man; I mean Big Black Carstairs. Most delightful form of naughtiness because gossip is absolutely forbidden by the chief who has very little sense of humour and cannot be teased. We wandered around the town considerably and even saw the three local prostitutes going into action.'

Meals didn't get any better. 'The food in Bolton', he reported, 'is really too awful – beyond a joke. Bill and I have now reached the stage where we cannot approach our lodgings without anxiety and we really dread our meals. Last night I ordered what I thought was an antiseptic meal. I mean a chop with boiled potatoes. What could be simpler, foolproof, but not bloody fool proof. She produced the most horrible concoction that has ever been seen which we had to wrap up in paper and put in a litter container. Fortunately there are a lot of these in Bolton and we are always putting our meals in them. Tonight we have been all round the town having drinks and trying to get something to eat and it was the

* A major British café/restaurant chain. Their cornerhouses were a feature of many towns and cities.

sheerest luck that we stumbled on this little haven of civilisation (the Swan Hotel). The food was really quite good and the waiter was anything but a Boltonian.'

After a week they moved their lodgings 'to a more frankly working-class area'. These, Bell wrote after a few days, were 'a great improvement, they have a certain air of refinement. Bill and I now have a double bed and I often snuggle up to him dreaming that it is you.' On the work front he reported, 'I have nearly finished my squalor scape and have started drawings for a series of street scenes. I shall be quite sorry to leave the gallery. The caretaker is such a charmer – talking with a very slow serious voice and sometimes rather drily humorous. Both he and his wife are most useful to us. They give us tea and an hour's rest in their parlour, a fine room with a very high ceiling and a noble roaring fire (coal paid for by the corporation). He was at Heligoland, Jutland, Delville Wood and a good many other actions during the war.'

Bell clearly liked the caretaker and his wife, but he didn't have a very high opinion of some of the observers. 'We also talk about wars', he wrote, 'to John Sommerfield the Spanish hero who is on the M-O staff up here. He is not a very sympathetic character – awfully ugly for one thing and a bit insensitive. Last night Bill and I went on his behalf to do counting in a dance hall (very charming place of which I hope to do a painting). We met him on our way home and he took us down what are called "backs" – the equivalent of mews in London except that there are no stables of course only coal sheds and rubbish – in these the street lights go out at eleven and they become the abode of perpendicular love.'

Coldstream was referred to in Bell's letters as 'the old master', and after just over a week in Bolton he was 'at last beginning to take an interest in the possibilities of painting in this town and he is making drawings of the dance hall, inside and out (the inside is a dream ice cream panache pink and green affair with belated classical dignity and a lovely low marzipan ceiling arching over the whole affair). The people enjoy dancing in a way no Southerner can imagine and though there is no drink and no unseemliness the shrieks of laughter and the high spirits are deafening. Bill and I sitting up in the balcony felt very much the spectators at a play, especially when one or two good-natured dancers took pity on us and asked us why we weren't dancing.'

When bad weather prevented them from working outside, they went to the dance hall and spent the afternoon drawing there. 'The orchestra came up to see what we were doing and were terribly disappointed not to find themselves included. To please Bill I had my hair cut this morning, an ordeal in an insanitary little shop. When I came out he really was pleased and now when we walk about the streets he points out with delight all the people who pass us without taking much interest. As a matter of fact it is quite remarkable how little attention one attracts. I have done things I certainly wouldn't dare do in London like drawing people in the street or standing opposite pubs drawing the doorway and the only reaction has been an occasional "Oh 'e's sketchin'" uttered in a most kindly and tolerant way.'

Two weeks into their stay they had to move into Davenport Street. 'Tom has to go to London and we can't afford these comfortable lodgings any more. We had Harrisson to dinner last night. We all parted the best of friends after he said that our kind of painting could be good and surrealism could only be retrogressive.' But the Worktown headquarters didn't suit them nor did some of the residents. 'There is not a single civilised being to talk to,' Bell complained.

> We share the house with Walter, almost the ugliest man in history and a dreadful bore. He tells me every day several times that when he was 18 he was union secretary over 1,800 men. He also tells a lot about himself as a boy orator, as an artist (he does the sort of work that would even make the *Daily Worker* blanch a bit) and of course about the terrible hard work he does on M-O. The hard work is a popular fiction here; they all like to think of themselves dropping with fatigue. But Walter is quite nice compared with Joe, also a working man originally who has turned into a dreadful snob, dresses in *Strand Magazine* plus fours. There is also awful Ethel, the cook, whom Mr Coldstream called Mrs Eyeballs. Charles Madge, the poet and Mass-Observer, has arrived here, very gentle and sheepish drove me almost mad last night by saying Yaas Yaas like a curate to everything I said and annoyed the old master by not answering his questions. We have nearly abolished the smell in the house by leaving all the windows open while the others were sleeping off the effects of their terrifyingly strenuous labours. But awful Ethel is a smell in herself, a host of awful smells rose from the kitchen as soon as she came. Poor Bill has had a bad time today. He rose early, lit the fire so as to heat the water for a bath. Ethel used the water for her astonishing pretence sometimes called washing up. Then awful Ethel let the fire out so he couldn't have his bath.

Despite all the trials and tribulations recorded by Bell, he and Coldstream both produced a panoramic view of the town. From their rooftop vantage point the scene each of them painted was deserted and lifeless. Harrisson, who was unsure about the relative merits of rival surrealist and realist approaches, was pleased with their work – 'decent straight stuff' he told his friend Trevelyan and well suited for illustrating his planned books. So enthusiastic was he that he produced a programme for a Bolton Series of paintings of social life which included: houses of the middle class with rubbish in the foreground, interior of cotton mill, chapel, pub, market, a Bolton wedding and a Bolton funeral, dance hall, derelict iron foundry, religious procession, mill workers.

Bell and Coldstream's stay in Bolton lasted for just three weeks. They expressed relief at returning to London after their stay in 'the hideous North'. They found it 'a fascinating if rather horrifying experience' and felt that it had brought them as artists closer to a relationship with the real world. Not everyone associated with the Worktown project would have agreed, and the contempt of some of the local observers for them was expressed by one who said, 'These English realists are not the tough guys they ought to be. They're just phoney left-wing revolutionaries only at home in their haven of comfort in the metropolis.'

While Coldstream and Bell were working on their paintings, Wickham and Trevelyan were out with their easels on Bolton's streets. Trevelyan's medium was collage, depicting an industrial landscape made from bits of newspaper, magazines and catalogues. In his autobiography he recalled carrying a suitcase full of scraps of paper, copies of the magazine *Picture Post*, scissors, glue and Indian ink with him to the site where he was going to make a collage. He would work on the spot, battling with the wind and his own shyness in front of an inquisitive audience. When all the work had been completed Harrisson took copies of the paintings on to the streets, saying to Trevelyan: 'I am having fun showing all you boyses pictures of Bolton to workers and getting their votes.'[7]

Harrisson reported on the experiment in a radio talk on 'Art and the Ordinary Chap' and in a newspaper article 'What They Think in Worktown'. 'I showed their pictures to all sorts of working people all over the town, and wrote down exactly what they said about each one. But because I wanted to show them to people in pubs and clubs, dance halls and at street corners, it wasn't practicable to use the canvases: I had to use photos of them. All the pictures one from each artist showed a typical view of the great smoky town, interpreted according to that particular painter's point of view. Wickham's impressionistic view was not liked: "Gives the impression of derelict places. It's gruesome" was one comment. A fish and chip shop proprietor declared: "It certainly looks like a distressed area," while a housewife was very decided in her view: "I don't like this. It's a flaming disgrace."'

The comments people made on the pictures by Coldstream and Bell were very different. An old man said: 'This is what I would call typical of here on a dirty and mucky rainy day.' Lots of people, though, said the pictures made the town look deserted, hollow, lifeless, yet all the chimneys were smoking. Bell and Goldstream hoped their realist paintings would have sufficient popular appeal to encourage some wealthy local benefactor to commission more work for them for the local Art Gallery. 'Success in the Bolton experiment', Bell said, 'could revolutionise the art galleries in England, bringing art to the people and income to the artists producing the realist portrayal of local scenes that, I assume, local people would be most likely to appreciate.' But no local benefactor appeared, and for Bell the Bolton experience did nothing to foster respect for his potential working-class audience. 'The real trouble about this town', he wrote in one of his letters, 'is that class distinction is unknown. It really is like Soviet Russia, an absolute hell of incompetence and awful food with a great deal of work going on and very nice people leading a very unpleasant life. The unpleasantness of the life has had an extraordinary effect upon the intelligence of the people which is just about as low as could be. The people here have less intelligence than any others I have ever met, even back home in Zululand.'

Of all the artists involved with Mass-Observation, Trevelyan was the most successful in tuning in with the ideals of the project.[8] Surprisingly it was his surrealist representation of Bolton that brought the best response. The picture was a collage, made up like a puzzle piece of newspaper, rag, canvas and calico, stuck on and sometimes painted over, to represent a weird landscape of factories and houses and park. The first thing people did when they saw this picture was to stare at it in speechless silence – sometimes for five minutes at a time. Here's what one man, unemployed, exclaimed after a period of intense contemplation: 'Great. That's great. One thing, it is us. You can tell that.' Another man: 'That's a remarkable picture, though. I can't place it.'[9]

Harrisson was particularly interested in the work Trevelyan was doing as he felt that his methods could easily be adopted as popular art forms. In a letter to him, Harrisson proposed an exhibition about Bolton in which he suggested they 'reconstruct an actual part of a street and the graphitti [sic] of one lavatory wall . . . Also serve Bolton meals with readings aloud on how to eat them. Fish and chips frying continually and soot falling constantly.' Trevelyan's work in Bolton was close to the politics of Mass-Observation's founders, but it was also personally liberating for him, and in his autobiography he gives his own assessment of what this period of work meant to him. 'I drew much profit from my contact with Mass-Observation. First of all it was largely through my experiences in it that I had the courage to find myself in painting, to leave the various clichés of Surrealism and Abstraction and to paint the things I cared about in the way I felt them.'[10]

While the painters were at work creating their images of Bolton, Humphrey Spender continued with his photographic work. But he was still ill at ease with the class gulf, feeling like 'a man from another planet' and, unlike the full-time investigators, unable to make contact with his subjects. When asked whether he treated his photographic work more as reporting or as that of an artist and whether he was considered on a par with Trevelyan and Coldstream he said: 'Tom thought of the photographic side as very important but saw it as pure recording. I was prepared to accept that. Tom would literally search the whole surface of a collection of photographs for information about small details – the number of rings that people were wearing, whether they were wearing horn-rimmed glasses, how many people had beards, how many people had cloth caps in a football crowd. It was factual data of every kind he wanted from photographs.'

Mass-Observation had now been in Bolton for more than a year, and there was no let-up in its recording of this sort of detail of everyday life. One observer on the top deck of the number 1 bus reported that at 5.30 a swarm of mill hands got on at a corner. Three mill girls aged about fifteen and a great many boys and men came on top. The three girls got on first and scrambled up to the front seats. They then turned round and shouted, 'Tommy! Tommy!' It was not obvious who Tommy was, but a man of about forty-five in a cap and overcoat came and sat behind them, while three or four young boys came too, and sat behind the middle-aged man. When Tommy came the girl with the loudest voice said, 'Thee sit there, Tommy, so we can see thee face!' There was continual chaff and laughter all the way especially from the girls. The boys grinned, and Tommy smiled quietly to himself. All the mill hands seemed very jolly and excited. At Victoria Square most of the men got off. The three girls remained. They yelled chaff after the men and boys, and went on shouting, 'Tommy!' as the men and boys ran across the square in the direction of the Art Gallery.[11]

As the observers listened in to conversations there was much light-hearted banter like this, but they also noted an increasingly sombre note creeping in to everyday chat as more and more conversations turned to the subject of war. In a small beerhouse all the men were talking at the tops of their voices: 'Now it's about the Wanderers and two are talking about the Army, then it gets to "Thee just see, before long they'll have us all on munitions, them and all the bloody women, they'll not let so many men this time on it, it'll be to the bloody front, theer's no beer theer." At this they all laughed, one said, "We bet 'em last time, and we'll a to do it again."' A woman at an exhibition of the Manchester Society of Women Artists declared, 'The common people don't want war. It's the politicians. Telling us they are making it safe for democracy and all that. We don't want to become like Italy. I believe the people there are dreadful rag tag and bobtail. They'll fall on your neck for a cigarette.' Her companion concurred: 'I believe they're spending every penny on armaments. The people must be having an awful time. We don't know half. We don't want to become mixed up in any of it. I say let us do without allies and just keep the Empire.'[12] In the Commercial Hotel the view was much more basic. Man with cap: 'There'll be a bleedin' war . . . be with the bloody Germans.' Man with cap and coat: 'Aye, yer right Bill . . . going to be some bloody trouble.'

Before the trouble, however, there were things to celebrate. On 20 May 1938 massive enthusiasm and excitement was aroused by the visit to Bolton of King George VI and Queen Elizabeth. Thousands of people were packed into Victoria Square as the royal cavalcade of cars approached the Town Hall in warm sunshine. Along Moor Lane a crowd of 6,000 lined the route, cheering and waving flags. The Queen responded with smiles and waves while the King bowed gravely. In the blue and gold enclosure in front of the Town Hall steps, the official reception party including Lord Derby and the Mayor and Mayoress waited. Standing opposite were the smart ranks of the Duke of Lancaster's Own Yeomanry. At 12.30 p.m. the royal party arrived at the Town Hall, where the King expressed his admiration for the new Civic Centre and enquired about the state of trade. Before entering the Town Hall the royal couple made their way across to chat to a group of Great War veterans, some of them severely disabled. One of them, James Grant, had served as a warrant engineer on HMS *Cumberland* where he was a shipmate of the King. To his great surprise the King remembered him and recognised him. Those present were later to praise the Queen's 'spontaneous friendliness' and the King's 'simple dignity'.

With the sun shining, Bolton was a much pleasanter place for visitors and residents alike. Moss Bank Park with its putting and bowling greens was a mecca for the entire town on fine weekends and holidays. The focal point was the fish pond surrounded by shrubs and terraced walkways. The council stressed the value of parks as an aid to public health. They provided open spaces and fresh air for Boltonians who had spent all week in the heat and noise and confinement of mill work. But their eyes, even on a sunny day, were permanently in shadow. Large peaks on flat caps and the brims on trilbys created the effect for men, while women pulled down their cloche hats over their heads with the same result.

Observers too took advantage of the greenery that provided a welcome respite from the general drabness of their surroundings. On a sunny Sunday afternoon, taking a break from their observations and report-writing, they'd take a walk. Few of them had lost their political convictions or the idealism that had brought them to Worktown, and their conversations would often turn to the issues of the day that preoccupied them. One that was of particular interest at this time was George Orwell's return from the Spanish Civil War and the views that he'd brought back with him. Orwell had survived a bullet through his neck in Spain, but his faith in socialist solidarity had not survived. While he was there he had witnessed the Republican cause being sabotaged by feuds between different factions within the Popular Front. The communists, acting on instructions from Moscow, seemed to be more intent on hunting down heretics within their own ranks who did not toe the party line than in taking on the fascists. Back home when he tried to write what he saw as the truth – that fascism and communism had more in common than most people realised – his work was inevitably rejected by pillars of the left. communist writers and critics like Harry Pollitt, the General Secretary of the Communist Party, criticised him as a 'little middle-class boy' who had dabbled in socialism only to come out showing his true colours as the imperialist reactionary he had always been. There was some sympathy for this view, but many of the people who had made their way to Bolton could see that there was a lot of truth in what Orwell had to say. This had been brought home by their observations of political meetings of the far right and the left, at many of which people had made the point that in their extremism there was little to choose between what either side was saying.

As well as being a place for recreation and a little debate, the parks provided Spender with a place where he felt more comfortable with his camera, and he took photographs of Worktowners enjoying their leisure. But the more he went to Bolton, the more uneasy he became about what he was doing at the *Mirror*. He came to believe that his work should make some kind of objective attempt to reflect real life, poverty, politics and all. Unfortunately the *Mirror* didn't seem to be very interested in showing this view of life. His art editor wanted pictures of rural landscapes, Morris dancing and harvest time, rather than photographs of mill workers in Bolton, derelict Welsh coal-mines or unemployed dock-workers walking the banks of the Tyne. Spender wasn't suited to the *Mirror* and the *Mirror* didn't suit him. The art editor found the excuse he was looking for to sack him when he refused to take a comic photograph of Edith Sitwell wearing a fruit-laden hat. The art editor's reaction was 'Orders is orders.' Spender recalled that Bartholomew, the paper's editorial director 'had me up in his office and said, "Obviously, you're fighting this man, and therefore the job is unsympathetic. Take three times your salary for three months and stay away."' Soon after leaving the *Mirror* he was asked to join the original team of photographers working for the new socially aware photojournalist magazine *Picture Post*, which was first published towards the end of 1938. Liberal, anti-fascist and, above all, populist in its editorial stance, it was a pioneering example of photojournalism and was an immediate success.

Over a period of five weeks on five or six visits to Bolton in 1937 and 1938, Spender had taken more than 900 pictures of the town's people, its street life, pubs, markets, religious services, parks and wastelands. A constant feature of taking these kind of photographs was, he confessed, 'a feeling that I was intruding and that I was exploiting the people I was photographing. What it taught me as a photographer was that practically all the photographs I've ever taken which have not included people are deadly boring.' His photographs of Bolton never appeared in any of Mass-Observation's publications. Spender said that it was too expensive to reproduce them and that Harrisson only had a vague idea about their possible use within the haphazard mountain of information he had amassed. He was always very enthusiastic about them and had a standard thing to say: 'One day these will be fantastic, they will be of great use. At the moment we haven't enough money to produce a book, but it's very important to keep them.'[13]

After he got the job on *Picture Post*, Spender didn't go back to Bolton, and Harrisson was also ready to move on. Forever restless and always looking for a new challenge, by the summer of 1938 he was fed up with Worktown and wanted to return to London. Madge, for very different reasons, was also ready for a change. It was a time of major upheaval in his personal life and this precipitated an exchange of roles and of locations with Harrisson. Madge had finally married Kathleen Raine in March at Lewisham Registry Office. But within weeks, in late April, Kathleen met Alastair MacDonald, a well-dressed man about town, and fell in love with him. 'It did not take me long', Madge recounted in his autobiography, 'to learn this uncomfortable state of affairs. Although at first I treated it as a passing fancy, I soon had to recognise that it had taken a strong hold. Arriving back in Blackheath from a day in London, I remember how my heart sank when I saw Alastair's hat in the hall . . . I was very upset, and at a party where I drank too much sherry, I passed out on the carpet from excess of emotion and alcohol.'[14]

It was not just the affair, however, that caused a rift between them. 'It was Mass-Observation', he said later, 'that broke up my marriage.'[15]

Kathleen became more and more antipathetic to the whole thing and to the sort of people who at that stage were coming to Grotes Buildings to give a hand. A great variety of people used to come there to help with the paperwork involved by the constant stream of reports from observers and requests for information that came through the post. Sometimes we put them up in makeshift fashion. It was an encroachment on the privacy of the home that Kathleen at times resented bitterly, especially when those who encroached were not at all glamorous or famous. In her autobiography she wrote of this time: 'There was something in the faces, in the spiritual atmosphere, of some of Charles's Communist friends which I sensed as evil.' When Kathleen and I first met, we had agreed or felt that we agreed on our political and religious beliefs, or lack of them. Now, in reaction to Mass-Observation she moved sharply away from materialism and into mysticism. This divergence must have been at work before she met Alastair; after she had met him, and fallen for him, it made it difficult, if not impossible, for us to get back to our old footing and preserve the marriage.[16]

The breakdown of his relationship with Raine was to lead Madge to look for a change of direction in his life, and this in its turn was set to provide the Worktown project with a new focus. Mass-Observation was about to enter a new phase of its operation.

18

ARRIVALS AND DEPARTURES

*'Tom was difficult sometimes and I began to feel
that I would like to do something else'*

Walter Hood

The second phase of Mass-Observation's work in Bolton began with the arrival of a thirty-three-year-old Austrian refugee, Gertrude Wagner, in July 1938. With a background in social psychology and previous research experience she was ideally suited to the organisation. In the late 1920s she began a law degree in Vienna, but also became interested in psychology and when a new unit concerned with the application of psychology to social and political problems was set up at Vienna University she joined in the work. The unit undertook a study of unemployment in the community of Marienthal in Austria during 1930 and Wagner was one of the fieldworkers.

In 1936 she left Austria and came to England, where she started work on an employment study which involved interviewing unemployed men in different British towns. She then obtained a grant to study social psychology at London University for a master's degree. Around the same time she heard about Mass-Observation and wrote to Harrisson expressing an interest in meeting him to tell him about her own research, which was on saving and spending. He invited her to Bolton to do some of the research for her thesis. At the same time she received an offer from Madge to make use of Mass-Observation's national panel. Her purpose was to describe the attitude, behaviour and motivation of two small groups towards two important economic actions, saving and spending. The two groups to be investigated were working-class people in Bolton and Mass-Observers from the national panel.

When she first arrived in Bolton she was taken to Harrisson's room and found him knee-deep in papers. The floor was covered with them. The place could never be cleaned because there was so much paper, and so it was rather squalid. Nothing was filed or organised. She thought the house was a dreadful mess, and she immediately cleaned the kitchen and bought fresh food. Soon after Wagner's arrival Brian Barefoot came back to Bolton and he immediately noticed the difference that she had made to the Davenport Street house. 'In keeping the house tidy and neat for a while, she must have been almost its only feminine influence.' He also noted that she was able to stand up to Harrisson without getting herself thrown out. Wagner herself found Harrisson 'an interesting man and odd; not easy to get on with'. She also found the observers odd but friendly. She thought the whole thing was an amazing set-up, but, bringing her academic eye to it, she decided that Mass-Observation had 'no method'.[1]

No method – and no money either. 'Originally,' Barefoot said, 'we had a reasonably adequate diet and a little money for expenses. In August 1938, however, there was very little money at all. The daily woman no longer "did" for us, and often we lived for several days at a time on fish and chips, bread and jam, and tea. Unpaid bills littered the house; Tom Harrisson was in the worst possible temper. It was about that time that I remember someone saying that if the stay in Bolton had taught him one thing it was the "littleness of great men", but someone else, probably Walter Hood replied: "Maybe, but they're still greater than you or I." At his best Tom was great company, witty, lively and compelling his audience to join in and feel almost great alongside him.' But later acquaintance with Harrisson brought Barefoot in contact with the darker side of his nature. 'He would demand of us', he recalled, 'far more work than we were capable of, and then get angry because we made small mistakes: he could not bear to be corrected or criticised, though he welcomed criticism of the work itself; and he was selfish in respect of others' rights to a little free time, rarely giving them a holiday. Finally signs of paranoia made their appearance. He suspected people of upsetting the progress of the work; he is supposed by some to have engineered himself a fire which destroyed a large proportion of his political material; he sacked people who were critical of him, and quarrelled with all of us at some time or another.'[2]

Finance or the lack of it had always been a problem. Another that stayed with the team for the length of the project was the hostility of the press. Mass-Observers were still described as private eyes or spies. 'They May Be Watching You' was a headline in *Everybody's*[*] in June 1938. Despite the critical press coverage, and perhaps rather surprisingly, more

* *Everybody's Weekly* was a tabloid founded in London in 1913. It was published until April 1959.

and more local people were showing a willingness to take the observers into their confidence and into their homes. Reporting on family relations, one observer went to 90 Westbourne Avenue and noticed immediately that the mother was the dominating person in the house. The husband did not talk at all but sat in his corner smoking a pipe.

> Looks very well fed, happy and quite intelligent, but she does all the talking. In the room are also her daughter, who can't talk very much and the son-in-law about whom she makes tactless remarks such as 'Yes my poor daughter she had a bad time with him (son-in-law) out of work for such a long time, he has stomach trouble.' Son-in-law rather embarrassed at this remark. Grandchild, six, terribly spoiled but very intelligent, talks the whole time, grandmother extremely proud. He is the son of her son and his mother died a month after his birth. Since then she has brought him up, and he says mammy to her. She whispers, 'He does not know that I am not his mother.' The child had a tremendous amount of playthings, got a comic every day and a book once a month. The woman's main conversation was about sicknesses. The grandchild was ill a lot and she told the observer that she had lost her daughter after an illness of two years.[3]

After more than a year in Bolton, Harrisson's team were building up a detailed picture of all aspects of life in the town, but central to it all was earning a living. Often when it was getting near payday in a Bolton household the kitchen cupboard would be nearly empty – only bread would be left and folk would have to borrow margarine off one another to make it edible. In the meanest of homes, meals were always 'scratch' and the table never seemed to be cleared. Some folk could only afford Nestlé's milk,* and bread and jam were the staples. Pigs were always popular and pig's trotter had such a special association with the town that the Bolton Wanderers football team was commonly known as 'the Trotters'. Also common was the meat and potato pie, while Lancashire hotpot (mutton and Sunday scraps) was also popular. Tuesdays and Fridays were 'fish days'. Plaice was the choice of those with money to spare, but the poorer families selected 'garnets' – large ugly fish notable for their incredible number of bones. Tinned salmon was kept until the weekend for the arrival of family and friends for tea.[4]

One of the things the observers were asking questions about was shopping. The working-class housewife, they found, rarely made a weekly

---

* Condensed milk that came in a can.

order for her groceries. Generally she would go out for them during the time when her husband was at work. She didn't have many activities outside her own home and didn't go out very much in the evening. When the wife did go out, coming into contact with people outside the home-circle represented one of the only means of social intercourse for her, so the journey to the shop was significant for her.[5] When observers wanted to go into some of the poorer districts to ask questions, Harry Gordon would often act as their guide. When people were brought to their doors, he recalled, 'They were afraid we were salesmen and did not want to be bothered but were soon put at their ease and answered the questions.' Many were very forthcoming, revealing in some cases quite intimate details: 'No changes of underclothes. When those we have on are washed we must stop in.' Another revealed that he couldn't afford tobacco, 'so buy smoking herbs – 2d a week', while a Roman Catholic lady was quite clear about her priorities: 'There's 3d for the Church. It's church money. Aa always pay that. I wouldn't miss it. I'd sooner starve.' Gordon emphasised the basic kindness and hospitality of the people who were being interviewed: 'There was a lot of poverty but people were kind and would offer you a cup of tea. More so when you told them that you were not selling Hoovers or something like that.'

Gertrude Wagner's research for her own thesis consisted mostly of interviews in Bolton, but, as Brian Barefoot recalled, she did 'work for M-O at the same time. She lived with the rest of the team at Davenport Street and was the only member of the team apart from myself with a love of the open air; one Sunday we undertook a long walk over the moors together.' The first stage of Wagner's work for her own study of 'The Psychological Aspect of Saving and Spending' was to devise a questionnaire to be sent to the national panel of observers and used for interviews with people in Bolton. It was a far cry from Harrisson's original 'you don't ask a bird any questions' anthropological approach, but Wagner was a very different observer to any who had previously been in Bolton. She had experience of market research, and earlier that year she had published a critical article on the newly emerging discipline, arguing for the replacement of tick-box questionnaires with methods that allowed a skilled investigator to record 'as much as possible the exact words of the interviewed person' along with 'his own shrewd and trained observations'. The best results, she argued, would be obtained by in-depth interviews, preceded by preliminary study of 'the impact of social environment and social institutions'.[6]

The move towards market research was a significant one for

Mass-Observation and it tied in with a trend that was already manifesting itself in the directives going out from Blackheath to the national panel. In June, Madge had sent one out on prejudices about margarine. The report that resulted from this found that while most people had no strong feelings against the taste of margarine, the overwhelming majority would hesitate to offer it to their friends. The work was paid for by Unilever's advertising agency, Lintas. Faced with rumblings of discontent from observers suspicious that work was being taken on for business firms, exploiting the volunteers to make money for themselves, Madge and Harrisson responded by saying that M-O undertook no research that wouldn't be published, that was not open to everyone.[7]

Most of the work in Blackheath was still being carried out by unpaid volunteers, which meant that the organisation did not have a lot of control over the ability or suitability of its workers. In August Madge wrote, 'I have three people working in the big room today. They are slow, incompetent and stupid.' Next day, though, things looked up and he wrote, 'Blackheath is buzzing with people. A marvellous coal bagger and an all-in wrestler arrived for breakfast, having come down from Bolton on a lorry all night. One of the nicest people I've met for a long time [Bill Naughton]. Also a crippled schoolteacher from Northumberland in a chair who is very good. And a boy and a girl from Lewisham. Not to mention Ralph Parker, the *Times* journalist, and Joe Wilcock, who has recently moved back to London.'[8]

Among Madge's more regular helpers was Bruce Watkin, who managed the office for a time and helped with the writing of reports, and nineteen-year-old Priscilla Feare, who came to work unpaid as a typist and filing clerk. The working environment contrasted starkly with conditions for the observers in Bolton, with relaxed working lunches on the terrace and Madge himself 'most charming and wonderful to work for'.[9] Madge's seemingly idyllic existence in Blackheath couldn't last. Harrisson was by this time itching to get back to London, while Madge's increasingly complicated personal relationships were beginning to make him feel that he needed to get away. 'The situation [with Kathleen]', he wrote in his autobiography, 'dragged on inconclusively throughout the summer. In mid-June we gave a party at 6 Grotes Buildings at which many of our friends were present – also Stephen and Inez Spender. It was a fine warm evening, the guests were absorbed into the shadows of the garden, wine was drunk freely, restraints were loosened. Stephen went home at about midnight, Inez remained overnight and we slept together, with Kathleen's knowledge.' On 1 August, Madge wrote, 'Dearest Inez, I love you very much and think about you all the time. This is Monday morning and frightfully hot; and I am just off to the Bank Holiday Zoo which is going to be a massacre and to Lambeth Walk this evening where I shall no doubt drink formidable amounts of beer.'[10]

Around this time Harrisson and Madge had begun work on what was to be one of the first Penguin Specials. Entitled *Britain by Mass-Observation*, it included a study of the popular Lupino Lane song 'The Lambeth Walk' and of the people who lived in the real Lambeth Walk. In the course of his research Madge went to Lambeth and enjoyed 'a wonderful party that went on till 2 a.m., where everyone could play piano or accordion by ear, where everyone handed round their glasses of beer for others to drink and where I also noticed transvestism and fine class-conscious songs like "What does it feel like to be poor?"' A week later Madge wrote to Inez that he had been for a walk by the Thames with the ornithologist James Fisher and his wife Angus along with [his old friends from the Blackheath group] the Leggs, and that 'we had drunk a lot of rum and beer. What I did not write was that Angus and I had left the others in the pub and had gone off along the towpath, in the rays of the setting sun. Arriving at a lonely stretch where there was a small wooden jetty, I took Angus in my arms. So urgent was our impulse that we lay down on the jetty and made love there and then, rather awkwardly because of the planks. Angus said we would make up for this later that night. She and James stayed the night at Grotes Buildings. She came to my room and leapt into bed beside me, and we were wonderfully happy.'[11]

Madge felt he needed to distance himself from this bohemian existence in London, so when Harrisson suggested that they should switch locations he readily agreed. Harrisson's idea was that Madge should go to Bolton to make a study of economic life in the same way that he had organised the pub, politics and religion studies there and that he would go to Grotes Buildings. Harrisson, it appeared, couldn't get away from Bolton quickly enough and, true to form, he did not show much concern for the observers he left behind there, as Brian Barefoot recalled.

Like most men of genius, Tom Harrisson could on occasions be extremely 'difficult' – a polite word for self-centredness, obstinacy and determination to put his own ideas in front of any other consideration. He could be quite extraordinarily selfish; the most striking example that comes to mind concerns his final departure from Bolton near the end of August 1938, when there were left in the house (apart from the Bolton residents who came in daily) only Walter Hood, Gertrude Wagner and myself. On that occasion he left in the middle of the night, with Julian Trevelyan in the latter's car; and he finished up all the milk before he left, so that we had none for breakfast.[12]

In this rather shabby fashion Harrisson's days in Worktown came to an end. The leading members of his team, if they had not already left, soon followed. Joe Wilcock was back in London trying to make sense of the vast archive of material that had been built up on religion and church services in Bolton. It was an unenviable task, not helped by Harrisson trying to impose his stamp on the shape of the proposed book on religion. 'It may be best', he suggested, 'to write as if a Melanesian had been sent over to Bolton by a cannibal tribe. The tribe are on the fringe of Missionary activity, which is pressing inland. They must decide between either preserving their own beliefs or dying out from introducing diseases, or accepting the new way of life which they do not understand. So they send delegates over to Bolton so that they may report on What is this Christianity. Does it do among the white men what the missionary says it will do among the black men? The greatest difference the delegates would find would be the numbers of people and what they are doing and wearing in the streets on Sunday.'[13] Harrisson wrote a draft for the first chapter himself formulated in this way, with his Melanesian cannibal arriving at the station in Bolton on a Sunday morning, walking through the deserted streets, puzzled at why there was nobody around. Wilcock may have been the ideal person to attend the many different religious services in Bolton and report factually on what he saw and heard, but he wasn't a particularly creative individual and this sort of approach to the book was not one for him.

With his research for the proposed 'Politics and the Non-Voter' book completed, Walter Hood was the next to leave. In the development of his own social and political consciousness he had found the time he had spent in Bolton of great value. While he was there he'd studied sociological works and began to realise that some of the romantic notions he had about working-class community, identity and solidarity were misled. He realised that people were much more individualised than he had once thought, so the message of socialism had to be interpreted to suit the audience and the needs of the people within society. But it was time to move on. Towards the end of the summer he began to get restless and decided to make plans to leave Mass-Observation. 'I was', he explained, 'looking after the money when we had any. There was a tremendous amount of pressure and stresses in our commune, which I had to try and help them ease. Tom was difficult sometimes and I began to feel that I would like to do something else.' For nearly eighteen months he had been a staunch lieutenant, but he had nothing to show for it. He had no money and was beginning to feel an element of resentment towards Harrisson.

Brian Barefoot, who'd done so much of the work with Hood for the politics book, was there for his departure and recorded it in his account of his time in Bolton.

> Walter left on August 30th. His departure was an epic. For the first time for eighteen months he could be a free man, for there was no more work to do. The night before he left, the Bolton Labour Party gave a supper in his honour; next day he spent all the time visiting friends and acquaintances, and in packing his few belongings. Then we had several beers in local pubs; a taxi arrived for Walter and his kit, and about a dozen people came to the station to see him off. Economy thrown to the winds, he had a porter to wheel his truck with his luggage on it, and had it put in the van, while he got into the Manchester train with only his tartan rug, his most valued – almost his only – personal possession. Finally the train pulled out (the wrong train, as we discovered later, but who cares!) and the last I saw of Walter was his small form leaning out of the carriage window, raised fist in salute to us all. It was a parting on a grand scale.

Barefoot left the following morning, quietly in his characteristic way, after saying goodbye to Gertrude Wagner, who was left in charge of the house, and to Bill Rigby, one of the Bolton residents who were still involved in the project. 'For some queer reason a friendship had sprung up between us, so different in age and outlook, and he would confide in me his complaints about how he was being treated. He was being treated very badly, scarcely being given any money for the work he did.'

With the departures of Hood and Barefoot, Wagner was for a time the only resident of Davenport Street. The original Worktown study of pubs, pools, religion, politics and holidays was being wound up to be replaced by a new study led by Madge and Wagner, 'Social Factors in Economic Projects'. All four books relating to the original study commissioned by Gollancz were scheduled for publication in the autumn and winter of 1938. Sommerfield and Wilcock were now back in London working on their books, so it seems strange that along with her own research Wagner continued to do reports on religious meetings and services. One of these was a Christadelphian meeting at the end of August which, she reported, should have started at 6.30 on the steps of the Town Hall. At 6.25 there were men going round with posters saying 'No more war. The Gospel of Christ'. As Wagner looked at the posters a middle-class man of about forty came up to her and asked whether she was from the press and whether she was interested in the movement. She told the man she was interested and he explained that they wanted to prove that the existing Churches didn't believe in the Bible. 'The clergymen', he said, 'have taken over too much power and there is nothing said about the power of clergymen in the Bible.'

About fifteen of those present were Christadelphians who had come from different towns to have a propaganda week. The group began their meeting with a prayer and in the talk that followed they repeated over and over again that everything they say is in the Bible and anybody who is interested can look it up. Anybody who had not got a Bible, they promised, could get one from them completely free. At the end of the meeting a girl approached Wagner and asked her whether she could help them to start a group in Bolton. She was then taken in a car where she was told that, although they had all sorts of people as members, their campaigns were done mostly by university and middle-class people. They were the only ones, she was told, 'who have the money; they have to pay their own expenses and the time they give up is part of their holidays. They think they are the only real Christians, because they are against war under all conditions. God has said love your enemy.'[14]

Groups like the Christadelphians, however, were no longer in tune with the majority view in the country. The various peace movements had experienced a falling away of support, with many people no longer believing that it was right to meet violence with inaction. But the anti-war sentiments expressed by the Christadelphians appealed to Wagner. Like the other observers before her, she was beginning to be known in Bolton and with the first-hand knowledge she had of the situation in Europe she was invited to give talks on Nazi Germany and Austria, especially by the Churches. With the *Anschluss* of Germany and Austria, Hitler had, by bluster and bullying, created a Greater Germany of seventy-four million people. Austria's former leaders, including the Chancellor, Kurt von Schuschnigg, who had opposed the union, were now being held in Dachau concentration camp and the 'great spring cleaning', as the Nazi newspapers were calling the planned pogrom, had begun. Jewish judges were dismissed, Jewish shops were placarded, and theatres and music halls were purged of Jews.

Wagner used her talks to establish her credentials and explain why she was in Bolton, always concluding the talk with a brief explanation of her research project and a request for people prepared to be interviewed at home. She also used the fact that she was making contact with people in Bolton to get other Austrians out of her homeland. Refugees could come to England if an English person agreed to be responsible for them. She recruited people whose names could be used as sponsors. In this way she was able to arrange for quite a few people to come in. Harrisson and Madge both sponsored people, including a cousin of Wagner's.

In London, Harrisson soon found a new focus. He set out to build up a new team of observers in Fulham – referred to as 'Metrop' in Mass-Observation publications. Before the Second World War Fulham was a working-class area and Harrisson envisaged it as a London counterpart to Worktown. He also redirected his search for art that the working man could associate with from the professional painters he had brought up to Bolton to a group of working-class painters in the Northumberland mining community of Ashington. He still wanted to find a popular aesthetic that would take art out of its ivory tower and make it accessible to the working man, and through an article in the *Listener* he found out about the men in Ashington. The group, who later found fame as the Pitmen Painters, had turned a WEA art-appreciation class into a painters' workshop, where they represented their everyday work and leisure in a primitive style untouched by the protocols of art-school education.[15] Harrisson was excited by their subject matter and style and by their indifference to the art market. Trevelyan was equally enthusiastic, so, intrigued by the naive realism of the group, they quickly made contact and arranged to meet them.

When Harrisson moved back to London he was immediately caught up in the escalating international crisis. Europe stood on the brink of war. The German advances throughout 1938 and the seizure of Austria and the Rhineland allied to the flow of Jewish refugees had brought home to the public the reality of Hitler's regime, of its anti-Semitism and of its territorial ambitions. 'In the last few years,' Mass-Observation reported, 'events have become increasingly spectacular and crises more frequent. As a result, a great many people started being interested in foreign affairs and political issues for the first time. As one crisis succeeds another, one might expect this interest would grow.' But when, at the end of August 1938, M-O asked 460 people if their interest in crises was increasing or decreasing, the results pointed quite clearly to a decrease of interest. 'Decreasing,' a twenty-seven-year-old toolmaker replied; 'for years we've heard so much of them that we're a trifle wary.' An eighteen-year-old clerk said he took little interest in any of the accounts of crises: 'I am getting tired of people talking about wars in Spain and China, and if people start talking about another war I feel like saying "For goodness sake shut up."'[16]

But, even as these interviews were being conducted, the biggest crisis so far was unfolding as Hitler threatened Czechoslovakia, ostensibly on behalf of the Sudeten Germans in the western fringe of Bohemia. Prime Minister Neville Chamberlain flew to Berlin to urge Hitler not to invade. Two meetings were held in mid-September, but the discussions were inconclusive. As the crisis unfolded Madge and Harrisson saw an opportunity for Mass-Observation. From early in the year they had come to regard the national panel as a useful source of information on a wide range of issues and relied heavily on it to monitor public response to the political events of the year.[17] Now they were perfectly placed to track public opinion on a matter of major national importance.

'Hanging over all our heads for years now', Mass-Observation stated,

> has been the threat of another general European war. Practically every grown-up person in this country must have been conscious of this threat at one time or another. Since it is so much a matter of life and death, they must have some definite attitude about it. How many people think there is going to be a war? One might have expected that the continuous bad news and the obvious preparations for war, re-armament, A.R.P. and the rest of it, would convince everybody that war was imminent. So it is interesting that the day after Hitler's Nuremberg speech on Monday, September 12 [in which he was unyielding in his refusal to accede to conciliatory Czech proposals along lines that Britain was suggesting], when war news filled the papers and the BBC was issuing special bulletins, questioning in working-class streets in Metrop showed a dominance of 'there won't be a war' statements.[18]

A possible explanation, the report went on, 'is that the worse things get, and the nearer the danger comes, the more necessary it is for people to put up a psychological defence in order to carry on with their daily lives. They have to hope for the best.'

Mass-Observation began to direct more and more of its attention to the worsening political crisis. During Chamberlain's toing and froing between London and Munich, the opinions of the man in the street were sought. Blackheath also encouraged observers to write about political issues in their diaries, and investigators in Bolton were asked to record overheard conversations in public places.[19] 'Right up to Chamberlain's return from his second visit to Hitler,' M-O reported, 'no one really knew what was happening. Everyone knew there was a crisis. And so an enormous frustration boiled up into a simmering mass of doubts and fears and furies. For the first time since the Abdication, an observer spending an hour in any town would have been almost sure to hear at least one conversation about politics.'[20]

Things came to a head towards the end of the month. By the last week in September, the Mass-Observation report on the crisis continued,

> tension, which many were finding almost unbearable, and which had really got into full swing on the evening of Monday, September 26, when the late newspaper placards announced that Hitler would march if he didn't get what he wanted by October 1, was acute. All the 'there won't be a war' statements were changing rapidly. War was now regarded as inevitable by the Press and MPs. An M-O snap survey over a number of towns showed that the public now agreed to an unprecedented degree. Out of 206 people whose answers had so far been received, 105 thought there would be war definitely on or before Saturday, 15 that there would be a war in a few weeks, 9 that there would be a war in a year or two, but 56 still believed that there would be no war at all, and 21 say they don't know or care.[21]

In Bolton new forms of greeting became popular: 'Have you got your gas mask?' 'Have you not measured for your Khaki yet?' 'Have you got a gun?' 'Have you got your papers yet?' A minority of 15 per cent of men questioned had firmly decided not to fight in any war, but more typical were sentiments such as these. Man of thirty: 'Yes, I am prepared to go and fight. Hitler has gone too bloody far this time, he needs teaching a lesson and I for one am prepared to give it him.' Man of thirty: 'Yes, I would fight. I'm a Britisher and proud of it. I'll fight to my last drop of blood. Some of these bloody pacifists want an operation and inject some British blood in them.' Man of forty: 'Yes, I will fight now. He wants his bloody clock knocking round. We shall have to show him who is boss. They talk about nothing else at work, it's a bloody pain.'[22] 'It's now or never to stop the bastard' was certainly one school of thought. But the more general consensus, according to Mass-Observation's national polls, was that the British public were more inclined to agree to Chamberlain letting Hitler have his way with Czechoslovakia rather than go to war against Germany, especially as Hitler was maintaining that 'This is the last territorial claim I shall make in Europe.'

As civil defence preparations were stepped up, M-O reported that there were mass fears. As one observer put it, 'With distribution of gas masks began real fear. All over the place one heard: "To think that one man is responsible for all this!" Along with fear went hate: "Everyone rages at Hitler. He will grace a good many bonfires on November 5th" was one comment, while a young English girl said: "I'd like to dig my scissors in him and twist it round and round."' On the evening of 27 September, Chamberlain broadcast to the nation: 'How horrible, fantastic, incredible, it is that we should be digging trenches and trying on gas masks here because of a quarrel in a faraway country between people of whom we know nothing.' He flew to Munich the next morning, convinced that the House of Commons wanted peace at any price, and by the afternoon of 30 September had agreed to Hitler's demands for the 'return' of the German-speaking parts of Czechoslovakia in exchange for a paper signed by him, renouncing any intention of going to war with Britain. This was the infamous piece of paper that Chamberlain announced, on his return, meant 'peace for our time'. Hitler was able to march into Czechoslovakia without having to fight for it, but the crisis was over and the settlement triggered a great tide of relief that swept over the country. For a brief moment it appeared that this policy of surrender mirrored the public's response. Without exception the media heaped praise on Chamberlain, but not everyone was in tune. His politics of avoiding war with Germany became the subject of intense public debate. On one side there was condemnation for allowing Hitler's Germany to grow too strong; others judged that Chamberlain had no alternative and was acting in Britain's best interests.

British communists, in particular, argued that appeasement was a pro-fascist policy and went as far as saying that the British ruling class would have preferred fascism to socialism. There was a view in many quarters that Munich and the whole policy of appeasement was one of granting from fear or cowardice unwarranted concessions in order to buy temporary peace at someone else's expense. The Left Book Club's Victor Gollancz, reflecting the true feelings of much of the population, distributed nearly two million leaflets analysing 'The Great Betrayal' within three days of Chamberlain's return from Munich. They were sentiments that Madge shared, and he recalled 'meeting Inez [Spender] in a pub in Leicester Square, and how totally downcast we both felt at the news of the Munich agreement'.[23]

Madge's personal life was a mess. Married to Kathleen Raine and still living with her and their children at Grotes Building, he was also carrying on with Angus Fisher, while declaring his love for Inez Spender. He and Inez would eventually divorce and marry each other, but even in the context of the open relationships enjoyed by bohemian intellectual couples like the Madges and the Spenders, there was already sufficient friction by October 1938 for Stephen Spender to brand Madge a 'crook' who seduced women with 'Wykehamist flattery'.[24] Madge was feeling the need to get away from the pressures of Blackheath, and the move to Bolton at this time would have suited him. But one of the consequences of Munich for him was that it delayed the move. Throughout the crisis he stayed in London, monitoring developments with Harrisson and analysing responses coming in to Blackheath from the national panel. Despite the continued deterioration in his relationship with Kathleen fuelled by the affairs they were both now very openly involved in, he continued to live in and work from 6 Grotes Buildings. The situation was further complicated by the fact that, without anywhere of his own to live, Harrisson had moved in there, adding to the pressures on Madge's marriage. He was never easy to be around when he was writing; he liked noise and always had a constant flow of visitors coming to see him. Many of their old friends like the Leggs and the Jenningses had never really liked him. Now Raine found the chaos created in their Blackheath home by his presence there, allied to her husband's continued dalliance with the two other women in his life, made her life intolerable.

In spite of these domestic difficulties Mass-Observation's founders were now enjoying one of the most fruitful periods of their partnership, and, working in closer collaboration than at any other time in their somewhat strained relationship, they wrote the book which more than anything else established the reputation of Mass-Observation. *Britain by Mass-Observation* was made up of an account of Keaw Yed – an ancient festival held in Westhoughton, Lancashire, all-in wrestling in Bolton and an account of the processes by which the Lambeth Walk became the latest craze in dance halls up and down the country. But the longest section of the Penguin Special was a detailed analysis of public opinion during the weeks of the Munich Crisis, based on responses from the national panel and random interviews conducted in London.[25] 'It was concerned', Madge said in his autobiography, 'with the way people responded to the events of this month. There were no opinion polls in those days, but newspaper leader writers and commentators, including some of the most intelligent, made confident assertions about what the man in the street was thinking. Although our methods of collecting people's reactions were hand-to-mouth and could claim no statistical exactness, we could draw on reports from the national panel of observers, and also from full-time observers both in Bolton and London. We were able to show shifts of opinion at different dates, differences in the reactions of men and women, striking differences in the level of interest in foreign politics as the crisis progressed, in a way which had not been tried before.'[26]

As he worked on the book in Blackheath, Harrisson also managed to find time to pursue his new-found interest in the coal-mining painters of Ashington, and he and Trevelyan went to Northumberland to meet the group. With characteristic enthusiasm he threw himself into working with them and promoting their work, believing that their subject matter and style combined with their indifference to the contemporary art world was of great significance to the ongoing debate about the social relevance of art. After a week spent with them, they arranged to mount an exhibition of 'Unprofessional Painting' in a Gateshead community centre, featuring the work of the group alongside work by other amateur artists from around the country. They also set up a series of lectures to accompany the exhibition, including one by Harrisson on social realism and another by Madge on poetry and everyday life.[27]

Bolton was never far from Harrisson's thoughts, and in October he revisited the town to discuss the economics project with Wagner. Observation of shops and shoppers, he said, would be one of the keystones of the project, and with regard to what he described as the shopping habit they agreed that total shopping behaviour must be observed over a period of time in order to discover what regularity existed, if any. How far, they needed to find out, did a shopper follow a beaten track in shopping, how far did they set out to get X commodity at the cheapest price and how far did social-psychological relationships with shop workers or owners affect economic relationships? The method, they agreed, would be for observers to go on shopping expeditions with shoppers over a period of three weeks or so – and through that to obtain notes on the varying roles of individual shopkeepers. They would also have to measure the time a woman spent shopping per week, on an hourly basis, and do this in relation to different social groups. Wagner suggested that a questionnaire should be sent to housewives to establish who bought what and to ask questions like 'Have you stopped shopping at your usual shops. If so: Why? How do you feel about it? Have you started at new shops etc?'[28] Wagner maintained that doing this sort of survey would be very labour intensive and they would need more observers for the work, so Harrisson agreed to make another approach to one of his old benefactors, Sir Ernest Simon, for funding for this new project.

When their work on *Britain* was completed, Madge was able to go along with Harrisson's earlier suggestion that the two of them should swap headquarters. 'These were my last days at Grotes Buildings,' he recalled in his autobiography. 'I wrote to my mother: October 27. Possibly I may arrange for Tom Harrisson to take over this house, paying the rent etc, and running the Blackheath end of M-O, while I live at Bolton.' Then on 31 October he wrote, 'I'm off to Bolton tonight.' Madge was at last able to take over from Harrisson in Worktown to investigate 'The Economics of Everyday Life' – the part that money played in the daily life of a Boltonian. The project and the book that was planned aimed to illustrate from conversations, personal documents, references in speeches, wayside pulpits and posters the attitudes to money of ordinary men and women with stories of generosity and meanness, saving, spending and gambling.

When he arrived at Davenport Street, he noted in a later memo to Harrisson, 'and saw the files and went through the stacks of index cards with your ideas and observations, it gave a vivid impression of energy and chaos'.[29] For his part Harrisson felt the same was true of the Blackheath end of the operation. From the start, despite the chaos that most visitors found at Davenport Street, he felt that it was Madge who was unsystematic. The panel material, he insisted, required good filing and analysis. But, he told Madge later, he found there were trunkloads of panel reports which were put together in any order, tied round with string and put away after Madge and Kathleen and others had read through the quotations, typed out some and put two or three in the private observers' bulletins. Harrisson felt that all his work had one central drive and that the great mass of it had been incorporated into new and stimulating material.[30] In spite of the Munich Crisis and their work on *Britain* bringing them closer together for a time, they were back on a collision course again.

19

SLEEPING WITH THE NATIVES

*'I have a houseful of bloody experts here now, and I foresee
that M-O is going to be a series of skirmishes and
battles between them and me and Tom'*

Charles Madge

Madge went up to Bolton with the very broad brief of studying economic life in the town. Within days of his arrival he was following people around Bolton's Victorian market hall, making very detailed notes on their movements and their purchases. '11.45 a.m. Woman about 50, with daughter, 12. Woman wears green hat, drab coat, grey fur collar. To Brooks stall; 45 secs examining muslin curtains, lifts between fingers, has a good look at them. Then 45 secs at neighbouring milliners stall – remnants.' And so the report goes on: 'at Schofields Pork Stall she buys a piece of gammon and a 1lb of sausages – total time 2 mins. Then Greenhalgh Grocery. 3 mins. 2 mins at Bailey's crockery, finally buying 6d sugar bowl. Then eggs at Charlsons, 1 min; buttons (1d) at Haynes – under 1 min.'[1]

Madge spent his early days in Bolton doing shopping follows like this – 'a rather Tom Harrisson like approach', as he put it. Prior to this he'd made only fleeting visits to Bolton and his initial impression of the town had been that it was about a hundred years behind the times.[2] Now he was there to stay and, like so many observers before him, he had to get used to the dampness, the grime, the monochrome townscapes and the all-pervading carboniferous atmosphere. Making his way back through the November gloom to the cheerless dinginess of Davenport Street after a long day of observations, everything was new to him. The trams rattled along the cobbled streets as workers and shoppers made their way home. Huddled figures in cloth caps, mufflers and clogs hurried past and the backdrop of great, gaunt spinning mills, bleach works and engineering workshops, smoking mill chimneys and row upon row of terraced houses gave it all, to his poetic eye, a dark and forbidding feel. Then a flash of brilliance from deep inside one of the mills, as he glimpsed the hundreds of yards of two-inch line-shafting with its chromium plate all shining in the dark, would appeal to his surrealistic vision.

Madge's move to Bolton distanced him from his increasingly complicated private life, but he couldn't get away from it for long, and within days of his arrival Angus was writing, 'I feel more deeply in love with you than I ever did and content to let it be a distant non-contacted love for the time being.' But on a visit to London it was Inez he went to see and on his return to Bolton he wrote: 'I am still aglow with you and want you so much . . . I am finding out why Boltonians buy so much coal at the New Year and what they do with their old bowlers.' But the next day 'Angus wrote that she had a week's holiday coming and did I want her to come to Bolton. I must have asked her to come because she wrote: "I am up in the air about next Wednesday. It will be heaven to kiss you again."' Before her visit he was in London for two days and saw Inez – 'I need hardly labour the point that I was playing a double game,' he admitted in his autobiography.

Angus Fisher went to Bolton to stay with Madge from 16 to 21 November. At the time we learn from a letter he wrote to Inez in the middle of this visit that he was 'working very hard and satisfactorily on the most basic possible problems, such as why the hardest-up working-class families buy fancy cakes, which have a really poetic range, variety and appeal in Bolton. This morning we were all trailing shoppers through the market. The proprietor of the Golden Lion said that England had lost its morals from the Prime-Minister downwards . . . Woolworth's had a Christmas display with a live girl in a sad Mickey Mouse mask doing hula-hula on top of a spangled house advertising 6d Monster Packets of Toys. It's a lovely place, though bread and butter and fish and chips becomes a devitalising diet.'[3]

'It was', Madge continued in his autobiography, 'a very rough sort of existence up there and not at all typical of the way other people lived in Bolton. It was more a version of the bohemian life – a rather curious version of it which we lived up there.' Madge shared this bohemian life with Wagner, who found him much easier to get on with than Harrisson. Together they discussed the methodology for their research project and devised terminology for their shop observations. They decided that shopping could be classified as purposive or non-purposive. 'A purposive purchase or walk through a shop is one in which it is evident that the purchaser has previously decided on what he or she needs, and has gone to get it. This can be decided by the speed with which he or she makes her way to the appropriate place for the purchase, and the way her desires are communicated to the shop assistant. A non-purposive purchase is one in which it is evident that the purchaser has not previously decided upon what he or she needs. This can be decided by the hesitancy of approach of the purchaser, the time he or she takes to decide upon an order, and the manner in which the order is given.'[4] For rough use in follows, they decided, the relationship between customer and shop assistant could be classed as: '(a) Matter of fact. The exchange of money and goods between customer and assistant takes place with no visible exchange of the customary expressions of friendliness, i.e. smiles, a few words, action of the hand. (b) Friendly. The exchange of smiles, and a few words in the course of the purchase. (c) Very friendly. The exchange of conversation, laughter and general attitude of ease in their relation.'[5]

To carry out these observations more bodies were needed. To do some of the trailing round Woolworth's Harrisson sent Geoffrey Thomas, an aspiring young novelist who had been working for Mass-Observation in Fulham, to join Wagner and Madge in Bolton. His brief was to conduct 'objective fieldwork and detailed outdoor studies of behaviour'.[6] Thomas spent his time following people around Bolton's shops and market, investigating how far the housewife 'knows beforehand exactly what she wants or is influenced by what she sees in the shop and noting her interactions with shop assistants and how she chooses what to buy'.[7] He put this into practice within days of arriving in Bolton as he followed people around Marks and Spencer's. At 11.40 a.m. he noted: 'woman 35 with boy of 12, lower middle class. Study shirts. Mother points to shirts and says "This is what you want isn't it?" . . . Along to boys' jackets hanging on pegs. Mother: "They didn't have these last time we were here did they?" Boy shook his head. From there they went to toy counter. Boy said "Oh, look at the aeroplanes" . . . Mother went off to look at women's dresses. Boy followed after a time, and said a dress was nice.' Eventually, Thomas reported, they went back to the toy counter where the woman bought two toy filling stations, costing 2/11d each.[8]

The main shops in Bolton town centre were Marks and Spencer's, Woolworth's and a local department store, Gregory and Porritt's. Follows were done in all of them. In Marks and Spencer's, Wagner reported: '12.30. Middle-class woman. About thirty-four. Tailored suit. Brown fur over her arm. Walks in straight to the stocking stall, looks at the 1/11d stockings. Takes one pair in her hands, investigates it from all sides feeling with her fingertips the strength of the material.' Altogether this woman spent seven minutes trying to decide which stockings to buy, examining different pairs, looking at different shades, investigating the strength of the material at the heel, asking another woman if she thinks they will wear well. All this was reported in minute detail by Wagner. By way of contrast she described 'a well-dressed working-class girl, blue suit, hair well done, about twenty . . . Goes straight to the counter for 1/6 stockings, looks for a second, points to a certain pair, gets it wrapped up, pays and walks immediately out. Not quite a minute altogether.'[9]

Shopping follows like these were very much in line with Harrisson's notion of 'objective fieldwork', but it was clear from the start that the work for the economics project would go beyond this as Wagner brought into play her social psychologist's focus on interviews as a key research tool. In addition to following people around shops, therefore, Thomas was briefed to arrange a series of interviews with shop owners to find out about their customers' shopping habits. Bromley's Confectioners was a small to medium-sized shop on Tonge Moor Road that sold confectionery and cooked meats. It was run by the owner and his wife, who took time off to tell Thomas about their business. A shop like this, he learned, might specialise in certain things like roast heart, on certain days, and people who like those things will come in for them at the right time. As for the regular day-to-day trade he learned that pies were a dinnertime trade, and custards and tarts also sold well at dinnertime. More confectionery, he was informed, was sold in the latter half of the week, the reason being 'if one's wife works she will probably bake on a Saturday and that will last the house until Tuesday'. What Thomas and the other observers were doing was early market research. He was able to find out that custards, made with eggs and sterilised milk, were a favourite because people buying them couldn't make their equal at the same price. Tarts, he learned, were a great favourite in summer; Eccles cakes, sultanas and Nelson cakes were more popular with men than women; children liked anything with chocolate. Women, he found, were the main customers, and at Bromley's the shop owner told him that he had got to know the neighbourhood well, 'since customers bring their troubles and gossip to him. Also has inquiries from hire-purchase firms to answer.'[10]

It was not just shops that were the focus of the economics project, and in taking her research work into individual houses and interviewing housewives, Wagner changed the whole focus of the Bolton operation and did much to redress the earlier male focus of the Worktown project. In studying the household economy she looked at the way the weekly money was divided up among the household, whether the housewife had a conscious plan for the way she used the household budget and whether she discussed it. It also involved the compromises of married life and sex differences in the standard of living. But, unlike Wilcock and his fellow Christians or Hood and his Labour Party friends, Wagner never got close to the people she interviewed. For the housewives who confided in her she remained somewhat superior, as was brought home to her when she recorded one of them meeting her in the street who was 'astonished to see me carrying a basket and [thought that] it may not agree with my role I am acting in Bolton to be seen with a shopping basket'.[11] She clearly felt Wagner was far too important to be out around town doing her own shopping.

Throughout November Wagner, Madge and Thomas watched people doing their shopping and noted their prejudices and habits: how, for example, people decided what sort of bread to buy – white or brown; what sort of spread – butter or margarine; and whether to buy fresh or tinned milk. They looked at habits with regard to eating fruit, meat and vegetables and at the ritual of tea – the family drink; at happiness in terms of extra spending, particularly on things like treats for children. They recorded the weekly cycle of spending and the compromises of married life. 'My wife is always bloody well grumbling about prices going up. I think she wants more money off me. I wonder if she realises that every bloody thing I buy's gone up too . . . beer, baccy.'

Their aim was to discover how ordinary people behaved – what they ate, what they spent, what they thought and how they lived. Nothing was considered too trivial to observe. Economics and the expenses of birth, children, marriage, old age, death and burial; education and the standard of living; housework, cooking, and the place of the fish and chip shop were all subjected to the gaze of the observers, as was the family budget. Housewives took them into their confidence, invited them into their homes and gave detailed breakdowns of their household finances right down to the last penny. In one house it was reported that there were ten people – man, woman, eight children – four boys and four girls. The oldest lad would be sixteen next birthday and working, serving his time. The only income came from the man, whose wages were £2 17/6d and the boy who earned 14/9d – a total of £3 12/3d.

The housewife gave a breakdown of their weekly outgoings: 'Rent 10/6d: Coal 3/6d sometimes it's more. Clubs. That's insurance for death. Oh we have one 4d a week, an endowment for £5.2.6. Then there's Union 4d for Bobby and 7d for Joe. Lighting is 1/6d a week. 2 shillings a week for a check so that the young lad that's working can have his overalls and footwear. 4/6d for the boy's dinner. You see they all have their dinners in the canteen an' you don't like the lad to feel he's out of it.

Wait a minute, there's 2/6d a week that I pay to a Scotsman that comes. That's for kiddies' clothes – an' they've got to be nice. I get 4 to 5 loaves of bread every day an' they're five pence each.'

The woman went on to list everything in her weekly shop and what it cost: tea, coffee, sugar, soap and soap powder, salt, pepper and starch, a quart of milk every day, self-raising flour, lard and thirty pounds of potatoes a week. All this came to £1 3/9d a week. At this point she sat down and said, 'Eh I stop an' think I don't know how I carry on.' The observer asked about butter – 'Oh we never see butter in this house. I get six pounds of marge at 5d' – she stopped. 'Do you know when I went into Townleys (hospital) for this last un it's the first time I've tasted butter for three years.' (Her last was only eight weeks old.) When the observer asked about meat, 'Oh I don't buy meat – perhaps I get a bit of mince meat.'

They have, the report went on, a crippled girl, with infantile paralysis in one leg – 'Oh yes I get malt and milk for her with the bad leg. An' I pay 1/6d a week so she can learn the violin. I generally get three tins of beans a week, that's another 1/6d – an' a packet of fags every day – them's luxuries – 1/2d. The gas runs 8d a week, but when there's no pennies we use the fire. I give the eldest lad 1/9d a week pocket money an' he's paying for the wireless 1s a week an' Joe pays the other 1/3. Am payin' a shilling a week for the squeezers (wringing machine) an' we get the B.E.N. [*Bolton Evening News*] every day. Sometimes kids get a penny pocket money.' At this point the woman sat still and said, 'Eh I don't know. We want to try to find the kids a job which will give them a chance we haven't got.' Then she continued: 'About once a fortnight I go to the pictures. It costs 4d.' Her husband, she said, had one suit, one pair of shoes, three sets of work clothes and clogs – 'Sometimes I buy him a new collar an' tie.' With regard to her own clothes she disclosed, 'I've got this dress – an' another old one. I have one coat that's worth wearing – I got from the minister's wife – it's black and that's a good colour. Also I've a change of underclothes – mind it's just a change – an' when I get them given they got to be altered – an' I keeps on washin' them. All the kiddies the same. I cuts an' contrives.'

'We got on talking about furniture,' the observer continued. The woman said, 'The piano husband got for 4/- – and carting it away. The two large chairs. Listen! Those two chairs were broken up – one was in pieces when we got it – they lay in a man's garden for eight months then his wash-house – then Joe got 'em. The square table I got from a friend. The two green plush chairs (no springs in them) I got them from a lady for helpin' her to move. An' the chairs which we are finishing with, we've given them to a friend – who's worse off than us. The old dresser – that was expensive, 22/-. I've paid for that at 1/- a week. Oh yes we're always in debt. The pans the same as we got married seventeen years ago – it's the same with the kettle – I generally spend 1d to 3d a week on odd cups or saucers. Bedding, we've got nothing of any value but I keeps on doin' them up.'

Then it was back to clothes. 'Husband', she said, 'has to depend on other people, on th' kindness of friends.' It was the same for the wife except 'Sometimes I buy some stockings 6d at Woolworth's – I got a good bargain t'other day off the rag-cart, three pairs of shoes for 6d. I gave one pair to the woman further up. Since the eldest boy started work he hasn't had a new suit – always second hand – an' the same as far as boots is concerned it's cut down, or a rag-cart, or a rummage sale. When the holidays come along we have to get straight by payin' a few shillings a week for months after.' Above the mantelpiece, the observer noted a verse:

Bless the four corners of this House
And be the lintel blest
And Bless the Hearth and Bless the Board
And Bless the Bed of Rest
And Bless the Door that opens wide
To Strangers and to Kin
And Bless the little window-pane that lets the
Sunshine in.

While Madge was in Bolton looking at the economics of everyday life, Harrisson took over direction of a small team of full-time Mass-Observation staff in Blackheath and the panel of volunteer observers and diarists, which by this time had grown to nearly 1,500. He was also supervising Mass-Observation's work in Fulham, where work included further observations of pubs and churchgoing along with surveys of the voting habits of shopkeepers and the leisure activities of young people. Joe Wilcock, now back in London, worked in Fulham, but Harrisson had no money to pay him and the best he could do for him was to persuade his contacts in the Labour Party to give him some work.[12]

While he had plenty to keep him occupied at the Blackheath end of the operation, Harrisson worried about what was happening in Bolton. He was particularly concerned about what he described as 'the somewhat academic tendencies of Wagner and Madge'.[13] It is perhaps surprising, therefore, that when he was approached by another academic he agreed to take him on to supplement the team in Bolton. Twenty-nine-year-old Dennis Chapman was the sociologist who had been so critical of the lack of awareness of the subject displayed by Harrisson and Madge when he'd first met them in early 1937. Instead of throwing in his lot with Mass-Observation he chose to work for Seebohm Rowntree on a study of poverty in York, then joined a team in the Department of Psychology in the University of St Andrews on a study of long-term unemployment among Dundee jute workers. But the money ran out and he became unemployed. Harrisson got in touch with him. 'Twenty pounds collected. Further sixty guaranteed and other money almost certain for Social Factors in Economics research, Bolton and Ashington. Would you start Bolton next week. We have every prospect of being able to secure you a decent income for at least six months. Reply Star and Garter, Putney. Harrisson. Second of November 1938.' 'It was typical!' Chapman said in a later interview: 'that a penniless Mass-Observation was staying at the Star and Garter Putney with a friend, and that an expensive telegram was written rather than a letter.'

Within days Chapman received a second telegram. 'I will bring you dough on Thursday. Things work well. I should like you to work some of the time here and in Ashington and be the moving part of the Bolton unit etc etc. Anyway, get to know the smells and accents of Bolton. That's the first thing I'm looking to you to counteract the somewhat academic tendencies of Wagner and Madge. Spend the next four days talking to working men, cotton operatives, tannery chaps, colliers, unemployed, all over Bolton.' Chapman was not impressed: 'The naivety of this', he asserted, 'is that I had served a craft apprenticeship. I had spent several years selling insurance all over the county of Somerset. I came from a working-class background and spent a year doing fieldwork in York for Rowntree with railway workers, chocolate workers, unemployed, the rest of it . . . including a very elaborate family budget survey, and I had just spent two years studying the life of what were probably the poorest of the unemployed in Britain of that time, the unemployed jute workers of Dundee. And here was Tom Harrisson telling me to get the sights and smells of the working class, which shows basically how totally ignorant he was.' In spite of his indignation about Harrisson's approach, Chapman needed the work and decided to accept the offer. 'In due course,' he recalled, 'A. D. Peters, who was the literary agent for Tom Harrisson, sent me £35, which is all I ever got.'

As Chapman started work in Bolton the news from the continent was not good. Anti-Semitic laws were passed in Italy, and in Germany widespread anti-Jewish violence broke out. In what became known as *Kristallnacht* – the night of broken glass – synagogues were bombed or burned out, Jewish shops and homes were ransacked and Jews were subjected to mob violence in the streets as the police stood by and watched. Some 35,000 Jews were arrested throughout the Reich. In Bolton, Chapman found 'the team consisted of Gertrude Wagner, Geoffrey Thomas, occasionally Charles Madge, myself and a mysterious character called Gerald Edwards who was also employed as a drama organiser by Bolton Corporation. So he had an income. Whether he had to pay rent or was allowed to live rent free in the attic I don't know. He gave us information and also brought other people in who were associated with drama. Geoffrey Thomas was using Mass-Observation as a source for a novel of working-class life that he was engaged on.'[14]

Looking for funding for the economics project in Bolton, Harrisson turned, as already agreed with Wagner, to Sir Ernest Simon, extolling in a letter to him the qualifications and experience of Wagner and Chapman. 'Both', he wrote, though he was being somewhat sparing with the truth, 'have refused good jobs to work with me on this book, because they believe it to be important. In order to keep them, I have got to be able to pay them a bit. I would ask you to put up two sums of forty pounds which would ensure the keep of Chapman and his family (wife and kids).'[15] Harrisson also started to look into potential new sources of income from the world of advertising by doing the sort of work that had been done for Lintas with the margarine survey. Mass-Observation was now beginning to carry out market research, in violation of its high scientific aims. Madge and some of the other observers had reservations about this course of action but Harrisson continued to set the agenda and was, as Chapman put it, 'still the dominant person in the organisation'. He was also still more inclined to put his own interests first and remained cavalier in his attitude to money and in the way he treated others. 'Still I think more likely to put his interest in his current girlfriend ahead of almost any other requirement of the time' was Chapman's view. 'Very, very careless about money and totally contemptuous of the interests of small tradesmen. He ran up bills everywhere and never paid them, which was the antithesis of the working-class ethic that he was supposed to be studying.'

Chapman referred to one occasion when Harrisson bought a small Pye portable radio.

I don't know how much it was at the time, but it was expensive ... £13 sticks in my mind ... and he bought it on the never-never. He paid the deposit and probably a small number of instalments. He hadn't paid the rest of the instalments and the man who had the little shop round the corner, who was obviously not a wealthy entrepreneur by any means, wanted to reclaim the radio set and Madge wrote to Harrisson saying he had either to pay up or he would lose the radio set. The following day Tom arrived having travelled overnight by first-class sleeper from London with a lady, in order to take the radio away so that it couldn't be reclaimed. Now the cost of two first-class fares, two sleepers, was much more than the amount outstanding on the radio. It amounted, I suppose, technically, to theft. This was the sort of absurd antithesis to what he was claiming, because he did rob an honest tradesman, and in order to do it spent much more than he would have had to do to have paid his debt. That, I think, was not untypical.

Chapman was working closely with Madge, who, he recalled, 'wrote poems while we were there'. Wagner 'was the academic and she was interested in the emotional substructure of working-class life. For this she depended very much on Bill Naughton to get information about the families he visited as a coalman.' Naughton was a participant observer in the true sense and his job gave him an entrée to a social field that would be closed to any other person. There were other local people who helped the team in this way. Chapman remembered two in particular: 'two women who were cotton workers. One was Joyce Mangnall and there was another girl whose name I never knew. She was a kind of Junoesque figure – a splendid physical specimen, very, very beautiful and a delightful cook. These two used to come in and look after us and give us their stories. They would often come in the evening and play cards. But these two girls were extremely bright, intelligent and in these days would be getting their A levels and going to university. It was a sort of little commune. For the fieldwork, there were people like this who were interested enough to come in and tell us things. Their interest was partly social. With Bill Naughton it was emotional; he formed an attachment and later fathered some of Wagner's children.'[16]

Madge and Wagner's Worktown was very different to the Worktown of Harrisson and his band of observers. With its new emphasis on social psychology and a mix of research methods, their approach had moved a long way from Harrisson's original unobserved observation. It was now the interview and questionnaire that formed the basis of their work, while observation of behaviour was supplementary. Undoubtedly the whole tenor of the work was now much more academic and no longer could they be described, with any justification, as spies or snoopers. But the whole Worktown set-up had changed immeasurably and Madge's Worktown team was much less integrated in the life of the town than Harrisson's original team had been. The leading investigators were now university-trained academics; no longer was there the kind of rapport that Sommerfield had with the men in the pub, that Wilcock had with the churchgoers or that Hood had with the local Labour Party and left-wing activists.

Madge was well aware of this and was anxious to supplement the team with, as he put it in a letter to Harrisson, 'a Walter Hood prolet-obs'.[17] The nearest he could come to finding such a person was Bill Naughton, who had become a frequent visitor to Davenport Street since forming his relationship with Wagner. Chapman appeared to have difficulty concealing his disdain for their affair. On one occasion, seeing Wagner's bedspread hanging up to dry in the kitchen, he scornfully remarked that it was 'the binding for a big portion of her thesis'.[18] But Chapman himself had no room to talk as he had his own liaison with one of the natives. From soon after his arrival he had been having an affair with Joyce Mangnall. Both parties would appear to have benefited from these liaisons. Although it is extremely unlikely that Chapman or Wagner were acting on Harrisson's suggestion that the anthropologist should not hesitate to sleep with the natives, the relationships that the observers had with these locals and their presence at Davenport Street no doubt improved their understanding of and contact with working-class culture. For Naughton and Mangnall, their relationship with Mass-Observation must have made a positive contribution to their subsequent upward social mobility.

Mangnall, the weaver whom Harrisson had first met during his time working in a mill just after he'd arrived in Bolton in 1936, was particularly active when Madge was in the town. Hundreds of her conversations with friends, neighbours and workmates were recorded, and she was an extremely useful contact because she always brought in people she knew and always did half a dozen or more questionnaires in her own circle. Madge found her presence and that of Naughton reassuring, keeping what had become an academic team in touch with grass-roots reality. Confronted by Wagner and Chapman, both academically trained sociologists, Madge wrote to Inez Spender, 'I have a houseful of bloody experts here now, and I foresee that M-O is going to be a series of skirmishes and battles between them and me and Tom.'[19]

Like Mangnall, Naughton had been known to the Mass-Observation team in Bolton since the early days of the project. He came from a coal-mining family and even into his late twenties, when he was a Co-op coalman, looked like a miner, as Harrisson recalled on first meeting him: 'he was always well bathed and spruced up but he had the dark-rimmed, coal-flecked eyelashes you see on miners. He told me it took longer to get those eyelashes clean than all the rest of him. You had to do it with olive oil, a cloth and a matchstick. To clean his hands he used a mixture of olive oil and sugar and that took ten minutes.'[20] He was, as Brian Barefoot had already found out, something of an aficionado of all-in wrestling, and he was soon taking his new girlfriend to the bouts at the Bolton Stadium.

'Monday at seven', Wagner reported, 'Naughton called for me as he had promised to take me to an all-in wrestling fight in the Worktown Stadium. He is quite an expert in wrestling, does it with his brother at home "for fun". Goes every Monday to the Stadium. In his ordinary life he is a coal driver, twenty-eight years of age, married with two kids to whom he reads at bedtime, poetry, selected with skill and taste of which an Oxford professor need not be ashamed.' It was early and they decided to walk down to the Stadium. 'Bill . . . tells me more about the game. He warns me not to be afraid that the men hurt each other too much. He thinks that I will not be able to understand the whole game properly, as it is very difficult art.' They walked through 'rather slummy districts along closed mills, one looked especially downfallen, all windows smashed'. Wagner made a remark about it. Naughton laughed and said, 'You know there is something about smashing windows. If I pass a closed mill and there is nobody about, I can't resist. I have to take a piece of coal from my van and smash a window; it seems such a pleasure.'

The stadium was in an old mill. 'Passing a small yard', Wagner recorded, 'and getting a ticket for 6d, 1/-, 2/- or 2/6d (the colour of the tickets is changed every week to hinder too much swindling) you are allowed into the hall. The first impression is what shabby elegance. The windows are curtained by red blue crepe paper rather worn and bleached by incoming rain. In the centre is the ring. Around it the 2/6 and 2/- seats, red plush with lots of holes in them, and evidently originating from very different sources. Then come the 1/- seats, plain chairs with red crepe coating. Five feet away, separated by a four foot high fence, the 6d stands where the whole audience room is slightly sloped.' As for the wrestling itself, Wagner reported that at first the whole affair seemed boring to her, but by the second fight she was beginning to enjoy now and again a quick movement, a skilful jump, a good defence movement, even though she disliked the brutality. She said that after the interval she got so involved and was so much in favour of one of the fighters that she found herself holding her breath back for fear he might lose.[21]

Although the primary focus of the work in Bolton was now on economics, Wagner's wrestling reports, which were to form the basis of a chapter in *Britain by Mass Observation*, show that the wider spectrum of life in the town was not forgotten. 'One of the things that was in mind at that time', Chapman said, 'was local humour – what made people laugh. So we started visiting cinemas where there were humorous films and seeing what it was that Bolton audiences laugh at and for how long they laughed.' Observers were also expected to go to the local dance halls and, according to Chapman,

> dance with the local girls and take them home afterwards and see how we got on. This was presumably some kind of bonus but anthropologists were apparently relieved of certain moral restraints because this was the only way you could get to know . . . I must say the young women of Bolton were far too intelligent and sophisticated to be taken in by any ploy of this kind. And again it showed the naivety because there was no one in Davenport Street who spoke with anything like a Northern accent. They certainly wouldn't have recognised my Cotswold accent as being a working-class accent. It would be Southern and toffee-nosed. I think we were tolerated in an amused kind of way by the people we saw out, but that we never penetrated very deeply into their lives or their interests.

On the economics front Chapman was also involved in the study of Bolton market. There, he said, 'my stint was to study the selling of potatoes. I was expected to be present in the market from dawn till closing time and observe one potato stall selling every day of the week and, it was hoped, every day of the month for every day of the year to be certain. I became a great European expert on the selling of potatoes in open markets in snow-bound Bolton. But this was Tom's approach. On the other hand he had no means of handling the data once it had been collected. It was just data, data, data. Then a commissioned book. Then the immense problem of trying to make some kind of coherent pattern out of it rather than deciding on a framework for your observations.'[22]

With no satisfactory way to determine what data was relevant, completion and delivery of the books was becoming more and more of a problem. By the end of the year Harrisson was claiming that the planned volumes on politics and the pub were ready for the publisher and that the third on religion was close to completion. But this was far from the true state of affairs. The three books on Bolton commissioned by Gollancz were proving very hard to pull into shape. One of the main problems was that, despite appointing Hood, Wilcock and Sommerfield as leaders of the fieldwork and authors of the planned books, Harrisson never appears to have had any intention of giving them any autonomy. Barefoot, who did so much work for the politics book with Walter Hood, realised from a very early stage that 'while Tom Harrisson would make his name from Bolton, no one else was likely to make a career from it'.[23] Bruce Watkin wrote later of the exploitation of Mass-Observation's less educated workers whom Harrisson had seduced into working for nothing by feeding them promises of future fame as authors.[24]

The book that was nearest to completion was *The Pub and the People*. In fact it was the only one that was anywhere near completion. This was almost certainly due to the fact that Sommerfield was the only one of the three proposed authors who had any real writing experience. But even he was having problems. He had completed a draft of the book on the pub by the autumn of 1938, but neither Gollancz nor Harrisson was happy with it. Revisions and rewrites meant that the final draft was not completed until shortly before the war. The religion book was delayed by tensions that had always existed between Wilcock and Harrisson over the approach to be taken in it. Harrisson was a non-believer and saw Wilcock as a far-out fundamentalist who was easily taken in by parsonic sentimentality, while Wilcock distrusted Harrisson and never overcame his fear that he would make 'some blasphemous use of the material'.[25] Such incompatible viewpoints made it difficult to move from the collection of information to the framing of any sort of coherent analysis. As ever money, or the lack of it, was probably the biggest problem. With no pay coming in from Harrisson, Wilcock had to find other work and was not prepared to work on the religion book on a voluntary basis in his spare time. But it was on the politics book that Harrisson's takeover was most blatant, holding back the Gollancz book on 'Politics and the Non-Voter' and making full use of the material for a book of his own, 'The Poverty of Freedom', which he did not acknowledge as a Mass-Observation study.

Having done his time in the North, Harrisson was now happy to be back in London – immersing himself in London life, or the life of the East End to be precise, as he'd swapped the refinements of Madge's Blackheath home for rented rooms in a bug-infested tenement building off Commercial Road.[26] It was the squalor of Davenport Street again in a different setting. Concerned about the growth of anti-Semitism, he wanted to subject prevailing stereotypes about the Jews – mean, money-grasping, loud and flashy – to objective examination and to investigate the causes and extent of anti-Semitism. To fund the research he secured a payment of £250 from the Jewish Board of Deputies.

Overseeing the operation in Bolton, Madge the poet was turning into Madge the sociologist and he was settling into his new role there, writing to Inez on 21 December,

> I am tenderly melancholy but happy this afternoon, with the usual chimney pouring out black smoke against a pale Christmas sky with a few pink clouds. I have just found out about 'Footings' which happen in all the mills on Christmas Eve – terrific unofficial bean feasts with pies, cakes and a great deal of rum, whisky, gin, vermouth and Pink Petal cocktails. They are organised and paid for by the mill girls, and the men expect to be treated. Foremen are bribed with drink, and if the manager walks through, everyone rushes back to their loom. As soon as he goes out, the signal is given and the fun starts again. It happens in every mill and they save up for twelve weeks to pay for it.[27]

Finances for the operation remained perilous, and on 23 December Madge wrote again to Inez.

> The money situation in Bolton got very bad so I made a dash to London – and secured £150. More important than this, I had an hour's talk to Karin Stephen* and a long talk with Kathleen which have quite suddenly, for me, cleared up a tangle which has been oppressing me for a long time. Briefly, the change is this – that though for a long time I have known – and Kathleen has known – that we couldn't get back to each other, yet for one reason or another it has always seemed necessary to leave a hypothetical Open Door for a return. When Karin had heard my story, she said that it was impossible to mend our marriage. This I accept, and more important still, Kathleen is now prepared to accept it, and not to maintain this deadly myth of the Open Door.[28]

With some of the turmoil in his private life resolved, a good working relationship with Wagner in Bolton and a modest level of funding secured for their project Madge was able to approach the New Year in a positive frame of mind.

---

* A psychoanalyst and psychologist who was one of Madge's circle and Virginia Woolf's sister-in-law.

20

SKIRMISHES AND BATTLES

*'Everything is blowing into our hands . . . We have
got what no one else has got, facts before the war'*

Tom Harrisson writing to Charles Madge

Mass-Observation was now well established and had by the beginning of 1939 become a household name. The status of the organisation was given a further boost when *Britain by Mass-Observation* was published to great acclaim as a Penguin Special in January. It contained an eighty-page analysis of the Munich Crisis that was highly critical not just of government but of media coverage. Material included interviews in Bolton and in Fulham, surveys made through the national panel of observers, observations and overheard comments in Whitehall and Downing Street, analysis also of how newspapers and radio treated the crisis and a study of rumours. As always with Mass-Observation, the human eye caught telling details. Before Chamberlain announced from a window in Downing Street that he had brought back from Munich a promise of 'peace for our time', he stretched out his arm to silence the people cheering below. An observer noted, 'Several in crowd appear to take this for a Fascist salute and stretch forth their arms likewise.'

'All this', Madge noted, 'could of course have been done better with bigger resources, and on a sounder statistical basis, but M-O could at least provide an alternative to newspaper accounts and speculations about public opinion which had no serious foundations of any kind.'[1] The book sold 100,000 copies in ten days and brought in a large number of recruits to the national panel. It also, as Madge observed in his autobiography, alerted key players in Whitehall to the potential value of Mass-Observation as an instrument for monitoring public opinion under war conditions.

In these early days of 1939 the news coming in from abroad wasn't good. On 26 January Franco's attack on the great bastion of Republicanism, Catalonia, led to another Nationalist triumph. His troops entered Barcelona and met with only sporadic resistance, as exhausted Republican armies crossed into France. Over the previous six months the Nationalists, heavily reinforced and supplied by Hitler and Mussolini, had won a series of victories. The fall of Madrid couldn't be delayed much longer and, with it, the Spanish Civil War would be over. At home the Labour Party had expelled the left-wing Sir Stafford Cripps for his campaign to widen the united front with the communists, which he had been advocating since 1936, into an anti-fascist Popular Front. That evening Geoffrey Thomas went to a Labour Party ward meeting and witnessed what he described as 'a fine example of what a ward meeting should not be. The atmosphere was pretty grim, with the fall of Barcelona, and the expulsion of Cripps. Ellis Clarke thought the party was done for now, sooner or later. The President of the ward association is a big white-haired Irishman, Kilcommins, who has no real interest in politics, but a lot in trade unions. He is fairly stupid, but has learned to speak. The whole meeting was frightful, and displayed a complete lack of knowledge of the elements of organising.'

Thomas was an aspiring novelist and during his time with Mass-Observation he kept a diary recording day-to-day life in Davenport Street. It reveals that life there was as dirty, as overcrowded and as underfunded as it had ever been. But above all it was still interesting and, without the domineering presence of Harrisson, it appeared to be more relaxed and convivial. After the Labour Party meeting he wrote that Charles had returned 'this afternoon and as a result we had a bottle of rum in the evening. The results were odd. Joyce had some rum toddy, and was badly sick. When Charles had cleared off to his room, we took her home with Mary, and walked back sliding through the slush. It was a vile night with bitter wind and rain. We got back to find Gerald sitting in the kitchen with a single candle, the light having gone out. There we also sat and were philosophical, to the extent of Dennis lighting twelve candles in a row along the mantelpiece.'

The following day Thomas recorded that there was another drinking session at Davenport Street. This time it was sherry and 'I went to bed with my boots on. It all happened because Dennis got his long awaited 35 quid from H., now, I hear, in love with a tough Mayfairite, just back from a long week-end in Paris, to see his millionaire friend Guthmann.' The tough Mayfairite was Betha Wolferstan Clayton, a rich, upper-class married woman who had a big house in Ladbroke Grove. Biddy, as she was known to her friends, was stylish and sophisticated. Her Ladbroke Grove house was a meeting place for people interested in or active in the theatre, journalism and the arts. She was married to Michael Clayton and they had a five-year-old son, but soon after they met she and Harrisson became lovers.

In Bolton, Thomas was doing his bit in getting to know the natives, recording in his diary that he 'met a girl at the Reform Club, and liked her, though she is not particularly good looking'. In the evening they were on the sherry again at Davenport Street. 'We had two bottles between five of us, for Bill Naughton came in the middle, fresh from coal-heaving. Presently, when neither Dennis nor I could drink more sherry we went and bought some fish and chips from the motherly woman down the road who once told Dennis I was delicate, like china, and returned to demolish them. Then I went up to my room and passed out.'

Communal life was working well for this set of observers, but if they were to stay together, money needed to be raised to keep the operation going. 'All through this time,' Chapman recalled, 'M-O was absolutely penniless. How the rent was paid at Davenport Street was a mystery. I think the coke was supplied by Bill Naughton. There was a desperate central-heating system which was run by coke. The ashes were never taken out of the cellar. Soon the space for coke began to diminish and the quantities of ash built up, and it became a duty to go down and do the thing. The only way in which you could do it was to go down naked and then have a bath because you were so filthy. There was the splendid sight of members of the commune going down to stoke the boiler which for some reason was called Martha.' They managed to feed very well at Davenport Street. 'There seemed to be unlimited credit at the butcher's which I never understood. Of course Tom spent a great deal of money, so any way of getting money was important. He got a commission to make a survey about public opinion about air-raid precautions for the *News Chronicle*. Gerald Edwards was having his hair cut that morning, so he interviewed the barber. He went on the tram so he interviewed the tram conductor. I forget how he got the other three interviews, but it made five anyhow. These appeared as percentages in the *News Chronicle* article. We got paid for that, quite a good fee. We got a splendid telegram the next day saying how deeply moved he was by this new spirit of co-operation. We sent five interview answers the previous day by telegram and they had duly appeared as an impressive contribution to human knowledge.'

Apart from small amounts like this raised by Harrisson, the brunt of finding the money needed to keep the project alive was now falling on Madge and Wagner, and they were not making very much progress. Despite several meetings with Sir Ernest Simon, he was still holding back from providing the funding that had been requested from him. He was particularly concerned that none of the Worktown books had yet appeared. Then there was a further worry when he learned that Chapman was leaving. To fill the gap he proposed that Hans Singer and another of Wagner's contacts in the Economics Department at Manchester University, Adolf Lowe, should be brought in as consulting economists to the project. Eventually in February, as cash was running out, following further negotiations with the university and Simon, Madge and Wagner clinched a deal with him.

More help came from Victor Gollancz who, despite the continued non-appearance of any of the original Worktown books, came in agreeing that the research into 'Social Factors in Economics' would provide the material for a fifth Mass-Observation book which he agreed to publish. With Simon's support and an advance of £150 from Gollancz, the future of the project was secured. By this time Chapman had left. 'When the £35 was up,' he said in a later interview, 'I had to depart and that was the end of it.'[2] Madge, somewhat surprisingly, appears to have been relieved. Writing to Harrisson he said, 'Though not anti-Mass-Observation, he is too deeply ingrained with the academic approach to get really right behind us.'[3]

Wagner and Madge were interested in saving as part of working-class behaviour, and together they devised a questionnaire to be used for a survey of attitudes to saving. For members of savings clubs, mill workers and Bible classes the main questions were: 'Do you save and if so why and by what method?', 'In saving, are you thinking of the next holidays or do you look beyond and if so how far?' and 'What would you sacrifice in your weekly spending in order to save?' Among the questions for the middle classes were: 'What do you think of the working-class attitude to money?', while working-class interviewees were to be asked: 'Which classes in society do you think are meanest about money; most generous; most thrifty; think most about money?'[4]

Much of the fieldwork for the savings survey was done by Geoffrey Thomas. Throughout January and February he visited works and schools every day to conduct interviews with the organisers of savings clubs. At Robert Watson, Construction Engineers, he learned that 90 per cent of the workers were in the club, and that their payments varied from one to five shillings, with an odd one who put in ten shillings a week. 'The idea of the club is to help them put something away for the June holiday.'[5] When he visited the town's Education Office to find out about their scheme, the organiser explained that this club was not confined to members of the office staff only, but was also available for members of their family. The scheme had thirty-two members and their payments varied from sixpence to eleven shillings a week. Reasons for saving, the organiser explained, were very complicated. His original incentive to save was provided by his children. He wanted his son to be able to go to university if he were cut out for it. As it happened his son won a scholarship and the money wasn't needed for that, so it went on buying furniture. 'The youngsters', he observed, 'save fairly well, and so do the elder men, but those who are young married men find it difficult to do so, since they earn only about £190 a year.'[6]

In London Harrisson was getting restless. He was supposed to be in charge of the national team of observers, but the task bored him, so in February it was agreed that Madge should take back responsibility for the panel while Harrisson would lead the Mass-Observation staff team in London analysing popular opinion with regard to the likelihood of war. Europe was now being torn apart by political and military tension, but in the face of ever more blatant German expansionism Chamberlain's government clung to its policy of appeasement. Italy, meanwhile, was pursuing its own expansionist aims against the almost defenceless African state of Ethiopia. In Spain loyalist Republicans continued to flee the country, escaping a conflict which, by the time it ended, had claimed some half a million lives and involved Italy and Germany on one side, and the Soviet Union on the other. The stage was set for the coming conflict, but for the Mass-Observers, as for most of Britain's population, life went on as normal while members of Chamberlain's government continued to say: 'We do not expect war either now or in the near future.'[7]

During the second stage of Mass-Observation's work in Bolton, Wagner had become the key figure. Her links with Manchester University helped to establish the academic respectability of the project, particularly through the contact she had with Hans Singer in the Economics Department.[8] Dennis Chapman's departure left Geoffrey Thomas as the main footsoldier for the research. It meant that he was not only conducting most of the interviews for the savings survey, but also having to do a lot of the shop follows which still formed an important part of the work. In February he was in Woolworth's making detailed observations of customers complete with all the terminology that had been identified by Madge and Wagner in abbreviated form and very precise timings of their movements: '3.38 pm. Two women enter. One 55 – other 28, neatly dressed. Younger goes to jewellery counter and looks at it for one or two minutes. Rejoins mother and stands talking to her further up the aisle.

They go to food counter and look for a time, then daughter selects packet of dates 3d and mother a tin of pepper 2d. P. [Purposive] M-of-f. [Matter of fact]. Average speed.'[9]

With shop observations on the Saturday there wasn't a great deal of time off for Thomas, and on the following Monday morning he had more interviews to do for the savings survey. The first was with Mr Kay of Holdsworth Mills on China Lane, who told him that the only rules were 'anything they like they put in. They can withdraw any time they like, but if they withdraw twice in any one year they are asked to close their account.' Kay said he knew very well how most of the money was spent. About 60 per cent went on holidays. 'Others buy furnishings – others use the club to pay their insurance premiums. A lot of people object to having a saving club in the mill. They don't like the management knowing what they save. They think it gives them an excuse for cutting wages.'[10]

When Thomas went into Bolton's schools to find out about their savings clubs, he also learned a lot about family finances, particularly about 'spends' and the amount of money older children had. At Folds Road Senior Girls School, the science mistress, who was the Secretary of the Savings Club, said 'she thought many of the girls earned as much as 2/- by minding babies and going errands, but they did not save it. Instead they used it for sweets and pictures, many girls going three times a week.'[11] At St Mary's Senior Boys School the teacher he was interviewing took Thomas along to the senior boys' classroom and asked them about pocket money. Two received more than a shilling a week, one got two shillings a week. These earned their money. Nine got sixpence to a shilling a week, given them by their mothers. All go to the cinema once, nine went twice, and three went three times a week. Three went to all-in wrestling, five to the Wanderers.[12]

In London Harrisson was feeling liberated. He'd done his time in the austere North and was now revelling in the glamour and excitement of metropolitan life. Biddy Clayton's house was a meeting place for people involved in theatre, journalism, art and antiques, and Harrisson was a frequent visitor. Through his old friend Mary Adams, whose husband Vyvyan was a Tory MP, he had access to the world of the press and politics, and at parties in their Regent's Park house he could pick up on the latest anti-appeasement stories. Prime Minister Chamberlain was still committed to an active, positive pursuit of a working accommodation with the fascist dictators, but there was a major rift on the right between the 'men of Munich' and their followers and their critics headed by Churchill who denounced the policy of appeasement as dishonourable.

Harrisson was also glad to be rid of his responsibilities for the national panel, and he was now able to focus his attention on the work in the East End. The group he had put together here to carry out his investigations was very different from his Bolton team. They were younger, better educated and much more middle class. None of them had the empathy with working-class life that Hood, Wilcock or Sommerfield brought to the Worktown project, but because they had parents who were able to support them, they came cheap – always a major consideration for Harrisson. Using techniques that had been employed in Bolton, members of the team infiltrated a number of local organisations, including the Young Jewish Communists and the Christian Socialist League. One observer hung out for a week with a group of Jewish lads, recording their attempts to pick up Cockney girls. They also used doorstep interviews to probe feelings about anti-Semitism and recorded the usual Mass-Observation bizarre statistics, such as the fact that Cockneys were three times more likely to whistle while peeing in public lavatories than Jews.[13]

It was not long before Harrisson abandoned the damp, bug-infested rooms where he had been living in the East End and moved in with Biddy Clayton. Her Ladbroke Grove house became the new headquarters for Mass-Observation. Here Harrisson worked in 'a big room with wide windows all along both sides, on to Spring and the trees, blackbirds on the lawn'.[14] Priscilla Feare, who had stayed in London working for Harrisson after Madge had gone to Bolton, recalled that 'Most of the house was taken over by MO, particularly the conservatory, full of Victoriana, where I worked for Tom. He dictated at fearful speeds, usually cutting out shorthand and talking straight on to the typewriter, suddenly coming out with "Read me back the last two pages." He was nice enough to work with, if impatient and in a rush. I swore at him once to his great surprise. He took it in good mood. It was useful to stand up to him occasionally. Lunches were always scrumptious. Biddy Clayton provided excellent fare for Tom and anyone else around. She was like "something out of [Evelyn] Waugh or [Antony]Powell" either drifting out of bath in a robe or floating around in an enormous fur coat.'[15]

At the grittier Bolton end of the operation work was now well advanced on Wagner's thesis, and most of the material on which it would be based had been gathered. In total it consisted of 200 interviews with people in Bolton and 341 sent in by the national panel of observers. The first question put to each group was 'Do you save?' Eighty per cent of Worktowners, it was found, did save. It was the worker in the mill, she found, who saved less, or was more often unable to save at all, than workers in other industries, which were usually better paid. The married Worktowner was less able to save than the single, and clerical workers showed a higher percentage of savers.[16] The collaboration between Madge and Wagner continued to flourish and it was Harrisson rather than this 'bloody expert' who provided most of the 'skirmishes and battles' that Madge had anticipated when he'd written to Inez. The first half of 1939 was marked by a series of increasingly hostile letters and long phone calls between the Mass-Observation founders about the direction the organisation should take and about their own roles in it. One of the reasons appears to have been Madge's growing confidence in his own academic development in the fields of economics and sociology and his conviction that this was the right direction for Mass-Observation.

It was this confidence and conviction that led him to write to the influential economist John Maynard Keynes. Keynes was leading a revolution in economic thinking, which overturned the old idea that free markets would automatically provide full employment as long as workers were flexible in their wage demands. Instead he advocated state intervention to moderate boom-and-bust cycles of economic activity. In his letter to Keynes, Madge outlined the work they were doing on working-class savings. He enclosed a copy of their questionnaire and asked Keynes whether he thought work like theirs might help the economist in 'forecasts which involve psychological assumptions'. In particular he wondered whether the growing international crisis would be likely to have a big effect on savings. 'We would', he said, 'gain immensely from having your opinion on these questions ... Possibly by modifying our research on savings we would make ourselves useful ... in wartime.'[17] Keynes responded positively and suggested an addition to the questionnaire. He also sent a copy of his book *A General Theory of Economics*.

Professionally everything was going well for Madge, but his private life was still in turmoil. On one of his visits to London he was with Harrisson on a bus and told him that never again would he get himself mixed up with any intellectual woman and that he was going to stay up North and not go to London any more, because he felt an interest in a similar person again. But Madge didn't keep to that, and according to various statements from observers, he was constantly coming down to London from Bolton throughout 1939, which, according to several people concerned, interfered with the work.[18]

The Worktown project was winding down. In April Brian Barefoot spent his last night at Davenport Street on his way north but, he recalled, 'There was only a shadow of the old pioneering spirit there

now.' While he was there he gave news of Walter Hood. After leaving
Mass-Observation the previous August Hood had put himself up as a parliamentary candidate for the Labour Party and also considered becoming
a Quaker teacher. But he also received a letter from Barrett Brown, his
former Principle at Ruskin, asking if he would be interested in becoming
one of the first Imperial Relations Trust scholars to go and investigate
in another Commonwealth country. Hood accepted the opportunity
and went to Australia to work with Melbourne University, researching
Australian culture, lifestyles and people for the Trust. He felt that with
his socialist philosophy and Mass-Observation experience he was fully
equipped for the job and left England in March 1939.

Within a period of two years over ninety people had come up to Bolton
to work full time for short periods and twelve for longer periods of between six and eighteen months, as well as innumerable part-time local
helpers and informants. Now it was all drawing to a close. By June the
end of the 'Social Factors in Economics' project was in sight and Madge
was planning to close down the Davenport Street house in the autumn.
Wagner had secured a research post in the Sociology Department at
Liverpool University, starting in October, and Madge planned to return
to London and move into the rooms that Harrisson had rented in the
East End.[19] That summer war was looking more and more inevitable.
Ending his non-interventionist policy, Chamberlain had entered into a
military commitment to defend Poland, which was being threatened by
Germany. As the threat of invasion increased, Madge wrote to the Ministry of Information setting out his ideas about how Mass-Observation
would be able to make itself useful in the event of war. He felt that
M-O could carry on if it had some measure of official recognition and he
proposed to continue the Bolton operation with Ministry support, and to
set up similar units in Newcastle, Liverpool, Manchester, Birmingham,
Cardiff and Bristol', while 'Tom would no doubt mobilise the London
people.' The intention was to monitor the reactions of lower professional
groups to the crisis.[20] While Madge courted the Ministry of Information,
Harrisson took on work for the Ministry of Labour, investigating the level
of commitment among people who volunteered for Air Raid Precautions
(ARP) work. The old ideals of independence from the Establishment
were rapidly disappearing.

As Madge and Harrisson negotiated to secure the future for Mass-
Observation and give it a wartime role, the last of the observers continued
their work in Bolton. Geoffrey Thomas recorded some of their final days
there in his diary. On Tuesday 4 July he wrote: 'At the weekend we did

intense observation of the town. There were crowds, drunks, an immense buying spirit, and after it all the seven of us went into the Golden Lion, and drank beer, whisky and sherry. Then we wandered home and had fish and chips for supper. Charles had his mistress, Inez Spender, up for the weekend, chaperoned by a plump, dark, handsome woman, Mary Elliot. She had a nice voice, though terribly middle-class. Inez Spender is rather handsome when one has seen her several times, but she is too, too striving to be intelligent.' On the surface all was harmonious in the Davenport Street 'commune', but Thomas revealed later that he found Wagner difficult and was disturbed by having to accept a woman acting on equal intellectual terms with a man. He wrote in his diary, 'She is an odd creature, mentally dishonest, and sometimes emotionally dishonest. She is a female who attempts to deal in the abstract, when she is not built for it. She is completely tactless in her relations with people and the most God-awful psycho that has ever taken a degree.'[21]

The country was on the brink of a war that would disrupt everything, but Harrisson was still coming up with proposals for ambitious new projects. One of them, Humphrey Spender recalled, was 'an idea that a whole collection of painters, writers, poets and so on would go on an expedition to New Guinea. He now wanted to repeat the Mass-Observation exercise there. I was asked to go and I was very keen to go and Tom said "Before you go it would be very good if you took a course of anthropology at the London School of Economics." And I went as far as taking a course there. So the whole thing was very serious. We even had injections for mysterious tropical diseases. So it came as a nasty shock when the outbreak of war put an end to the whole thing. Quite a lot of money was collected. Whether it was ever given back to the people who gave it I don't know.'

In August, as reports flooded in of German troops massing on the Polish border, mobilisation papers went out and the Admiralty issued orders closing the Mediterranean and the Baltic to British shipping. Bolton Artillery soldiers marched up Trinity Street in readiness for war. Germany had become an armed camp and troops were everywhere. As Europe raced towards a second great war, differences between Madge and Harrisson were forgotten for a time and they were of one accord in looking to the newly established Ministry of Information to keep Mass-Observation going. They both felt they had good reason to believe that the Ministry would want to make use of their services. Their prospects were greatly enhanced when John Hilton, a long-time friend and ally of Mass-Observation, was appointed Director of Home Publicity. Arguing that, unless money could be provided MO would probably disintegrate and all the expertise it had acquired would be lost, Hilton secured funding for a trial, starting with a report on the Ministry's leaflets and posters.[22]

Madge continued with his work in Bolton for a short time, but on 1 September Hitler took the fateful step of invading Poland and Chamberlain announced in a radio broadcast on 3 September that Britain had declared war on Germany. Harrisson, writing to Madge, was very upbeat: 'Everything is blowing into our hands . . . We have got what no one else has got, facts before the war.'[23] But the war disrupted the activities of Mass-Observation. 'At the outbreak of war,' Madge remembered, 'I was in Bolton, but by mid-September I was back in London collaborating with Tom Harrisson on a study of government propaganda for the Ministry of Information, itself only a few days old.'[24] It wasn't just work that brought him back, however, there were also personal reasons. In the summer Inez Spender had left her husband, Stephen, and Madge returned to London to his Blackheath home to be with her. Although he and Harrisson were now both in London, the outbreak of war put paid to the earlier plan to close Davenport Street down, since it was felt that having a Northern base as well as a London presence would help in their pitch for wartime work from the Ministry of Information.

When Britain declared war, Mass-Observation asked its volunteers to keep diaries of their experiences. To raise money, Madge and Harrisson wrote a book based on these and other wartime observations, *War Begins at Home*, which was published by Chatto and Windus in January 1940. They reported that people hated and resisted the blackout, perhaps because the Blitz had not yet begun, and the point of it was not apparent. The dark made people afraid of assault and theft, including the theft of pets. 'They do say there is cats in pies,' a charwoman in Hampstead explained. With the promise of funding, plans were drawn up for work in London and Bolton involving counting the number of people who looked at war posters and conducting interviews with them. But the contract did not materialise and the commission to carry out the work was withdrawn.

If anything Harrisson was even more excited by the prospect of observing humanity at war than he had been in peacetime. 'Apart from its dramatic and deathly qualities, its terrible fascination and the fears it evokes in every human mind, war is invaluable (if we dare call it that) to the student of psychology and behaviour,' he wrote in a Mass-Observation report called *Recording the War*.[25] 'Keeping Mass-Observation afloat at this time, Priscilla Feare recalled, 'was difficult, and became even more complicated by wartime imperatives. I think we all recognised that he [Harrisson] led a very exhausting, stressful life, trying to get money to keep us all going and writing books and articles. Apart from basic food or travel, the most pressing expense for observers was the cost of shoe-leather repairs. £2 per week was the basic wage, but Tom had to pay up for shoe maintenance.'[26]

As well as diaries and reports from the national panel that were still flooding in, the Mass-Observation archive contained all the reports and observations from Bolton made by more than eighty observers over a period of two and a half years. But there was not much to show for it. The result of all their activity was a single book, *The Pub and the People*, and even this wasn't published until 1943. It celebrated the pub as an active and social form of leisure, a way of life, Orwell wrote when he reviewed it, that was in danger of being 'gradually replaced by the passive, drug-like pleasures of the cinema and the radio'. The books that Gollancz had commissioned on religion and on politics never appeared, and Madge, it seems from correspondence with Harrisson, had not even seen drafts of them.[27]

The disappointing end result of all the work in Bolton could be put down first of all to the fact that the two and a half years of the project had been filled with such hectic activity that it produced far more material than could ever be processed into books, and secondly to the apparently chaotic way Harrisson had of managing the project. But it is much more likely that he was just overtaken by events. It is clear that, despite the promises he gave to the would-be authors, he always intended that he would make the biggest input to each of the books himself. But the international crisis leading up to the war and the actual outbreak of war meant that there were always more pressing reports to be written, and the Worktown books had to be put on the back burner.

It wasn't just the books that suffered. The outbreak of war had severely disrupted the activities of Mass-Observation and brought to a head the differences in opinion between the founders. Harrisson was campaigning for more government contracts, but Madge had misgivings. He didn't want Mass-Observation to degenerate into a government department. Harrisson now saw the role of M-O as being a kind of war barometer – monitoring the effects of war upon the morale of the masses. During the first few months all aspects of a country going to war were looked at, from assessing the success of public information to jazz lyrics and attendance at dance halls. One thing they both still agreed on was that the study of popular culture could yield insights into trends in underlying social attitudes which were vital to the future of democracy. Dance halls and the lyrics of popular songs, they argued, had mass appeal, and politicians could learn from the entrepreneurial skills of the dance-hall proprietors and the people who devised popular songs.

In the reports that were commissioned from Bolton and from the national panel, particular emphasis was now placed on gathering people's reactions to the possible effects of air raids, the use of gas masks and bomb-proof shelters, the blackout and the upheavals of evacuation. This was the period of the Phoney War and, in Madge's judgement, 'inquiry such as these would probably not have been possible when the war escalated in May. A few months remained in which Mass-Observation could deploy itself as an independent organisation. During this time I produced seventeen issues of a weekly bulletin called *US*. After the first issue had appeared, Cecil King, then a director of the *Daily Mirror*, telephoned me to say that he had lunched with Winston Churchill, had shown him the book and the bulletin and that Winston had been greatly interested – he became a subscriber to the bulletin.'

By tacit consent, Madge went on,

> Harrisson now concentrated on questions of morale and I on questions of economic behaviour. In January 1940, Sir John Reith took over as Minister of Information, and soon after that a small new department, Home Intelligence, was established to monitor public opinion. It was headed by Mary Adams, seconded from the BBC. Guided by her, and with a group of interviewer observers, Harrisson was assessing morale on the home front. Meanwhile I and another group of interviewer-observers had begun to investigate working-class saving and spending in Islington. In mid-March I saw Keynes, economic adviser at the Treasury, and he suggested our inquiry was a suitable object of support for the newly formed National Institute of Economic and Social Research. In mid-April the Council of the Institute agreed to give us their support.[28]

Harrisson saw his collaboration with the Ministry of Information as helping to achieve a true democratic unity in Britain where the interests of the ordinary people were paramount. Mass-Observation could, he believed, indicate to the government the people's wishes and at the same time help the government explain its own actions to the people. The morale on the home front project was taken over by Duff Cooper, the wartime Minister of Information, and Mass-Observation was used increasingly to monitor public opinion and morale and to gauge the effectiveness of public-information campaigns. But the national press was critical of the organisation's involvement with the government and the *Daily Express* coined the phrase 'Cooper's Snoopers' to describe anyone working on what had become the government's 'Wartime Social Survey'. The controversy fuelled further the arguments Madge and Harrisson were now having. Madge still believed the main aim of Mass-Observation should be to provide facts for political change, not to join forces with the government and become part of its propaganda campaign. He did not approve of the direction that the organisation was taking. 'When he [Harrisson] told me that he proposed to place himself and M-O at the disposal of a government department,' he recalled, 'rightly or wrongly I had misgivings and said I would prefer to opt out of M-O rather than join in what, as I then saw it, looked like a sort of home-front espionage.'[29]

Harrisson had always been difficult, but Madge could be equally intractable in his own way and he certainly wasn't the gentle soul he has sometimes been portrayed as. In the contest of wills they were engaged in, he could be as self-centred as Harrisson. But in spite of their differences, they had stayed together at the head of the organisation for three years, established it as a household name and produced significant work like *Britain by Mass-Observation*. It was only when these wartime differences surfaced that the tempestuous relationship between them that had stood at the centre of the organisation throughout this time was finally blown apart. In July 1940 Madge left the organisation he had been instrumental in founding to oversee a research project set up to study trends in the wartime domestic economy for the Institute of Economic and Social Research. The work he did and the understanding he gained of the social needs of the working class through his research into patterns of saving and spending helped Keynes persuade Parliament that workers would not mind having taxes taken out of their wages, thus making it easier for Britain to finance the war. Ultimately it led to some of the thinking behind the Beveridge Report and the formation of the Welfare State.

Soon after Madge's departure, Mass-Observation moved out of 85 Davenport Street and the Worktown project came to an end. The last reports from Bolton, dated August 1940, were filed by Alec Hughes, a new recruit who had grown up and gone to university in Liverpool before he joined M-O. Without Madge, Mass-Observation became Harrisson's property and project. He took over the direction of the organisation and committed it to more research work for the Ministry of Information until he was called up in 1942, producing during this time Mass-Observation's most substantial work, *People in Production* – a comprehensive survey of wartime factory life. After his call-up he continued to keep up Mass-Observation's profile through his work as a journalist and broadcaster, but he was never to work for Mass-Observation again in a full-time capacity.

Although the three founders had left and the Worktown project had come to an end, Mass-Observation continued to operate throughout the Second World War, and it was the war that gave more focus to the organisation's activity. All the enigmatic trivia it had been collecting now made sense in relation to the need to study factors bearing on British morale in what became total war. As the war went on, the government itself came to appreciate the value of social surveys. Mass-Observation looked at every wartime by-election, and by early 1944 Harrisson was confidently predicting Churchill's defeat in 1945, though few believed him. Despite many difficulties, the organisation survived all through the war years, and it re-entered peace as Britain's most famous social survey organisation.

Ever restless and forever looking for a new challenge, Harrisson himself had moved on. In 1945 he was parachuted into Borneo, where he led a guerrilla force of native tribesmen. After the war he made his home there, becoming an amateur expert in a wide range of fields from conservation and palaeontology to museum administration and local security. Madge took a very different direction as Keynes's sponsorship brought him into the academic establishment, and he later became a professor of sociology at the University of Birmingham. Within his three years with Mass-Observation Madge had converted himself from surrealist poet to rigorous social scientist. Of the other founders, Jennings consolidated his reputation as a leading documentary film-maker during the war, directing a series of classic wartime propaganda films, such as *London Can Take It* and *Listen to Britain* – the work for which he is chiefly remembered today. But his work as a documentary-maker was to be short lived. In 1950, while location-scouting on the Greek island of Poros, he lost his life when he fell off a cliff.

Without its founders Mass-Observation gradually lost its subversive eccentricity. In 1949, it was incorporated as a market-research firm and was registered as a limited company. Moving on into the early 1950s, despite the sheer surrealistic daftness attached to a lot of the ideas at the outset, it developed into a serious enterprise, treated with respect even at government level. Gradually, however, the emphasis shifted away from social issues towards consumer behaviour as the social-survey techniques the organisation had been the first to use in Britain in the 1930s became the tools of the new market-research industry. Its archives lay unread in the basement of Mass-Observation's South Kensington headquarters until the late 1960s, when two research students came across them and took them to the University of Sussex, where the Vice-Chancellor, Asa

Briggs, recognised their value. He agreed to the archive being housed at the university, where it was opened up as a resource for historical research. The original Mass-Observation idea of a national panel was revived in 1981 and new volunteer writers were recruited from all over Britain. This continues today, providing a programme in which ordinary people can write about their lives in the knowledge that their contributions will be archived and kept for future social historians as a record of daily life and attitudes in the late twentieth and early twenty-first centuries.

The Worktown project itself enjoyed a very brief revival in 1960 when Harrisson, back in Britain on leave, called on some of the old team to spend time with him in Bolton, going back to the streets, the shops, the pubs and the churches where they had carried out their observations in the 1930s. Humphrey Spender, John Sommerfield, Julian Trevelyan, Michael Wickham, Woodrow Wyatt and Bill Naughton all responded to the call and came back to revisit their old haunts between July and September. Their brief was to observe the mass of ordinary people and record what they saw and heard in order to provide Harrisson with data to compare with the observations from the 1930s. The result of their efforts was a book by Harrisson, *Britain Revisited*, which was published by Gollancz in 1961.

Among those who went back to Bolton in 1960, Humphrey Spender, who had been so uneasy trying to capture his images of Worktown, spoke eloquently of the town and its people. 'I think I speak for most of the eighty people who came especially to Worktown to help in these studies, when I say that we found an almost unfailing pleasure, honour and hospitality, among the hundred thousand people of this great, smoky, anonymous industrial town. Whatever we thought of the pubs individually, all of us found there friendliness and the company of British working life. Whatever these people's limitations and whatever our own, there emerges unmistakable through this research a basic goodness of heart in the individual . . .'

At a time when writers and artists saw it as their duty to get in touch with the masses and ally themselves with working-class movements, Worktown can now be seen within the context of this mobilisation of progressive forces and middle-class radicalism that was eventually to lay the basis for the 1945 Labour victory. The project and the vast archive it amassed have been described variously as a people's history and as a well-intentioned, idealistic attempt at a kind of general sociological study rarely conducted today. It has also been criticised as a middle-class adventure at the expense of the working class – nice young men attempting to penetrate into working-class pubs and institutions to try to get to know the workers. But this criticism is not entirely justified. Although there were lots of touches of the dilettante and the Oxbridge effete about the project and, for Harrisson in particular, of cannibals and just popping up north, the presence of men like Sommerfield, Hood and Wilcock, working alongside local helpers like Letchford and Naughton, ensured that the project kept a firm footing in working-class life and culture. Between them they collected an astonishing amount of material, recording in great detail how ordinary people worked, lived and enjoyed themselves. Chaotic, disorganised and lacking in focus it may have appeared but it was the chaos that comes from vision and high aspiration on a shoe-string – taking on a wildly ambitious project without ever having the real funding, resources and infrastructure to carry it through. In spite of these shortcomings there can be no doubt that Mass-Observation made an important contribution to the ways in which the British people saw themselves in the turbulent days just before the outbreak of the Second World War. And today, in times of economic hardship for many working people in Britain the observations of the Worktown team and the stories they recorded help us to appreciate the much greater levels of deprivation endured by many working people in the 1930s. Whatever the view, the Worktown observers along with the national panel of diarists collected a huge amount of material that all adds up to provide a fascinating insight into the lives of ordinary people living and working in a pre-war British industrial town.

NOTES

1: Going Native

1 Adapted from MOA1/5/40/G/1, Cotton, TH, 1937, Script for BBC radio programme on the cotton industry
2 MOA, Work, TH, Draft for book
3 Biographical details in this and the following paragraphs taken from Judith M. Heimann, *The Most Offending Soul Alive: Tom Harrisson and his Remarkable Life*, University of Hawaii Press, 1997
4 ibid.
5 Juliet Gardiner, *The Thirties: An Intimate History*, Harper Press, 2010
6 MOA 32/109/10, Tom Harrisson, Interview by Stuart Wavell, September 1960
7 *Britain in the 1930s: Photographs by Humphrey Spender in association with Mass-Observation*. Introduction and commentary by Tom Harrisson, Lion and Unicorn Press, Royal College of Art, London, 1975
8 TH quoted in Heimann, *The Most Offending Soul Alive*
9 Based on Humphrey Spender and Jeremy Mulford, *Worktown People: Photographs from Northern England, 1937–38*, Falling Wall Press, 1982
10 MOA, Cotton, TH, 1937, Script for BBC radio programme
11 Account of meal at the Tillotsons' is based on MOA 42, Assorted short reports (1), Upperclass Drunk, JS, 20.6, An account of an evening with the Tillotsons
12 Based on a letter written by Harrisson to the authorities of Oxford University 1933, quoted by Charles Madge in draft for a book on Mass-Observation 1937–49, Charles Madge papers, University of Sussex Library
13 Based on MOA 32/109/10, Tom Harrisson, Interview by Stuart Wavell, September 1960
14 James Hinton, *The Mass Observers: A History, 1937–1949*, Oxford University Press, 2013
15 Based on MOA 32/109/10, Tom Harrisson, Interview by Stuart Wavell, September 1960 and *Britain in the 1930s: Photographs by Humphrey Spender in association with the Mass Observation Archive*
16 Gardiner, *The Thirties*
17 Richard Crossman archive, University of Warwick
18 Adapted from MOA 31, Christmas is coming to Worktown
19 Based on *Britain in the 1930s: Photographs by Humphrey Spender in association with the Mass Observation Archive*

2: Anthropology at Home

1 Judith M. Heimann, *The Most Offending Soul Alive: Tom Harrisson and his Remarkable Life*, University of Hawaii Press, 1997

2   Charles Madge, 'Birth of Mass-Observation', *Times Literary Supplement*, December 1979
3   MOA 28/7/17, Charles Madge, Interview by Angus Calder, March 1979
4   J. B. Priestley quoted on BFI, screenonline.org.uk, 'The definitive guide to Britain's film and TV history'
5   Charles Madge, review of Tom Harrisson, *Living through the Blitz*, Charles Madge papers, University of Sussex Library
6   MOA 28/7/19, Charles Madge notes
7   In an Ideal World, Charles Madge speaks to Madeleine Kingsley, Charles Madge papers, University of Sussex Library
8   *Mass-Observation in Bolton: Humphrey Spender's Worktown Photographs*, exhibition catalogue, Watermans Arts Centre, 1994
9   Charles Madge, Draft of unpublished autobiography. CMpap, 71/1/6 University of Sussex Library
10 Heimann, *The Most Offending Soul Alive*
11 David Gascoyne, *Journal 1936–1937*, Enitharmon Press, 1981
12 Angus Calder, 'Mass-Observation 1937–1949', BAAS Annual Meeting, 1981
13 *Dictionary of National Biography*
14 Gascoyne, *Journal 1936–1937*
15 CM to Malinowski, 3.12.37, Bronisław Malinowski papers
16 MOA 28/7/19, Charles Madge notes
17 *Mass-Observation in Bolton*, exhibition catalogue
18 Calder, 'Mass-Observation 1937–1949'
19 MOA 32/15, Dennis Chapman, Interview by Nick Stanley, February 1979
20 Quoted in Heimann, *The Most Offending Soul Alive*
21 ibid.

3: You Don't Ask a Bird Any Questions

1   Based on Judith M. Heimann, *The Most Offending Soul Alive: Tom Harrisson and his Remarkable Life*, University of Hawaii Press, 1997
2   Detail about funding in this and the following paragraphs taken from James Hinton, *The Mass Observers: A History, 1937–1949*, Oxford University Press, 2013
3   Details about observers in this and the following paragraphs taken from ibid.
4   MOA 32/44, Walter Hood memoir, 1974
5   MOA 32/44, Mass-Observation interview with Walter Hood, 1975
6   Information on local observers from Hinton, *The Mass Observers*
7   *Mass-Observation in Bolton: Humphrey Spender's Worktown Photographs*, exhibition catalogue, Watermans Arts Centre, 1994
8   'The Rebel: A Short Biography of Tom Harrisson', in Timothy Green, *The Adventurers*, Michael Joseph, 1970
9   MOA 15/48, Leisure Activities, JW, 11.12.37, Budgerigar Society
10 Deborah Frizzell, *Humphrey Spender's Humanist Landscapes: Photo-documents 1932–1942*, Yale University Press, 1997
11 Quoted in *Stranger Than Fiction*, a Mass-Observation film by Ian Potts and Angus Calder, 1985
12 MOA 35/15, Dennis Chapman, Interview by Nick Stanley, February 1979

13 Mass-Observation, *The Pub and the People: A Worktown Study*, Victor Gollancz, 1943
14 Heimann, *The Most Offending Soul Alive*
15 Charles Madge, Draft of unpublished autobiography. CMpap, 71/1/6, University of Sussex Library
16 Hinton, *The Mass Observers*
17 *Britain in the 1930s: Photographs by Humphrey Spender in Association with the Mass Observation Archive*, introduction and commentary by Tom Harrisson, Lion and Unicorn Press, Royal College of Art, London, 1975
18 MOA, Anthony West, *New Statesman*, 13.4.73

4: Where Cotton Was King

1 Quoted in Deborah Frizzell, *Humphrey Spender's Humanist Landscapes: Photo-documents 1932–1942*, Yale University Press, 1997
2 David Hall, *Working Lives*, Bantam Press, 2012
3 MOA, Work, TH, Draft for book
4 Adapted from David Wray, *Cotton Times: Understanding the Industrial Revolution*; www.cottontimes.co.uk. Fred Dibnah and David Hall, *Fred Dibnah's Age of Steam*, BBC Books, 2003
5 W. R. Mitchell, *Life in the Lancashire Mill Towns*, Dalesman Publishing. 1982
6 Hall, *Working Lives*
7 MOA 1/5/6/26/H/1 Tom Harrisson, *Industrial Spring*,
8 MOA 37/4 Mass-Observation interview with Harry Gordon, Dorothy Sheridan 1980
9 MOA, Municipal Politics, Untitled document
10 James Hinton, *The Mass Observers: A History, 1937–1949*, Oxford University Press, 2013
11 Humphrey Jennings and Charles Madge (eds), *May 12 1937: Mass-Observation Day-Survey*, Faber & Faber, 1937, Mill hand, Bolton

5: The Coronation

1 *Daily Telegraph*, 4.3.37
2 *Manchester Evening News*, 15.4.37
3 *Daily Express*, 27.4.37
4 Humphrey Jennings and Charles Madge (eds), *May 12 1937: Mass-Observation Day-Survey*, Faber & Faber, 1937
5 *News Chronicle*, 6.4.37
6 Based on draft for *First Year's Work*, Bronislaw Malinowski papers
7 Mass-Observation, *The Pub and the People: A Worktown Study*, Victor Gollancz, 1943
8 Charles Madge and Tom Harrisson (eds), *First Year's Work, 1937–38, by Mass-Observation*, Lindsay Drummond, 1938
9 MOA 3, Public Houses, TH, 4.3.37, The Royal, Vernon Street
10 Mass-Observation, *The Pub and the People: A Worktown Study*, Victor Gollancz, 1943
11 MOA 3, Public Houses, TH, PJ and JF, 3.4.37, The Good Samaritan
12 Angus Calder, 'Mass-Observation 1937–1949', BAAS Annual Meeting, 1981

13 Jennings and Madge (eds), *May 12 1937: Mass-Observation Day-Survey*

14 MOA, Directive to observers, June 1937

15 ibid.

16 MOA 28/7/25, W. R. Lee, Interview by Angus Calder at the Royal Commonwealth Society, 22 April 1980

17 MOA 28/2/46, Priscilla McNamara (Feare), Interview by Angus Calder, 10 January 1980

18 MOA 28/7/10, Photocopied letter and memo correspondence between Tom Harrisson and Charles Madge. TH, 18.1.40, Memo to CM

19 ibid.

20 MOA 42-B, Miscellaneous conversations and overheards, 22.3.37, Conversation at girls' school staff meeting

21 *Daily Express*, 10.5.37

22 Jennings and Madge (eds), *May 12 1937: Mass-Observation Day-Survey*

23 MOA 3, Public Houses, JS, Coronation Day

24 MOA 20, Church Services, TH, 23.5.37, Trinity Sunday Catholic processions

25 MOA 28/2/25, Interview with John Sommerfield

26 Quoted by Marie-Louise Jennings in her Introduction to Humphrey Jennings, *Pandaemonium 1660–1886*, Icon Books, 2012

6: Across the Class Divide

1 MOA 32, Food and Shopping, Questionnaires and interviews about food shopping and household budget for food

2 MOA 36/C/1, Cinema Observations, WH, 19.4.38, Outing with a girl stranger

3 Based on MOA 28/7/35, Notes on Mass-Observation in Bolton by Harry Gordon, 08/10/80, and MOA 32/37/2, Interview with Harry Gordon with Dorothy Sheridan 08/10/80

4 Judith M. Heimann, *The Most Offending Soul Alive: Tom Harrisson and his Remarkable Life*, University of Hawaii Press, 1997

5 The account of Brian Barefoot's involvement with M-O in this and the following paragraphs is taken from MOA 32/7/1, Brian Barefoot, Account of work done with Mass-Observation, 1937–41, 1979

6 Kevin Jackson, *Humphrey Jennings*, Picador, London, 2004

7 Mass-Observation, *The Pub and the People: A Worktown Study*, Victor Gollancz, 1943

8 Based on MOA 28/2/25, Interview with John Sommerfield

9 Adapted from MOA 43/1, Tom Honeyford Autobiography

10 Madge and Harrisson (eds), *First Year's Work, 1937–38*

11 MOA 32/7/1, BB 21.8.38 All-in Wrestling, Bolton stadium

12 MOA 32/44/10, *Walter Hood and the Development of Mass-Observation Methods*, Mandy Manners, Dissertation, 2002

13 ibid.

14 MOA 7, Party Politics, BB, 24.9.37, Labour Party Crusade meeting

15 MOA 8, Political Activities, Remarks made to house collectors during Spain week

7: The Secret Photographer

1   Humphrey Spender, *Worktown: Photographs of Bolton and Blackpool Taken for Mass-Observation 1937/38*, Gardner Centre Gallery, University of Sussex, Brighton, 1977

2   Unless otherwise noted the biographical details in this and the following paragraphs are taken from Deborah Frizzell, *Humphrey Spender's Humanist Landscapes: Photo-documents 1932–1942*, Yale University Press, 1997

3   Spender, *Worktown: Photographs of Bolton and Blackpool*

4   Interviewed for Jeremy Mulford (ed.), *Worktown People: Photographs from Northern England 1937–38*, Bristol, 1982

5   Interview with Spender in *Worktown: Photographs of Bolton and Blackpool*

6   ibid.

7   ibid.

8   Humphrey Spender, *Lensman: Photographs 1932–52*, Chatto & Windus, London, 1987

9   Interview for Spender, *Worktown: Photographs of Bolton and Blackpool*

10 ibid.

11 Spender, *Lensman: Photographs 1932–52*

12 Mulford (ed.), *Worktown People*

13 Julian Trevelyan, *Indigo Days: The Art and Memoirs of Julian Trevelyan*, Scolar Press, 1957

14 Spender, *Worktown: Photographs of Bolton and Blackpool*

15 Juliet Gardiner, *The Thirties: An Intimate History*, Harper Press, 2010

16 MOA 32/44/3, Interview between Walter Hood and Tom Harrisson, 4.5.1974, University of Sussex Library

17 Details of Michael Wickham in this and the following paragraphs taken from interview by Nick Stanley, 8 February 1980, MOA 28/2/14

18 Spender, *Lensman: Photographs 1932–52*

19 MOA 28/2/41, Humphrey Spender, Interview by Robert Melville

20 MOA 24, BB, 21.9.37, Secular Funeral

21 MOA 28/2/41, Humphrey Spender, Interview by Robert Melville

22 Charles Madge and Tom Harrisson, *Mass-Observation*, Frederick Muller, June 1937

8: A Day in the Life

1   MOA 28/7/34, Interview with Harry Gordon and Louie Davies

2   Angus Calder, 'Mass-Observation 1937–1949', BAAS Annual Meeting, 1981

3   MOA 28/2/14, Michael Wickham, Interview by Nick Stanley, 8 February 1980

4   James Hinton, *The Mass Observers: A History, 1937–1949*, Oxford University Press, 2013

5   MOA 32/44/3, Walter Hood interviewed by Harrisson, 4.5.1974, University of Sussex Library

6   Hinton, *The Mass Observers*

7   MOA 32/44, Walter Hood memoir, 1974, University of Sussex Library

8   MOA 28/2/25, Interview with John Sommerfield

9   MOA 28/2/41, Humphrey Spender, Interview by Robert Melville

10 MOA 32/7/5, Brian Barefoot, Account of work done with Mass-Observation, 1937–41, 1979
11 MOA 42, Assorted short reports (1) EL, 21.8.37, Street Row
12 MOA 37B, Byelaws, Police, Public Health, HP, 9.4.38, Police in Bolton Streets
13 A working-class housewife, Mrs Duckworth, quoted in Peter Gurney (ed.), *Bolton Working-Class Life in the 1930s: A Mass-Observation Anthology*, University of Sussex, 1988
14 MOA 32/7/1, Brian Barefoot Account of work carried out with Mass Observation, 1979
15 MOA 37, Harry Gordon, Notes from Bolton
16 MOA 29-C, Shopping Report, BP & JS
17 David Pocock, 'Afterword' to 1987 reprint of Humphrey Jennings and Charles Madge (eds), *May 12 1937: Mass-Observation Day-Survey*, Faber & Faber, 1937; *Left Review*, 1 July 1937
18 Kevin Jackson, *Humphrey Jennings*, Picador, London, 2004
19 Julian Trevelyan, *Indigo Days: The Art and Memoirs of Julian Trevelyan*, Scolar Press, 1957
20 Pocock, 'Afterword' to 1987 reprint of Jennings and Madge (eds), *May 12 1937: Mass-Observation Day-Survey*
21 Charles Madge, Review of Tom Harrisson, *Living through the Blitz*. Charles Madge papers, University of Sussex Library
22 Jackson, *Humphrey Jennings*

9: Health, Housing and Politics

1   MOA 47.1, Leisure, TH, 28.8.37, Report on Saturday afternoon
2   James Hinton, *The Mass Observers: A History, 1937–1949*, Oxford University Press, 2013
3   MOA 32/7/1, Brian Barefoot, Account of work done with Mass-Observation, 1937–41, 1979
4   MOA 7, Party Politics, BB, 24.9.37, Labour Party Crusade meeting
5   *People*, 24.4.38
6   Andrew Rigby, 'The Peace Pledge Union: From Peace to War, 1936–1945', from *Challenge to Mars: Essays on Pacifism from 1918 to 1945*, Peter Brock and Thomas P. Socknat (eds), University of Toronto Press, 1999
7   MOA 1/5/9/38/A/1, Booklet *Housing Conditions in East Ward*, Bolton Housing Committee Survey Report, 1931
8   Juliet Gardiner, *The Thirties: An Intimate History*, Harper Press, 2010
9   Mass-Observation, SxRefLibrary/3/23, *An Enquiry into People's Homes*
10 Top o'th'Brow Housing Estate, in Peter Gurney (ed.), *Bolton Working-Class Life in the 1930s: A Mass-Observation Anthology*, University of Sussex, 1988
11 ibid.
12 Mass-Observation, *The Pub and the People: A Worktown Study*, Victor Gollancz, 1943
13 MOA 37E, Baths and Wash Houses, HP, 5.4.38, Bridgeman Street Swimming Baths
14 Report included in MOA 32/7/1, Brian Barefoot Account, 1979
15 ibid.

16   MOA 28/2/14, Michael Wickham, Interview by Nick Stanley, 8 February 1980
17   MOA 8, Political Activities, JW, 12.10.37, Spanish Medical Aid committee sale of work

10: Politics and the Non-Voter

1   This and the account of the council meeting in the following paragraphs are taken from MOA, Municipal Politics, Untitled document
2   James Hinton, *The Mass Observers: A History, 1937–1949*, Oxford University Press, 2013
3   Nick Hubble, *Mass-Observation and Everyday Life*, Palgrave Macmillan, 2006
4   MOA, Tom Harrisson, 'The Poverty of Freedom', 1939 unpublished
5   MOA 32/44, Mass-Observation interview with Walter Hood, 1975
6   Hinton, *The Mass Observers*
7   MOA 11, TH, Great Lever Election Experiment
8   Judith M. Heimann, *The Most Offending Soul Alive: Tom Harrisson and his Remarkable Life*, University of Hawaii Press, 1997
9   Interview in *Stranger Than Fiction*, a Mass-Observation film by Ian Potts and Angus Calder, 1985
10   MOA 7, Party Politics, ZB, 27.10.37, Labour Party meeting, Great Lever Ward
11   MOA 32/7/1, Brian Barefoot, Account of work done with Mass-Observation, 1937–41, 1979
12   MOA 11, TH, The Great Lever Election Experiment
13   MOA 11, TH, 1.11.37, Vote counting in Town Hall
14   MOA 3, JS, Labour Club on election day
15   MOA 11, TH, The Great Lever Election Experiment
16   MOA 40/19/10, Barbara Phillipson, Interview in *Stranger than Fiction*, DVD of film directed by Ian Potts, University of Sussex
17   MOA 7, Party Politics, TH, 3.11.37, Delegate meeting of the Bolton Labour Party
18   Hinton, *The Mass Observers*
19   Tom Harrisson, 'Remembrance Day in Bolton, 7 November 1939', in Angus Calder and Dorothy Sheridan (eds), *Speak for Yourself: A Mass-Observation Anthology 1937–1949*, Jonathan Cape, 1984
20   MOA 12, Voting, Parliamentary By-election, TH, 14.12.37 Tonge by-election
21   MOA 32/44/10, *Walter Hood and the Development of Mass-Observation Methods*, Mandy Manners, Dissertation, 2002
22   MOA 32/44/3, Walter Hood interviewed by Tom Harrisson, 4.5.1974
23   MOA 32/44, Walter Hood memoir, 1974, University of Sussex Library

11: The Pub and the People

1   MOA 3, JS, Labour Club on election day
2   MOA 3, Public Houses, Suggestions for pub observers
3   MOA 3, Public Houses, JS, 23.4.37, A round of pubs
4   MOA 3, Public Houses, JS, 24.4.37, The Grapes
5   Mass-Observation, *The Pub and the People: A Worktown Study*, Victor Gollancz, 1943
6   ibid.

7   ibid.

8   ibid.

9   MOA 28/2/25, Interview with John Sommerfield

10   MOA 3, Public Houses, JS, 19.4.37, The One Horseshoe

11   MOA 3, Public Houses, JS, 23.4.37, The Dog and Partridge

12   MOA 3, Public Houses, JS, 5.5.37, The Dog and Partridge

13   MOA 3, Public Houses, JS, 22.4.37, Yates's Wine Lodge and The George

14   Angus Calder and Dorothy Sheridan (eds), *Speak for Yourself: A Mass-Observation Anthology 1937–1949*, Jonathan Cape, 1984

15   MOA 3.1, EL, 25.4.37

16   ibid.

17   ibid.

18   MOA 3, Public Houses, 7.10.37, Observation in a Bolton Pub, quoted in Peter Gurney (ed.), *Bolton Working-Class Life in the 1930s: A Mass-Observation Anthology*, University of Sussex, 1988

19   Charles Madge and Tom Harrisson (eds), *First Year's Work, 1937–38, by Mass-Observation*, Lindsay Drummond, 1938

20   MOA 3, Public Houses, JS, 19.4.37, Conversation about pubs in chip shop

21   MOA 3, Public Houses, JS, 7.5.37, The Globe

22   MOA 3, Public Houses, JS, 7.5.37, Moses Gate pubs

12: Snoopers

1   Humphrey Spender, *Lensman: Photographs 1932–52*, Chatto & Windus, London, 1987

2   Quoted in Jeremy Mulford (ed.), *Worktown People: Photographs from Northern England 1937–38*, Falling Wall Press, 1982

3   Humphrey Spender, 'Tribulations of a Photographer, 1938', in Angus Calder and Dorothy Sheridan (eds), *Speak for Yourself: A Mass-Observation Anthology 1937–1949*, Jonathan Cape, 1984

4   Mulford (ed.), *Worktown People*

5   Interview for Humphrey Spender, *Worktown: Photographs of Bolton and Blackpool Taken for Mass-Observation 1937/38*, Gardner Centre Gallery, University of Sussex, Brighton, 1977

6   MOA 28/2/41, Humphrey Spender, Interview by Robert Melville

7   Spender, *Lensman: Photographs 1932–52*

8   ibid.

9   MOA28/7/10, Photocopied letter and memo correspondence between Tom Harrisson and Charles Madge, CM, 21.1.40, memo to TH

10   ibid.

11   Mulford (ed.), *Worktown People*

12   ibid.

13   MOA 42, Assorted Short Reports (1), JAS, 4.3.38, Bog Graphiti (sic)

14   MOA 42, Assorted Short Reports (1), Is the Bible right? An attempt to give a scientific basis to 'piss' and 'shit'

15   Mulford (ed.), *Worktown People*

16   *Britain in the 1930s: Photographs by Humphrey Spender in association with the Mass-Observation Archive*. introduction and commentary by Tom Harrisson, Lion and Unicorn Press, Royal College of Art, London, 1975

17 MOA 28/2/14, Michael Wickham, Interview by Nick Stanley, 8 February 1980

18 MOA 3, Public Houses, JS, 9.5.37, Nag's Head

19 MOA 3, Public Houses, EL, 26.7.37, Pub prostitutes

20 James Hinton, *The Mass Observers: A History, 1937–1949*, Oxford University Press, 2013

21 Peter Gurney, '"Intersex" and "Dirty Girls": Mass-Observation and Working-Class Sexuality in England in the 1930s', *Journal of the History of Sexuality*, 8.2. 1997

22 MOA 3, Public Houses, JS, 23.4.37, A round of pubs

23 Mulford (ed.), *Worktown People*

13: Worktown Women

1 This and the account of mill work in the following paragraphs are taken from MOA 40-B, Book Drafts, Mill Work, PB, November 1937, detailed observations at Musgrave's Spinning Company

2 MOA 27, Armistice Day etc., ZB, 11.11.37, Armistice Morning

3 MOA 30, Shopping, ZB, 19/5.37, Corsets

4 Juliet Gardiner, *The Thirties: An Intimate History*, Harper Press, 2010

5 MOA 47, Leisure, ZB, 18.11.37, Bolton Women's Citizens' Association

6 MOA 22, Fetes, Bazaars, Jumble Sales, ZB, 17.11.37, Enterprise Bazaar

7 MOA28/2/14, Michael Wickham interview by Nick Stanley, 8 February 1980

8 MOA 22, Fetes, Bazaars, Jumble Sales, ZB, 21.10.37, Bazaar, Girls' Moral Welfare Association

9 MOA 40-B, Book Drafts, Mill Work, PB, November 1937

10 *Britain in the 1930s: Photographs by Humphrey Spender in association with the Mass-Observation Archive*, introduction and commentary by Tom Harrisson, Lion and Unicorn Press, Royal College of Art, London, 1975

11 MOA 8, Political Activities, ZB, 17.11.37, Fascist meeting

12 MOA 8, Political Activities, ZB, 9.11.37, Spanish Aid meeting

13 Judith M. Heimann, *The Most Offending Soul Alive: Tom Harrisson and his Remarkable Life*, University of Hawaii Press, 1997

14: Pinch the Sermon

1 MOA 19, Church Finances and Social Events, TH, 19.12.37, St George's Road Congregational Church Nativity Play

2 MOA 27, Christmas is Coming to Worktown

3 Mass-Observation, *The Pub and the People: A Worktown Study*, Victor Gollancz, 1943

4 Juliet Gardiner, *The Thirties: An Intimate History*, Harper Press, 2010

5 Mass-Observation, *The Pub and the People*

6 MOA 20-B, Church Services, JW, December 1937, Bolton Parish church services

7 MOA 24, FC, 5.4.38, Funeral of Town Clerk

8 MOA 24, Meetings, Lectures, Funerals, TH, 23.4.38, C of E Confirmation

9 MOA 20, Church Services, JW, 27.2.38, St Mary's Catholic

10 MOA 20, Church Services, JW, 13.3.38, Catholic Mission, Grand Theatre

11 MOA 17, Non-Conformists, JW, 27.2.38, Beulah Hall

12 Angus Calder and Dorothy Sheridan (eds), *Speak for Yourself: A Mass-Observation Anthology 1937–1949*, Jonathan Cape, 1984

13 MOA 17-C, Mazdaznan, JW, 12.4.37

14 MOA 17, Non-Conformists, BB, 8.1.38, Pentecostal League of Prayer

15 MOA 32/7/1, Brian Barefoot, Account of work done with Mass-Observation, 1937–41, 1979

16 MOA 17, Directions for observers

17 MOA 16-D, Church Bells, Parish church bells, People questioned about why the bells are ringing

18 MOA 16-D, Church Bells, JS, 19.4.37, Conversation with proprietor of Savoy Supper Bar about church bells

19 James Hinton, *The Mass Observers: A History, 1937–1949*, Oxford University Press, 2013

20 MOA 17, Non-Conformists, JW, 1.5.38, Quaker meeting

15: Compromised

1 MOA 32/7/1, Brian Barefoot, Account of work done with Mass-Observation, 1937–41, 1979

2 Julian Trevelyan, *Indigo Days: The Art and Memoirs of Julian Trevelyan*, Scolar Press, 1957

3 MOA 1/5/6/26/H/1, Tom Harrisson, *Industrial Spring*

4 MOA 32/16/2, Frank Cawson, Interview by Angus Calder, Torquay, 29 February 1980

5 MOA 36, Cinema Observations WH 19.4 Outing with a Girl Stranger,

6 MOA 32-D, Eating Places, JS, 17.4.38, Fish and Chip Shops

7 MOA 32/16/2, Frank Cawson, Interview by Angus Calder, Torquay, 29 February 1980

8 MOA 7, Party Politics, FC, 7.2.38, communist meeting

9 MOA 7, Party Politics, FC, 22.3.38, Junior Imperial League

10 MOA32/16/2, Frank Cawson, Interview by Angus Calder, Torquay, 29 February 1980

11 MOA 7, Party Politics, APW, 27.2.38, Morrison's Speech

12 Charles Madge and Tom Harrisson (eds), *Britain by Mass-Observation*, Penguin, 1939

13 MOA 32/7, Analysis of Austria Day Surveys, BB, 9.4.38

14 Madge and Harrisson (eds), *Britain by Mass-Observation*

15 MOA 32/115, Interview with Woodrow Wyatt

16 MOA 32/16/2, Frank Cawson, Interview by Angus Calder, Torquay, 29 February 1980

17 MOA 40/19/10, Barbara Phillipson, Interview in *Stranger than Fiction*, DVD of film directed by Ian Potts, University of Sussex

18 MOA 17-C, Mazdaznans, BP, March 1938

19 MOA 17, Non-Conformists, BP, 17.4.38, Hebron Hall

20 Barbara Phillipson, Interview for *Stranger Than Fiction* film

21 Charles Madge, Draft of unpublished autobiography. CMpap, 71/1/6, University of Sussex Library

22 Juliet Gardiner, *The Thirties: An Intimate History*, Harper Press, 2010

23 James Hinton, *The Mass Observers: A History, 1937–1949*, Oxford University Press, 2013
24 MOA 32/16/4, Frank Cawson, Interview by Angus Calder. Torquay, 29 February 1980
25 Hinton, *The Mass Observers*
26 MOA 32/16/4, Frank Cawson, Interview by Angus Calder. Torquay, 29 February 1980

16: A Night on the Town

1   MOA 17, Non-Conformists, FC, 3.4.38, Salvation Army
2   MOA 23, FC, 15.1.38–16.3.38, Bradshawgate
3   Mass-Observation, *The Pub and the People: A Worktown Study*, Victor Gollancz, 1943
4   This and the following paragraphs on dance halls are taken from MOA 28, Leisure Activities, Report on Worktown Dance Hall
5   MOA 28, Leisure Activities, WH, 31.3.38, The Co-operative Comrades Circle Dance in Co-op Hall, Bridge Street
6   MOA 28, Leisure Activities, BB, 13.7.38, Harlem Night at Aspin Hall
7   MOA 37/B/7, Humphrey Pease 13.4.38, Police Activities
8   James Hinton, *The Mass Observers: A History, 1937–1949*, Oxford University Press, 2013
9   Juliet Gardiner, *The Thirties: An Intimate History*, Harper Press, 2010
10 MOA 8, Political Activities, FC, 23.2.38, Collection at film Spanish Earth
11 MOA 8, Political Activities, TH, 19.2.38, Interview with cinema manager re Spanish Earth
12 Mass-Observation, *The Pub and the People*
13 Madge and Harrisson (eds), *First Year's Work*
14 MOA 28/7/18, Mass-Observation interview with Charles Madge, 23 March 1978
15 MOA 28/2/25, Interview with John Sommerfield
16 MOA 32/120/3, Tom Harrisson Articles and Papers

17: Art and the Ordinary Chap

1   Based on Tom Harrisson, 'The Poverty of Freedom', Unpublished book, 1939, MOA
2   ibid.
3   Tom Harrisson, 'What they think in "Worktown"', *Listener*, 25.8.38
4   MOA 32/19/1, Notes of a conversation between Sir William Coldstream, Lawrence Gowing and Nick Stanley at University College London, 19 May 1980
5   ibid.
6   ibid.
7   TH to Trevelyan, August 1938, Julian Tevelyan papers
8   Judith M. Heimann, *The Most Offending Soul Alive: Tom Harrisson and his Remarkable Life*, University of Hawaii Press, 1997
9   Harrisson, 'What they think in "Worktown"'
10 Julian Trevelyan, *Indigo Days: The Art and Memoirs of Julian Trevelyan*, Scolar Press, 1957

11 MOA 42-B, Miscellaneous Conversations and Overheards, On top of No. 1 bus from Escrick Street to Victoria Square, 29.4.38, overheard comments and conversation
12 MOA 42-B, Conversation overheard at the Annual Exhibition of the Manchester Society of Women Artists, 28.4.38
13 Jeremy Mulford (ed.), *Worktown People: Photographs from Northern England 1937–38*, Falling Wall Press, 1982
14 MOA 28/7/18, Mass-Observation interview with Charles Madge, 23 March 1978
15 MOA 32/66/6, Charles Madge, Interview by Angus Calder, March 1979
16 MOA 28/7/18, Mass-Observation interview with Charles Madge, March 1978

18: Arrivals and Departures

1 MOA, Gertrude Wagner, Interview by Derek Smith, 27 April 1988. St Martin's crypt Trafalgar Square
2 MOA 32/7/1, Brian Barefoot, Account of work done with Mass-Observation, 1937–41, 1979
3 MOA 41, Study of a small area
4 W. R. Mitchell, *Life in the Lancashire Mill Towns*, Dalesman Publishing, 1982
5 MOA 29-A, Shopping Report
6 Gertrude Wagner, 'Market Research: A Critical Study', *Review of Economic Studies*, February 1938
7 James Hinton, *The Mass Observers: A History, 1937–1949*, Oxford University Press, 2013
8 CM to Inez Spender, 2 and 3.8.38, Charles Madge papers
9 MOA 28/2/46, Priscilla McNamara, interviewed by Angus Calder, 10 January 1980.
10 Charles Madge, Draft of unpublished autobiography. CMpap 71/1/6, University of Sussex Library
11 ibid.
12 MOA 32/7/1, Brian Barefoot Account, 1979
13 MOA 14-C, Christianity in Industrial Bolton
14 MOA 17, Non-Conformists, GW, 31.8.38, Christadelphian meeting
15 William Feaver, *Pitman Painters: The Ashington Group, 1934–1984*, Ashington Group Trustees, 2009
16 Charles Madge and Tom Harrisson (eds), *Britain by Mass-Observation*, Penguin, 1939
17 Angus Calder and Dorothy Sheridan (eds), *Speak for Yourself: A Mass-Observation Anthology 1937–1949*, Jonathan Cape, 1984
18 Madge and Harrisson (eds), *Britain by Mass-Observation*
19 *Mass-Observation in Bolton: Humphrey Spender's Worktown Photographs*, exhibition catalogue, Watermans Arts Centre, 1994
20 Madge and Harrisson (eds), *Britain by Mass-Observation*
21 ibid.
22 ibid.
23 Charles Madge, Draft of unpublished autobiography. CMpap 71/1/6, University of Sussex Library
24 Nick Hubble, *Mass-Observation and Everyday Life*, Palgrave Macmillan, 2006

25 Hinton, *The Mass Observers*
26 Charles Madge, Draft of unpublished autobiography. CMpap 71/1/6, University of Sussex Library
27 Calder and Sheridan (eds), *Speak for Yourself*
28 MOA 29-A, Shop Observation, Shops and Shoppers, The Shopping Habit
29 MOA 28/7/10, Photocopied letter and memo correspondence between Tom Harrisson and Charles Madge CM, 21.1.40, memo to TH
30 MOA 28/7/10, Photocopied letter and memo correspondence between Tom Harrisson and Charles Madge TH, 18.1.40, memo to CM

19: Sleeping with the Natives

1   MOA 29-C, CM, 18.11.38, Market Hall follows
2   Barbara Phillipson, Interview in *Stranger Than Fiction*, a Mass-Observation film by Ian Potts and Angus Calder, 1985
3   Charles Madge, Draft of unpublished autobiography. CMpap 71/1/6, University of Sussex Library
4   MOA 29-A, Shop Observation, Shop Observation Terminology
5   MOA 29-A, Shop Observation, Guidelines for observers for counts
6   MOA 28/7/17, Charles Madge, Interview by Angus Calder, March 1979
7   MOA 28/A/6, Saving and Spending in Worktown
8   MOA 30, Shopping, GT, 11.11.38, Marks and Spencer's
9   MOA 30, GW, 19.11.38, Marks and Spencer's
10 MOA 32-C, GT, 18.11.38, Confectioners
11 MOA 29-A, GW, 13.3.39, Shopping Expedition
12 James Hinton, *The Mass Observers: A History, 1937–1949*, Oxford University Press, 2013
13 MOA 32/17, Letter Harrisson to Chapman, October 1938
14 MOA 32/15, Dennis Chapman, Interview by Nick Stanley at Liverpool University School of Business Studies, 23 February 1979
15 MOA 1-B, Letter from TH to Sir Ernest Simon reporting on progress and observers two years in
16 MOA 32/15, Dennis Chapman, Interview by Nick Stanley, 23 February 1979
17 MOA 1-C, CM letter to TH, January 1939
18 MOA32/102, Geoffrey Thomas diary, 27 January–11 February 1939
19 Ms 71/2/5, Letter CM to IS, November 1938, University of Sussex Library
20 MOA 32/120/3, Tom Harrisson, Articles and Papers
21 MOA4-E, All-in wrestling, GW Worktown Stadium, Match attended with BN
22 MOA 32/15, Dennis Chapman, Interview by Nick Stanley, 23 February 1979
23 MOA 32/7/1, Brian Barefoot, Account of work done with Mass-Observation, 1937–41, 1979
24 MOA32/110/2, Correspondence between Dorothy Sheridan, Joy Eldridge and Bruce Watkin, January 1995
25 Quoted in Hinton, *The Mass Observers*
26 MOA 28/7/10, Photocopied letter and memo correspondence between Tom Harrisson and Charles Madge. TH letter to CM, 17.1.39
27 Quoted in MOA 71/3/1, Charles Madge, Draft of unpublished autobiography
28 ibid.

20: Skirmishes and Battles

1   MOA 28/7/19, Charles Madge notes
2   MOA 32/15, Dennis Chapman, Interview by Nick Stanley, February 1979
3   MOA 28/7/10, Photocopied letter and memo correspondence between Tom Harrisson and Charles Madge. CM to TH, January 1938
4   MOA 19/65/E/2, Draft questions on savings and trade, CM, 17.1.39
5   MOA 33-B, GT, 6.2.39, Interview with Hoole
6   MOA 33-B, GT, 10.2.39, Education office
7   Sir John Anderson, Launch of Government Scheme of Voluntary National Service, 24.1.39
8   Ms71/2/5, Letter, CM letters to Inez Spender, 3 and 12.12.38, University of Sussex Library
9   MOA 29, GT, 11.2.39, Follows in Woolworth's
10 MOA 33-B, Savings Clubs, GT, 13.2.39, Interview with H. Kay of Holdsworth Mills, China Lane
11 MOA 33-B, Interview, Folds Road Girls Senior School, WG, 13.3.39
12 MOA 38-B, Savings Clubs, GT, March 1939, Interview with Byrne, St Mary's Senior Boys
13 James Hinton, *The Mass Observers: A History, 1937–1949*, Oxford University Press, 2013
14 MOA, Tom Harrisson, 'Poverty of Freedom', unpublished
15 Priscilla McNamara (MOA28/2/46), Interview by Angus Calder, 10 January 1980
16 MOA32/107, Gertrude Wagner, 'The Psychological Aspect of Saving and Spending'
17 CM to Keynes, 18 April 1939, Charles Madge papers, University of Sussex Special Collections
18 TH, 18.1.40, Memo to CM. MOA28/7/10, Photocopied letter and memo correspondence between Tom Harrisson and Charles Madge
19 Hinton, *The Mass Observers*
20 CM letter to Max Nicholson, 23.8.39, Charles Madge papers, University of Sussex Special Collections
21 MOA 32/102, Geoffrey Thomas diary, 11 February 1939
22 Hinton, *The Mass Observers*
23 MOA, Letter from TH to CM, 20.9.39
24 MOA 28/7/19, Charles Madge notes
25 'The Rebel: A Short Biography of Tom Harrisson', in Timothy Green, *The Adventurers*, Michael Joseph, 1970
26 MOA 28/2/46, Priscilla McNamara (Feare), Interview by Angus Calder, 10 January 1980
27 CM, 21.1.40, Memo to TH. OA28/7/10 Photocopied letter and memo correspondence between Tom Harrisson and Charles Madge
28 MOA 28/7/19, Charles Madge notes
29 Quoted in Angus Calder, 'Mass-Observation 1937–1949', BAAS Annual Meeting, 1981

BIBLIOGRAPHY

Angus Calder, 'Mass-Observation 1937–1949', BAAS Annual Meeting, 1981

Angus Calder and Dorothy Sheridan (eds), *Speak for Yourself: A Mass-Observation Anthology 1937–1949*, Jonathan Cape, 1984

Fred Dibnah and David Hall, *Fred Dibnah's Age of Steam*, BBC Books, 2003

William Feaver, *Pitman Painters: The Ashington Group, 1934–1984*, Ashington Group Trustees, 2009

Deborah Frizzell, *Humphrey Spender's Humanist Landscapes: Photo-documents 1932–1942*, Yale University Press, 1997

Juliet Gardiner, *The Thirties: An Intimate History*, Harper Press, 2010

David Gascoyne, *Journal 1936–1937*, Enitharmon Press, 1981

Timothy Green, *The Adventurers*, Michael Joseph, 1970

Peter Gurney (ed.), *Bolton Working-Class Life in the 1930s: A Mass-Observation Anthology*, University of Sussex, 1988

David Hall, *Working Lives*, Bantam Press, 2012

Judith M. Heimann, *The Most Offending Soul Alive: Tom Harrisson and his Remarkable Life*, University of Hawaii Press, 1997

James Hinton, *The Mass Observers: A History, 1937–1949*, Oxford University Press, 2013

Nick Hubble, *Mass-Observation and Everyday Life*, Palgrave Macmillan, 2006

Kevin Jackson, *Humphrey Jennings*, Picador, 2004

Tom Jeffrey. *Mass-Observation: A Short History*, Centre for Contemporary Cultural Studies, University of Birmingham, 1978

Humphrey Jennings, *Pandaemonium 1660–1886*, Icon Books, 2012

Humphrey Jennings and Charles Madge (eds), *May 12 1937: Mass-Observation Day-Survey*, Faber & Faber, 1937

Charles Madge and Tom Harrisson (eds), *Britain by Mass-Observation*, Penguin, 1939

Charles Madge and Tom Harrisson (eds), *First Year's Work, 1937–38, by Mass-Observation*, Lindsay Drummond, 1938

Charles Madge and Tom Harrisson, *Mass-Observation*, Frederick Muller, June 1937

Mass-Observation, *The Pub and the People: A Worktown Study*, Victor Gollancz, 1943

Mass-Observation in Bolton: Humphrey Spender's Worktown Photographs, exhibition catalogue, Waterman's Arts Centre, 1994

W. R. Mitchell, *Life in the Lancashire Mill Towns*, Dalesman Publishing, 1982

Jeremy Mulford (ed.), *Worktown People: Photographs from Northern England 1937–38*, Falling Wall Press, 1982

Andrew Rigby, 'The Peace Pledge Union: From Peace to War, 1936–1945' Peter Brook and Thomas P Socknat (eds), in *Challenge to Mars: Essays on Pacifism from 1918 to 1945*, University of Toronto Press, 1999

Humphrey Spender, *Lensman: Photographs 1932–52*, Chatto & Windus, London, 1987

Humphrey Spender, *Worktown: Photographs of Bolton and Blackpool Taken for Mass-Observation 1937/38*, Gardner Centre Gallery, University of Sussex, Brighton, 1977

Humphrey Spender and Jeremy Mulford, *Worktown People: Photographs from Northern England, 1937–38*, Falling Wall Press, 1982

Julian Trevelyan, *Indigo Days: The Art and Memoirs of Julian Trevelyan*, Scolar Press, 1957

David Wray, *Cotton Times: Understanding the Industrial Revolution*. www.cottontimes. co.uk

ACKNOWLEDGEMENTS

I wish to express my gratitude to: the Trustees of the Mass-Observation Archive for permission to quote extensively from M-O material; Fiona Courage, the curator of the M-O archive; Jessica Scantlebury at the University of Sussex Special Collections; the counter staff at the Keep, where the archive is housed, for their unfailing help in fetching all the material for me to look at; Martha Fogg at Adam Matthew Digital for arranging for me to have access to Mass-Observation Online; Bob Snape and Caroline Edge at the Centre for Worktown Studies, University of Bolton, for pointing me in the right direction during the early stages of my research; and Matthew Watson at Bolton Library and Museum Service. I was also greatly helped by Brian Barefoot's account of the time he spent with Mass-Observation in Bolton and by the interviews conducted by Angus Calder and Nick Stanley with the surviving members of the Worktown team in the 1970s and 1980s. Without this account and these interviews this book would not have been possible.

I would also like to thank my agent Gordon Wise at Curtis Brown who first made me aware of the Mass-Observation Archive, suggested that I might want to write a book based on it and offered practical support throughout the project. Special thanks to my editor Bea Hemming who commissioned the book, encouraged me throughout the writing and improved it immeasurably with her advice and edits, and to my copy-editor Peter James who did a terrific job on getting my text and references into presentable form. Finally, my thanks, as always, to my wife Fran for her support and encouragement and for helping with transcriptions of some of the material.

INDEX

and 'pick-ups', 221–3, 287; in pubs,
70, 77–8, 152–3, 162, 174; and male
observers, 174–5, 181
see also mill girls; prostitutes
Woolworth's, 4, 267, 272, 285–6
Workers' Bookshop, 106
'Worktown' (the name), 22
wrestling, 45, 88–9, 100, 263, 277–8, 286

Wyatt, Woodrow, 7–8, 47, 107, 159, 213,
296

Yates's Wine Lodge, 60, 77, 152–3,
157–8
Young Jewish Communists, 287
Your Bolton, 140